Elasticsearch Server
Third Edition

Leverage Elasticsearch to create a robust, fast, and flexible search solution with ease

Rafał Kuć

Marek Rogoziński

BIRMINGHAM - MUMBAI

Elasticsearch Server
Third Edition

First published: October 2013

Second edition: February 2015

Third edition: February 2016

Production reference: 1230216

Published by Packt Publishing Ltd.
Livery Place
35 Livery Street
Birmingham B3 2PB, UK.

ISBN 978-1-78588-881-6

www.packtpub.com

Credits

Authors
Rafał Kuć

Marek Rogoziński

Reviewer
Paige Cook

Commissioning Editor
Nadeem Bagban

Acquisition Editor
Divya Poojari

Content Development Editor
Kirti Patil

Technical Editor
Utkarsha S. Kadam

Copy Editor
Alpha Singh

Project Coordinator
Nidhi Joshi

Proofreader
Safis Editing

Indexer
Rekha Nair

Graphics
Jason Monteiro

Production Coordinator
Manu Joseph

Cover Work
Manu Joseph

About the Authors

Rafał Kuć is a software engineer, trainer, speaker and consultant. He is working as a consultant and software engineer at Sematext Group Inc. where he concentrates on open source technologies such as Apache Lucene, Solr, and Elasticsearch. He has more than 14 years of experience in various software domains—from banking software to e-commerce products. He is mainly focused on Java; however, he is open to every tool and programming language that might help him to achieve his goals easily and quickly. Rafał is also one of the founders of the `solr.pl` site, where he tries to share his knowledge and help people solve their Solr and Lucene problems. He is also a speaker at various conferences around the world such as Lucene Eurocon, Berlin Buzzwords, ApacheCon, Lucene/Solr Revolution, Velocity, and DevOps Days.

Rafał began his journey with Lucene in 2002; however, it wasn't love at first sight. When he came back to Lucene in late 2003, he revised his thoughts about the framework and saw the potential in search technologies. Then Solr came and that was it. He started working with Elasticsearch in the middle of 2010. At present, Lucene, Solr, Elasticsearch, and information retrieval are his main areas of interest.

Rafał is also the author of the Solr Cookbook series, *ElasticSearch Server* and its second edition, and the first and second editions of *Mastering ElasticSearch*, all published by *Packt Publishing*.

Marek Rogoziński is a software architect and consultant with more than 10 years of experience. His specialization concerns solutions based on open source search engines, such as Solr and Elasticsearch, and the software stack for big data analytics including Hadoop, Hbase, and Twitter Storm.

He is also a cofounder of the solr.pl site, which publishes information and tutorials about Solr and Lucene libraries. He is the coauthor of *ElasticSearch Server* and its second edition, and the first and second editions of *Mastering ElasticSearch*, all published by *Packt Publishing*.

He is currently the chief technology officer and lead architect at ZenCard, a company that processes and analyzes large quantities of payment transactions in real time, allowing automatic and anonymous identification of retail customers on all retailer channels (m-commerce/e-commerce/brick&mortar) and giving retailers a customer retention and loyalty tool.

About the Reviewer

Paige Cook works as a software architect for Videa, part of the Cox Family of Companies, and lives near Atlanta, Georgia. He has twenty years of experience in software development, primarily with the Microsoft .NET Framework. His career has been largely focused on building enterprise solutions for the media and entertainment industry. He is especially interested in search technologies using the Apache Lucene search engine and has experience with both Elasticsearch and Apache Solr. Apart from his work, he enjoys DIY home projects and spending time with his wife and two daughters.

www.PacktPub.com

eBooks, discount offers, and more

Did you know that Packt offers eBook versions of every book published, with PDF and ePub files available? You can upgrade to the eBook version at www.PacktPub.com and as a print book customer, you are entitled to a discount on the eBook copy. Get in touch with us at customercare@packtpub.com for more details.

At www.PacktPub.com, you can also read a collection of free technical articles, sign up for a range of free newsletters and receive exclusive discounts and offers on Packt books and eBooks.

https://www2.packtpub.com/books/subscription/packtlib

Do you need instant solutions to your IT questions? PacktLib is Packt's online digital book library. Here, you can search, access, and read Packt's entire library of books.

Why subscribe?

- Fully searchable across every book published by Packt
- Copy and paste, print, and bookmark content
- On demand and accessible via a web browser

Table of Contents

Preface	**xv**
Chapter 1: Getting Started with Elasticsearch Cluster	**1**
Full text searching	**2**
The Lucene glossary and architecture	2
Input data analysis	4
Indexing and querying	5
Scoring and query relevance	6
The basics of Elasticsearch	**6**
Key concepts of Elasticsearch	7
Index	7
Document	7
Document type	8
Mapping	8
Key concepts of the Elasticsearch infrastructure	9
Nodes and clusters	9
Shards	9
Replicas	9
Gateway	10
Indexing and searching	10
Installing and configuring your cluster	**12**
Installing Java	12
Installing Elasticsearch	12
Running Elasticsearch	13
Shutting down Elasticsearch	15
The directory layout	15
Configuring Elasticsearch	16
The system-specific installation and configuration	18
Installing Elasticsearch on Linux	18
Configuring Elasticsearch as a system service on Linux	20
Elasticsearch as a system service on Windows	20

Manipulating data with the REST API   **21**

Understanding the REST API   21

Storing data in Elasticsearch   22

Creating a new document   22

Retrieving documents   25

Updating documents   26

Dealing with non-existing documents   28
Adding partial documents   29

Deleting documents   31

Versioning   32

Usage example   32
Versioning from external systems   33

Searching with the URI request query   **34**

Sample data   34

URI search   35

Elasticsearch query response   38

Query analysis   40

URI query string parameters   41

The query   42
The default search field   42
Analyzer   42
The default operator property   42
Query explanation   42
The fields returned   45
Sorting the results   45
The search timeout   45
The results window   46
Limiting per-shard results   46
Ignoring unavailable indices   46
The search type   46
Lowercasing term expansion   46
Wildcard and prefix analysis   47

Lucene query syntax   47

Summary   **48**

Chapter 2: Indexing Your Data   **49**

Elasticsearch indexing   **50**

Shards and replicas   50

Write consistency   52

Creating indices   52

Altering automatic index creation   53
Settings for a newly created index   55
Index deletion   55

Mappings configuration   **56**

Type determining mechanism   56

Disabling the type determining mechanism   57

Tuning the type determining mechanism for numeric types	58
Tuning the type determining mechanism for dates	59
Index structure mapping	**61**
Type and types definition	62
Fields	63
Core types	63
Multi fields	70
The IP address type	70
Token count type	71
Using analyzers	**71**
Out-of-the-box analyzers	72
Defining your own analyzers	73
Default analyzers	76
Different similarity models	**76**
Setting per-field similarity	77
Available similarity models	78
Batch indexing to speed up your indexing process	**80**
Preparing data for bulk indexing	81
Indexing the data	82
The _all field	84
The _source field	85
Additional internal fields	86
Introduction to segment merging	**86**
Segment merging	87
The need for segment merging	87
The merge policy	87
The merge scheduler	88
Throttling	89
Introduction to routing	**89**
Default indexing	90
Default searching	90
Routing	92
The routing parameters	93
Routing fields	94
Summary	**95**
Chapter 3: Searching Your Data	**97**
Querying Elasticsearch	**97**
The example data	98
A simple query	100
Paging and result size	101
Returning the version value	103
Limiting the score	104
Choosing the fields that we want to return	105

Source filtering 106
Using the script fields 108
Passing parameters to the script fields 110
Understanding the querying process **111**
Query logic 111
Search type 112
Search execution preference 113
Search shards API 114
Basic queries **116**
The term query 116
The terms query 117
The match all query 118
The type query 118
The exists query 119
The missing query 119
The common terms query 119
The match query 121
The Boolean match query 121
The phrase match query 123
The match phrase prefix query 124
The multi match query 124
The query string query 125
Running the query string query against multiple fields 128
The simple query string query 128
The identifiers query 129
The prefix query 129
The fuzzy query 130
The wildcard query 132
The range query 133
Regular expression query 134
The more like this query 134
Compound queries **137**
The bool query 137
The dis_max query 139
The boosting query 140
The constant_score query 141
The indices query 141
Using span queries **142**
A span 143
Span term query 143
Span first query 144
Span near query 145

Span or query   147
Span not query   148
Span within query   149
Span containing query   150
Span multi query   151
Performance considerations   151
Choosing the right query   **151**
The use cases   152
Limiting results to given tags   152
Searching for values in a range   152
Boosting some of the matched documents   153
Ignoring lower scoring partial queries   154
Using Lucene query syntax in queries   157
Handling user queries without errors   157
Autocomplete using prefixes   159
Finding terms similar to a given one   160
Matching phrases   160
Spans, spans everywhere   160
Summary   **162**
Chapter 4: Extending Your Querying Knowledge   **163**
Filtering your results   **164**
The context is the key   165
Explicit filtering with bool query   165
Highlighting   **169**
Getting started with highlighting   170
Field configuration   172
Under the hood   172
Forcing highlighter type   172
Configuring HTML tags   173
Controlling highlighted fragments   175
Global and local settings   175
Require matching   176
Custom highlighting query   179
The Postings highlighter   180
Validating your queries   **183**
Using the Validate API   183
Sorting data   **186**
Default sorting   186
Selecting fields used for sorting   187
Sorting mode   189
Specifying behavior for missing fields   191
Dynamic criteria   191

Calculate scoring when sorting	192
Query rewrite	**193**
Prefix query as an example	193
Getting back to Apache Lucene	195
Query rewrite properties	197
Summary	**199**
Chapter 5: Extending Your Index Structure	**201**
Indexing tree-like structures	**201**
Data structure	202
Analysis	203
Indexing data that is not flat	**204**
Data	204
Objects	205
Arrays	205
Mappings	206
Final mappings	207
Sending the mappings to Elasticsearch	207
To be or not to be dynamic	208
Disabling object indexing	209
Using nested objects	**209**
Scoring and nested queries	213
Using the parent-child relationship	**213**
Index structure and data indexing	214
Child mappings	214
Parent mappings	214
The parent document	215
Child documents	215
Querying	216
Querying data in the child documents	216
Querying data in the parent documents	219
Performance considerations	221
Modifying your index structure with the update API	**221**
The mappings	222
Adding a new field to the existing index	222
Modifying fields of an existing index	223
Summary	**225**
Chapter 6: Make Your Search Better	**227**
Introduction to Apache Lucene scoring	**227**
When a document is matched	228
Default scoring formula	228
Relevancy matters	229

Scripting capabilities of Elasticsearch   **230**

  Objects available during script execution   230

  Script types   232

    In file scripts   232

    Inline scripts   233

    Indexed scripts   234

  Querying with scripts   235

  Scripting with parameters   236

  Script languages   237

  Using other than embedded languages   237

  Using native code   238

    The factory implementation   238

    Implementing the native script   239

    The plugin definition   240

    Installing the plugin   242

    Running the script   242

Searching content in different languages   **243**

  Handling languages differently   243

  Handling multiple languages   243

  Detecting the language of the document   244

  Sample document   244

  The mappings   245

  Querying   247

    Queries with an identified language   247

    Queries with an unknown language   248

  Combining queries   249

Influencing scores with query boosts   **250**

  The boost   250

  Adding the boost to queries   250

  Modifying the score   254

    Constant score query   254

    Boosting query   255

    The function score query   255

When does index-time boosting make sense?   **262**

  Defining boosting in the mappings   263

Words with the same meaning   **263**

  Synonym filter   263

    Synonyms in the mappings   264

    Synonyms stored on the file system   265

  Defining synonym rules   265

    Using Apache Solr synonyms   265

    Using WordNet synonyms   267

  Query or index-time synonym expansion   267

Understanding the explain information   **267**
  Understanding field analysis   267
  Explaining the query   269
Summary   **272**
Chapter 7: Aggregations for Data Analysis   **273**
Aggregations   **273**
  General query structure   274
  Inside the aggregations engine   277
Aggregation types   **278**
  Metrics aggregations   278
    Minimum, maximum, average, and sum   278
    Field value statistics and extended statistics   281
    Value count   283
    Field cardinality   283
    Percentiles   284
    Percentile ranks   286
    Top hits aggregation   287
    Geo bounds aggregation   292
    Scripted metrics aggregation   292
  Buckets aggregations   294
    Filter aggregation   294
    Filters aggregation   296
    Terms aggregation   298
    Range aggregation   301
    Date range aggregation   305
    IPv4 range aggregation   308
    Missing aggregation   309
    Histogram aggregation   310
  Date histogram aggregation   312
    Time zones   312
  Geo distance aggregations   313
  Geohash grid aggregation   315
  Global aggregation   315
  Significant terms aggregation   316
    Choosing significant terms   319
    Multiple value analysis   319
  Sampler aggregation   321
  Children aggregation   322
  Nested aggregation   323
  Reverse nested aggregation   324
  Nesting aggregations and ordering buckets   326
    Buckets ordering   329
Pipeline aggregations   **330**
    Available types   330
    Referencing other aggregations   330

Gaps in the data	330
Pipeline aggregation types	331
Summary	**344**
Chapter 8: Beyond Full-text Searching	**345**
Percolator	**345**
The index	346
Percolator preparation	347
Getting deeper	350
Controlling the size of returned results	352
Percolator and score calculation	352
Combining percolators with other functionalities	353
Getting the number of matching queries	354
Indexed document percolation	355
Elasticsearch spatial capabilities	**355**
Mapping preparation for spatial searches	356
Example data	356
Additional geo_field properties	357
Sample queries	358
Distance-based sorting	358
Bounding box filtering	360
Limiting the distance	362
Arbitrary geo shapes	363
Point	364
Envelope	364
Polygon	365
Multipolygon	365
An example usage	366
Storing shapes in the index	367
Using suggesters	**369**
Available suggester types	369
Including suggestions	370
Suggester response	371
Term suggester	372
Term suggester configuration options	373
Additional term suggester options	373
Phrase suggester	374
Completion suggester	376
Custom weights	380
Context suggester	381
The Scroll API	**388**
Problem definition	388
Scrolling to the rescue	388
Summary	**390**

Chapter 9: Elasticsearch Cluster in Detail 391

Understanding node discovery 392
Discovery types 392
Node roles 392
Master node 393
Data node 393
Client node 393
Configuring node roles 394
Setting the cluster's name 394
Zen discovery 395
Master election configuration 395
Configuring unicast 396
Fault detection ping settings 397
Cluster state updates control 397
Dealing with master unavailability 398
Adjusting HTTP transport settings 398
Disabling HTTP 398
HTTP port 398
HTTP host 399

The gateway and recovery modules 399
The gateway 399
Recovery control 400
Additional gateway recovery options 401
Indices recovery API 401
Delayed allocation 403
Index recovery prioritization 404

Templates and dynamic templates 405
Templates 405
An example of a template 405
Dynamic templates 406
The matching pattern 408
Field definitions 408

Elasticsearch plugins 408
The basics 409
Installing plugins 409
Removing plugins 411

Elasticsearch caches 412
Fielddata cache 412
Fielddata size 412
Circuit breakers 413
Fielddata and doc values 413
Shard request cache 414
Enabling and configuring the shard request cache 414
Per request shard request cache disabling 415
Shard request cache usage monitoring 415

Node query cache   416
Indexing buffers   416
When caches should be avoided   417
The update settings API   **417**
The cluster settings API   418
The indices settings API   418
Summary   **419**
Chapter 10: Administrating Your Cluster   **421**
Elasticsearch time machine   **421**
Creating a snapshot repository   422
Creating snapshots   424
Additional parameters   425
Restoring a snapshot   425
Cleaning up – deleting old snapshots   427
Monitoring your cluster's state and health   **427**
Cluster health API   428
Controlling information details   429
Additional parameters   429
Indices stats API   430
Docs   431
Store   431
Indexing, get, and search   431
Additional information   432
Nodes info API   433
Returned information   434
Nodes stats API   434
Cluster state API   435
Cluster stats API   436
Pending tasks API   436
Indices recovery API   437
Indices shard stores API   439
Indices segments API   439
Controlling the shard and replica allocation   **440**
Explicitly controlling allocation   440
Specifying node parameters   441
Configuration   441
Index creation   441
Excluding nodes from allocation   442
Requiring node attributes   443
Using the IP address for shard allocation   443
Disk-based shard allocation   443
The number of shards and replicas per node   445
Allocation throttling   445

Cluster-wide allocation	446
Allocation awareness	447
Forcing allocation awareness	449
Filtering	449
Manually moving shards and replicas	451
Moving shards	451
Canceling shard allocation	452
Forcing shard allocation	452
Multiple commands per HTTP request	453
Allowing operations on primary shards	453
Handling rolling restarts	453
Controlling cluster rebalancing	**454**
Understanding rebalance	454
Cluster being ready	455
The cluster rebalance settings	455
Controlling when rebalancing will be allowed	455
Controlling the number of shards being moved between nodes concurrently	455
Controlling which shards may be rebalanced	456
The Cat API	**456**
The basics	456
Using Cat API	458
Common arguments	458
The examples	459
Getting information about the master node	459
Getting information about the nodes	460
Retrieving recovery information for an index	460
Warming up	**460**
Defining a new warming query	461
Retrieving the defined warming queries	462
Deleting a warming query	463
Disabling the warming up functionality	464
Choosing queries for warming	464
Index aliasing and using it to simplify your everyday work	**465**
An alias	466
Creating an alias	466
Modifying aliases	467
Combining commands	467
Retrieving aliases	468
Removing aliases	469
Filtering aliases	469
Aliases and routing	470
Zero downtime reindexing and aliases	470
Summary	**471**

Chapter 11: Scaling by Example   473
Hardware   473
Physical servers or a cloud   474
CPU   475
RAM memory   475
Mass storage   476
The network   476
How many servers   476
Cost cutting   477
Preparing a single Elasticsearch node   477
The general preparations   478
   Avoiding swapping   478
   File descriptors   479
   Virtual memory   479
The memory   480
Field data cache and breaking the circuit   480
Use doc values   481
RAM buffer for indexing   481
Index refresh rate   481
Thread pools   482
Horizontal expansion   483
Automatically creating the replicas   486
Redundancy and high availability   486
Cost and performance flexibility   488
Continuous upgrades   488
Multiple Elasticsearch instances on a single physical machine   489
   Preventing a shard and its replicas from being on the same node   489
Designated node roles for larger clusters   490
   Query aggregator nodes   491
   Data nodes   492
   Master eligible nodes   492
Preparing the cluster for high indexing and querying throughput   492
Indexing related advice   492
   Index refresh rate   493
   Thread pools tuning   493
   Automatic store throttling   494
   Handling time-based data   494
   Multiple data paths   495
   Data distribution   495
   Bulk indexing   497
   RAM buffer for indexing   498
Advice for high query rate scenarios   498
   Shard request cache   499
   Think about the queries   499

Parallelize your queries	501
Field data cache and breaking the circuit	501
Keep size and shard size under control	502
Monitoring	**502**
Elasticsearch HQ	502
Marvel	504
SPM for Elasticsearch	505
Summary	**506**
Index	**507**

Preface

Welcome to Elasticsearch Server, Third Edition. This is the third instalment of the book dedicated to yet another major release of Elasticsearch—this time version 2.2. In the third edition, we have decided to go on a similar route that we took when we wrote the second edition of the book. We not only updated the content to match the new version of Elasticsearch, but also restructured the book by removing and adding new sections and chapters. We read the suggestions we got from you—the readers of the book, and we carefully tried to incorporate the suggestions and comments received since the release of the first and second editions.

While reading this book, you will be taken on a journey to the wonderful world of full-text search provided by the Elasticsearch server. We will start with a general introduction to Elasticsearch, which covers how to start and run Elasticsearch, its basic concepts, and how to index and search your data in the most basic way. This book will also discuss the query language, so called Query DSL, that allows you to create complicated queries and filter returned results. In addition to all of this, you'll see how you can use the aggregation framework to calculate aggregated data based on the results returned by your queries. We will implement the autocomplete functionality together and learn how to use Elasticsearch spatial capabilities and prospective search.

Finally, this book will show you Elasticsearch's administration API capabilities with features such as shard placement control, cluster handling, and more, ending with a dedicated chapter that will discuss Elasticsearch's preparation for small and large deployments— both ones that concentrate on indexing and also ones that concentrate on indexing.

What this book covers

Chapter 1, Getting Started with Elasticsearch Cluster, covers what full-text searching is, what Apache Lucene is, what text analysis is, how to run and configure Elasticsearch, and finally, how to index and search your data in the most basic way.

Chapter 2, Indexing Your Data, shows how indexing works, how to prepare index structure, what data types we are allowed to use, how to speed up indexing, what segments are, how merging works, and what routing is.

Chapter 3, Searching Your Data, introduces the full-text search capabilities of Elasticsearch by discussing how to query it, how the querying process works, and what types of basic and compound queries are available. In addition to this, we will show how to use position-aware queries in Elasticsearch.

Chapter 4, Extending Your Query Knowledge, shows how to efficiently narrow down your search results by using filters, how highlighting works, how to sort your results, and how query rewrite works.

Chapter 5, Extending Your Index Structure, shows how to index more complex data structures. We learn how to index tree-like data types, how to index data with relationships between documents, and how to modify index structure.

Chapter 6, Make Your Search Better, covers Apache Lucene scoring and how to influence it in Elasticsearch, the scripting capabilities of Elasticsearch, and its language analysis capabilities.

Chapter 7, Aggregations for Data Analysis, introduces you to the great world of data analysis by showing you how to use the Elasticsearch aggregation framework. We will discuss all types of aggregations—metrics, buckets, and the new pipeline aggregations that have been introduced in Elasticsearch.

Chapter 8, Beyond Full-text Searching, discusses non full-text search-related functionalities such as percolator—reversed search, and the geo-spatial capabilities of Elasticsearch. This chapter also discusses suggesters, which allow us to build a spellchecking functionality and an efficient autocomplete mechanism, and we will show how to handle deep-paging efficiently.

Chapter 9, Elasticsearch Cluster in Detail, discusses nodes discovery mechanism, recovery and gateway Elasticsearch modules, templates, caches, and settings update API.

Chapter 10, Administrating Your Cluster, covers the Elasticsearch backup functionality, rebalancing, and shards moving. In addition to this, you will learn how to use the warm up functionality, use the Cat API, and work with aliases.

Chapter 11, Scaling by Example, is dedicated to scaling and tuning. We will start with hardware preparations and considerations and a single Elasticsearch node-related tuning. We will go through cluster setup and vertical scaling, ending the chapter with high querying and indexing use cases and cluster monitoring.

What you need for this book

This book was written using Elasticsearch server 2.2 and all the examples and functions should work with this. In addition to this, you'll need a command that allows you to send HTTP request such as curl, which is available for most operating systems. Please note that all the examples in this book use the previously mentioned curl tool. If you want to use another tool, please remember to format the request in an appropriate way that is understood by the tool of your choice.

In addition to this, some chapters may require additional software, such as Elasticsearch plugins, but when needed it has been explicitly mentioned.

Who this book is for

If you are a beginner to the world of full-text search and Elasticsearch, then this book is especially for you. You will be guided through the basics of Elasticsearch and you will learn how to use some of the advanced functionalities.

If you know Elasticsearch and you worked with it, then you may find this book interesting as it provides a nice overview of all the functionalities with examples and descriptions. However, you may encounter sections that you already know.

If you know the Apache Solr search engine, this book can also be used to compare some functionalities of Apache Solr and Elasticsearch. This may give you the knowledge about which tool is more appropriate for your use case.

If you know all the details about Elasticsearch and you know how each of the configuration parameters work, then this is definitely not the book you are looking for.

Conventions

In this book, you will find a number of text styles that distinguish between different kinds of information. Here are some examples of these styles and an explanation of their meaning.

Code words in text, database table names, folder names, filenames, file extensions, pathnames, dummy URLs, user input, and Twitter handles are shown as follows: "If you use the Linux or OS X command, the cURL package should already be available."

A block of code is set as follows:

```
{
   "mappings": {
      "post": {
         "properties": {
            "id": { "type":"long" },
            "name": { "type":"string" },
            "published": { "type":"date" },
            "contents": { "type":"string" }
         }
      }
   }
}
```

When we wish to draw your attention to a particular part of a code block, the relevant lines or items are set in bold:

```
{
   "mappings": {
      "post": {
         "properties": {
            "id": { "type":"long" },
            "name": { "type":"string" },
            "published": { "type":"date" },
            "contents": { "type":"string" }
         }
      }
   }
}
```

Any command-line input or output is written as follows:

```
curl -XPUT http://localhost:9200/users/?pretty -d '{
  "mappings" : {
    "user": {
      "numeric_detection" : true
    }
  }
}'
```

Warnings or important notes appear in a box like this.

Reader feedback

Feedback from our readers is always welcome. Let us know what you think about this book—what you liked or disliked. Reader feedback is important for us as it helps us develop titles that you will really get the most out of.

To send us general feedback, simply e-mail feedback@packtpub.com, and mention the book's title in the subject of your message.

If there is a topic that you have expertise in and you are interested in either writing or contributing to a book, see our author guide at www.packtpub.com/authors.

Customer support

Now that you are the proud owner of a Packt book, we have a number of things to help you to get the most from your purchase.

Downloading the example code

You can download the example code files for this book from your account at http://www.packtpub.com. If you purchased this book elsewhere, you can visit http://www.packtpub.com/support and register to have the files e-mailed directly to you.

You can download the code files by following these steps:

1. Log in or register to our website using your e-mail address and password.
2. Hover the mouse pointer on the **SUPPORT** tab at the top.
3. Click on **Code Downloads & Errata**.
4. Enter the name of the book in the **Search** box.
5. Select the book for which you're looking to download the code files.
6. Choose from the drop-down menu where you purchased this book from.
7. Click on **Code Download**.

Once the file is downloaded, please make sure that you unzip or extract the folder using the latest version of:

- WinRAR / 7-Zip for Windows
- Zipeg / iZip / UnRarX for Mac
- 7-Zip / PeaZip for Linux

Downloading the color images of this book

We also provide you with a PDF file that has color images of the screenshots/diagrams used in this book. The color images will help you better understand the changes in the output. You can download this file from `https://www.packtpub.com/sites/default/files/downloads/ElasticsearchServerThirdEdition_ColorImages.pdf`.

Errata

Although we have taken every care to ensure the accuracy of our content, mistakes do happen. If you find a mistake in one of our books—maybe a mistake in the text or the code—we would be grateful if you could report this to us. By doing so, you can save other readers from frustration and help us improve subsequent versions of this book. If you find any errata, please report them by visiting `http://www.packtpub.com/submit-errata`, selecting your book, clicking on the **Errata Submission Form** link, and entering the details of your errata. Once your errata are verified, your submission will be accepted and the errata will be uploaded to our website or added to any list of existing errata under the Errata section of that title.

To view the previously submitted errata, go to `https://www.packtpub.com/books/content/support` and enter the name of the book in the search field. The required information will appear under the **Errata** section.

Piracy

Piracy of copyrighted material on the Internet is an ongoing problem across all media. At Packt, we take the protection of our copyright and licenses very seriously. If you come across any illegal copies of our works in any form on the Internet, please provide us with the location address or website name immediately so that we can pursue a remedy.

Please contact us at copyright@packtpub.com with a link to the suspected pirated material.

We appreciate your help in protecting our authors and our ability to bring you valuable content.

Questions

If you have a problem with any aspect of this book, you can contact us at questions@packtpub.com, and we will do our best to address the problem.

1
Getting Started with Elasticsearch Cluster

Welcome to the wonderful world of Elasticsearch—a great full text search and analytics engine. It doesn't matter if you are new to Elasticsearch and full text searches in general, or if you already have some experience in this. We hope that, by reading this book, you'll be able to learn and extend your knowledge of Elasticsearch. As this book is also dedicated to beginners, we decided to start with a short introduction to full text searches in general, and after that, a brief overview of Elasticsearch.

Please remember that Elasticsearch is a rapidly changing of software. Not only are features added, but the Elasticsearch core functionality is also constantly evolving and changing. We try to keep up with these changes, and because of this we are giving you the third edition of the book dedicated to Elasticsearch 2.x.

The first thing we need to do with Elasticsearch is install and configure it. With many applications, you start with the installation and configuration and usually forget the importance of these steps. We will try to guide you through these steps so that it becomes easier to remember. In addition to this, we will show you the simplest way to index and retrieve data without going into too much detail. The first chapter will take you on a quick ride through Elasticsearch and the full text search world. By the end of this chapter, you will have learned the following topics:

- Full text searching
- The basics of Apache Lucene
- Performing text analysis
- The basic concepts of Elasticsearch
- Installing and configuring Elasticsearch

- Using the Elasticsearch REST API to manipulate data
- Searching using basic URI requests

Full text searching

Back in the days when full text searching was a term known to a small percentage of engineers, most of us used SQL databases to perform search operations. Using SQL databases to search for the data stored in them was okay to some extent. Such a search wasn't fast, especially on large amounts of data. Even now, small applications are usually good with a standard LIKE `%phrase%` search in a SQL database. However, as we go deeper and deeper, we start to see the limits of such an approach—a lack of scalability, not enough flexibility, and a lack of language analysis. Of course, there are additional modules that extend SQL databases with full text search capabilities, but they are still limited compared to dedicated full text search libraries and search engines such as Elasticsearch. Some of those reasons led to the creation of Apache Lucene (`http://lucene.apache.org/`), a library written completely in Java (`http://java.com/en/`), which is very fast, light, and provides language analysis for a large number of languages spoken throughout the world.

The Lucene glossary and architecture

Before going into the details of the analysis process, we would like to introduce you to the glossary and overall architecture of Apache Lucene. We decided that this information is crucial for understanding how Elasticsearch works, and even though the book is not about Apache Lucene, knowing the foundation of the Elasticsearch analytics and indexing engine is vital to fully understand how this great search engine works.

The basic concepts of the mentioned library are as follows:

- **Document**: This is the main data carrier used during indexing and searching, comprising one or more fields that contain the data we put in and get from Lucene.
- **Field**: This a section of the document, which is built of two parts: the name and the value.
- **Term**: This is a unit of search representing a word from the text.
- **Token**: This is an occurrence of a term in the text of the field. It consists of the term text, start and end offsets, and a type.

Apache Lucene writes all the information to a structure called the **inverted index**. It is a data structure that maps the terms in the index to the documents and not the other way around as a relational database does in its tables. You can think of an inverted index as a data structure where data is term-oriented rather than document-oriented. Let's see how a simple inverted index will look. For example, let's assume that we have documents with only a single field called title to be indexed, and the values of that field are as follows:

- Elasticsearch Server (document 1)
- Mastering Elasticsearch Second Edition (document 2)
- Apache Solr Cookbook Third Edition (document 3)

A very simplified visualization of the Lucene inverted index could look as follows:

Term	Count	Document
apache	1	<3>
cookbook	1	<3>
edition	2	<2>, <3>
elasticsearch	2	<1>, <2>
mastering	1	<2>
second	1	<2>
server	1	<1>
solr	1	<3>
third	1	<3>

Each term points to the number of documents it is present in. For example, the term edition is present twice in the second and third documents. Such a structure allows for very efficient and fast search operations in term-based queries (but not exclusively). Because the occurrences of the term are connected to the terms themselves, Lucene can use information about the term occurrences to perform fast and precise scoring information by giving each document a value that represents how well each of the returned documents matched the query.

Of course, the actual index created by Lucene is much more complicated and advanced because of additional files that include information such as term vectors (per document inverted index), doc values (column oriented field information), stored fields (the original and not the analyzed value of the field), and so on. However, all you need to know for now is how the data is organized and not what exactly is stored.

Each index is divided into multiple write-once and read-many-time structures called segments. Each segment is a miniature Apache Lucene index on its own. When indexing, after a single segment is written to the disk it can't be updated, or we should rather say it can't be fully updated; documents can't be removed from it, they can only be marked as deleted in a separate file. The reason that Lucene doesn't allow segments to be updated is the nature of the inverted index. After the fields are analyzed and put into the inverted index, there is no easy way of building the original document structure. When deleting, Lucene would have to delete the information from the segment, which translates to updating all the information within the inverted index itself.

Because of the fact that segments are write-once structures Lucene is able to merge segments together in a process called segment merging. During indexing, if Lucene thinks that there are too many segments falling into the same criterion, a new and bigger segment will be created — one that will have data from the other segments. During that process, Lucene will try to remove deleted data and get back the space needed to hold information about those documents. Segment merging is a demanding operation both in terms of the I/O and CPU. What we have to remember for now is that searching with one large segment is faster than searching with multiple smaller ones holding the same data. That's because, in general, searching translates to just matching the query terms to the ones that are indexed. You can imagine how searching through multiple small segments and merging those results will be slower than having a single segment preparing the results.

Input data analysis

The transformation of a document that comes to Lucene and is processed and put into the inverted index format is called **indexation**. One of the things Lucene has to do during this is data analysis. You may want some of your fields to be processed by a language analyzer so that words such as car and cars are treated as the same be your index. On the other hand, you may want other fields to be divided only on the white space character or be only lowercased.

Analysis is done by the analyzer, which is built of a tokenizer and zero or more token filters, and it can also have zero or more character mappers.

A tokenizer in Lucene is used to split the text into tokens, which are basically the terms with additional information such as its position in the original text and its length. The results of the tokenizer's work is called a token stream, where the tokens are put one by one and are ready to be processed by the filters.

Apart from the tokenizer, the Lucene analyzer is built of zero or more token filters that are used to process tokens in the token stream. Some examples of filters are as follows:

- **Lowercase filter**: Makes all the tokens lowercased
- **Synonyms filter**: Changes one token to another on the basis of synonym rules
- **Language stemming filters**: Responsible for reducing tokens (actually, the text part that they provide) into their root or base forms called the stem (`https://en.wikipedia.org/wiki/Word_stem`)

Filters are processed one after another, so we have almost unlimited analytical possibilities with the addition of multiple filters, one after another.

Finally, the character mappers operate on non-analyzed text—they are used before the tokenizer. Therefore, we can easily remove HTML tags from whole parts of text without worrying about tokenization.

Indexing and querying

You may wonder how all the information we've described so far affects indexing and querying when using Lucene and all the software that is built on top of it. During indexing, Lucene will use an analyzer of your choice to process the contents of your document; of course, different analyzers can be used for different fields, so the name field of your document can be analyzed differently compared to the summary field. For example, the name field may only be tokenized on whitespaces and lowercased, so that exact matches are done and the summary field is stemmed in addition to that. We can also decide to not analyze the fields at all—we have full control over the analysis process.

During a query, your query text can be analyzed as well. However, you can also choose not to analyze your queries. This is crucial to remember because some Elasticsearch queries are analyzed and some are not. For example, prefix and term queries are not analyzed, and match queries are analyzed (we will get to that in *Chapter 3, Searching Your Data*). Having queries that are analyzed and not analyzed is very useful; sometimes, you may want to query a field that is not analyzed, while sometimes you may want to have a full text search analysis. For example, if we search for the `LightRed` term and the query is being analyzed by the standard analyzer, then the terms that would be searched are light and red. If we use a query type that has not been analyzed, then we will explicitly search for the `LightRed` term. We may not want to analyze the content of the query if we are only interested in exact matches.

What you should remember about indexing and querying analysis is that the index should match the query term. If they don't match, Lucene won't return the desired documents. For example, if you use stemming and lowercasing during indexing, you need to ensure that the terms in the query are also lowercased and stemmed, or your queries won't return any results at all. For example, let's get back to our LightRed term that we analyzed during indexing; we have it as two terms in the index: light and red. If we run a LightRed query against that data and don't analyze it, we won't get the document in the results—the query term does not match the indexed terms. It is important to keep the token filters in the same order during indexing and query time analysis so that the terms resulting from such an analysis are the same.

Scoring and query relevance

There is one additional thing that we only mentioned once till now—scoring. What is the score of a document? The score is a result of a scoring formula that describes how well the document matches the query. By default, Apache Lucene uses the TF/IDF (term frequency/inverse document frequency) scoring mechanism, which is an algorithm that calculates how relevant the document is in the context of our query. Of course, it is not the only algorithm available, and we will mention other algorithms in the *Mappings configuration* section of *Chapter 2*, *Indexing Your Data*.

> If you want to read more about the Apache Lucene TF/IDF scoring formula, please visit Apache Lucene Javadocs for the TFIDF. The similarity class is available at http://lucene.apache.org/core/5_4_0/core/org/apache/lucene/search/similarities/TFIDFSimilarity.html.

The basics of Elasticsearch

Elasticsearch is an open source search server project started by Shay Banon and published in February 2010. During this time, the project grew into a major player in the field of search and data analysis solutions and is widely used in many common or lesser-known search and data analysis platforms. In addition, due to its distributed nature and real-time search and analytics capabilities, many organizations use it as a document store.

Key concepts of Elasticsearch

In the next few pages, we will get you through the basic concepts of Elasticsearch. You can skip this section if you are already familiar with Elasticsearch architecture. However, if you are not familiar with Elasticsearch, we strongly advise you to read this section. We will refer to the key words used in this section in the rest of the book, and understanding those concepts is crucial to fully utilize Elasticsearch.

Index

An index is the logical place where Elasticsearch stores the data. Each index can be spread onto multiple Elasticsearch nodes and is divided into one or more smaller pieces called **shards** that are physically placed on the hard drives. If you are coming from the relational database world, you can think of an index like a table. However, the index structure is prepared for fast and efficient full text searching and, in particular, does not store original values. That structure is called an inverted index (https://en.wikipedia.org/wiki/Inverted_index).

If you know MongoDB, you can think of the Elasticsearch index as a collection in MongoDB. If you are familiar with CouchDB, you can think about an index as you would about the CouchDB database. Elasticsearch can hold many indices located on one machine or spread them over multiple servers. As we have already said, every index is built of one or more shards, and each shard can have many replicas.

Document

The main entity stored in Elasticsearch is a document. A document can have multiple fields, each having its own type and treated differently. Using the analogy to relational databases, a document is a row of data in a database table. When you compare an Elasticsearch document to a MongoDB document, you will see that both can have different structures. The thing to keep in mind when it comes to Elasticsearch is that fields that are common to multiple types in the same index need to have the same type. This means that all the documents with a field called title need to have the same data type for it, for example, string.

Documents consist of fields, and each field may occur several times in a single document (such a field is called **multivalued**). Each field has a type (text, number, date, and so on). The field types can also be complex—a field can contain other subdocuments or arrays. The field type is important to Elasticsearch because type determines how various operations such as analysis or sorting are performed. Fortunately, this can be determined automatically (however, we still suggest using mappings; take a look at what follows).

Unlike the relational databases, documents don't need to have a fixed structure—every document may have a different set of fields, and in addition to this, fields don't have to be known during application development. Of course, one can force a document structure with the use of schema. From the client's point of view, a document is a JSON object (see more about the JSON format at `https://en.wikipedia.org/wiki/JSON`). Each document is stored in one index and has its own unique identifier, which can be generated automatically by Elasticsearch, and document type. The thing to remember is that the document identifier needs to be unique inside an index and should be for a given type. This means that, in a single index, two documents can have the same unique identifier if they are not of the same type.

Document type

In Elasticsearch, one index can store many objects serving different purposes. For example, a blog application can store articles and comments. The document type lets us easily differentiate between the objects in a single index. Every document can have a different structure, but in real-world deployments, dividing documents into types significantly helps in data manipulation. Of course, one needs to keep the limitations in mind. That is, different document types can't set different types for the same property. For example, a field called title must have the same type across all document types in a given index.

Mapping

In the section about the basics of full text searching (the *Full text searching* section), we wrote about the process of analysis—the preparation of the input text for indexing and searching done by the underlying Apache Lucene library. Every field of the document must be properly analyzed depending on its type. For example, a different analysis chain is required for the numeric fields (numbers shouldn't be sorted alphabetically) and for the text fetched from web pages (for example, the first step would require you to omit the HTML tags as it is useless information). To be able to properly analyze at indexing and querying time, Elasticsearch stores the information about the fields of the documents in so-called mappings. Every document type has its own mapping, even if we don't explicitly define it.

Key concepts of the Elasticsearch infrastructure

Now, we already know that Elasticsearch stores its data in one or more indices and every index can contain documents of various types. We also know that each document has many fields and how Elasticsearch treats these fields is defined by the mappings. But there is more. From the beginning, Elasticsearch was created as a distributed solution that can handle billions of documents and hundreds of search requests per second. This is due to several important key features and concepts that we are going to describe in more detail now.

Nodes and clusters

Elasticsearch can work as a standalone, single-search server. Nevertheless, to be able to process large sets of data and to achieve fault tolerance and high availability, Elasticsearch can be run on many cooperating servers. Collectively, these servers connected together are called a cluster and each server forming a cluster is called a node.

Shards

When we have a large number of documents, we may come to a point where a single node may not be enough—for example, because of RAM limitations, hard disk capacity, insufficient processing power, and an inability to respond to client requests fast enough. In such cases, an index (and the data in it) can be divided into smaller parts called **shards** (where each shard is a separate Apache Lucene index). Each shard can be placed on a different server, and thus your data can be spread among the cluster nodes. When you query an index that is built from multiple shards, Elasticsearch sends the query to each relevant shard and merges the result in such a way that your application doesn't know about the shards. In addition to this, having multiple shards can speed up indexing, because documents end up in different shards and thus the indexing operation is parallelized.

Replicas

In order to increase query throughput or achieve high availability, shard replicas can be used. A replica is just an exact copy of the shard, and each shard can have zero or more replicas. In other words, Elasticsearch can have many identical shards and one of them is automatically chosen as a place where the operations that change the index are directed. This special shard is called a primary shard, and the others are called replica shards. When the primary shard is lost (for example, a server holding the shard data is unavailable), the cluster will promote the replica to be the new primary shard.

Gateway

The cluster state is held by the gateway, which stores the cluster state and indexed data across full cluster restarts. By default, every node has this information stored locally; it is synchronized among nodes. We will discuss the gateway module in *The gateway and recovery modules* section of *Chapter 9, Elasticsearch Cluster*, in detail.

Indexing and searching

You may wonder how you can tie all the indices, shards, and replicas together in a single environment. Theoretically, it would be very difficult to fetch data from the cluster when you have to know where your document is: on which server, and in which shard. Even more difficult would be searching when one query can return documents from different shards placed on different nodes in the whole cluster. In fact, this is a complicated problem; fortunately, we don't have to care about this at all—it is handled automatically by Elasticsearch. Let's look at the following diagram:

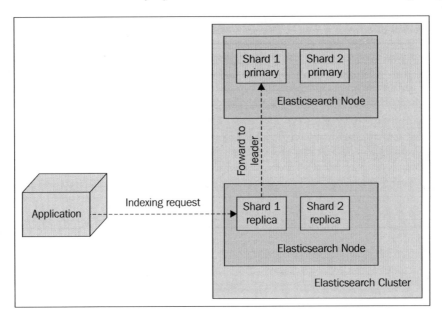

When you send a new document to the cluster, you specify a target index and send it to any of the nodes. The node knows how many shards the target index has and is able to determine which shard should be used to store your document. Elasticsearch can alter this behavior; we will talk about this in the *Introduction to routing* section in *Chapter 2, Indexing Your Data*. The important information that you have to remember for now is that Elasticsearch calculates the shard in which the document should be placed using the unique identifier of the document—this is one of the reasons each document needs a unique identifier. After the indexing request is sent to a node, that node forwards the document to the target node, which hosts the relevant shard.

Now, let's look at the following diagram on searching request execution:

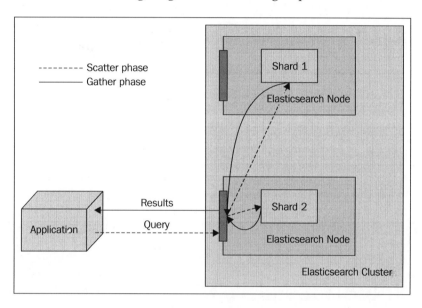

When you try to fetch a document by its identifier, the node you send the query to uses the same routing algorithm to determine the shard and the node holding the document and again forwards the request, fetches the result, and sends the result to you. On the other hand, the querying process is a more complicated one. The node receiving the query forwards it to all the nodes holding the shards that belong to a given index and asks for minimum information about the documents that match the query (the identifier and score are matched by default), unless routing is used, when the query will go directly to a single shard only. This is called the scatter phase. After receiving this information, the aggregator node (the node that receives the client request) sorts the results and sends a second request to get the documents that are needed to build the results list (all the other information apart from the document identifier and score). This is called the gather phase. After this phase is executed, the results are returned to the client.

Now the question arises: what is the replica's role in the previously described process? While indexing, replicas are only used as an additional place to store the data. When executing a query, by default, Elasticsearch will try to balance the load among the shard and its replicas so that they are evenly stressed. Also, remember that we can change this behavior; we will discuss this in the *Understanding the querying process* section in *Chapter 3, Searching Your Data*.

Installing and configuring your cluster

Installing and running Elasticsearch even in production environments is very easy nowadays, compared to how it was in the days of Elasticsearch 0.20.x. From a system that is not ready to one with Elasticsearch, there are only a few steps that one needs to go. We will explore these steps in the following section:

Installing Java

Elasticsearch is a Java application and to use it we need to make sure that the Java SE environment is installed properly. Elasticsearch requires Java Version 7 or later to run. You can download it from `http://www.oracle.com/technetwork/java/javase/downloads/index.html`. You can also use OpenJDK (`http://openjdk.java.net/`) if you wish. You can, of course, use Java Version 7, but it is not supported by Oracle anymore, at least without commercial support. For example, you can't expect new, patched versions of Java 7 to be released. Because of this, we strongly suggest that you install Java 8, especially given that Java 9 seems to be right around the corner with the general availability planned to be released in September 2016.

Installing Elasticsearch

To install Elasticsearch you just need to go to `https://www.elastic.co/downloads/elasticsearch`, choose the last stable version of Elasticsearch, download it, and unpack it. That's it! The installation is complete.

At the time of writing, we used a snapshot of Elasticsearch 2.2. This means that we've skipped describing some properties that were marked as deprecated and are or will be removed in the future versions of Elasticsearch.

The main interface to communicate with Elasticsearch is based on the HTTP protocol and REST. This means that you can even use a web browser for some basic queries and requests, but for anything more sophisticated you'll need to use additional software, such as the cURL command. If you use the Linux or OS X command, the cURL package should already be available. If you use Windows, you can download the package from http://curl.haxx.se/download.html.

Running Elasticsearch

Let's run our first instance that we just downloaded as the ZIP archive and unpacked. Go to the bin directory and run the following commands depending on the OS:

- **Linux** or **OS X**: ./elasticsearch
- **Windows**: elasticsearch.bat

Congratulations! Now, you have your Elasticsearch instance up-and-running. During its work, the server usually uses two port numbers: the first one for communication with the REST API using the HTTP protocol, and the second one for the transport module used for communication in a cluster and between the native Java client and the cluster. The default port used for the HTTP API is 9200, so we can check search readiness by pointing the web browser to http://127.0.0.1:9200/. The browser should show a code snippet similar to the following:

```
{
  "name" : "Blob",
  "cluster_name" : "elasticsearch",
  "version" : {
    "number" : "2.2.0",
    "build_hash" : "5b1dd1cf5a1957682d84228a569e124fedf8e325",
    "build_timestamp" : "2016-01-13T18:12:26Z",
    "build_snapshot" : true,
    "lucene_version" : "5.4.0"
  },
  "tagline" : "You Know, for Search"
}
```

The output is structured as a **JavaScript Object Notation (JSON)** object. If you are not familiar with JSON, please take a minute and read the article available at https://en.wikipedia.org/wiki/JSON.

Elasticsearch is smart. If the default port is not available, the engine binds to the next free port. You can find information about this on the console during booting as follows:

```
[2016-01-13 20:04:49,953][INFO ][http
] [Blob] publish_address {127.0.0.1:9201},
bound_addresses {[fe80::1]:9200}, {[::1]:9200},
{127.0.0.1:9201}
```

Note the fragment with `[http]`. Elasticsearch uses a few ports for various tasks. The interface that we are using is handled by the HTTP module.

Now, we will use the cURL program to communicate with Elasticsearch. For example, to check the cluster health, we will use the following command:

```
curl -XGET http://127.0.0.1:9200/_cluster/health?pretty
```

The `-X` parameter is a definition of the HTTP request method. The default value is GET (so in this example, we can omit this parameter). For now, do not worry about the GET value; we will describe it in more detail later in this chapter.

As a standard, the API returns information in a JSON object in which new line characters are omitted. The `pretty` parameter added to our requests forces Elasticsearch to add a new line character to the response, making the response more user-friendly. You can try running the preceding query with and without the `?pretty` parameter to see the difference.

Elasticsearch is useful in small and medium-sized applications, but it has been built with large clusters in mind. So, now we will set up our big two-node cluster. Unpack the Elasticsearch archive in a different directory and run the second instance. If we look at the log, we will see the following:

```
[2016-01-13 20:07:58,561][INFO ][cluster.service          ] [Big
Man] detected_master {Blob}{5QPh00RUQraeLHAInbR4Jw}{127.0.0.1}
{127.0.0.1:9300}, added {{Blob}{5QPh00RUQraeLHAInbR4Jw}{127.0.0.1}
{127.0.0.1:9300},}, reason: zen-disco-receive(from master [{Blob}
{5QPh00RUQraeLHAInbR4Jw}{127.0.0.1}{127.0.0.1:9300}])
```

This means that our second instance (named Big Man) discovered the previously running instance (named Blob). Here, Elasticsearch automatically formed a new two-node cluster. Starting from Elasticsearch 2.0, this will only work with nodes running on the same physical machine—because Elasticsearch 2.0 no longer supports multicast. To allow your cluster to form, you need to inform Elasticsearch about the nodes that should be contacted initially using the `discovery.zen.ping.unicast.hosts` array in `elasticsearch.yml`. For example, like this:

```
discovery.zen.ping.unicast.hosts: ["192.168.2.1", "192.168.2.2"]
```

Shutting down Elasticsearch

Even though we expect our cluster (or node) to run flawlessly for a lifetime, we may need to restart it or shut it down properly (for example, for maintenance). The following are the two ways in which we can shut down Elasticsearch:

- If your node is attached to the console, just press *Ctrl + C*

- The second option is to kill the server process by sending the TERM signal (see the `kill` command on the Linux boxes and Program Manager on Windows)

 The previous versions of Elasticsearch exposed a dedicated shutdown API but, in 2.0, this option has been removed because of security reasons.

The directory layout

Now, let's go to the newly created directory. We should see the following directory structure:

Directory	Description
Bin	The scripts needed to run Elasticsearch instances and for plugin management
Config	The directory where configuration files are located
Lib	The libraries used by Elasticsearch
Modules	The plugins bundled with Elasticsearch

After Elasticsearch starts, it will create the following directories (if they don't exist):

Directory	Description
Data	The directory used by Elasticsearch to store all the data
Logs	The files with information about events and errors
Plugins	The location to store the installed plugins
Work	The temporary files used by Elasticsearch

Configuring Elasticsearch

One of the reasons — of course, not the only one — why Elasticsearch is gaining more and more popularity is that getting started with Elasticsearch is quite easy. Because of the reasonable default values and automatic settings for simple environments, we can skip the configuration and go straight to indexing and querying (or to the next chapter of the book). We can do all this without changing a single line in our configuration files. However, in order to truly understand Elasticsearch, it is worth understanding some of the available settings.

We will now explore the default directories and the layout of the files provided with the Elasticsearch tar.gz archive. The entire configuration is located in the config directory. We can see two files here: elasticsearch.yml (or elasticsearch.json, which will be used if present) and logging.yml. The first file is responsible for setting the default configuration values for the server. This is important because some of these values can be changed at runtime and can be kept as a part of the cluster state, so the values in this file may not be accurate. The two values that we cannot change at runtime are cluster.name and node.name.

The cluster.name property is responsible for holding the name of our cluster. The cluster name separates different clusters from each other. Nodes configured with the same cluster name will try to form a cluster.

The second value is the instance (the node.name property) name. We can leave this parameter undefined. In this case, Elasticsearch automatically chooses a unique name for itself. Note that this name is chosen during each startup, so the name can be different on each restart. Defining the name can helpful when referring to concrete instances by the API or when using monitoring tools to see what is happening to a node during long periods of time and between restarts. Think about giving descriptive names to your nodes.

Other parameters are commented well in the file, so we advise you to look through it; don't worry if you do not understand the explanation. We hope that everything will become clearer after reading the next few chapters.

Remember that most of the parameters that have been set in the elasticsearch.yml file can be overwritten with the use of the Elasticsearch REST API. We will talk about this API in *The update settings API* section of *Chapter 9, Elasticsearch Cluster in Detail*.

The second file (`logging.yml`) defines how much information is written to system logs, defines the log files, and creates new files periodically. Changes in this file are usually required only when you need to adapt to monitoring or backup solutions or during system debugging; however, if you want to have a more detailed logging, you need to adjust it accordingly.

Let's leave the configuration files for now and look at the base for all the applications — the operating system. Tuning your operating system is one of the key points to ensure that your Elasticsearch instance will work well. During indexing, especially when having many shards and replicas, Elasticsearch will create many files; so, the system cannot limit the open file descriptors to less than 32,000. For Linux servers, this can usually be changed in `/etc/security/limits.conf` and the current value can be displayed using the `ulimit` command. If you end up reaching the limit, Elasticsearch will not be able to create new files; so merging will fail, indexing may fail, and new indices will not be created.

> On Microsoft Windows platforms, the default limit is more than 16 million handles per process, which should be more than enough. You can read more about file handles on the Microsoft Windows platform at `https://blogs.technet.microsoft.com/markrussinovich/2009/09/29/pushing-the-limits-of-windows-handles/`.

The next set of settings is connected to the **Java Virtual Machine (JVM)** heap memory limit for a single Elasticsearch instance. For small deployments, the default memory limit (1,024 MB) will be sufficient, but for large ones it will not be enough. If you spot entries that indicate `OutOfMemoryError` exceptions in a log file, set the `ES_HEAP_SIZE` variable to a value greater than 1024. When choosing the right amount of memory size to be given to the JVM, remember that, in general, no more than 50 percent of your total system memory should be given. However, as with all the rules, there are exceptions. We will discuss this in greater detail later, but you should always monitor your JVM heap usage and adjust it when needed.

The system-specific installation and configuration

Although downloading an archive with Elasticsearch and unpacking it works and is convenient for testing, there are dedicated methods for Linux operating systems that give you several advantages when you do production deployment. In production deployments, the Elasticsearch service should be run automatically with a system boot; we should have dedicated start and stop scripts, unified paths, and so on. Elasticsearch supports installation packages for various Linux distributions that we can use. Let's see how this works.

Installing Elasticsearch on Linux

The other way to install Elasticsearch on a Linux operating system is to use packages such as RPM or DEB, depending on your Linux distribution and the supported package type. This way we can automatically adapt to system directory layout; for example, configuration and logs will go into their standard places in the /etc/ or /var/log directories. But this is not the only thing. When using packages, Elasticsearch will also install startup scripts and make our life easier. What's more, we will be able to upgrade Elasticsearch easily by running a single command from the command line. Of course, the mentioned packages can be found at the same URL address as we mentioned previously when we talked about installing Elasticsearch from zip or tar.gz packages: https://www.elastic. co/downloads/elasticsearch. Elasticsearch can also be installed from remote repositories via standard distribution tools such as apt-get or yum.

 Before installing Elasticsearch, make sure that you have a proper version of Java Virtual Machine installed.

Installing Elasticsearch using RPM packages

When using a Linux distribution that supports RPM packages such as Fedora Linux, (https://getfedora.org/) Elasticsearch installation is very easy. After downloading the RPM package, we just need to run the following command as root:

```
yum elasticsearch-2.2.0.noarch.rpm
```

Alternatively, you can add the remote repository and install Elasticsearch from it (this command needs to be run as root as well):

```
rpm --import https://packages.elastic.co/GPG-KEY-elasticsearch
```

This command adds the GPG key and allows the system to verify that the fetched package really comes from Elasticsearch developers. In the second step, we need to create the repository definition in the `/etc/yum.repos.d/elasticsearch.repo` file. We need to add the following entries to this file:

```
[elasticsearch-2.2]
name=Elasticsearch repository for 2.2.x packages
baseurl=http://packages.elastic.co/elasticsearch/2.x/centos
gpgcheck=1
gpgkey=http://packages.elastic.co/GPG-KEY-elasticsearch
enabled=1
```

Now it's time to install the Elasticsearch server, which is as simple as running the following command (again, don't forget to run it as root):

```
yum install elasticsearch
```

Elasticsearch will be automatically downloaded, verified, and installed.

Installing Elasticsearch using the DEB package

When using a Linux distribution that supports DEB packages (such as Debian), installing Elasticsearch is again very easy. After downloading the DEB package, all you need to do is run the following command:

```
sudo dpkg -i elasticsearch-2.2.0.deb
```

It is as simple as that. Another way, which is similar to what we did with RPM packages, is by creating a new packages source and installing Elasticsearch from the remote repository. The first step is to add the public GPG key used for package verification. We can do that using the following command:

```
wget -qO - https://packages.elastic.co/GPG-KEY-elasticsearch | sudo apt-key add -
```

The second step is by adding the DEB package location. We need to add the following line to the `/etc/apt/sources.list` file:

```
deb http://packages.elastic.co/elasticsearch/2.2/debian stable main
```

This defines the source for the Elasticsearch packages. The last step is updating the list of remote packages and installing Elasticsearch using the following command:

```
sudo apt-get update && sudo apt-get install elasticsearch
```

Elasticsearch configuration file localization

When using packages to install Elasticsearch, the configuration files are in slightly different directories than the default `conf` directory. After the installation, the configuration files should be stored in the following location:

- `/etc/sysconfig/elasticsearch` or `/etc/default/elasticsearch`: A file with the configuration of the Elasticsearch process as a user to run as, directories for logs, data and memory settings
- `/etc/elasticsearch/`: A directory for the Elasticsearch configuration files, such as the `elasticsearch.yml` file

Configuring Elasticsearch as a system service on Linux

If everything goes well, you can run Elasticsearch using the following command:

```
/bin/systemctl start elasticsearch.service
```

If you want Elasticsearch to start automatically every time the operating system starts, you can set up Elasticsearch as a system service by running the following command:

```
/bin/systemctl enable elasticsearch.service
```

Elasticsearch as a system service on Windows

Installing Elasticsearch as a system service on Windows is also very easy. You just need to go to your Elasticsearch installation directory, then go to the `bin` subdirectory, and run the following command:

```
service.bat install
```

You'll be asked for permission to do so. If you allow the script to run, Elasticsearch will be installed as a Windows service.

If you would like to see all the commands exposed by the `service.bat` script file, just run the following command in the same directory as earlier:

```
service.bat
```

For example, to start Elasticsearch, we will just run the following command:

```
service.bat start
```

Manipulating data with the REST API

Elasticsearch exposes a very rich REST API that can be used to search through the data, index the data, and control Elasticsearch behavior. You can imagine that using the REST API allows you to get a single document, index or update a document, get the information on Elasticsearch current state, create or delete indices, or force Elasticsearch to move around shards of your indices. Of course, these are only examples that show what you can expect from the Elasticsearch REST API. For now, we will concentrate on using the **create**, **retrieve**, **update**, **delete** (**CRUD**) part of the Elasticsearch API (https://en.wikipedia.org/wiki/Create,_read,_update_ and_delete), which allows us to use Elasticsearch in a fashion similar to how we would use any other NoSQL (https://en.wikipedia.org/wiki/NoSQL) data store.

Understanding the REST API

If you've never used an application exposing the REST API, you may be surprised how easy it is to use such applications and remember how to use them. In REST-like architectures, every request is directed to a concrete object indicated by a path in the address. For example, let's assume that our hypothetical application exposes the /books REST end-point as a reference to the list of books. In such case, a call to /books/1 could be a reference to a concrete book with the identifier 1. You can think of it as a data-oriented model of an API. Of course, we can nest the paths—for example, a path such as /books/1/chapters could return the list of chapters of our book with identifier 1 and a path such as /books/1/chapters/6 could be a reference to the sixth chapter in that particular book.

We talked about paths, but when using the HTTP protocol, (https://en.wikipedia.org/wiki/Hypertext_Transfer_Protocol) we have some additional verbs (such as POST, GET, PUT, and so on.) that we can use to define system behavior in addition to paths. So if we would like to retrieve the book with identifier 1, we would use the GET request method with the /books/1 path. However, we would use the PUT request method with the same path to create a book record with the identifier or one, the POST request method to alter the record, DELETE to remove that entry, and the HEAD request method to get basic information about the data referenced by the path.

Now, let's look at example HTTP requests that are sent to real Elasticsearch REST API endpoints, so the preceding hypothetical information will be turned into something real:

GET http://localhost:9200/: This retrieves basic information about Elasticsearch, such as the version, the name of the node that the command has been sent to, the name of the cluster that node is connected to, the Apache Lucene version, and so on.

GET `http://localhost:9200/_cluster/state/nodes/` This retrieves information about all the nodes in the cluster, such as their identifiers, names, transport addresses with ports, and additional node attributes for each node.

DELETE `http://localhost:9200/books/book/123`: This deletes a document that is indexed in the books index, with the book type and an identifier of 123.

We now know what REST means and we can start concentrating on Elasticsearch to see how we can store, retrieve, alter, and delete the data from its indices. If you would like to read more about REST, please refer to `http://en.wikipedia.org/wiki/Representational_state_transfer`.

Storing data in Elasticsearch

In Elasticsearch, every document is represented by three attributes — the index, the type, and the identifier. Each document must be indexed into a single index, needs to have its type correspond to the document structure, and is described by the identifier. These three attributes allows us to identify any document in Elasticsearch and needs to be provided when the document is physically written to the underlying Apache Lucene index. Having the knowledge, we are now ready to create our first Elasticsearch document.

Creating a new document

We will start learning the Elasticsearch REST API by indexing one document. Let's imagine that we are building a CMS system (`http://en.wikipedia.org/wiki/Content_management_system`) that will provide the functionality of a blogging platform for our internal users. We will have different types of documents in our indices, but the most important ones are the articles that will be published and are readable by users.

Because we talk to Elasticsearch using JSON notation and Elasticsearch responds to us again using JSON, our example document could look as follows:

```
{
  "id": "1",
  "title": "New version of Elasticsearch released!",
  "content": "Version 2.2 released today!",
  "priority": 10,
  "tags": ["announce", "elasticsearch", "release"]
}
```

As you can see in the preceding code snippet, the JSON document is built with a set of fields, where each field can have a different format. In our example, we have a set of text fields (id, title, and content), we have a number (the priority field), and an array of text values (the tags field). We will show documents that are more complicated in the next examples.

> One of the changes introduced in Elasticsearch 2.0 has been that field names can't contain the dot character. Such field names were possible in older versions of Elasticsearch, but could result in serialization errors in certain cases and thus Elasticsearch creators decided to remove that possibility.

One thing to remember is that by default Elasticsearch works as a schema-less data store. This means that it can try to guess the type of the field in a document sent to Elasticsearch. It will try to use numeric types for the values that are not enclosed in quotation marks and strings for data enclosed in quotation marks. It will try to guess the date and index them in dedicated fields and so on. This is possible because the JSON format is semi-typed. Internally, when the first document with a new field is sent to Elasticsearch, it will be processed and mappings will be written (we will talk more about mappings in the *Mappings configuration* section of *Chapter 2, Indexing Your Data*).

> A schema-less approach and dynamic mappings can be problematic when documents come with a slightly different structure—for example, the first document would contain the value of the priority field without quotation marks (like the one shown in the discussed example), while the second document would have quotation marks for the value in the priority field. This will result in an error because Elasticsearch will try to put a text value in the numeric field and this is not possible in Lucene. Because of this, it is advisable to define your own mappings, which you will learn in the *Mappings configuration* section of *Chapter 2, Indexing Your Data*.

Let's now index our document and make it available for retrieval and searching. We will index our articles to an index called `blog` under a type named `article`. We will also give our document an identifier of 1, as this is our first document. To index our example document, we will execute the following command:

```
curl -XPUT 'http://localhost:9200/blog/article/1' -d '{"title": "New
version of Elasticsearch released!", "content": "Version 2.2 released
today!", "priority": 10, "tags": ["announce", "elasticsearch", "release"]
}'
```

Note a new option to the `curl` command, the `-d` parameter. The value of this option is the text that will be used as a request payload—a request body. This way, we can send additional information such as the document definition. Also, note that the unique identifier is placed in the URL and not in the body. If you omit this identifier (while using the HTTP PUT request), the indexing request will return the following error:

```
No handler found for uri [/blog/article] and method [PUT]
```

If everything worked correctly, Elasticsearch will return a JSON response informing us about the status of the indexing operation. This response should be similar to the following one:

```
{
 "_index":"blog",
 "_type":"article",
 "_id":"1",
 "_version":1,
 "_shards":{
  "total":2,
  "successful":1,
  "failed":0},
 "created":true
}
```

In the preceding response, Elasticsearch included information about the status of the operation, index, type, identifier, and version. We can also see information about the shards that took part in the operation—all of them, the ones that were successful and the ones that failed.

Automatic identifier creation

In the previous example, we specified the document identifier manually when we were sending the document to Elasticsearch. However, there are use cases when we don't have an identifier for our documents—for example, when handling logs as our data. In such cases, we would like some application to create the identifier for us and Elasticsearch can be such an application. Of course, generating document identifiers doesn't make sense when your document already has them, such as data in a relational database. In such cases, you may want to update the documents; in this case, automatic identifier generation is not the best idea. However, when we are in need of such functionality, instead of using the HTTP PUT method we can use POST and omit the identifier in the REST API path. So if we would like Elasticsearch to generate the identifier in the previous example, we would send a command like this:

```
curl -XPOST 'http://localhost:9200/blog/article/' -d '{"title": "New
version of Elasticsearch released!", "content": "Version 2.2 released
today!", "priority": 10, "tags": ["announce", "elasticsearch", "release"]
}'
```

We've used the HTTP POST method instead of PUT and we've omitted the identifier. The response produced by Elasticsearch in such a case would be as follows:

```
{
  "_index":"blog",
  "_type":"article",
  "_id":"AU1y-s6w2WzST_RhTvCJ",
  "_version":1,
  "_shards":{
   "total":2,
   "successful":1,
   "failed":0},
  "created":true
}
```

As you can see, the response returned by Elasticsearch is almost the same as in the previous example, with a minor difference—the _id field is returned. Now, instead of the 1 value, we have a value of AU1y-s6w2WzST_RhTvCJ, which is the identifier Elasticsearch generated for our document.

Retrieving documents

We now have two documents indexed into our Elasticsearch instance—one using a explicit identifier and one using a generated identifier. Let's now try to retrieve one of the documents using its unique identifier. To do this, we will need information about the index the document is indexed in, what type it has, and of course what identifier it has. For example, to get the document from the blog index with the article type and the identifier of 1, we would run the following HTTP GET request:

```
curl -XGET 'localhost:9200/blog/article/1?pretty'
```

> The additional URI property called pretty tells Elasticsearch to include new line characters and additional white spaces in response to make the output easier to read for users.

Elasticsearch will return a response similar to the following:

```
{
   "_index" : "blog",
   "_type" : "article",
   "_id" : "1",
   "_version" : 1,
   "found" : true,
   "_source" : {
     "title" : "New version of Elasticsearch released!",
     "content" : "Version 2.2 released today!",
```

```
    "priority" : 10,
    "tags" : [ "announce", "elasticsearch", "release" ]
  }
}
```

As you can see in the preceding response, Elasticsearch returned the _source field, which is the original document sent to Elasticsearch and a few additional fields that tell us about the document, such as the index, type, identifier, document version, and of course information as towhether the document was found or not (the found property).

If we try to retrieve a document that is not present in the index, such as the one with the 12345 identifier, we get a response like this:

```
{
  "_index" : "blog",
  "_type" : "article",
  "_id" : "12345",
  "found" : false
}
```

As you can see, this time the value of the found property was set to false and there was no _source field because the document has not been retrieved.

Updating documents

Updating documents in the index is a more complicated task compared to indexing. When the document is indexed and Elasticsearch flushes the document to a disk, it creates segments—an immutable structure that is written once and read many times. This is done because the inverted index created by Apache Lucene is currently impossible to update (at least most of its parts). To update a document, Elasticsearch internally first fetches the document using the GET request, modifies its _source field, removes the old document, and indexes a new document using the updated content. The content update is done using scripts in Elasticsearch (we will talk more about scripting in Elasticsearch in the *Scripting capabilities of Elasticsearch* section in *Chapter 6, Make Your Search Better*).

Please note that the following document update examples require you to put the script.inline: on property into your elasticsearch.yml configuration file. This is needed because inline scripting is disabled in Elasticsearch for security reasons. The other way to handle updates is to store the script content in the file in the Elasticsearch configuration directory, but we will talk about that in the *Scripting capabilities of Elasticsearch* section in *Chapter 6, Make Your Search Better*.

Let's now try to update our document with identifier 1 by modifying its content field to contain the This is the updated document sentence. To do this, we need to run a POST HTTP request on the document path using the _update REST end-point. Our request to modify the document would look as follows:

```
curl -XPOST 'http://localhost:9200/blog/article/1/_update' -d '{
  "script" : "ctx._source.content = new_content",
  "params" : {
   "new_content" : "This is the updated document"
  }
}'
```

As you can see, we've sent the request to the /blog/article/1/_update REST end-point. In the request body, we've provided two parameters—the update script in the script property and the parameters of the script. The script is very simple; it takes the _source field and modifies the content field by setting its value to the value of the new_content parameter. The params property contains all the script parameters.

For the preceding update command execution, Elasticsearch would return the following response:

```
{"_index":"blog","_type":"article","_id":"1","_version":2,"_shards":{"
total":2,"successful":1,"failed":0}}
```

The thing to look at in the preceding response is the _version field. Right now, the version is 2, which means that the document has been updated (or re-indexed) once. Basically, each update makes Elasticsearch update the _version field.

We could also update the document using the doc section and providing the changed field, for example:

```
curl -XPOST 'http://localhost:9200/blog/article/1/_update' -d '{
  "doc" : {
   "content" : "This is the updated document"
  }
}'
```

We now retrieve the document using the following command:

```
curl -XGET 'http://localhost:9200/blog/article/1?pretty'
```

And we get the following response from Elasticsearch:

```
{
  "_index" : "blog",
  "_type" : "article",
  "_id" : "1",
  "_version" : 2,
  "found" : true,
  "_source" : {
    "title" : "New version of Elasticsearch released!",
    "content" : "This is the updated document",
    "priority" : 10,
    "tags" : [ "announce", "elasticsearch", "release" ]
  }
}
```

As you can see, the document has been updated properly.

The thing to remember when using the update API of Elasticsearch is that the _source field needs to be present because this is the field that Elasticsearch uses to retrieve the original document content from the index. By default, that field is enabled and Elasticsearch uses it to store the original document.

Dealing with non-existing documents

The nice thing when it comes to document updates, which we would like to mention as it can come in handy when using Elasticsearch Update API, is that we can define what Elasticsearch should do when the document we try to update is not present.

For example, let's try incrementing the priority field value for a non-existing document with identifier 2:

```
curl -XPOST 'http://localhost:9200/blog/article/2/_update' -d '{
  "script" : "ctx._source.priority += 1"
}'
```

The response returned by Elasticsearch would look more or less as follows:

```
{"error":{"root_cause":[{"type":"document_missing_
exception","reason":"[article][2]: document missing","shard":"2","in
dex":"blog"}],"type":"document_missing_exception","reason":"[article]
[2]: document missing","shard":"2","index":"blog"},"status":404}
```

As you can imagine, the document has not been updated because it doesn't exist. So now, let's modify our request to include the upsert section in our request body that will tell Elasticsearch what to do when the document is not present. The new command would look as follows:

```
curl -XPOST 'http://localhost:9200/blog/article/2/_update' -d '{
 "script" : "ctx._source.priority += 1",
 "upsert" : {
  "title" : "Empty document",
  "priority" : 0,
  "tags" : ["empty"]
 }
}'
```

With the modified request, a new document would be indexed; if we retrieve it using the GET API, it will look as follows:

```
{
   "_index" : "blog",
   "_type" : "article",
   "_id" : "2",
   "_version" : 1,
   "found" : true,
   "_source" : {
     "title" : "Empty document",
     "priority" : 0,
     "tags" : [ "empty" ]
   }
}
```

As you can see, the fields from the upsert section of our update request were taken by Elasticsearch and used as document fields.

Adding partial documents

In addition to what we already wrote about the update API, Elasticsearch is also capable of merging partial documents from the update request to already existing documents or indexing new documents using information about the request, similar to what we saw seen with the upsert section.

Let's imagine that we would like to update our initial document and add a new field called **count to it** (setting it to 1 initially). We would also like to index the document under the specified identifier if the document is not present. We can do this by running the following command:

```
curl -XPOST 'http://localhost:9200/blog/article/1/_update' -d '{
  "doc" : {
    "count" : 1
  },
  "doc_as_upsert" : true
}
```

We specified the new field in the doc section and we said that we want the doc section to be treated as the upsert section when the document is not present (with the doc_as_upsert property set to true).

If we now retrieve that document, we see the following response:

```
{
  "_index" : "blog",
  "_type" : "article",
  "_id" : "1",
  "_version" : 3,
  "found" : true,
  "_source" : {
    "title" : "New version of Elasticsearch released!",
    "content" : "This is the updated document",
    "priority" : 10,
    "tags" : [ "announce", "elasticsearch", "release" ],
    "count" : 1
  }
}
```

 For a full reference on document updates, please refer to the official Elasticsearch documentation on the Update API, which is available at https://www.elastic.co/guide/en/elasticsearch/reference/current/docs-update.html.

Deleting documents

Now that we know how to index documents, update them, and retrieve them, it is time to learn about how we can delete them. Deleting a document from an Elasticsearch index is very similar to retrieving it, but with one major difference — instead of using the HTTP GET method, we have to use HTTP DELETE one.

For example, if we would like to delete the document indexed in the blog index under the article type and with an identifier of 1, we would run the following command:

```
curl -XDELETE 'localhost:9200/blog/article/1'
```

The response from Elasticsearch indicates that the document has been deleted and should look as follows:

```
{
  "found":true,
  "_index":"blog",
  "_type":"article",
  "_id":"1",
  "_version":4,
  "_shards":{
   "total":2,
   "successful":1,
   "failed":0
  }
}
```

Of course, this is not the only thing when it comes to deleting. We can also remove all the documents of a given type. For example, if we would like to delete the entire blog index, we should just omit the identifier and the type, so the command would look like this:

```
curl -XDELETE 'localhost:9200/blog'
```

The preceding command would result in the deletion of the blog index.

Versioning

Finally, there is one last thing that we would like to talk about when it comes to data manipulation in Elasticsearch — the great feature of versioning. As you may have already noticed, Elasticsearch increments the document version when it does updates to it. We can leverage this functionality and use optimistic locking (http://en.wikipedia.org/wiki/Optimistic_concurrency_control), and avoid conflicts and overwrites when multiple processes or threads access the same document concurrently. You can assume that your indexing application may want to try to update the document, while the user would like to update the document while doing some manual work. The question that arises is: Which document should be the correct one — the one updated by the indexing application, the one updated by the user, or the merged document of the changes? What if the changes are conflicting? To handle such cases, we can use versioning.

Usage example

Let's index a new document to our blog index — one with an identifier of 10, and let's index its second version soon after we do that. The commands that do this look as follows:

```
curl -XPUT 'localhost:9200/blog/article/10' -d '{"title":"Test
document"}'
curl -XPUT 'localhost:9200/blog/article/10' -d '{"title":"Updated test
document"}'
```

Because we've indexed the document with the same identifier, it should have a version 2 (you can check it using the GET request).

Now, let's try deleting the document we've just indexed but let's specify a version property equal to 1. By doing this, we tell Elasticsearch that we are interested in deleting the document with the provided version. Because the document is a different version now, Elasticsearch shouldn't allow indexing with version 1. Let's check if what we say is true. The command we will use to send the delete request looks as follows:

```
curl -XDELETE 'localhost:9200/blog/article/10?version=1'
```

The response generated by Elasticsearch should be similar to the following one:

```
{
  "error" : {
    "root_cause" : [ {
      "type" : "version_conflict_engine_exception",
      "reason" : "[article][10]: version conflict, current [2],
        provided [1]",
      "shard" : 1,
```

```
        "index" : "blog"
    } ],
    "type" : "version_conflict_engine_exception",
    "reason" : "[article][10]: version conflict, current [2],
      provided [1]",
    "shard" : 1,
    "index" : "blog"
  },
  "status" : 409
}
```

As you can see, the `delete` operation was not successful—the versions didn't match. If we set the version property to 2, the `delete` operation would be successful:

curl -XDELETE 'localhost:9200/blog/article/10?version=2&pretty'

The response this time will look as follows:

```
{
  "found" : true,
  "_index" : "blog",
  "_type" : "article",
  "_id" : "10",
  "_version" : 3,
  "_shards" : {
    "total" : 2,
    "successful" : 1,
    "failed" : 0
  }
}
```

This time the delete operation has been successful because the provided version was proper.

Versioning from external systems

The very good thing about Elasticsearch versioning capabilities is that we can provide the version of the document that we would like Elasticsearch to use. This allows us to provide versions from external data systems that are our primary data stores. To do this, we need to provide an additional parameter during indexing— `version_type=external` and, of course, the version itself. For example, if we would like our document to have the `12345` version, we could send a request like this:

**curl -XPUT 'localhost:9200/blog/article/20?version=12345&version_
type=external' -d '{"title":"Test document"}'**

The response returned by Elasticsearch is as follows:

```
{
  "_index" : "blog",
  "_type" : "article",
  "_id" : "20",
  "_version" : 12345,
  "_shards" : {
    "total" : 2,
    "successful" : 1,
    "failed" : 0
  },
  "created" : true
}
```

We just need to remember that, when using `version_type=external`, we need to provide the version in cases where we index the document. In cases where we would like to change the document and use optimistic locking, we need to provide a version parameter equal to, or higher than, the version present in the document.

Searching with the URI request query

Before getting into the wonderful world of the Elasticsearch query language, we would like to introduce you to the simple but pretty flexible URI request search, which allows us to use a simple Elasticsearch query combined with the Lucene query language. Of course, we will extend our search knowledge using Elasticsearch in *Chapter 3, Searching Your Data*, but for now we will stick to the simplest approach.

Sample data

For the purpose of this section of the book, we will create a simple index with two document types. To do this, we will run the following six commands:

```
curl -XPOST 'localhost:9200/books/es/1' -d '{"title":"Elasticsearch
Server", "published": 2013}'

curl -XPOST 'localhost:9200/books/es/2' -d '{"title":"Elasticsearch
Server Second Edition", "published": 2014}'

curl -XPOST 'localhost:9200/books/es/3' -d '{"title":"Mastering
Elasticsearch", "published": 2013}'

curl -XPOST 'localhost:9200/books/es/4' -d '{"title":"Mastering
Elasticsearch Second Edition", "published": 2015}'

curl -XPOST 'localhost:9200/books/solr/1' -d '{"title":"Apache Solr 4
Cookbook", "published": 2012}'
```

```
curl -XPOST 'localhost:9200/books/solr/2' -d '{"title":"Solr Cookbook
Third Edition", "published": 2015}'
```

Running the preceding commands will create the book's index with two types: es and solr. The title and published fields will be indexed and thus, searchable.

URI search

All queries in Elasticsearch are sent to the _search endpoint. You can search a single index or multiple indices, and you can restrict your search to a given document type or multiple types. For example, in order to search our book's index, we will run the following command:

```
curl -XGET 'localhost:9200/books/_search?pretty'
```

The results returned by Elasticsearch will include all the documents from our book's index (because no query has been specified) and should look similar to the following:

```
{
  "took" : 3,
  "timed_out" : false,
  "_shards" : {
    "total" : 5,
    "successful" : 5,
    "failed" : 0
  },
  "hits" : {
    "total" : 6,
    "max_score" : 1.0,
    "hits" : [ {
      "_index" : "books",
      "_type" : "es",
      "_id" : "2",
      "_score" : 1.0,
      "_source" : {
        "title" : "Elasticsearch Server Second Edition",
        "published" : 2014
      }
    }, {
      "_index" : "books",
      "_type" : "es",
      "_id" : "4",
      "_score" : 1.0,
      "_source" : {
        "title" : "Mastering Elasticsearch Second Edition",
```

```
          "published" : 2015
        }
      }, {
        "_index" : "books",
        "_type" : "solr",
        "_id" : "2",
        "_score" : 1.0,
        "_source" : {
          "title" : "Solr Cookbook Third Edition",
          "published" : 2015
        }
      }, {
        "_index" : "books",
        "_type" : "es",
        "_id" : "1",
        "_score" : 1.0,
        "_source" : {
          "title" : "Elasticsearch Server",
          "published" : 2013
        }
      }, {
        "_index" : "books",
        "_type" : "solr",
        "_id" : "1",
        "_score" : 1.0,
        "_source" : {
          "title" : "Apache Solr 4 Cookbook",
          "published" : 2012
        }
      }, {
        "_index" : "books",
        "_type" : "es",
        "_id" : "3",
        "_score" : 1.0,
        "_source" : {
          "title" : "Mastering Elasticsearch",
          "published" : 2013
        }
      } ]
    }
  }
```

As you can see, the response has a header that tells you the total time of the query and the shards used in the query process. In addition to this, we have documents matching the query—the top 10 documents by default. Each document is described by the index, type, identifier, score, and the source of the document, which is the original document sent to Elasticsearch.

We can also run queries against many indices. For example, if we had another index called `clients`, we could also run a single query against these two indices as follows:

```
curl -XGET 'localhost:9200/books,clients/_search?pretty'
```

We can also run queries against all the data in Elasticsearch by omitting the index names completely or setting the queries to `_all`:

```
curl -XGET 'localhost:9200/_search?pretty'
curl -XGET 'localhost:9200/_all/_search?pretty'
```

In a similar manner, we can also choose the types we want to use during searching. For example, if we want to search only in the `es` type in the book's index, we run a command as follows:

```
curl -XGET 'localhost:9200/books/es/_search?pretty'
```

Please remember that, in order to search for a given type, we need to specify the index or multiple indices. Elasticsearch allows us to have quite a rich semantics when it comes to choosing index names. If you are interested, please refer to `https://www.elastic.co/guide/en/elasticsearch/reference/current/multi-index.html`; however, there is one thing we would like to point out. When running a query against multiple indices, it may happen that some of them do not exist or are closed. In such cases, the `ignore_unavailable` property comes in handy. When set to `true`, it tells Elasticsearch to ignore unavailable or closed indices.

For example, let's try running the following query:

```
curl -XGET 'localhost:9200/books,non_existing/_search?pretty'
```

The response would be similar to the following one:

```
{
  "error" : {
    "root_cause" : [ {
      "type" : "index_missing_exception",
      "reason" : "no such index",
      "index" : "non_existing"
    } ],
    "type" : "index_missing_exception",
```

```
        "reason" : "no such index",
        "index" : "non_existing"
      },
      "status" : 404
    }
```

Now let's check what will happen if we add the `ignore_unavailable=true` to our request and execute the following command:

```
curl -XGET 'localhost:9200/books,non_existing/_search?pretty&ignore_
unavailable=true'
```

In this case, Elasticsearch would return the results without any error.

Elasticsearch query response

Let's assume that we want to find all the documents in our book's index that contain the `elasticsearch` term in the title field. We can do this by running the following query:

```
curl -XGET 'localhost:9200/books/_search?pretty&q=title:elasticsearch'
```

The response returned by Elasticsearch for the preceding request will be as follows:

```
{
  "took" : 37,
  "timed_out" : false,
  "_shards" : {
    "total" : 5,
    "successful" : 5,
    "failed" : 0
  },
  "hits" : {
    "total" : 4,
    "max_score" : 0.625,
    "hits" : [ {
      "_index" : "books",
      "_type" : "es",
      "_id" : "1",
      "_score" : 0.625,
      "_source" : {
        "title" : "Elasticsearch Server",
        "published" : 2013
      }
    }, {
```

```
        "_index" : "books",
        "_type" : "es",
        "_id" : "2",
        "_score" : 0.5,
        "_source" : {
          "title" : "Elasticsearch Server Second Edition",
          "published" : 2014
        }
      }, {
        "_index" : "books",
        "_type" : "es",
        "_id" : "4",
        "_score" : 0.5,
        "_source" : {
          "title" : "Mastering Elasticsearch Second Edition",
          "published" : 2015
        }
      }, {
        "_index" : "books",
        "_type" : "es",
        "_id" : "3",
        "_score" : 0.19178301,
        "_source" : {
          "title" : "Mastering Elasticsearch",
          "published" : 2013
        }
      } ]
  }
}
```

The first section of the response gives us information about how much time the request took (the `took` property is specified in milliseconds), whether it was timed out (the `timed_out` property), and information about the shards that were queried during the request execution—the number of queried shards (the total property of the `_shards` object), the number of shards that returned the results successfully (the successful property of the `_shards` object), and the number of failed shards (the failed property of the `_shards` object). The query may also time out if it is executed for a longer period than we want. (We can specify the maximum query execution time using the timeout parameter.) The failed shard means that something went wrong with that shard or it was not available during the search execution.

Of course, the mentioned information can be useful, but usually, we are interested in the results that are returned in the hits object. We have the total number of documents returned by the query (in the `total` property) and the maximum score calculated (in the `max_score` property). Finally, we have the `hits` array that contains the returned documents. In our case, each returned document contains its index name (the `_index` property), the type (the `_type` property), the identifier (the `_id` property), the score (the `_score` property), and the `_source` field (usually, this is the JSON object sent for indexing.

Query analysis

You may wonder why the query we've run in the previous section worked. We indexed the Elasticsearch term and ran a query for Elasticsearch and even though they differ (capitalization), the relevant documents were found. The reason for this is the analysis. During indexing, the underlying Lucene library analyzes the documents and indexes the data according to the Elasticsearch configuration. By default, Elasticsearch will tell Lucene to index and analyze both string-based data as well as numbers. The same happens during querying because the URI request query maps to the `query_string` query (which will be discussed in *Chapter 3, Searching Your Data*), and this query is analyzed by Elasticsearch.

Let's use the indices-analyze API (`https://www.elastic.co/guide/en/ elasticsearch/reference/current/indices-analyze.html`). It allows us to see how the analysis process is done. With this, we can see what happened to one of the documents during indexing and what happened to our query phrase during querying.

In order to see what was indexed in the title field of the Elasticsearch server phrase, we will run the following command:

```
curl -XGET 'localhost:9200/books/_analyze?pretty&field=title' -d
'Elasticsearch Server'
```

The response will be as follows:

```
{
  "tokens" : [ {
    "token" : "elasticsearch",
    "start_offset" : 0,
    "end_offset" : 13,
    "type" : "<ALPHANUM>",
    "position" : 0
  }, {
    "token" : "server",
    "start_offset" : 14,
```

```
      "end_offset" : 20,
      "type" : "<ALPHANUM>",
      "position" : 1
    } ]
  }
```

You can see that Elasticsearch has divided the text into two terms—the first one has a token value of elasticsearch and the second one has a token value of the server.

Now let's look at how the query text was analyzed. We can do this by running the following command:

```
curl -XGET 'localhost:9200/books/_analyze?pretty&field=title' -d
'elasticsearch'
```

The response of the request will look as follows:

```
  {
    "tokens" : [ {
      "token" : "elasticsearch",
      "start_offset" : 0,
      "end_offset" : 13,
      "type" : "<ALPHANUM>",
      "position" : 0
    } ]
  }
```

We can see that the word is the same as the original one that we passed to the query. We won't get into the Lucene query details and how the query parser constructed the query, but in general the indexed term after the analysis was the same as the one in the query after the analysis; so, the document matched the query and the result was returned.

URI query string parameters

There are a few parameters that we can use to control URI query behavior, which we will discuss now. The thing to remember is that each parameter in the query should be concatenated with the & character, as shown in the following example:

```
curl -XGET 'localhost:9200/books/_search?pretty&q=published:2013&df=title
&explain=true&default_operator=AND'
```

Please remember to enclose the URL of the request using the ' characters because, on Linux-based systems, the & character will be analyzed by the Linux shell.

The query

The q parameter allows us to specify the query that we want our documents to match. It allows us to specify the query using the Lucene query syntax described in the Lucene query syntax section later in this chapter. For example, a simple query would look like this: q=title:elasticsearch.

The default search field

Using the df parameter, we can specify the default search field that should be used when no field indicator is used in the q parameter. By default, the _all field will be used. (This is the field that Elasticsearch uses to copy the content of all the other fields. We will discuss this in greater depth in *Chapter 2, Indexing Your Data*). An example of the df parameter value can be df=title.

Analyzer

The analyzer property allows us to define the name of the analyzer that should be used to analyze our query. By default, our query will be analyzed by the same analyzer that was used to analyze the field contents during indexing.

The default operator property

The default_operator property that can be set to OR or AND, allows us to specify the default Boolean operator used for our query (http://en.wikipedia.org/wiki/Boolean_algebra). By default, it is set to OR, which means that a single query term match will be enough for a document to be returned. Setting this parameter to AND for a query will result in returning the documents that match all the query terms.

Query explanation

If we set the explain parameter to true, Elasticsearch will include additional explain information with each document in the result—such as the shard from which the document was fetched and the detailed information about the scoring calculation (we will talk more about it in the *Understanding the explain information* section in *Chapter 6, Make Your Search Better*). Also remember not to fetch the explain information during normal search queries because it requires additional resources and adds performance degradation to the queries. For example, a query that includes explain information could look as follows:

```
curl -XGET 'localhost:9200/books/_search?pretty&explain=true&q=title:solr'
```

The results returned by Elasticsearch for the preceding query would be as follows:

```
{
  "took" : 2,
  "timed_out" : false,
  "_shards" : {
    "total" : 5,
    "successful" : 5,
    "failed" : 0
  },
  "hits" : {
    "total" : 2,
    "max_score" : 0.70273256,
    "hits" : [ {
      "_shard" : 2,
      "_node" : "v5iRsht9SOWVzu-GY-YH1A",
      "_index" : "books",
      "_type" : "solr",
      "_id" : "2",
      "_score" : 0.70273256,
      "_source" : {
        "title" : "Solr Cookbook Third Edition",
        "published" : 2015
      },
      "_explanation" : {
        "value" : 0.70273256,
        "description" : "weight(title:solr in 0)
          [PerFieldSimilarity], result of:",
        "details" : [ {
          "value" : 0.70273256,
          "description" : "fieldWeight in 0, product of:",
          "details" : [ {
            "value" : 1.0,
            "description" : "tf(freq=1.0), with freq of:",
            "details" : [ {
              "value" : 1.0,
              "description" : "termFreq=1.0",
              "details" : [ ]
            } ]
          }, {
            "value" : 1.4054651,
            "description" : "idf(docFreq=1, maxDocs=3)",
            "details" : [ ]
          }, {
```

```
            "value" : 0.5,
            "description" : "fieldNorm(doc=0)",
            "details" : [ ]
          } ]
        } ]
      }
    }, {
      "_shard" : 3,
      "_node" : "v5iRsht9SOWVzu-GY-YHlA",
      "_index" : "books",
      "_type" : "solr",
      "_id" : "1",
      "_score" : 0.5,
      "_source" : {
        "title" : "Apache Solr 4 Cookbook",
        "published" : 2012
      },
      "_explanation" : {
        "value" : 0.5,
        "description" : "weight(title:solr in 1)
          [PerFieldSimilarity], result of:",
        "details" : [ {
          "value" : 0.5,
          "description" : "fieldWeight in 1, product of:",
          "details" : [ {
            "value" : 1.0,
            "description" : "tf(freq=1.0), with freq of:",
            "details" : [ {
              "value" : 1.0,
              "description" : "termFreq=1.0",
              "details" : [ ]
            } ]
          }, {
            "value" : 1.0,
            "description" : "idf(docFreq=1, maxDocs=2)",
            "details" : [ ]
          }, {
            "value" : 0.5,
            "description" : "fieldNorm(doc=1)",
            "details" : [ ]
          } ]
        } ]
      }
    } ]
  }
}
```

The fields returned

By default, for each document returned, Elasticsearch will include the index name, the type name, the document identifier, score, and the _source field. We can modify this behavior by adding the fields parameter and specifying a comma-separated list of field names. The field will be retrieved from the stored fields (if they exist; we will discuss them in *Chapter 2, Indexing Your Data*) or from the internal _source field. By default, the value of the fields parameter is _source. An example is: fields=title,priority.

We can also disable the fetching of the _source field by adding the _source parameter with its value set to false.

Sorting the results

Using the sort parameter, we can specify custom sorting. The default behavior of Elasticsearch is to sort the returned documents in descending order of the value of the _score field. If we want to sort our documents differently, we need to specify the sort parameter. For example, adding sort=published:desc will sort the documents in descending order of published field. By adding the sort=published:asc parameter, we will tell Elasticsearch to sort the documents on the basis of the published field in ascending order.

If we specify custom sorting, Elasticsearch will omit the _score field calculation for the documents. This may not be the desired behavior in your case. If you want to still keep a track of the scores for each document when using a custom sort, you should add the track_scores=true property to your query. Please note that tracking the scores when doing custom sorting will make the query a little bit slower (you may not even notice the difference) due to the processing power needed to calculate the score.

The search timeout

By default, Elasticsearch doesn't have timeout for queries, but you may want your queries to timeout after a certain amount of time (for example, 5 seconds). Elasticsearch allows you to do this by exposing the timeout parameter. When the timeout parameter is specified, the query will be executed up to a given timeout value and the results that were gathered up to that point will be returned. To specify a timeout of 5 seconds, you will have to add the timeout=5s parameter to your query.

The results window

Elasticsearch allows you to specify the results window (the range of documents in the results list that should be returned). We have two parameters that allow us to specify the results window size: `size` and `from`. The size parameter defaults to 10 and defines the maximum number of results returned. The `from` parameter defaults to 0 and specifies from which document the results should be returned. In order to return five documents starting from the 11th one, we will add the following parameters to the query: `size=5&from=10`.

Limiting per-shard results

Elasticsearch allows us to specify the maximum number of documents that should be fetched from each shard using `terminate_after` property and specifying the maximum number of documents. For example, if we want to get no more than 100 documents from each shard, we can add `terminate_after=100` to our URI request.

Ignoring unavailable indices

When running queries against multiple indices, it is handy to tell Elasticsearch that we don't care about the indices that are not available. By default, Elasticsearch will throw an error if one of the indices is not available, but we can change this by simply adding the `ignore_unavailable=true` parameter to our URI request.

The search type

The URI query allows us to specify the search type using the `search_type` parameter, which defaults to `query_then_fetch`. Two values that we can use here are: `dfs_query_then_fetch` and `query_then_fetch`. The rest of the search types available in older Elasticsearch versions are now deprecated or removed. We'll learn more about search types in the *Understanding the querying process* section of *Chapter 3, Searching Your Data*.

Lowercasing term expansion

Some queries, such as the prefix query, use query expansion. We will discuss this in the *Query rewrite* section in *Chapter 4, Extending Your Querying Knowledge*. We are allowed to define whether the expanded terms should be lowercased or not using the `lowercase_expanded_terms` property. By default, the `lowercase_expanded_terms` property is set to `true`, which means that the expanded terms will be lowercased.

Wildcard and prefix analysis

By default, wildcard queries and prefix queries are not analyzed. If we want to change this behavior, we can set the `analyze_wildcard` property to `true`.

 If you want to see all the parameters exposed by Elasticsearch as the URI request parameters, please refer to the official documentation available at: `https://www.elastic.co/guide/en/elasticsearch/reference/current/search-uri-request.html`.

Lucene query syntax

We thought that it would be good to know a bit more about what syntax can be used in the q parameter passed in the URI query. Some of the queries in Elasticsearch (such as the one currently being discussed) support the Lucene query parser syntax—the language that allows you to construct queries. Let's take a look at it and discuss some basic features.

A query that we pass to Lucene is divided into terms and operators by the query parser. Let's start with the terms; you can distinguish them into two types—single terms and phrases. For example, to query for a `book` term in the `title` field, we will pass the following query:

```
title:book
```

To query for the `elasticsearch book` phrase in the title field, we will pass the following query:

```
title:"elasticsearch book"
```

You may have noticed the name of the field in the beginning and in the term or the phrase later.

As we already said, the Lucene query syntax supports operators. For example, the + operator tells Lucene that the given part must be matched in the document, meaning that the term we are searching for must present in the field in the document. The - operator is the opposite, which means that such a part of the query can't be present in the document. A part of the query without the + or - operator will be treated as the given part of the query that can be matched but it is not mandatory. So, if we want to find a document with the `book` term in the title field and without the `cat` term in the description field, we send the following query:

```
+title:book -description:cat
```

We can also group multiple terms with parentheses, as shown in the following query:

```
title:(crime punishment)
```

We can also boost parts of the query (this increases their importance for the scoring algorithm — the higher the boost, the more important the query part is) with the ^ operator and the boost value after it, as shown in the following query:

```
title:book^4
```

These are the basics of the Lucene query language and should allow you to use Elasticsearch and construct queries without any problems. However, if you are interested in the Lucene query syntax and you would like to explore that in depth, please refer to the official documentation of the query parser available at `http://lucene.apache.org/core/5_4_0/queryparser/org/apache/lucene/queryparser/classic/package-summary.html`.

Summary

In this chapter, we learned what full text search is and the contribution Apache Lucene makes to this. In addition to this, we are now familiar with the basic concepts of Elasticsearch and its top-level architecture. We used the Elasticsearch REST API not only to index data, but also to update, retrieve, and finally delete it. We've learned what versioning is and how we can use it for optimistic locking in Elasticsearch. Finally, we searched our data using the simple URI query.

In the next chapter, we'll focus on indexing our data. We will see how Elasticsearch indexing works and what the role of primary shards and replicas is. We'll see how Elasticsearch handles data that it doesn't know and how to create our own mappings—the JSON structure that describes the structure of our index. We'll also learn how to use batch indexing to speed up the indexing process and what additional information can be stored along with our index to help us achieve our goal. In addition, we will discuss what an index segment is, what segment merging is, and how to tune a segment. Finally, we'll see how routing works in Elasticsearch and what options we have when it comes to both indexing and querying routing.

2
Indexing Your Data

In the previous chapter, we learned what full text search is and how Apache Lucene fits there. We were introduced to the basic concepts of Elasticsearch and we are now familiar with its top-level architecture, so we know how it works. We used the REST API to index data, to update it, to delete it, and of course to retrieve it. We searched our data with the simple URI query and we used versioning that allowed us to use optimistic locking functionality. By the end of this chapter, you will have learned the following topics:

- Basic information about Elasticsearch indexing
- Adjusting Elasticsearch schema-less behavior
- Creating your own mappings
- Using out of the box analyzers
- Configuring your own analyzers
- Index data in batches
- Adding additional internal information to indices
- Segment merging
- Routing

Elasticsearch indexing

So far we have our Elasticsearch cluster up and running. We also know how to use Elasticsearch REST API to index our data, we know how to retrieve it, and we also know how to remove the data that we no longer need. We've also learned how to search in our data by using the URI request search and Apache Lucene query language. However, until now we've used Elasticsearch functionality that allows us not to care about indices, shards, and data structure. This is not something that you may be used to when you are coming from the world of SQL databases, where you need the database and the tables with all the columns created upfront. In general, you needed to describe the data structure to be able to put data into the database. Elasticsearch is schema-less and by default creates indices automatically and because of that we can just install it and index data without the need of any preparations. However, this is usually not the best situation when it comes to production environments where you want to control the analysis of your data. Because of that we will start with showing you how to manage your indices and then we will get you through the world of mappings in Elasticsearch.

Shards and replicas

In *Chapter 1, Getting Started with Elasticsearch Cluster*, we told you that indices in Elasticsearch are built from one or more shards. Each of those shards contains part of the document set and each shard is a separate Lucene index. In addition to that, each shard can have replicas – physical copies of the primary shard itself. When we create an index, we can tell Elasticsearch how many shards it should be built from.

> The default number of shards that Elasticsearch uses is 5 and each index will also contain a single replica. The default configuration can be changed by setting the `index.number_of_shards` and `index.number_of_replicas` properties in the `elasticsearch.yml` configuration file.

When defaults are used, we will end up with five Apache Lucene indices that our Elasticsearch index is built of and one replica for each of those. So, with five shards and one replica, we would actually get 10 shards. This is because each shard would get its own copy, so the total number of shards in the cluster would be 10.

Dividing indices in such a way allows us to spread the shards across the cluster. The nice thing about that is that all the shards will be automatically spread throughout the cluster. If we have a single node, Elasticsearch will put the five primary shards on that node and will leave the replicas unassigned, because Elasticsearch doesn't assign shards and their replicas to the same node. The reason for that is simple – if a node would crash, we would lose both the primary source of the data and all the copies. So, if you have one Elasticsearch node, don't worry about replicas not being assigned – it is something to be expected. Of course when you have enough nodes for Elasticsearch to assign all the replicas (in addition to shards), it is not good to not have them assigned and you should look for the probable causes of that situation.

The thing to remember is that having shards and replicas is not free. First of all, each replica needs additional disk space, exactly the same amount of space that the original shard needs. So if we have 3 replicas for our index, we will actually need 4 times more space. If our primary shard weighs 100GB in total, with 3 replicas we would need 400GB – 100GB for each replica. However, this is not the only cost. Each replica is a Lucene index on its own and Elasticsearch needs some memory to handle that. The more shards in the cluster, the more memory is being used. And finally, having replicas means that we will have to do indexation on each of the replica, in addition to the indexation on the primary shard. There is a notion of shadow replicas which can copy the whole binary index, but, in most cases, each replica will do its own indexation. The good thing about replicas is that Elasticsearch will try to spread the query and get requests evenly between the shards and their replicas, which means that we can scale our cluster horizontally by using them.

So to sum up the conclusions:

- Having more shards in the index allows us to spread the index between more servers and parallelize the indexing operations and thus have better indexing throughput.

- Depending on your deployment, having more shards may increase query throughput and lower queries latency – especially in environments that don't have a large number of queries per second.

- Having more shards may be slower compared to a single shard query, because Elasticsearch needs to retrieve the data from multiple servers and combine them together in memory, before returning the final query results.

- Having more replicas results in a more resilient cluster, because when the primary shard is not available, its copy will take that role. Basically, having a single replica allows us to lose one copy of a shard and still serve the whole data. Having two replicas allows us to lose two copies of the shard and still see the whole data.

- The higher the replica count, the higher queries throughput the cluster will have. That's because each replica can serve the data it has independently from all the others.

- The higher number of shards (both primary and replicas) will result in more memory needed by Elasticsearch.

Of course, these are not the only relationships between the number of shards and replicas in Elasticsearch. We will talk about most of them later in the book.

So, how many shards and replicas should we have for our indices? That depends. We believe that the defaults are quite good but nothing can replace a good test. Note that the number of replicas is not very important because you can adjust it on a live cluster after index creation. You can remove and add them if you want and have the resources to run them. Unfortunately, this is not true when it comes to the number of shards. Once you have your index created, the only way to change the number of shards is to create another index and re-index your data.

Write consistency

Elasticsearch allows us to control the write consistency to prevent writes happening when they should not. By default, Elasticsearch indexing operation is successful when the write is successful on the quorum on active shards – meaning 50% of the active shards plus one. We can control this behavior by adding `action.write_consitency` to our `elasticsearch.yml` file or by adding the consistency parameter to our index request. The mentioned properties can take the following values:

- `quorum`: The default value, requiring 50% plus 1 active shards to be successful for the index operation to succeed

- `one`: Requires only a single active shard to be successful for the index operation to succeed

- `all`: Requires all the active shards to be successful for the index operation to succeed

Creating indices

When we were indexing our documents in *Chapter 1, Getting Started with Elasticsearch Cluster*, we didn't care about index creation at all. We assumed that Elasticsearch will do everything for us and actually it was true; we just used the following command:

```
curl -XPUT 'http://localhost:9200/blog/article/1' -d '{"title": "New
version of Elasticsearch released!", "content": "Version 1.0 released
today!", "tags": ["announce", "elasticsearch", "release"] }'
```

This is just fine. If such an index does not exist, Elasticsearch automatically creates the index for us. However, there are times when we want to create indices ourselves for various reasons. Maybe we would like to have control over which indices are created to avoid errors or maybe we have some non default settings that we would like to use when creating a particular index. The reasons may differ, but it's good to know that we can create indices without indexing documents.

The simplest way to create an index is to run a PUT HTTP request with the name of the index we want to create. For example, to create an index called blog, we could use the following command:

```
curl -XPUT http://localhost:9200/blog/
```

We just told Elasticsearch that we want to create the index with the name blog. If everything goes right, you will see the following response from Elasticsearch:

```
{"acknowledged":true}
```

Altering automatic index creation

We already mentioned that automatic index creation is not the best idea in some cases. For example, a simple typo during index creation can lead to creating hundreds of unused indices and make cluster state information larger than it should be, putting more pressure on Elasticsearch and the underlying JVM. Because of that, we can turn off automatic index creation by adding a simple property to the elasticsearch.yml configuration file:

```
action.auto_create_index: false
```

Let's stop for a while and discuss the action.auto_create_index property, because it allows us to do more complicated things than just allowing (setting it to true) and disabling (setting it to false) automatic index creation. The mentioned property allows us to use patterns that specify the index names which should be allowed to be automatically created and which should be disallowed. For example, let's assume that we would like to allow automatic index creation for indices starting with logs and we would like to disallow all the others. To do something like this, we would set the action.auto_create_index property to something as follows:

```
action.auto_create_index: +logs*,-*
```

Now if we would like to create an index called logs_2015-10-01, we would succeed. To create such an index, we would use the following command:

```
curl -XPUT http://localhost:9200/logs_2015-10-01/log/1 -d '{"message":
"Test log message" }'
```

Elasticsearch would respond with:

```
{
  "_index" : "logs_2015-10-01",
  "_type" : "log",
  "_id" : "1",
  "_version" : 1,
  "_shards" : {
    "total" : 2,
    "successful" : 1,
    "failed" : 0
  },
  "created" : true
}
```

However, suppose we now try to create the `blog` using the following command:

```
curl -XPUT http://localhost:9200/blog/article/1 -d '{"title": "Test
article title" }'
```

Elasticsearch would respond with an error similar to the following one:

```
{
  "error" : {
    "root_cause" : [ {
      "type" : "index_not_found_exception",
      "reason" : "no such index",
      "resource.type" : "index_expression",
      "resource.id" : "blog",
      "index" : "blog"
    } ],
    "type" : "index_not_found_exception",
    "reason" : "no such index",
    "resource.type" : "index_expression",
    "resource.id" : "blog",
    "index" : "blog"
  },
  "status" : 404
}
```

One thing to remember is that the order of pattern definitions matters. Elasticsearch checks the patterns up to the first pattern that matches, so if we move -* as the first pattern, the +logs* pattern won't be used at all.

Settings for a newly created index

Manual index creation is also necessary when we want to pass non default configuration options during index creation; for example, initial number of shards and replicas. We can do that by including JSON payload with settings as the PUT HTTP request body. For example, if we would like to tell Elasticsearch that our blog index should only have a single shard and two replicas initially, the following command could be used:

```
curl -XPUT http://localhost:9200/blog/ -d '{
    "settings" : {
        "number_of_shards" : 1,
        "number_of_replicas" : 2
    }
}'
```

The preceding command will result in the creation of the blog index with one shard and two replicas, making a total of three physical Lucene indices – called shards as we already know. Of course there are a lot more settings that we can use, but what we did is enough for now and we will learn about the rest throughout the book.

Index deletion

Of course, similar to how we handled documents, Elasticsearch allows us to delete indices as well. Deleting an index is very similar to creating it, but instead of using the PUT HTTP method, we use the DELETE one. For example, if we would like to delete our previously created blog index, we would run the following command:

```
curl -XDELETE http://localhost:9200/blog
```

The response will be the same as the one we saw earlier when we created an index and should look as follows:

```
{"acknowledged":true}
```

Now that we know what an index is, how to create it, and how to delete it, we are ready to create indices with the mappings we have defined. Even though Elasticsearch is schema–less, there are a lot of situations where we would like to manually create the schema, to avoid any problems with the index structure.

Mappings configuration

If you are used to SQL databases, you may know that before you can start inserting the data in the database, you need to create a schema, which will describe what your data looks like. Although Elasticsearch is a schema-less (we rather call it data driven schema) search engine and can figure out the data structure on the fly, we think that controlling the structure and thus defining it ourselves is a better way. The field type determining mechanism is not going to guess the future. For example, if you first send an `integer` value, such as 60, and you send a `float` value such as 70.23 for the same field, an error can happen or Elasticsearch will just cut off the decimal part of the `float` value (which is actually what happens). This is because Elasticsearch will first set the field type to integer and will try to index the `float` value to the `integer` field which will cause cutting of the decimal point in the floating point number. In the next few pages you'll see how to create mappings that suit your needs and match your data structure.

> Note that we didn't include all the information about the available types in this chapter and some features of Elasticsearch, such as nested type, parent-child handling, storing geographical points, and search, are described in the following chapters of this book.

Type determining mechanism

Before we start describing how to create mappings manually, we want to get back to the automatic type determining algorithm used in Elasticsearch. As we already said, Elasticsearch can try guessing the schema for our documents by looking at the JSON that the document is built from. Because JSON is structured, that seems easy to do. For example, strings are surrounded by quotation marks, Booleans are defined using specific words, and numbers are just a few digits. This is a simple trick, but it usually works. For example, let's look at the following document:

```
{
  "field1": 10,
  "field2": "10"
}
```

The preceding document has two fields. The `field1` field will be given a type number (to be precise, that field will be given a long type). The second field, called `field2` will be given a string type, because it is surrounded by quotation marks. Of course, for some use cases this can be the desired behavior. However, if somehow we would surround all the data using quotation mark (which is not the best idea anyway) our index structure would contain only string type fields.

Don't worry about the fact that you are not familiar with what are the numeric types, the string types, and so on. We will describe them after we show you what you can do to tune the automatic type determining mechanism in Elasticsearch.

Disabling the type determining mechanism

The first solution is to completely disable the schema-less behavior in Elasticsearch. We can do that by adding the `index.mapper.dynamic` property to our index properties and setting it to `false`. We can do that by running the following command to create the index:

```
curl -XPUT 'localhost:9200/sites' -d '{
  "index.mapper.dynamic": false
}'
```

By doing that we told Elasticsearch that we don't want it to guess the type of our documents in the site's index and that we will provide the mappings ourselves. If we will try indexing some example document to the site's index, we will get the following error:

```
{
    "error" : {
      "root_cause" : [ {
        "type" : "type_missing_exception",
        "reason" : "type[[doc, trying to auto create mapping, but
          dynamic mapping is disabled]] missing",
        "index" : "sites"
      } ],
      "type" : "type_missing_exception",
      "reason" : "type[[doc, trying to auto create mapping, but
        dynamic mapping is disabled]] missing",
      "index" : "sites"
    },
    "status" : 404
}
```

This is because we didn't create any mappings – no schema for documents was created. Elasticsearch couldn't create one for us because we didn't allow it and the indexation command failed.

Of course this is not the only thing we can do when it comes to configuring how the type determining mechanism works. We can also tune it or disable it for a given type on the object level. We will talk about the second case in *Chapter 5, Extending Your Index Structure*. For now, let's look at the possibilities of tuning type determining mechanism in Elasticsearch.

Tuning the type determining mechanism for numeric types

One of the solutions to the problems with JSON documents and type guessing is that we are not always in control of the data. The documents that we are indexing can come from multiple places and some systems in our environment may include quotation marks for all the fields in the document. This can lead to problems and bad guesses. Because of that, Elasticsearch allows us to enable more aggressive fields value checking for numeric fields by setting the `numeric_detection` property to `true` in the mappings definition. For example, let's assume that we want to create an index called users and we want it to have the user type on which we will want more aggressive numeric fields parsing. To do that, we will use the following command:

```
curl -XPUT http://localhost:9200/users/?pretty -d '{
  "mappings" : {
    "user": {
      "numeric_detection" : true
    }
  }
}'
```

Now let's run the following command to index a single document to the users index:

```
curl -XPOST http://localhost:9200/users/user/1 -d '{"name": "User 1",
"age": "20"}'
```

Earlier, with the default settings, the age field would be set to string type. With the `numeric_detection` property set to `true`, the type of the age field will be set to long. We can check that by running the following command (it will retrieve the mappings for all the types in the users index):

```
curl -XGET 'localhost:9200/users/_mapping?pretty'
```

The preceding command should result in the following response returned by Elasticsearch:

```
{
  "users" : {
    "mappings" : {
      "user" : {
        "numeric_detection" : true,
        "properties" : {
          "age" : {
            "type" : "long"
          },
          "name" : {
            "type" : "string"
          }
        }
      }
    }
  }
}
```

As we can see, the age field was really set to be of type long.

Tuning the type determining mechanism for dates

Another type of data that causes trouble are fields with dates. Dates can come in different flavors, for example, 2015-10-01 11:22:33 is a proper date and so is 2015-10-01T11:22:33+00. Because of that, Elasticsearch tries to match the fields to timestamps or strings that match some given date format. If that matching operation is successful, the field is treated as a date based one. If we know how our date fields look, we can help Elasticsearch by providing a list of recognized date formats using the dynamic_date_formats property, which allows us to specify the formats array. Let's look at the following command for creating an index:

```
curl -XPUT 'http://localhost:9200/blog/' -d '{
  "mappings" : {
    "article" : {
      "dynamic_date_formats" : ["yyyy-MM-dd hh:mm"]
    }
  }
}'
```

The preceding command will result in the creation of an index called blog with the single type called article. We've also used the `dynamic_date_formats` property with a single date format that will result in Elasticsearch using the date core type (refer to the `Core types` section in this chapter for more information about field types) for fields matching the defined format. Elasticsearch uses the `joda-time` library to define the date formats, so visit `http://joda-time.sourceforge.net/api-release/org/joda/time/format/DateTimeFormat.html` if you are interested in knowing about them.

> Remember that the `dynamic_date_format` property accepts an array of values. That means that we can handle several date formats simultaneously.

With the preceding index, we can now try indexing a new document using the following command:

```
curl -XPUT localhost:9200/blog/article/1 -d '{"name": "Test", "test_field":"2015-10-01 11:22"}'
```

Elasticsearch will of course index that document, but let's look at the mappings created for our index:

```
curl -XGET 'localhost:9200/blog/_mapping?pretty'
```

The response for the preceding command will be as follows:

```
{
  "blog" : {
    "mappings" : {
      "article" : {
        "dynamic_date_formats" : [ "yyyy-MM-dd hh:mm" ],
        "properties" : {
          "name" : {
            "type" : "string"
          },
          "test_field" : {
            "type" : "date",
            "format" : "yyyy-MM-dd hh:mm"
          }
        }
      }
    }
  }
}
```

As we can see, the `test_field` field was given a date type, so our tuning works.

Unfortunately, the problem still exists if we want the Boolean type to be guessed. There is no option to force the guessing of Boolean types from the text. In such cases, when a change of source format is impossible, we can only define the field directly in the mappings definition.

Index structure mapping

Each data has its own structure – some are very simple, and some include complicated object relations, children documents, and nested properties. In each case, we need to have a schema in Elasticsearch called mappings that define how the data looks. Of course, we can use the schema-less nature of Elasticsearch, but we can and we usually want to prepare the mappings upfront, so we know how the data is handled.

For the purposes of this chapter, we will use a single type in the index. Of course, Elasticsearch as a multitenant system allows us to have multiple types in a single index, but we want to simplify the example, to make it easier to understand. So, for the purpose of the next few pages, we will create an index called posts that will hold data for documents in a post type. We also assume that the index will hold the following information:

- Unique identifier of the blog post
- Name of the blog post
- Publication date
- Contents – text of the post itself

In Elasticsearch, mappings, as with almost all communication, are sent as JSON objects in the request body. So, if we want to create the simplest mappings that matches our need, it will look as follows (we stored the mappings in the posts.json file, so we can easily send it):

```
{
  "mappings": {
    "post": {
      "properties": {
        "id": { "type":"long" },
        "name": { "type":"string" },
        "published": { "type":"date" },
        "contents": { "type":"string" }
      }
    }
  }
}
```

To create our posts index with the preceding mappings file, we will just run the following command:

```
curl -XPOST 'http://localhost:9200/posts' -d @posts.json
```

 Note that you can store your mappings and set a file name to whatever name you like. The `curl` command will just take the contents of it.

And again, if everything goes well, we see the following response:

```
{"acknowledged":true}
```

Elasticsearch reported that our index has been created. If we look at the Elasticsearch node – on the current master, we will see something as follows:

```
[2015-10-14 15:02:12,840] [INFO ] [cluster.metadata        ] [Shalla-
Bal] [posts] creating index, cause [api], templates [], shards [5]/[1],
mappings [post]
```

We can see that the posts index has been created, with 5 shards and 1 replica (shards [5]/[1]) and with mappings for a single post type (mappings [post]). Let's now discuss the contents of the posts.json file and the possibilities when it comes to mappings.

Type and types definition

The mappings definition in Elasticsearch is just another JSON object, so it needs to be properly started and ended with curly brackets. All the mappings definitions are nested inside a single mappings object. In our example, we had a single post type, but we can have multiple of them. For example, if we would like to have more than a single type in our mappings, we just need to separate them with a comma character. Let's assume that we would like to have an additional user type in our posts index. The mappings definition in such case will look as follows (we stored it in the posts_ with_user.json file):

```
{
    "mappings": {
        "post": {
            "properties": {
                "id": { "type":"long" },
                "name": { "type":"string" },
                "published": { "type":"date" },
                "contents": { "type":"string" }
            }
```

```
      },
      "user": {
        "properties": {
          "id": { "type":"long" },
          "name": { "type":"string" }
        }
      }
    }
  }
```

As you can see, we can name the types with the names we want. Under each type we have the `properties` object in which we store the actual name of the fields and their definition.

Fields

Each field in the mappings definition is just a name and an object describing the properties of the field. For example, we can have a field defined as the following:

```
"body": { "type":"string", "store":"yes", "index":"analyzed" }
```

The preceding field definition starts with a name – `body`. After that we have an object with three properties – the type of the field (the `type` property), if the original field value should be stored (the `store` property), and if the field should be indexed and how (the `index` property). And, of course, multiple field definitions are separated from each other using the comma character, just like other JSON objects.

Core types

Each field type in Elasticsearch can be given one of the provided core types. The core types in Elasticsearch are as follows:

- String
- Number (`integer`, `long`, `float`, `double`)
- Date
- Boolean
- Binary

In addition to the core types, Elasticsearch provides additional types that can handle more complicated data – such as nested documents, object, and so on. We will talk about them in *Chapter 5, Extending Your Index Structure*.

Common attributes

Before continuing with all the core type descriptions, we would like to discuss some common attributes that you can use to describe all the types (except for the binary one):

- `index_name`: This attribute defines the name of the field that will be stored in the index. If this is not defined, the name will be set to the name of the object that the field is defined with. Usually, you don't need to set this property, but it may be useful in some cases; for example, when you don't have control over the name of the fields in the JSON documents that are sent to Elasticsearch.

- `index`: This attribute can take the values `analyzed` and `no` and, for string-based fields, it can also be set to the additional `not_analyzed` value. If set to `analyzed`, the field will be indexed and thus searchable. If set to `no`, you won't be able to search on such a field. The default value is `analyzed`. In case of string-based fields, there is an additional option, `not_analyzed`. This, when set, will mean that the field will be indexed but not analyzed. So, the field is written in the index as it was sent to Elasticsearch and only a perfect match will be counted during a search – the query will have to include exactly the same value as the value in the index. If we compare it to the SQL databases world, setting the index property of a field to `not_analyzed` would work just like using where `field = value`. Also remember that setting the index property to no will result in the disabling inclusion of that field in `include_in_all` (the `include_in_all` property is discussed as the last property in the list).

- `store`: This attribute can take the values `yes` and `no` and specifies if the original value of the field should be written into the index. The default value is `no`, which means that Elasticsearch won't store the original value of the field and will try to use the `_source` field (the JSON representing the original document that has been sent to Elasticsearch) when you want to retrieve the field value. Stored fields are not used for searching, however they can be used for highlighting if enabled (which may be more efficient that loading the `_source` field in case it is big).

- `doc_values`: This attribute can take the values of `true` and `false`. When set to `true`, Elasticsearch will create a special on disk structure during indexation for not tokenized fields (like not analyzed string fields, number based fields, Boolean fields, and date fields). This structure is highly efficient and is used by Elasticsearch for operations that require un-inverted data, such as aggregations, sorting, or scripting. Starting with Elasticsearch 2.0 the default value of this is `true` for not tokenized fields. Setting this value to `false` will result in Elasticsearch using field data cache instead of doc values, which has higher memory demand, but may be faster in some rare situations.

- `boost`: This attribute defines how important the field is inside the document; the higher the boost, the more important the values in the field are. The default value of this attribute is 1, which means a neutral value – anything above 1 will make the field more important, anything less than 1 will make it less important.

- `null_value`: This attribute specifies a value that should be written into the index in case that field is not a part of an indexed document. The default behavior will just omit that field.

- `copy_to`: This attribute specifies an array of fields to which the original value will be copied to. This allows for different kind of analysis of the same data. For example, you could imagine having two fields – one called title and one called `title_sort`, each having the same value but processed differently. We could use `copy_to` to copy the title field value to `title_sort`.

- `include_in_all`: This attribute specifies if the field should be included in the _all field. The _all field is a special field used by Elasticsearch to allow easy searching in the contents of the whole indexed document. Elasticsearch creates the content of the _all field by copying all the document fields there. By default, if the _all field is used, all the fields will be included in it.

String

String is the basic text type which allows us to store one or more characters inside it. A sample definition of such a field is as follows:

```
"body" : { "type" : "string", "store" : "yes", "index" : "analyzed" }
```

In addition to the common attributes, the following attributes can also be set for the string-based fields:

- `term_vector`: This attribute can take the values no (the default one), yes, `with_offsets`, `with_positions`, and `with_positions_offsets`. It defines whether or not to calculate the Lucene term vectors for that field. If you are using highlighting (distinction which terms where matched in a document during the query), you will need to calculate the term vector for the so called fast vector highlighting – a more efficient highlighting version.

- `analyzer`: This attribute defines the name of the analyzer used for indexing and searching. It defaults to the globally-defined analyzer name.

- `search_analyzer`: This attribute defines the name of the analyzer used for processing the part of the query string that is sent to a particular field.

- `norms.enabled`: This attribute specifies whether the norms should be loaded for a field. By default, it is set to `true` for analyzed fields (which means that the norms will be loaded for such fields) and to `false` for non-analyzed fields. Norms are values inside of Lucene index that are used when calculating a score for a document – usually not needed for not analyzed fields and used only during query time. An example index creation command that disables norm for a single field present would look as follows:

```
curl -XPOST 'localhost:9200/essb' -d '{
 "mappings" : {
  "book" : {
   "properties" : {
    "name" : {
     "type" : "string",
     "norms" : {
      "enabled" : false
     }
    }
   }
  }
 }
}'
```

- `norms.loading`: This attribute takes the values `eager` and `lazy` and defines how Elasticsearch will load the norms. The first value means that the norms for such fields are always loaded. The second value means that the norms will be loaded only when needed. Norms are useful for scoring, but may require a vast amount of memory for large data sets. Having norms loaded eagerly (property set to `eager`) means less work during query time, but will lead to more memory consumption. An example index creation command that eagerly load norms for a single field present look as follows:

```
curl -XPOST 'localhost:9200/essb_eager' -d '{
 "mappings" : {
  "book" : {
   "properties" : {
    "name" : {
     "type" : "string",
     "norms" : {
      "loading" : "eager"
     }
    }
   }
  }
 }
}'
```

- `position_offset_gap`: This attribute defaults to 0 and specifies the gap in the index between instances of the given field with the same name. Setting this to a higher value may be useful if you want position-based queries (such as phrase queries) to match only inside a single instance of the field.

- `index_options`: This attribute defines the indexing options for the postings list – the structure holding the terms (we talk more about it in the `Postings format` section of this chapter). The possible values are docs (only document numbers are indexed), `freqs` (document numbers and term frequencies are indexed), `positions` (document numbers, term frequencies, and their positions are indexed), and `offsets` (document numbers, term frequencies, their positions, and offsets are indexed). The default value for this property is `positions` for analyzed fields and `docs` for fields that are indexed but not analyzed.

- `ignore_above`: This attribute defines the maximum size of the field in characters. A field whose size is above the specified value will be ignored by the analyzer.

> In one of the upcoming Elasticsearch versions, the string type may be deprecated and may be replaced by two new types, text and keyword, to better indicate what the string based field is representing. The text type will be used for analyzed text fields and the keyword type will be used for not analyzed text fields. If you are interested in the incoming changes, refer to the following GitHub issue: `https://github.com/elastic/elasticsearch/issues/12394`.

Number

This is the common name for a few core types that gather all the numeric field types that are available and waiting to be used. The following types are available in Elasticsearch (we specify them by using the type property):

- `byte`: This type defines a `byte` value; for example, 1. It allows for values between -128 and 127 inclusive.

- `short`: This type defines a `short` value; for example, 12. It allows for values between -32768 and 32767 inclusive.

- `integer`: This type defines an `integer` value; for example, 134. It allows for values between -231 and 231-1 inclusive up to Java 7 and values between 0 and 232-1 in Java 8.

- `long`: This type defines a `long` value; for example, 123456789. It allows for values between -263 and 263-1 inclusive up to Java 7 and values between 0 and 264-1 in Java 8.

- `float`: This type defines a `float` value; for example, `12.23`. For information about the possible values, refer to https://docs.oracle.com/javase/specs/jls/se8/html/jls-4.html#jls-4.2.3.

- `double`: This type defines a double value; for example, `123.45`. For information about the possible values, refer to https://docs.oracle.com/javase/specs/jls/se8/html/jls-4.html#jls-4.2.3.

> You can learn more about the mentioned Java types at http://docs.oracle.com/javase/tutorial/java/nutsandbolts/datatypes.html.

A sample definition of a field based on one of the numeric types is as follows:

```
"price" : { "type" : "float", "precision_step" : "4" }
```

In addition to the common attributes, the following ones can also be set for the numeric fields:

- `precision_step`: This attribute defines the number of terms generated for each value in the numeric field. The lower the value, the higher the number of terms generated. For fields with a higher number of terms per value, range queries will be faster at the cost of a slightly larger index. The default value is `16` for long and double, `8` for integer, short, and float, and `2147483647` for byte.

- `coerce`: This attribute defaults to true and can take the value of `true` or `false`. It defines if Elasticsearch should try to convert the string values to numbers for a given field and if the decimal parts of the `float` value should be truncated for the integer based fields.

- `ignore_malformed`: This attribute can take the value `true` or `false` (which is the default). It should be set to `true` in order to omit the badly formatted values.

Boolean

The `boolean` core type is designed for indexing the Boolean values (`true` or `false`). A sample definition of a field based on the `boolean` type is as follows:

```
"allowed" : { "type" : "boolean", "store": "yes" }
```

Binary

The binary field is a BASE64 representation of the binary data stored in the index. You can use it to store data that is normally written in binary form, such as images. Fields based on this type are by default stored and not indexed, so you can only retrieve them and not perform search operations on them. The binary type only supports the `index_name`, `type`, `store`, and `doc_values` properties. The sample field definition based on the binary field may look like the following:

```
"image" : { "type" : "binary" }
```

Date

The date core type is designed to be used for date indexing. The date in the field allows us to specify a format that will be recognized by Elasticsearch. It is worth noting that all the dates are indexed in UTC and are internally indexed as long values. In addition to that, for the date based fields, Elasticsearch accepts long values representing UTC milliseconds since epoch regardless of the format specified for the date field.

The default date format recognized by Elasticsearch is quite universal and allows us to provide the date and optionally the time; for example, 2012-12-24T12:10:22. A sample definition of a field based on the date type is as follows:

```
"published" : { "type" : "date", "format" : "YYYY-mm-dd" }
```

A sample document that uses the above date field with the specified format is as follows:

```
{
   "name" : "Sample document",
   "published" : "2012-12-22"
}
```

In addition to the common attributes, the following ones can also be set for the fields based on the `date` type:

- `format`: This attribute specifies the format of the date. The default value is `dateOptionalTime`. For a full list of formats, visit https://www.elastic.co/guide/en/elasticsearch/reference/current/mapping-date-format.html.

- `precision_step`: This attribute defines the number of terms generated for each value in the numeric field. Refer to the numeric core type description for more information about this parameter.

- `numeric_resolution`: This attribute defines the unit of time that Elasticsearch will use when a numeric value is passed to the date based field instead of the date following a format. By default, Elasticsearch uses the milliseconds value, which means that the numeric value will be treated as milliseconds since epoch. Another value is seconds.

- `ignore_malformed`: This attribute can take the value `true` or `false`. The default value is `false`. It should be set to `true` in order to omit badly formatted values.

Multi fields

There are situations where we need to have the same field analyzed differently. For example, one for sorting, one for searching, and one for analysis with aggregations, but all using the same field value, just indexed differently. We could of course use the previously described field value copying, but we can also use so called multi fields. To be able to use that feature of Elasticsearch, we need to define an additional property in our field definition called `fields`. The `fields` is an object that can contain one or more additional fields that will be present in our index and will have the value of the field that they are assigned to. For example, if we would like to have aggregations done on the `name` field and in addition to that search on that field, we would define it as follows:

```
"name": {
  "type": "string",
  "fields": {
    "agg": { "type" : "string", "index": "not_analyzed" }
  }
}
```

The preceding definition will create two fields – one called name and the second called `name.agg`. Of course, you don't have to specify two separate fields in the data you are sending to Elasticsearch – a single one named `name` is enough. Elasticsearch will do the rest, which means copying the value of the field to all the fields from the preceding definition.

The IP address type

The `ip` field type was added to Elasticsearch to simplify the use of IPv4 addresses in a numeric form. This field type allows us to search data that is indexed as an IP address, sort on such data, and use range queries using IP values.

A sample definition of a field based on one of the numeric types is as follows:

```
"address" : { "type" : "ip" }
```

In addition to the common attributes, the `precision_step` attribute can also be set for the `ip` type based fields. Refer to the numeric type description for more information about that property.

A sample document that uses the `ip` based field looks as follows:

```
{
  "name" : "Tom PC",
  "address" : "192.168.2.123"
}
```

Token count type

The `token_count` field type allows us to store and index information about how many tokens the given field has instead of storing and indexing the text provided to the field. It accepts the same configuration options as the number type, but in addition to that, we need to specify the analyzer which will be used to divide the field value into tokens. We do that by using the `analyzer` property.

A sample definition of a field based on the `token_count` field type looks as follows:

```
"title_count" : { "type" : "token_count", "analyzer" : "standard" }
```

Using analyzers

The great thing about Elasticsearch is that it leverages the analysis capabilities of Apache Lucene. This means that for fields that are based on the `string` type, we can specify which analyzer Elasticsearch should use. As you remember from the *Full text searching* section of *Chapter 1, Getting Started with Elasticsearch Cluster*, the analyzer is a functionality that is used to analyze data or queries in the way we want. For example, when we divide words on the basis of whitespaces and lowercase characters, we don't have to worry about the users sending words that are lowercased or uppercased. This means that Elasticsearch, elasticsearch, and ElAstIcSeaRCh will be treated as the same word. What's more is that Elasticsearch allows us to use not only the analyzers provided out of the box, but also create our own configurations. We can also use different analyzers at the time of indexing and different analyzers at the time of querying—we can choose how we want our data to be processed at each stage of the search process. Let's now have a look at the analyzers provided by Elasticsearch and at Elasticsearch analysis functionality in general.

Out-of-the-box analyzers

Elasticsearch allows us to use one of the many analyzers defined by default. The following analyzers are available out of the box:

- `standard`: This analyzer is convenient for most European languages (refer to `https://www.elastic.co/guide/en/elasticsearch/reference/current/analysis-standard-analyzer.html` for the full list of parameters).

- `simple`: This analyzer splits the provided value on non-letter characters and converts them to lowercase.

- `whitespace`: This analyzer splits the provided value on the basis of whitespace characters.

- `stop`: This is similar to a simple analyzer, but in addition to the functionality of the simple analyzer, it filters the data on the basis of the provided set of stop words (refer to `https://www.elastic.co/guide/en/elasticsearch/reference/current/analysis-stop-analyzer.html` for the full list of parameters).

- `keyword`: This is a very simple analyzer that just passes the provided value. You'll achieve the same by specifying a particular field as `not_analyzed`.

- `pattern`: This analyzer allows flexible text separation by the use of regular expressions (refer to `https://www.elastic.co/guide/en/elasticsearch/reference/current/analysis-pattern-analyzer.html` for the full list of parameters). The key point to remember when it comes to the pattern analyzer is that the provided pattern should match the separators of the words, not the words themselves.

- `language`: This analyzer is designed to work with a specific language. The full list of languages supported by this analyzer can be found at `https://www.elastic.co/guide/en/elasticsearch/reference/current/analysis-lang-analyzer.html`.

- `snowball`: This is an analyzer that is similar to standard, but additionally provides the stemming algorithm (refer to `https://www.elastic.co/guide/en/elasticsearch/reference/current/analysis-snowball-analyzer.html` for the full list of parameters).

Stemming is the process of reducing the inflected and derived words to their stem or base form. Such a process allows for the reduction of words, for example, with cars and car. For the mentioned words, stemmer (which is an implementation of the stemming algorithm) will produce a single stem, car. After indexing, the documents containing such words will be matched while using any of them. Without stemming, the documents with the word "cars" will only be matched by a query containing the same word. You can find more information about stemming on Wikipedia at https://en.wikipedia.org/wiki/Stemming.

Defining your own analyzers

In addition to the analyzers mentioned previously, Elasticsearch allows us to define new ones without the need for writing a single line of Java code. In order to do that, we need to add an additional section to our mappings file; that is, the settings section, which holds additional information used by Elasticsearch during index creation. The following code snippet shows how we can define our custom settings section:

```
"settings" : {
  "index" : {
    "analysis": {
      "analyzer": {
        "en": {
          "tokenizer": "standard",
          "filter": [
            "asciifolding",
            "lowercase",
            "ourEnglishFilter"
          ]
        }
      },
      "filter": {
        "ourEnglishFilter": {
          "type": "kstem"
        }
      }
    }
  }
}
```

We specified that we want a new analyzer named en to be present. Each analyzer is built from a single tokenizer and multiple filters. A complete list of the default filters and tokenizers can be found at https://www.elastic.co/guide/en/ elasticsearch/reference/current/analysis-tokenizers.html. Our en analyzer includes the standard tokenizer and three filters: asciifolding and lowercase, which are the ones available by default, and a custom ourEnglishFilter, which is a filter we have defined.

To define a filter, we need to provide its name, its type (the type property), and any number of additional parameters required by that filter type. The full list of filter types available in Elasticsearch can be found at https://www.elastic.co/guide/ en/elasticsearch/reference/current/analysis-tokenfilters.html. Please be aware, that we won't be discussing each filter as the list of filters is constantly changing. If you are interested in the full filters list, please refer to the mentioned page in the documentation.

So, the final mappings file with our custom analyzer defined will be as follows:

```
{
  "settings" : {
    "index" : {
      "analysis": {
        "analyzer": {
          "en": {
            "tokenizer": "standard",
            "filter": [
              "asciifolding",
              "lowercase",
              "ourEnglishFilter"
            ]
          }
        },
        "filter": {
          "ourEnglishFilter": {
            "type": "kstem"
          }
        }
      }
    }
  },
  "mappings" : {
    "post" : {
      "properties" : {
        "id": { "type" : "long" },
```

```
                "name": { "type" : "string", "analyzer": "en" }
            }
        }
    }
}
```

If we save the preceding mappings to a file called posts_mappings.json, we can run the following command to create the posts index:

```
curl -XPOST 'http://localhost:9200/posts' -d @posts_mappings.json
```

We can see how our analyzer works by using the Analyze API (https://www.elastic.co/guide/en/elasticsearch/reference/current/indices-analyze.html). For example, let's look at the following command:

```
curl -XGET 'localhost:9200/posts/_analyze?pretty&field=name' -d 'robots cars'
```

The command asks Elasticsearch to show the content of the analysis of the given phrase (robots cars) with the use of the analyzer defined for the post type and its name field. The response that we will get from Elasticsearch is as follows:

```
{
    "tokens" : [ {
        "token" : "robot",
        "start_offset" : 0,
        "end_offset" : 6,
        "type" : "<ALPHANUM>",
        "position" : 0
    }, {
        "token" : "car",
        "start_offset" : 7,
        "end_offset" : 11,
        "type" : "<ALPHANUM>",
        "position" : 1
    } ]
}
```

As you can see, the robots cars phrase was divided into two tokens. In addition to that, the robots word was changed to robot and the cars word was changed to car.

Default analyzers

There is one more thing to say about analyzers. Elasticsearch allows us to specify the analyzer that should be used by default if no analyzer is defined. This is done in the same way as we configured a custom analyzer in the settings section of the mappings file, but instead of specifying a custom name for the analyzer, a default keyword should be used. So to make our previously defined analyzer the default, we can change the en analyzer to the following:

```
{
  "settings" : {
    "index" : {
      "analysis": {
        "analyzer": {
          "default": {
            "tokenizer": "standard",
            "filter": [
              "asciifolding",
              "lowercase",
              "ourEnglishFilter"
            ]
          }
        },
        "filter": {
          "ourEnglishFilter": {
            "type": "kstem"
          }
        }
      }
    }
  }
}
```

We can also choose a different default analyzer for searching and a different one for indexing. If we would like to do that instead of using the default keyword for the analyzer name, we should use default_search and default_index respectively.

Different similarity models

With the release of Apache Lucene 4.0 in 2012, all the users of this great full text search library were given the opportunity to alter the default TF/IDF-based algorithm and use a different one (we've mentioned it in the *Full text searching* section of *Chapter 1, Getting Started with Elasticsearch Cluster*). Because of that we are able to choose a similarity model in Elasticsearch, which basically allows us to use different scoring formulas for our documents.

Note that the similarity models topic ranges from intermediate to advanced and in most cases the TF/IDF based algorithm will be sufficient for your use case. However, we decided to have it described in the book, so you know that you have the possibility of changing the scoring algorithm behavior if needed.

Setting per-field similarity

Since Elasticsearch 0.90, we are allowed to set a different similarity for each of the fields that we have in our mappings file. For example, let's assume that we have the following simple mappings that we use in order to index the blog posts:

```
{
  "mappings" : {
    "post" : {
      "properties" : {
        "id" : { "type" : "long" },
        "name" : { "type" : "string" },
        "contents" : { "type" : "string" }
      }
    }
  }
}
```

To do this, we will use the BM25 similarity model for the name field and the contents field. In order to do that, we need to extend our field definitions and add the similarity property with the value of the chosen similarity name. Our changed mappings will look like the following:

```
{
  "mappings" : {
    "post" : {
      "properties" : {
        "id" : { "type" : "long" },
        "name" : { "type" : "string", "similarity" : "BM25" },
        "contents" : { "type" : "string", "similarity" : "BM25" }
      }
    }
  }
}
```

And that's all, nothing more is needed. After the above change, Apache Lucene will use the BM25 similarity to calculate the score factor for the name and the contents fields.

Available similarity models

There are at least five new similarity models available. For most of the use cases, apart from the default one, you may find the following models useful:

- **Okapi BM25 model**: This similarity model is based on a probabilistic model that estimates the probability of finding a document for a given query. In order to use this similarity in Elasticsearch, you need to use the BM25 name. Okapi BM25 similarity is said perform best when dealing with short text documents where term repetitions are especially hurtful to the overall document score. To use this similarity, one needs to set the similarity property for a field to BM25. This similarity is defined out of the box and doesn't need additional properties to be set.

- **Divergence from randomness model**: This similarity model is based on the probabilistic model of the same name. In order to use this similarity in Elasticsearch, you need to use the DFR name. It is said that the divergence from randomness similarity model performs well on text that is similar to natural language.

- **Information-based model**: This is the last model of the newly introduced similarity models and is very similar to the divergence from randomness model. In order to use this similarity in Elasticsearch, you need to use the IB name. Similar to the DFR similarity, it is said that the information-based model performs well on data similar to natural language text.

The two other similarity models currently available are LM Dirichlet similarity (to use it, set the `type` property to `LMDirichlet`) and LM Jelinek Mercer similarity (to use it, set the `type` property to `LMJelinekMercer`). You can find more about these similarity models in *Apache Lucene Javadocs*, `Mastering Elasticsearch Second Edition`, published by Packt Publishing or in official documentation of Elasticsearch available at `https://www.elastic.co/guide/en/elasticsearch/reference/current/index-modules-similarity.html`.

Configuring default similarity

The default similarity allows us to provide an additional `discount_overlaps` property. It allows us to control if the tokens on the same positions in the token stream (with position increment of 0) are omitted during score calculation. By default, it is set to `true`, which means that the tokens on the same positions are omitted; if you want them to be counted, you can set that property to `false`. For example, the following command shows how to create an index with the `discount_overlaps` property changed for the default similarity:

```
curl -XPUT 'localhost:9200/test_similarity' -d '{
  "settings" : {
```

```
   "similarity" : {
    "altered_default": {
     "type" : "default",
     "discount_overlaps" : false
    }
   }
  },
  "mappings": {
   "doc": {
    "properties": {
     "name": { "type" : "string", "similarity": "altered_default" }
    }
   }
  }
 }'
```

Configuring BM25 similarity

Even though we don't need to configure the BM25 similarity, we can provide some additional options to tune its behavior. The BM25 similarity allows us to provide the discount_overlaps property similar to the default similarity and two additional properties: k1 and b. The k1 property specifies the term frequency normalization factor and the b property value determines to what degree the document length will normalize the term frequency values.

Configuring DFR similarity

In case of the DFR similarity, we can configure the basic_model property (which can take the value be, d, g, if, in, p, or ine), the after_effect property (with values of no, b, or l), and the normalization property (which can be no, h1, h2, h3, or z). If we choose a normalization value other than no, we need to set the normalization factor.

Depending on the chosen normalization value, we should use normalization.h1.c (the float value) for h1 normalization, normalization.h2.c (the float value) for h2 normalization, normalization.h3.c (the float value) for h3 normalization, and normalization.z.z (the float value) for z normalization. For example, the following is how the example similarity configuration will look (we put this into the settings section of our mappings file):

```
    "similarity" : {
      "esserverbook_dfr_similarity" : {
        "type" : "DFR",
```

```
        "basic_model" : "g",
        "after_effect" : "l",
        "normalization" : "h2",
        "normalization.h2.c" : "2.0"
      }
    }
```

Configuring IB similarity

In case of IB similarity, we have the following parameters through which we can configure the distribution property (which can take the value of `ll` or `spl`) and the lambda property (which can take the value of `df` or `tff`). In addition to that, we can choose the normalization factor, which is the same as for the DFR similarity, so we'll omit describing it a second time. The following is how the example IB similarity configuration will look (we put this into the settings section of our mappings file):

```
"similarity" : {
  "esserverbook_ib_similarity" : {
    "type" : "IB",
    "distribution" : "ll",
    "lambda" : "df",
    "normalization" : "z",
    "normalization.z.z" : "0.25"
  }
}
```

Batch indexing to speed up your indexing process

In *Chapter 1, Getting Started with Elasticsearch Cluster*, we saw how to index a particular document into Elasticsearch. It required opening an HTTP connection, sending the document, and closing the connection. Of course, we were not responsible for most of that as we used the `curl` command, but in the background this is what happened. However, sending the documents one by one is not efficient. Because of that, it is now time to find out how to index a large number of documents in a more convenient and efficient way than doing so one by one.

Preparing data for bulk indexing

Elasticsearch allows us to merge many requests into one package. This package can be sent as a single request. What's more, we are not limited to having a single type of request in the so called bulk – we can mix different types of operations together, which include:

- Adding or replacing the existing documents in the index (`index`)
- Removing documents from the index (`delete`)
- Adding new documents into the index when there is no other definition of the document in the index (`create`)
- Modifying the documents or creating new ones if the document doesn't exist (`update`)

The format of the request was chosen for processing efficiency. It assumes that every line of the request contains a JSON object with the description of the operation followed by the second line with a document – another JSON object itself. We can treat the first line as a kind of information line and the second as the data line. The exception to this rule is the `delete` operation, which contains only the information line, because the document is not needed. Let's look at the following example:

```
{ "index": { "_index": "addr", "_type": "contact", "_id": 1 }}
{ "name": "Fyodor Dostoevsky", "country": "RU" }
{ "create": { "_index": "addr", "_type": "contact", "_id": 2 }}
{ "name": "Erich Maria Remarque", "country": "DE" }
{ "create": { "_index": "addr", "_type": "contact", "_id": 2 }}
{ "name": "Joseph Heller", "country": "US" }
{ "delete": { "_index": "addr", "_type": "contact", "_id": 4 }}
{ "delete": { "_index": "addr", "_type": "contact", "_id": 1 }}
```

It is very important that every document or action description is placed in one line (ended by a newline character). This means that the document cannot be pretty-printed. There is a default limitation on the size of the bulk indexing file, which is set to 100 megabytes and can be changed by specifying the `http.max_content_length` property in the Elasticsearch configuration file. This lets us avoid issues with possible request timeouts and memory problems when dealing with requests that are too large.

 Note that with a single batch indexing file, we can load the data into many indices and documents in the bulk request can have different types.

Indexing the data

In order to execute the bulk request, Elasticsearch provides the `_bulk` endpoint. This can be used as `/_bulk` or with an index name as `/index_name/_bulk` or even with a type and index name as `/index_name/type_name/_bulk`. The second and third forms define the default values for the index name and the type name. We can omit these properties in the information line of our request and Elasticsearch will use the default values from the URI. It is also worth knowing that the default URI values can be overwritten by the values in the information lines.

Assuming we've stored our data in the `documents.json` file, we can run the following command to send this data to Elasticsearch:

```
curl -XPOST 'localhost:9200/_bulk?pretty' --data-binary @documents.json
```

The `?pretty` parameter is of course not necessary. We've used this parameter only for the ease of analyzing the response of the preceding command. What is important, in this case, is using `curl` with the `--data-binary` parameter instead of using `-d`. This is because the standard `-d` parameter ignores new line characters, which, as we said earlier, are important for parsing the bulk request content by Elasticsearch. Now let's look at the response returned by Elasticsearch:

```
{
  "took" : 469,
  "errors" : true,
  "items" : [ {
    "index" : {
      "_index" : "addr",
      "_type" : "contact",
      "_id" : "1",
      "_version" : 1,
      "_shards" : {
        "total" : 2,
        "successful" : 1,
        "failed" : 0
      },
      "status" : 201
    }
  }, {
    "create" : {
      "_index" : "addr",
      "_type" : "contact",
      "_id" : "2",
      "_version" : 1,
      "_shards" : {
```

```
      "total" : 2,
      "successful" : 1,
      "failed" : 0
    },
    "status" : 201
  }
}, {
  "create" : {
    "_index" : "addr",
    "_type" : "contact",
    "_id" : "2",
    "status" : 409,
    "error" : {
      "type" : "document_already_exists_exception",
      "reason" : "[contact][2]: document already exists",
      "shard" : "2",
      "index" : "addr"
    }
  }
}, {
  "delete" : {
    "_index" : "addr",
    "_type" : "contact",
    "_id" : "4",
    "_version" : 1,
    "_shards" : {
      "total" : 2,
      "successful" : 1,
      "failed" : 0
    },
    "status" : 404,
    "found" : false
  }
}, {
  "delete" : {
    "_index" : "addr",
    "_type" : "contact",
    "_id" : "1",
    "_version" : 2,
    "_shards" : {
      "total" : 2,
      "successful" : 1,
      "failed" : 0
    },
    "status" : 200,
```

```
            "found" : true
        }
    } ]
}
```

As we can see, every result is a part of the items array. Let's briefly compare these results with our input data. The first two commands, named index and create, were executed without any problems. The third operation failed because we wanted to create a record with an identifier that already existed in the index. The next two operations were deletions. Both succeeded. Note that the first of them tried to delete a nonexistent document; as you can see, this wasn't a problem for Elasticsearch – the thing worth noting though is that for the nonexisting document we saw a status of 404, which in the HTTP response code means not found (http://www.w3.org/Protocols/rfc2616/rfc2616-sec10.html). As you can see, Elasticsearch returns information about each operation, so for large bulk requests the response can be massive.

The _all field

The _all field is used by Elasticsearch to store data from all the other fields in a single field for ease of searching. This kind of field may be useful when we want to implement a simple search feature and we want to search all the data (or only the fields we copy to the _all field), but we don't want to think about the field names and things like that. By default, the _all field is enabled and contains all the data from all the fields from the document. However, this field makes the index a bit bigger and that is not always needed.

For example, when you input a search phrase into a search box in the library catalog site, you expect that you can search using the author's name, the ISBN number, and the words that the book title contains, but searching for the number of pages or the cover type usually does not make sense. We can either disable the _all field completely or exclude the copying of certain fields to it. In order not to include a certain field in the _all field, we use the include_in_all property, which was discussed earlier in this chapter. To completely turn off the _all field functionality, we modify our mappings file as follows:

```
{
  "book" : {
    "_all" : {
      "enabled" : false
    },
    "properties" : {
        .  .  .
    }
  }
}
```

In addition to the `enabled` property, the _all field supports the following ones:

- `store`
- `term_vector`
- `analyzer`

For information about the preceding properties, refer to the *Mappings configuration* section in this chapter.

The _source field

The _source field allows us to store the original JSON document that was sent to Elasticsearch during indexation. By default, the _source field is turned on as some of the Elasticsearch functionalities depend on it (for example, the partial update feature). In addition to that, the _source field can be used as the source of data for the highlighting functionality if a field is not stored. However, if we don't need such a functionality, we can disable the _source field as it causes some storage overhead. In order to do that, we need to set the _source object's enabled property to `false`, as follows:

```
{
  "book" : {
    "_source" : {
      "enabled" : false
    },
    "properties" : {
      . . .
    }
  }
}
```

We can also tell Elasticsearch which fields we want to exclude from the _source field and which fields we want to include. We do that by adding the `includes` and `excludes` properties to the _source field definition. For example, if we want to exclude all the fields in the author path from the _source field, our mappings will look as follows:

```
{
  "book" : {
    "_source" : {
      "excludes" : [ "author.*" ]
    },
    "properties" : {
      . . .
    }
  }
}
```

Additional internal fields

There are additional fields that are internally used by Elasticsearch, but which we can't configure. Those fields are:

- `_id`: This field is used to hold the identifier of the document inside the index and type

- `_uid`: This field is used to hold the unique identifier of the document in the index and is built of `_id` and `_type` (this allows to have documents with the same identifier with different types inside the same index)

- `_type`: This field is the type name for the document

- `_field_names`: This field is the list of fields existing in the document

Introduction to segment merging

In the *Full text searching* section of *Chapter 1, Getting Started with Elasticsearch Cluster*, we mentioned segments and their immutability. We wrote that the Lucene library, and thus Elasticsearch, writes data to certain structures that are written once and never change. This allows for some simplification, but also introduces the need for additional work. One such example is deletion. Because segment, cannot be altered, information about deletions must be stored alongside and dynamically applied during search. This is done by filtering deleted documents from the returned result set. The other example is the inability to modify the documents (however, some modifications are possible, such as modifying numeric doc values). Of course, one can say that Elasticsearch supports document updates (refer to the *Manipulating data with the REST API* section of *Chapter 1, Getting Started with Elasticsearch Cluster*). However, under the hood, the old document is marked as deleted and the one with the updated contents is indexed.

As time passes and you continue to index or delete your data, more and more segments are created. Depending on how often you modify the index, Lucene creates segments with various numbers of documents - thus, segments have different sizes. Because of that, the search performance may be lower and your index may be larger than it should be – it still contains the deleted documents. The equation is simple - the more segments your index has, the slower the search speed is. This is when segment merging comes into play. We don't want to describe this process in detail; in the current Elasticsearch version, this part of the engine was simplified but it is still a rather advanced topic. We decided to mention merging because we think that it is handy to know where to look for the cause of troubles connected with too many open files, suspicious CPU usage, expanding indices, or searching and indexing speed degrading with time.

Segment merging

Segment merging is the process during which the underlying Lucene library takes several segments and creates a new segment based on the information found in them. The resulting segment has all the documents stored in the original segments except the ones that were marked for deletion. After the merge operation, the source segments are deleted from the disk. Because segment merging is rather costly in terms of CPU and I/O usage, it is crucial to appropriately control when and how often this process is invoked.

The need for segment merging

You may ask yourself why you have to bother with segment merging. First of all, the more segments the index is built from, the slower the search will be and the more memory Lucene will use. The second is the disk space and resources, such as file descriptors, used by the index. If you delete many documents from your index then, until the merge happens, those documents are only marked as deleted and not deleted physically. So, it may happen that most of the documents that use our CPU and memory don't exist! Fortunately, Elasticsearch uses reasonable defaults for segment merging and it is very probable that no changes are necessary.

The merge policy

The merge policy defines when the merging process should be performed. Elasticsearch merges segments of approximately similar sizes, taking into account the maximum number of segments allowed per tier. The algorithm of merging can find segments with the lowest cost of merge and the most impact on the resulting segment.

The basic properties of the tiered merge policy are as follows:

- `index.merge.policy.expunge_deletes_allowed`: This property tells Elasticsearch to merge segments with percentage of the deleted documents higher than this value, defaults to 10.

- `index.merge.policy.floor_segment`: This property defaults to 2mb and tells Elasticsearch to treat smaller segments as ones with size equal to the value of this property. It prevents flushing of tiny segments to avoid their high number.

- `index.merge.policy.max_merge_at_once`: In this property, the maximum number of segments to be merged at once defaults to 10.

- `index.merge.policy.max_merge_at_once_explicit`: In this property, the maximum number of segments merged at once during expunge deletes or optimize operations defaults to `10`.

- `index.merge.policy.max_merged_segment`: In this property, the maximum size of segment that can be produced during normal merging defaults to 5gb.

- `index.merge.policy.segments_per_tier`: This property defaults to `10` and roughly defines the number of segments. Smaller values mean more merging but fewer segments, which results in higher search speed but lower indexing speed and more I/O pressure. Higher values of the property will result in higher segments count, thus slower search speed but higher indexing speed.

- `index.merge.policy.reclaim_deletes_weight` – This property tells Elasticsearch how important it is to choose segments with many deleted documents. It defaults to `2.0`.

  For example, to update merge policy settings of already created index we could run a command like this:

  ```
  curl -XPUT 'localhost:9200/essb/_settings' -d '{
  "index.merge.policy.max_merged_segment" : "10gb"
  }'
  ```

To get deeper into segment merging, refer to our book *Mastering Elasticsearch Second Edition*, published by Packt Publishing. You can also find more information about the tiered merge policy at `https://www.elastic.co/guide/en/elasticsearch/reference/current/index-modules-merge.html`.

> Up to the 2.0 version of Elasticsearch, we were able to choose between three merge policies: `tiered`, `log_byte_size`, and `log_doc`. The currently used merge policy is based on the tiered merge policy and we are forced to use it.

The merge scheduler

The merge scheduler tells Elasticsearch how the merge process should occur. The current implementation is based on a concurrent merge scheduler that is started in a separate thread and uses the defined number of threads doing merges in parallel. Elasticsearch allows you to set the number of threads that can be used for simultaneous merging by using the `index.merge.scheduler.max_thread_count` property.

Throttling

As we have already mentioned, merging may be expensive when it comes to server resources. The merge process usually works in parallel to other operations, so theoretically it shouldn't have too much influence. In practice, the number of disk input/output operations can be so large as to significantly affect the overall performance. In such cases, throttling is something that may help. In fact, this feature can be used for limiting the speed of the merge, but it may also be used for all the operations using the data store. Throttling can be set in the Elasticsearch configuration file (the `elasticsearch.yml` file) or dynamically by using the settings API (refer to the *The update settings API* section of *Chapter 9, Elasticsearch Cluster,* for detail). There are two settings that adjust throttling: **type** and **value**.

To set the throttling type, set the `indices.store.throttle.type` property, which allows us to use the following values:

- `none`: This value defines that no throttling is on
- `merge`: This value defines that throttling affects only the merge process
- `all`: This value defines that throttling is used for all the data store activities

The second property, `indices.store.throttle.max_bytes_per_sec`, describes how much the throttling limits the I/O operations. As its name suggests, it tells us how many bytes can be processed per second. For example, let's look at the following configuration:

```
indices.store.throttle.type: merge
indices.store.throttle.max_bytes_per_sec: 10mb
```

In this example, we limit the merge operations to 10 megabytes per second. By default, Elasticsearch uses the merge throttling type with the `max_bytes_per_sec` property set to `20mb`. This means that all the merge operations are limited to 20 megabytes per second.

Introduction to routing

By default, Elasticsearch will try to distribute your documents evenly among all the shards of the index. However, that's not always the desired situation. In order to retrieve the documents, Elasticsearch must query all the shards and merge the results. What if we could divide our data on some basis (for example, the client identifier) and use that information to put data with the same properties in the same place in the cluster. Elasticsearch allows us to do that by exposing a powerful document and query distribution control mechanism routing. In short, it allows us to choose a shard to be used to index or search the data.

Default indexing

During indexing operations, when you send a document for indexing, Elasticsearch looks at its identifier to choose the shard in which the document should be indexed. By default, Elasticsearch calculates the hash value of the document's identifier and, on the basis of that, it puts the document in one of the available primary shards. Then, those documents are redistributed to the replicas. The following diagram shows a simple illustration of how indexing works by default:

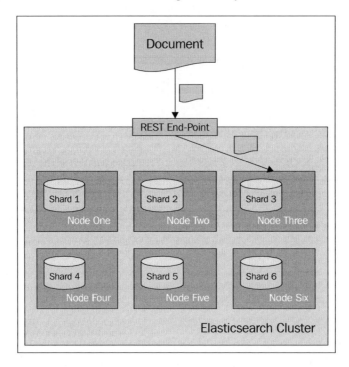

Default searching

Searching is a bit different from indexing, because in most situations you need to query all the shards to get the data you are interested in (we will talk about that in *Chapter 3, Searching Your Data*), at least in the initial scatter phase of the query. Imagine a situation when you have the following mappings describing your index:

```
{
    "mappings" : {
        "post" : {
            "properties" : {
                "id" : { "type" : "long" },
```

```
        "name" : { "type" : "string" },
        "contents" : { "type" : "string" },
        "userId" : { "type" : "long" }
  } }
} }
```

As you can see, our index consists of four fields: the identifier (the id field), name of the document (the name field), contents of the document (the contents field), and the identifier of the user to which the documents belong (the userId field). To get all the documents for a particular user, one with userId equal to 12, you can run the following query:

```
curl -XGET 'http://localhost:9200/posts/_search?q=userId:12'
```

Depending on the search type (we will talk more about it in *Chapter 3, Searching Your Data*), Elasticsearch will run your query. It usually means that it will first query all the nodes for the identifiers and score of the matching documents and then it will send an internal query again, but only to the relevant shards (the ones containing the needed documents) to get the documents needed to build the response.

A very simplified view of how the default searching works during its initial phase is shown in the following illustration:

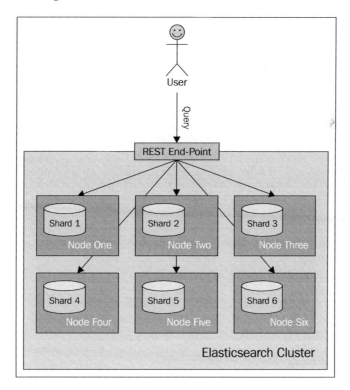

What if we could put all the documents for a single user into a single shard and query on that shard? Wouldn't that be wise for performance? Yes, that is handy and that is what routing allows you do to.

Routing

Routing can control which shard your documents and queries will be forwarded to. By now, you will probably have guessed that we can specify the routing value both during indexing and during querying and, in fact, if you decide to specify explicit routing values, you'll probably want to do that during indexing and searching.

In our case, we will use the `userId` value to set `routing` during indexing and the same value will be used during searching. Because we will use the same routing value for all the documents for a single user, the same hash value will be calculated and thus all the documents for that particular user will be placed in the same shard. Using the same value during search will result in searching a single shard instead of the whole index.

There is one thing you should remember when using routing when searching. When searching, you should add a query part that will limit the returned documents to the ones for the given user. Routing is not enough. This is because you'll probably have more distinct routing values than the number of shards your index will be built with. For example, you can have 10 shards building your index, but at the same time have hundreds of users. It is physically impossible to dedicate a single shard to only a single user. It is usually not good from a scaling point for view as well. Because of that, a few distinct values can point to the same shard – in our case data of a few users will be placed in the same shard. Because of that, we need a query part that will limit the data to a particular user identifier, such as a term query.

The following diagram shows a very simple illustration of how searching works with a provided custom routing value:

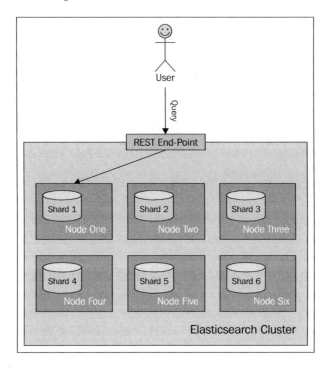

As you can see, Elasticsearch will send our query to a single shard. Now let's look at how we can specify the routing values.

The routing parameters

The idea is very simple. The endpoint used for all the operations connected with fetching or storing documents in Elasticsearch allows us to use additional parameter called routing. You can add it to your HTTP or set it by using the client library of your choice.

So, in order to index a sample document to the previously shown index, we will use the following command:

```
curl -XPUT 'http://localhost:9200/posts/post/1?routing=12' -d '{
  "id": "1",
  "name": "Test document",
  "contents": "Test document",
  "userId": "12"
}'
```

If we now get back to our previous query fetching our user's data and we modify it to use routing, it would look as follows:

```
curl -XGET 'http://localhost:9200/posts/_search?routing=12&q=userId:12'
```

As you can see, the same routing value was used during indexing and querying. This is possible in most cases when routing is used. We know which user data we are indexing and we will probably know which user is searching for the data. In our case, our imaginary user was given the identifier of 12 and we used that value during indexing and searching.

Note that during searching you can specify multiple routing values separated by commas. For example, if we want the preceding query to be additionally routed by the value of the section parameter (if it existed) and we also want to filter by this parameter, our query will look like the following:

```
curl -XGET 'http://localhost:9200/posts/_search?routing=12,6654&q=userId:
12+AND+section:6654'
```

Of course, the preceding command can match multiple shards now as the values given to routing can point to multiple shards. Because of that you need to provide only a single routing value during indexation (Elasticsearch needs to be pointed to a single shard or indexation will fail). You can of course query multiple shards at the same time and because of that multiple routing values can be provided during searching.

Remember that routing is not the only thing that is required to get results for a given user. That's because usually we have few shards that have unique routing values. This means that we will have data from multiple users in a single shard. So, when using routing, you should also narrow down your results to the ones for a given user. You'll learn more about how you can do that in *Chapter 3, Searching Your Data*.

Routing fields

Specifying the routing value with each request is critical when using an index operation. Without it, Elasticsearch uses the default way of determining where the document should be stored – it uses the hash value of the document identifier. This may lead to a situation where one document exists in many versions on different shards. A similar situation may occur when fetching the document. When a document is stored with a given routing value, we may hit the wrong shard and the document may be not found.

In fact, Elasticsearch allows us to change the default behavior and forces us to use routing when querying a given index. To do that, we need to add the following section to our type definition:

```
"_routing" : {
   "required" : true
}
```

The preceding definition means that the routing value needs to be provided (the `"required": true` property); without it, an index request will fail.

Summary

In this chapter, we've learned a lot when it comes to indexation and data handling in Elasticsearch. We started with basic information about Elasticsearch and we proceeded to tuning the schema-less behavior in Elasticsearch. We learned how to configure our mappings, use out of the box language analysis capabilities of Elasticsearch, and create our own mappings. We looked at batch indexing to speed up indexation and we added additional internal information to the documents in our indices. Finally, we looked at segment merging and routing.

In the next chapter, we will fully concentrate on searching and the extensive query language of Elasticsearch. We will start with how to query Elasticsearch and how the Elasticsearch query process works. We will learn about all the basic queries and compound queries to be able to use them in our applications. Finally, we will see which query should be chosen for the given use case.

3
Searching Your Data

In the previous chapter, we dived into Elasticsearch indexing. We learned a lot when it comes to data handling. We saw how to tune Elasticsearch schema-less mechanism and we now know how to create our own mappings. We also saw the core types of Elasticsearch and we used analyzers – both the one that comes out of the box with Elasticsearch and the one we defined ourselves. We used bulk indexing and we added additional internal information to our indices. Finally, we learned what segment merging is, how we can fine tune it, and how to use routing in Elasticsearch and what it gives us. This chapter is fully dedicated to querying. By the end of this chapter, you will have learned the following topics:

- How to query Elasticsearch
- What happens internally when queries are run
- What are the basic queries in Elasticsearch
- What are the compound queries in Elasticsearch that allow us to group other queries
- How to use position aware queries – span queries
- How to choose the right query for the job

Querying Elasticsearch

So far, when we havesearched our data, we used the REST API and a simple query or the GET request. Similarly, when we were changing the index, we also used the REST API and sent the JSON-structured data to Elasticsearch. Regardless of the type of operation we wanted to perform, whether it was a mapping change or document indexation, we used JSON structured request body to inform Elasticsearch about the operation details.

A similar situation happens when we want to send more than a simple query to Elasticsearch, we structure it using the JSON objects and send it to Elasticsearch in the request body. This is called the query DSL. In a broader view, Elasticsearch supports two kinds of queries: basic ones and compound ones. Basic queries, such as the `term` query, are used for querying the actual data. We will cover these in the *Basic queries* section of this chapter. The second type of query is the compound query, such as the `bool` query, which can combine multiple queries. We will cover these in the *Compound queries* section of this chapter.

However, this is not the whole picture. In addition to these two types of queries, certain queries can have filters that are used to narrow down your results with certain criteria. Filter queries don't affect scoring and are usually very efficient and easily cached.

To make it even more complicated, queries can contain other queries (don't worry; we will try to explain all this!). Furthermore, some queries can contain filters and others can contain both queries and filters. Although this is not everything, we will stick with this working explanation for now. We will go over this in greater detail in the *Compound queries* section in this chapter and the *Filtering your results* section in *Chapter 4, Extending Your Querying Knowledge*.

The example data

If not stated otherwise, the following mappings will be used for the rest of the chapter:

```
{
  "book" : {
    "properties" : {
      "author" : {
        "type" : "string"
      },
      "characters" : {
        "type" : "string"
      },
      "copies" : {
        "type" : "long",
        "ignore_malformed" : false
      },
      "otitle" : {
        "type" : "string"
      },
      "tags" : {
```

```
      "type" : "string",
      "index" : "not_analyzed"
    },
    "title" : {
      "type" : "string"
    },
    "year" : {
      "type" : "long",
      "ignore_malformed" : false,
      "index" : "analyzed"
    },
    "available" : {
      "type" : "boolean"
    }
  }
 }
}
```

The preceding mappings represent a simple library and were used to create the library index. One thing to remember is that Elasticsearch will analyze the string based fields if we don't configure it differently.

The preceding mappings were stored in the mapping.json file and, in order to create the mentioned library index, we can use the following commands:

```
curl -XPOST 'localhost:9200/library'
curl -XPUT 'localhost:9200/library/book/_mapping' -d @mapping.json
```

We also used the following sample data as the example ones for this chapter:

```
{ "index": {"_index": "library", "_type": "book", "_id": "1"}}
{ "title": "All Quiet on the Western Front","otitle": "Im
Westen nichts Neues","author": "Erich Maria Remarque","year":
1929,"characters": ["Paul Bäumer", "Albert Kropp", "Haie Westhus",
"Fredrich Müller", "Stanislaus Katczinsky", "Tjaden"],"tags":
["novel"],"copies": 1, "available": true, "section" : 3}
{ "index": {"_index": "library", "_type": "book", "_id": "2"}}
{ "title": "Catch-22","author": "Joseph Heller","year":
1961,"characters": ["John Yossarian", "Captain Aardvark",
"Chaplain Tappman", "Colonel Cathcart", "Doctor Daneeka"],"tags":
["novel"],"copies": 6, "available" : false, "section" : 1}
{ "index": {"_index": "library", "_type": "book", "_id": "3"}}
{ "title": "The Complete Sherlock Holmes","author": "Arthur Conan
Doyle","year": 1936,"characters": ["Sherlock Holmes","Dr. Watson", "G.
Lestrade"],"tags": [],"copies": 0, "available" : false, "section" :
12}
```

```
{ "index": {"_index": "library", "_type": "book", "_id": "4"}}
{ "title": "Crime and Punishment","otitle": "Преступлéние и
наказáние","author": "Fyodor Dostoevsky","year": 1886,"characters":
["Raskolnikov", "Sofia Semyonovna Marmeladova"],"tags": [],"copies":
0, "available" : true}
```

We stored our sample data in the documents.json file and we use the following command to index it:

```
curl -s -XPOST 'localhost:9200/_bulk' --data-binary @documents.json
```

This command runs bulk indexing. You can learn more about it in the *Batch indexing to speed up your indexing process* section in *Chapter 2, Indexing Your Data*.

A simple query

The simplest way to query Elasticsearch is to use the URI request query. We already discussed it in the *Searching with the URI request query* section of *Chapter 1, Getting Started with Elasticsearch Cluster*. For example, to search for the word crime in the title field, you could send a query using the following command:

```
curl -XGET 'localhost:9200/library/book/_search?q=title:crime&pretty'
```

This is a very simple, but limited, way of submitting queries to Elasticsearch. If we look from the point of view of the Elasticsearch query DSL, the preceding query is a query_string query. It searches for the documents that have the term crime in the title field and can be rewritten as follows:

```
{
  "query" : {
    "query_string" : { "query" : "title:crime" }
  }
}
```

Sending a query using the query DSL is a bit different, but still not rocket science. We send the GET (POST is also accepted in case your tool or library doesn't allow sending request body in HTTP GET requests) HTTP request to the _search REST endpoint as earlier and include the query in the request body. Let's take a look at the following command:

```
curl -XGET 'localhost:9200/library/book/_search?pretty' -d '{
  "query" : {
    "query_string" : { "query" : "title:crime" }
  }
}'
```

As you can see, we used the request body (the -d switch) to send the whole JSON-structured query to Elasticsearch. The pretty request parameter tells Elasticsearch to structure the response in such a way that we humans can read it more easily. In response to the preceding command, we get the following output:

```
{
  "took" : 4,
  "timed_out" : false,
  "_shards" : {
    "total" : 5,
    "successful" : 5,
    "failed" : 0
  },
  "hits" : {
    "total" : 1,
    "max_score" : 0.5,
    "hits" : [ {
      "_index" : "library",
      "_type" : "book",
      "_id" : "4",
      "_score" : 0.5,
      "_source" : {
        "title" : "Crime and Punishment",
        "otitle" : "Преступление и наказание",
        "author" : "Fyodor Dostoevsky",
        "year" : 1886,
        "characters" : [ "Raskolnikov", "Sofia Semyonovna
          Marmeladova" ],
        "tags" : [ ],
        "copies" : 0,
        "available" : true
      }
    } ]
  }
}
```

Nice! We got our first search results with the query DSL.

Paging and result size

Elasticsearch allows us to control how many results we want to get (at most) and from which result we want to start. The following are the two additional properties that can be set in the request body:

- from: This property specifies the document that we want to have our results from. Its default value is 0, which means that we want to get our results from the first document.

- `size`: This property specifies the maximum number of documents we want as the result of a single query (which defaults to `10`). For example, if we are only interested in aggregations results and don't care about the documents returned by the query, we can set this parameter to `0`.

If we want our query to get documents starting from the tenth item on the list and fetch 20 documents, we send the following query:

```
curl -XGET 'localhost:9200/library/book/_search?pretty' -d '{
  "from" :    9,
  "size" : 20,
  "query" : {
    "query_string" : { "query" : "title:crime" }
  }
}'
```

Downloading the example code

You can download the example code files for this book from your account at http://www.packtpub.com. If you purchased this book elsewhere, you can visit http://www.packtpub.com/support and register to have the files e-mailed directly to you.

You can download the code files by following these steps:

- Log in or register to our website using your e-mail address and password
- Hover the mouse pointer on the SUPPORT tab at the top
- Click on Code Downloads & Errata
- Enter the name of the book in the Search box
- Select the book for which you're looking to download the code files
- Choose from the drop-down menu where you purchased this book from
- Click on Code Download

Once the file is downloaded, make sure that you unzip or extract the folder using the latest version of:

- WinRAR / 7-Zip for Windows
- Zipeg / iZip / UnRarX for Mac
- 7-Zip / PeaZip for Linux

Returning the version value

In addition to all the information returned, Elasticsearch can return the version of the document (we mentioned about versioning in *Chapter 1, Getting Started with Elasticsearch Cluster*. To do this, we need to add the version property with the value of true to the top level of our JSON object. So, the final query, which requests the version information, will look as follows:

```
curl -XGET 'localhost:9200/library/book/_search?pretty' -d '{
    "version" : true,
    "query" : {
      "query_string" : { "query" : "title:crime" }
    }
}'
```

After running the preceding query, we get the following results:

```
{
    "took" : 4,
    "timed_out" : false,
    "_shards" : {
      "total" : 5,
      "successful" : 5,
      "failed" : 0
    },
    "hits" : {
      "total" : 1,
      "max_score" : 0.5,
      "hits" : [ {
        "_index" : "library",
        "_type" : "book",
        "_id" : "4",
        "_version" : 1,
        "_score" : 0.5,
        "_source" : {
          "title" : "Crime and Punishment",
          "otitle" : "Преступление и наказание",
          "author" : "Fyodor Dostoevsky",
          "year" : 1886,
          "characters" : [ "Raskolnikov", "Sofia Semyonovna
            Marmeladova" ],
          "tags" : [ ],
          "copies" : 0,
```

```
                "available" : true
              }
           } ]
       }
    }
```

As you can see, the _version section is present for the single hit we got.

Limiting the score

For nonstandard use cases, Elasticsearch provides a feature that lets us filter the results on the basis of a minimum score value that the document must have to be considered a match. In order to use this feature, we must provide the min_score value at the top level of our JSON object with the value of the minimum score. For example, if we want our query to only return documents with a score higher than 0.75, we send the following query:

```
curl -XGET 'localhost:9200/library/book/_search?pretty' -d '{
  "min_score" : 0.75,
  "query" : {
    "query_string" : { "query" : "title:crime" }
  }
}'
```

We get the following response after running the preceding query:

```
{
   "took" : 3,
   "timed_out" : false,
   "_shards" : {
      "total" : 5,
      "successful" : 5,
      "failed" : 0
   },
   "hits" : {
      "total" : 0,
      "max_score" : null,
      "hits" : [ ]
   }
}
```

If you look at the previous examples, the score of our document was 0.5, which is lower than 0.75, and thus we didn't get any documents in response.

Limiting the score usually doesn't make much sense because comparing scores between the queries is quite hard. However, maybe in your case, this functionality will be needed.

Choosing the fields that we want to return

With the use of the fields array in the request body, Elasticsearch allows us to define which fields to include in the response. Remember that you can only return these fields if they are marked as stored in the mappings used to create the index, or if the _source field was used (Elasticsearch uses the _source field to provide the stored values and the _source field is turned on by default).

So, for example, to return only the title and the year fields in the results (for each document), send the following query to Elasticsearch:

```
curl -XGET 'localhost:9200/library/book/_search?pretty' -d '{
  "fields" : [ "title", "year" ],
  "query" : {
    "query_string" : { "query" : "title:crime" }
  }
}'
```

In response, we get the following output:

```
{
  "took" : 5,
  "timed_out" : false,
  "_shards" : {
    "total" : 5,
    "successful" : 5,
    "failed" : 0
  },
  "hits" : {
    "total" : 1,
    "max_score" : 0.5,
    "hits" : [ {
      "_index" : "library",
      "_type" : "book",
      "_id" : "4",
      "_score" : 0.5,
      "fields" : {
        "title" : [ "Crime and Punishment" ],
        "year" : [ 1886 ]
      }
    } ]
  }
}
```

As you can see, everything worked as we wanted to. There are four things we would like to share with you at this point, which are as follows:

- If we don't define the fields array, it will use the default value and return the _source field if available.

- If we use the _source field and request a field that is not stored, then that field will be extracted from the _source field (however, this requires additional processing).

- If we want to return all the stored fields, we just pass an asterisk (*) as the field name.

- From a performance point of view, it's better to return the _source field instead of multiple stored fields. This is because getting multiple stored fields may be slower compared to retrieving a single _source field.

Source filtering

In addition to choosing which fields are returned, Elasticsearch allows us to use so-called **source filtering**. This functionality allows us to control which fields are returned from the _source field. Elasticsearch exposes several ways to do this. The simplest source filtering allows us to decide whether a document should be returned or not. Consider the following query:

```
curl -XGET 'localhost:9200/library/book/_search?pretty' -d '{
  "_source" : false,
  "query" : {
    "query_string" : { "query" : "title:crime" }
  }
}'
```

The result retuned by Elasticsearch should be similar to the following one:

```
{
  "took" : 12,
  "timed_out" : false,
  "_shards" : {
    "total" : 5,
    "successful" : 5,
    "failed" : 0
  },
  "hits" : {
    "total" : 1,
    "max_score" : 0.5,
```

```
    "hits" : [ {
      "_index" : "library",
      "_type" : "book",
      "_id" : "4",
      "_score" : 0.5
    } ]
  }
}
```

Note that the response is limited to base information about a document and the _source field was not included. If you use Elasticsearch as a second source of data and content of the document is served from SQL database or cache, the document identifier is all you need.

The second way is similar to that described in the preceding fields, although we define which fields should be returned in the document source itself. Let's see that using the following example query:

```
curl -XGET 'localhost:9200/library/book/_search?pretty' -d '{
  "_source" : ["title", "otitle"],
  "query" : {
    "query_string" : { "query" : "title:crime" }
  }
}'
```

We wanted to get the title and the otitle document fields in the returned _source field. Elasticsearch extracted those values from the original _source value and included the _source field only with the requested fields. The whole response returned by Elasticsearch looked as follows:

```
{
  "took" : 2,
  "timed_out" : false,
  "_shards" : {
    "total" : 5,
    "successful" : 5,
    "failed" : 0
  },
  "hits" : {
    "total" : 1,
    "max_score" : 0.5,
    "hits" : [ {
      "_index" : "library",
      "_type" : "book",
```

```
      "_id" : "4",
      "_score" : 0.5,
      "_source" : {
        "otitle" : "Преступле́ние и наказа́ние",
        "title" : "Crime and Punishment"
      }
    } ]
  }
}
```

We can also use an asterisk to select which fields should be returned in the _source field; for example, title* will return values for the title field and for title10 (if we have such field in our data). If we have documents with nested parts, we can use notation with a dot; for example, title.* to select all the fields nested under the title object.

Finally, we can also specify explicitly which fields we want to include and which to exclude from the _source field. We can include fields using the include property and we can exclude fields using the exclude property (both of them are arrays of values). For example, if we want the returned _source field to include all the fields starting with the letter t but not the title field, we will run the following query:

```
curl -XGET 'localhost:9200/library/book/_search?pretty' -d '{
  "_source" : {
    "include" : [ "t*"],
    "exclude" : ["title"]
  },
  "query" : {
    "query_string" : { "query" : "title:crime" }
  }
}'
```

Using the script fields

Elasticsearch allows us to use script-evaluated values that will be returned with the result documents (we will discuss Elasticsearch scripting capabilities in greater detail in the *Scripting capabilities of Elasticsearch* section in *Chapter 6, Make Your Search Better*). To use the script fields functionality, we add the script_fields section to our JSON query object and an object with a name of our choice for each scripted value that we want to return. For example, to return a value named correctYear, which is calculated as the year field minus 1800, we run the following query:

```
curl -XGET 'localhost:9200/library/book/_search?pretty' -d '{
  "script_fields" : {
```

```
      "correctYear" : {
        "script" : "doc[\"year\"].value - 1800"
      }
    },
    "query" : {
      "query_string" : { "query" : "title:crime" }
    }
}'
```

> By default, Elasticsearch doesn't allow us to use dynamic
> scripting. If you tried the preceding query, you probably got an
> error with information stating that the scripts of type [inline]
> with operation [search] and language [groovy] are disabled.
> To make this example work, you should add the script.
> inline: on property to the elasticsearch.yml file.
> However, this exposes a security threat. Make sure to read the
> *Scripting capabilities of Elasticsearch* section in *Chapter 6, Make Your
> Search Better*, to learn about the consequences.

Using the doc notation, like we did in the preceding example, allows us to catch
the results returned and speed up script execution at the cost of higher memory
consumption. We also get limited to single-valued and single term fields. If we
care about memory usage, or if we are using more complicated field values, we
can always use the _source field. The same query using the _source field looks
as follows:

```
curl -XGET 'localhost:9200/library/book/_search?pretty' -d '{
  "script_fields" : {
    "correctYear" : {
      "script" : "_source.year - 1800"
    }
  },
  "query" : {
    "query_string" : { "query" : "title:crime" }
  }
}'
```

The following response is returned by Elasticsearch with dynamic scripting enabled:

```
{
  "took" : 76,
  "timed_out" : false,
  "_shards" : {
    "total" : 5,
    "successful" : 5,
    "failed" : 0
  },
  "hits" : {
    "total" : 1,
    "max_score" : 0.5,
    "hits" : [ {
      "_index" : "library",
      "_type" : "book",
      "_id" : "4",
      "_score" : 0.5,
      "fields" : {
        "correctYear" : [ 86 ]
      }
    } ]
  }
}
```

As you can see, we got the calculated `correctYear` field in response.

Passing parameters to the script fields

Let's take a look at one more feature of the script fields - the passing of additional parameters. Instead of having the value `1800` in the equation, we can use a variable name and pass its value in the `params` section. If we do this, our query will look as follows:

```
curl -XGET 'localhost:9200/library/book/_search?pretty' -d '{
  "script_fields" : {
    "correctYear" : {
      "script" : "_source.year - paramYear",
      "params" : {
        "paramYear" : 1800
      }
    }
```

```
  },
  "query" : {
    "query_string" : { "query" : "title:crime" }
  }
}'
```

As you can see, we added the `paramYear` variable as part of the scripted equation and provided its value in the `params` section. This allows Elasticsearch to execute the same script with different parameter values in a slightly more efficient way.

Understanding the querying process

After reading the previous section, we now know how querying works in Elasticsearch. You know that Elasticsearch, in most cases, needs to scatter the query across multiple nodes, get the results, merge them, fetch the relevant documents from one or more shards, and return the final results to the client requesting the documents. What we didn't talk about are two additional things that define how queries behave: search type and query execution preference. We will now concentrate on these functionalities of Elasticsearch.

Query logic

Elasticsearch is a distributed search engine and so all functionality provided must be distributed in its nature. It is exactly the same with querying. Because we would like to discuss some more advanced topics on how to control the query process, we first need to know how it works.

Let's now get back to how querying works. We started the theory in the first chapter and we would like to get back to it. By default, if we don't alter anything, the query process will consist of two phases: the scatter and the gather phase. The aggregator node (the one that receives the request) will run the scatter phase first. During that phase, the query is distributed to all the shards that our index is built from (of course if routing is not used). For example, if it is built of 5 shards and 1 replica then 5 physical shards will be queried (we don't need to query a shard and its replica as they contain the same data). Each of the queried shards will only return the document identifier and the score of the document. The node that sent the scatter query will wait for all the shards to complete their task, gather the results, and sort them appropriately (in this case, from top scoring to the lowest scoring ones).

After that, a new request will be sent to build the search results. However, now only to those shards that held the documents to build the response. In most cases, Elasticsearch won't send the request to all the shards but to its subset. That's because we usually don't get the complete result of the query but only a portion of it. This phase is called the gather phase. After all the documents are gathered, the final response is built and returned as the query result. This is the basic and default Elasticsearch behavior but we can change it.

Search type

Elasticsearch allows us to choose how we want our query to be processed internally. We can do that by specifying the search type. There are different situations where different search types are appropriate: sometimes one can care only about the performance while sometimes query relevance is the most important factor. You should remember that each shard is a small Lucene index and, in order to return more relevant results, some information, such as frequencies, needs to be transferred between the shards. To control how the queries are executed, we can pass the `search_type` request parameter and set it to one of the following values:

- `query_then_fetch`: In the first step, the query is executed to get the information needed to sort and rank the documents. This step is executed against all the shards. Then only the relevant shards are queried for the actual content of the documents. This is the search type used by default if no search type is provided with the query and this is the query type we described previously.

- `dfs_query_then_fetch`: This is similar to `query_then_fetch`. However, it contains an additional query phase comparing to `query_then_fetch` which calculates distributed term frequencies.

There are also two deprecated search types: count and scan. The first one is deprecated starting from Elasticsearch 2.0 and the second one starting with Elasticsearch 2.1. The first search type used to provide benefits where only aggregations or the number of documents was relevant, but now it is enough to add size equal to 0 to your queries. The scan request was used for scrolling functionality.

So if we would like to use the simplest search type, we would run the following command:

```
curl -XGET 'localhost:9200/library/book/_search?pretty&search_type=query_
then_fetch' -d '{
 "query" : {
  "term" : { "title" : "crime" }
 }
}'
```

Search execution preference

In addition to the possibility of controlling how the query is executed, we can also control on which shards to execute the query. By default, Elasticsearch uses shards and replicas on any node in a round robin manner – so that each shard is queried a similar number of times. The default behavior is the proper method of shard execution preference for most use cases. But there may be times when we want to change the default behavior. For example, you may want the search to only be executed on the primary shards. To do that, we can set the preference request parameter to one of the following values:

- `_primary`: The operation will be only executed on the primary shards, so the replicas won't be used. This can be useful when we need to use the latest information from the index but our data is not replicated right away.

- `_primary_first`: The operation will be executed on the primary shards if they are available. If not, it will be executed on the other shards.

- `_replica`: The operation will be executed only on the replica shards.

- `_replica_first`: This operation is similar to `_primary_first`, but uses replica shards. The operation will be executed on the replica shards if possible and on the primary shards if the replicas are not available.

- `_local`: The operation will be executed on the shards available on the node which the request was sent from and, if such shards are not present, the request will be forwarded to the appropriate nodes.

- `_only_node:node_id`: This operation will be executed on the node with the provided node identifier.

- `_only_nodes:nodes_spec`: This operation will be executed on the nodes that are defined in `nodes_spec`. This can be an IP address, a name, a name or IP address using wildcards, and so on. For example, if `nodes_spec` is set to `192.168.1.*`, the operation will be run on the nodes with IP addresses starting with `192.168.1`.

- `_prefer_node:node_id`: Elasticsearch will try to execute the operation on the node with the provided identifier. However, if the node is not available, it will be executed on the nodes that are available.

- `_shards:1,2`: Elasticsearch will execute the operation on the shards with the given identifiers; in this case, on shards with identifiers 1 and 2. The `_shards` parameter can be combined with other preferences, but the shards identifiers need to be provided first. For example, `_shards:1,2;_local`.

- `Custom value`: Any custom, string value may be passed. Requests with the same values provided will be executed on the same shards.

For example, if we would like to execute a query only on the local shards, we would run the following command:

```
curl -XGET 'localhost:9200/library/_search?pretty&preference=_local' -d
'{
 "query" : {
  "term" : { "title" : "crime" }
 }
}'
```

Search shards API

When discussing the search preference, we would also like to mention the search shards API exposed by Elasticsearch. This API allows us to check which shards the query will be executed on. In order to use this API, run a request against the search_shards rest end point. For example, to see how the query will be executed, we run the following command:

```
curl -XGET 'localhost:9200/library/_search_shards?pretty' -d
'{"query":"match_all":{}}'
```

The response to the preceding command will be as follows:

```
{
   "nodes" : {
     "my0DcA_MTImm4NE3cG3ZIg" : {
       "name" : "Cloud 9",
       "transport_address" : "127.0.0.1:9300",
       "attributes" : { }
     }
   },
   "shards" : [ [ {
     "state" : "STARTED",
     "primary" : true,
     "node" : "my0DcA_MTImm4NE3cG3ZIg",
     "relocating_node" : null,
     "shard" : 0,
     "index" : "library",
     "version" : 4,
     "allocation_id" : {
       "id" : "9ayLDbL1RVSyJRYIJkuAxg"
     }
   } ], [ {
     "state" : "STARTED",
```

```
      "primary" : true,
      "node" : "my0DcA_MTImm4NE3cG3ZIg",
      "relocating_node" : null,
      "shard" : 1,
      "index" : "library",
      "version" : 4,
      "allocation_id" : {
        "id" : "wfpvtaLER-KVyOsuD46Yqg"
      }
    } ], [ {
      "state" : "STARTED",
      "primary" : true,
      "node" : "my0DcA_MTImm4NE3cG3ZIg",
      "relocating_node" : null,
      "shard" : 2,
      "index" : "library",
      "version" : 4,
      "allocation_id" : {
        "id" : "zrLPWhCOSTmjlb8TY5rYQA"
      }
    } ], [ {
      "state" : "STARTED",
      "primary" : true,
      "node" : "my0DcA_MTImm4NE3cG3ZIg",
      "relocating_node" : null,
      "shard" : 3,
      "index" : "library",
      "version" : 4,
      "allocation_id" : {
        "id" : "efnvY7YcSz6X8X8USacA7g"
      }
    } ], [ {
      "state" : "STARTED",
      "primary" : true,
      "node" : "my0DcA_MTImm4NE3cG3ZIg",
      "relocating_node" : null,
      "shard" : 4,
      "index" : "library",
      "version" : 4,
      "allocation_id" : {
        "id" : "XJHW2J63QUKdh3bK3T2nzA"
      }
    } ] ]
}
```

As you can see, in the response returned by Elasticsearch, we have the information about the shards that will be used during the query process. Of course, with the search shards API, we can use additional parameters that control the querying process. These properties are `routing`, `preference`, and `local`. We are already familiar with the first two. The `local` parameter is a Boolean (values `true` or `false`), one that allows us to tell Elasticsearch to use the cluster state information stored on the `local` node (setting `local` to `true`) instead of the one from the `master` node (setting `local` to `false`). This allows us to diagnose problems with cluster state synchronization.

Basic queries

Elasticsearch has extensive search and data analysis capabilities that are exposed in forms of different queries, filters, aggregates, and so on. In this section, we will concentrate on the basic queries provided by Elasticsearch. By basic queries we mean the ones that don't combine the other queries together but run on their own.

The term query

The term query is one of the simplest queries in Elasticsearch. It just matches the document that has a term in a given field - the exact, not analyzed term. The simplest term query is as follows:

```
{
  "query" : {
  "term" : {
    "title" : "crime"
  }
  }
}
```

It will match the documents that have the term crime in the title field. Remember that the term query is not analyzed, so you need to provide the exact term that will match the term in the indexed document. Note that in our input data, we have the `title` field with the value of `Crime` and `Punishment` (upper cased), but we are searching for `crime`, because the `Crime` terms becomes `crime` after analysis during indexing.

In addition to the term we want to find, we can also include the boost attribute to our term query, which will affect the importance of the given term. We will talk more about boosts in the *Introduction to Apache Lucene scoring* section of *Chapter 6, Make Your Search Better*. For now, we just need to remember that it changes the importance of the given part of the query.

For example, to change our previous query and give our term query a boost of 10.0, send the following query:

```
{
  "query" : {
  "term" : {
    "title" : {
    "value" : "crime",
    "boost" : 10.0
    }
  }
  }
}
```

As you can see, the query changed a bit. Instead of a simple term value, we nested a new JSON object which contains the value property and the boost property. The value of the value property should contain the term we are interested in and the boost property is the boost value we want to use.

The terms query

The terms query is an extension to the term query. It allows us to match documents that have certain terms in their contents instead of a single term. The term query allowed us to match a single, not analyzed term and the terms query allows us to match multiple of those. For example, let's say that we want to get all the documents that have the terms novel or book in the tags field. To achieve this, we will run the following query:

```
{
  "query" : {
  "terms" : {
    "tags" : [ "novel", "book" ]
  }
  }
}
```

The preceding query returns all the documents that have one or both of the searched terms in the tags field. This is a key point to remember – the terms query will find documents having any of the provided terms.

The match all query

The match all query is one of the simplest queries available in Elasticsearch. It allows us to match all of the documents in the index. If we want to get all the documents from our index, we just run the following query:

```
{
  "query" : {
  "match_all" : {}
  }
}
```

We can also include boost in the query, which will be given to all the documents matched by it. For example, if we want to add a boost of 2.0 to all the documents in our match all query, we will send the following query to Elasticsearch:

```
{
  "query" : {
  "match_all" : {
    "boost" : 2.0
  }
  }
}
```

The type query

A very simple query that allows us to find all the documents with a certain type. For example, if we would like to search for all the documents with the book type in our library index, we will run the following query:

```
{
  "query" : {
  "type" : {
    "value" : "book"
  }
  }
}
```

The exists query

A query that allows us to find all the documents that have a value in the defined field. For example, to find the documents that have a value in the `tags` field, we will run the following query:

```
{
  "query" : {
  "exists" : {
    "field" : "tags"
  }
  }
}
```

The missing query

Opposite to the exists query, the missing query returns the documents that have a null value or no value at all in a given field. For example, to find all the documents that don't have a value in the `tags` field, we will run the following query:

```
{
  "query" : {
  "missing" : {
    "field" : "tags"
  }
  }
}
```

The common terms query

The common terms query is a modern Elasticsearch solution for improving query relevance and precision with common words when we are not using stop words (`http://en.wikipedia.org/wiki/Stop_words`). For example, a crime and punishment query results in three term queries and each of them have a cost in terms of performance. However, the and term is a very common one and its impact on the document score will be very low. The solution is the common terms query which divides the query into two groups. The first group is the one with important terms, which are the ones that have lower frequency. The second group is the one with less important terms, which are the ones with high frequency. The first query is executed first and Elasticsearch calculates the score for all of the terms from the first group. This way the low frequency terms, which are usually the ones that have more importance, are always taken into consideration. Then Elasticsearch executes the second query for the second group of terms, but calculates the score only for the documents matched for the first query. This way the score is only calculated for the relevant documents and thus higher performance can be achieved.

An example of the common terms query is as follows:

```
{
  "query" : {
   "common" : {
    "title" : {
      "query" : "crime and punishment",
      "cutoff_frequency" : 0.001
    }
   }
  }
}
```

The query can take the following parameters:

- query: The actual query contents.

- cutoff_frequency: The percentage (0.001 means 0.1%) or an absolute value (when property is set to a value equal to or larger than 1). High and low frequency groups are constructed using this value. Setting this parameter to 0.001 means that the low frequency terms group will be constructed for terms having a frequency of 0.1% and lower.

- low_freq_operator: This can be set to or or and, but defaults to or. It specifies the Boolean operator used for constructing queries in the low frequency term group. If we want all the terms to be present in a document for it to be considered a match, we should set this parameter to and.

- high_freq_operator: This can be set to or or and, but defaults to or. It specifies the Boolean operator used for constructing queries in the high frequency term group. If we want all the terms to be present in a document for it to be considered a match, we should set this parameter to and.

- minimum_should_match: Instead of using low_freq_operator and high_freq_operator, we can use minimum_should_match. Just like with the other queries, it allows us to specify the minimum number of terms that should be found in a document for it to be considered a match. We can also specify high_freq and low_freq inside the minimum_should_match object, which allows us to define the different number of terms that need to be matched for the high and low frequency terms.

- boost: The boost given to the score of the documents.

- analyzer: The name of the analyzer that will be used to analyze the query text, which defaults to the default analyzer.

- disable_coord: Defaults to `false` and allows us to enable or disable the score factor computation that is based on the fraction of all the query terms that a document contains. Set it to `true` for less precise scoring, but slightly faster queries.

 Unlike the `term` and `terms` queries, the common terms query is analyzed by Elasticsearch.

The match query

The `match` query takes the values given in the `query` parameter, analyzes it, and constructs the appropriate query out of it. When using a `match` query, Elasticsearch will choose the proper analyzer for the field we choose, so you can be sure that the terms passed to the `match` query will be processed by the same analyzer that was used during indexing. Remember that the `match` query (and the `multi_match` query) doesn't support Lucene query syntax; however, it perfectly fits as a query handler for your search box. The simplest match (and the default) query will look like the following:

```
{
  "query" : {
    "match" : {
      "title" : "crime and punishment"
    }
  }
}
```

The preceding query will match all the documents that have the terms `crime`, and, or `punishment` in the `title` field. However, the previous query is only the simplest one; there are multiple types of match query which we will discuss now.

The Boolean match query

The `Boolean match` query is a query which analyzes the provided text and makes a Boolean query out of it. This is also the default type for the match query. There are a few parameters which allow us to control the behavior of the `Boolean match` queries:

- `operator`: This parameter can take the value of `or` or `and`, and controls which Boolean operator is used to connect the created Boolean clauses. The default value is `or`. If we want all the terms in our query to be matched, we should use the `and` Boolean operator.

- `analyzer`: This specifies the name of the analyzer that will be used to analyze the query text and defaults to the default analyzer.

- `fuzziness`: Providing the value of this parameter allows us to construct fuzzy queries. The value of this parameter can vary. For numeric fields, it should be set to numeric value; for date based field, it can be set to `millisecond` or `time` value, such as `2h`; and for text fields, it can be set to `0`, `1`, or `2` (the edit distance in the Levenshtein algorithm – `https://en.wikipedia.org/wiki/Levenshtein_distance`), `AUTO` (which allows Elasticsearch to control how fuzzy queries are constructed and which is a preferred value). Finally, for text fields, it can also be set to values from 0.0 to 1.0, which results in edit distance being calculated as term length minus 1.0 multiplied by the provided fuzziness value. In general, the higher the fuzziness, the more difference between terms will be allowed.

- `prefix_length`: This allows control over the behavior of the fuzzy query. For more information on the value of this parameter, refer to the *The fuzzy query* section in this chapter.

- `max_expansions`: This allows control over the behavior of the fuzzy query. For more information on the value of this parameter, refer to the *The fuzzy query* section in this chapter.

- `zero_terms_query`: This allows us to specify the behavior of the query, when all the terms are removed by the analyzer (for example, because of stop words). It can be set to none or all, with none as the default. When set to none, no documents will be returned when the analyzer removes all the query terms. If set it to all, all the documents will be returned.

- `cutoff_frequency`: It allows dividing the query into two groups: one with high frequency terms and one with low frequency terms. Refer to the description of the common terms query to see how this parameter can be used.

- `lenient`: When set to `true` (by default it is `false`), it allows us to ignore the exceptions caused by data incompatibility, such as trying to query numeric fields using string value.

The parameters should be wrapped in the name of the field we are running the query against. So if we want to run a sample Boolean match query against the `title` field, we send a query as follows:

```
{
  "query" : {
  "match" : {
    "title" : {
```

```
   "query" : "crime and punishment",
   "operator" : "and"
   }
  }
  }
}
```

The phrase match query

A `phrase match` query is similar to the `Boolean` query, but, instead of constructing the Boolean clauses from the analyzed text, it constructs the `phrase` query. You may wonder what phrase is when it comes to Lucene and Elasticsearch – well, it is two or more terms positioned one after another in an order. The following parameters are available:

- `slop`: An integer value that defines how many unknown words can be put between the terms in the `text` query for a match to be considered a phrase. The default value of this parameter is `0`, which means that no additional words are allowed.

- `analyzer`: This specifies the name of the analyzer that will be used to analyze the query text and defaults to the default analyzer.

A sample `phrase match` query against the title field looks like the following code:

```
{
  "query" : {
  "match_phrase" : {
    "title" : {
    "query" : "crime punishment",
    "slop" : 1
    }
  }
  }
}
```

Note that we removed the `and` term from our query, but because the slop is set to `1`, it will still match our document because we allowed one term to be present between our terms.

The match phrase prefix query

The last type of the match query is the `match phrase prefix` query. This query is almost the same as the `phrase match` query, but in addition, it allows prefix matches on the last term in the query text. Also, in addition to the parameters exposed by the match phrase query, it exposes an additional one – the `max_expansions` parameter, which controls how many prefixes the last term will be rewritten to. Our example query changed to the `match_phrase_prefix` query will look as follows:

```
{
  "query" : {
  "match_phrase_prefix" : {
    "title" : {
    "query" : "crime punishm",
    "slop" : 1,
    "max_expansions" : 20
    }
  }
  }
}
```

Note that we didn't provide the full crime and punishment phrase, but only `crime punishm` and still the query would match our document. This is because we used the `match_phrase_prefix` query combined with slop set to `1`.

The multi match query

It is the same as the `match` query, but instead of running against a single field, it can be run against multiple fields with the use of the `fields` parameter. Of course, all the parameters you use with the `match` query can be used with the `multi match` query. So if we would like to modify our `match` query to be run against the `title` and `otitle` fields, we will run the following query:

```
{
  "query" : {
    "multi_match" : {
      "query" : "crime punishment",
      "fields" : [ "title^10", "otitle" ]
    }
  }
}
```

As shown in the preceding example, the nice thing about the `multi match` query is that the fields defined in it support boosting, so we can increase or decrease the importance of matches on certain fields.

However, this is not the only difference when it comes to comparison with the match query. We can also control how the query is run internally by using the type property and setting it to one of the following values:

- best_fields: This is the default behavior, which finds documents having matches in any field from the defined ones, but setting the document score to the score of the best matching field. The most useful type when searching for multiple words and wanting to boost documents that have those words in the same field.

- most_fields: This value finds documents that match any field and sets the score of the document to the combined score from all the matched fields.

- cross_fields: This value treats the query as if all the terms were in one, big field, thus returning documents matching any field.

- phrase: This value uses the match_phrase query on each field and sets the score of the document to the score combined from all the fields.

- phrase_prefix: This value uses the match_phrase_prefix query on each field and sets the score of the document to the score combined from all the fields.

In addition to the parameters mentioned in the match query and type, the multi match query exposes some additional ones allowing more control over its behavior:

- tie_breaker: This allows us to specify the balance between the minimum and the maximum scoring query items and the value can be from 0.0 to 1.0. When used, the score of the document is equal to the best scoring element plus the tie_breaker multiplied by the score of all the other matching fields in the document. So, when set to 0.0, Elasticsearch will only use the score of the most scoring matching element. You can read more about it in *The dis_max query* section in this chapter.

The query string query

In comparison to the other queries available, the query string query supports full Apache Lucene query syntax, which we discussed earlier in the *Lucene query syntax* section of *Chapter 1, Getting Started with Elasticsearch Cluster*. It uses a query parser to construct an actual query using the provided text. An example query string query will look like the following code:

```
{
   "query" : {
   "query_string" : {
```

```
    "query" : "title:crime^10 +title:punishment -otitle:cat
        +author:(+Fyodor +dostoevsky)",
    "default_field" : "title"
  }
 }
}
```

Because we are familiar with the basics of the Lucene query syntax, we can discuss how the preceding query works. As you can see, we wanted to get the documents that may have the term crime in the title field and such documents should be boosted with the value of 10. Next, we wanted only the documents that have the term punishment in the title field and we didn't want documents with the term cat in the otitle field. Finally, we told Lucene that we only wanted the documents that had the fyodor and dostoevsky terms in the author field.

Similar to most of the queries in Elasticsearch, the query string query provides quite a few parameters that allow us to control the query behavior and the list of parameters for this query is rather extensive:

- query: This specifies the query text.
- default_field: This specifies the default field the query will be executed against. It defaults to the index.query.default_field property, which is by default set to _all.
- default_operator: This specifies the default logical operator (or or and) used when no operator is specified. The default value of this parameter is or.
- analyzer: This specifies the name of the analyzer used to analyze the query provided in the query parameter.
- allow_leading_wildcard: This specifies if a wildcard character is allowed as the first character of a term. It defaults to true.
- lowercase_expand_terms: This specifies if the terms that are a result of query rewrite should be lowercased. It defaults to true, which means that the rewritten terms will be lowercased.
- enable_position_increments: This specifies if position increments should be turned on in the result query. It defaults to true.
- fuzzy_max_expansions: This specifies the maximum number of terms into which fuzzy query will be expanded, if fuzzy query is used. It defaults to 50.
- fuzzy_prefix_length: This specifies the prefix length for the generated fuzzy queries and defaults to 0. To learn more about it, look at the fuzzy query description.

- `phrase_slop`: This specifies the phrase slop and defaults to `0`. To learn more about it, look at the `phrase match` query description.

- `boost`: This specifies the `boost` value which will be used and defaults to `1.0`.

- `analyze_wildcard`: This specifies if the terms generated by the wildcard query should be analyzed. It defaults to `false`, which means that those terms won't be analyzed.

- `auto_generate_phrase_queries`: specifies if the phrase queries will be automatically generated from the query. It defaults to `false`, which means that the phrase queries won't be automatically generated.

- `minimum_should_match`: This controls how many of the generated Boolean `should` clauses should be matched against a document for the document to be considered a hit. The value can be provided as a percentage; for example, 50%, which would mean that at least 50 percent of the given terms should match. It can also be provided as an integer value, such as 2, which means that at least 2 terms must match.

- `fuzziness`: This controls the behavior of the generated `fuzzy` query. Refer to the `match` query description for more information.

- `max_determined_states`: This defaults to 10000 and sets the number of states that the automaton can have for handling regular expression queries. It is used to disallow very expensive queries using regular expressions.

- `locale`: This sets the locale that should be used for the conversion of string values. By default, it is set to `ROOT`.

- `time_zone`: This sets the time zone that should be used by range queries that are run on date based fields.

- `lenient`: This can take the value of `true` or `false`. If set to `true`, format-based failures will be ignored. By default, it is set to `false`.

Note that Elasticsearch can rewrite the `query string` query and, because of that, Elasticsearch allows us to pass additional parameters that control the rewrite method. However, for more details about this process, go to the *Understanding the querying process* section in this chapter.

Running the query string query against multiple fields

It is possible to run the `query string` query against multiple fields. In order to do that, one needs to provide the fields parameter in the query body, which should hold the array of the field names. There are two methods of running the query string query against multiple fields: the default method uses the `Boolean` query to make queries and the other method can use the `dis_max` query.

In order to use the `dis_max` query, one should add the `use_dis_max` property in the query body and set it to `true`. An example query will look like the following code:

```
{
 "query" : {
  "query_string" : {
   "query" : "crime punishment",
   "fields" : [ "title", "otitle" ],
   "use_dis_max" : true
  }
 }
}
```

The simple query string query

The simple query string query uses one of the newest query parsers in Lucene - the SimpleQueryParser (`https://lucene.apache.org/core/5_4_0/queryparser/org/apache/lucene/queryparser/simple/SimpleQueryParser.html`). Similar to the query string query, it accepts Lucene query syntax as the query; however, unlike it, it never throws an exception when a parsing error happens. Instead of throwing an exception, it discards the invalid parts of the query and runs the rest.

An example simple query string query will look like the following code:

```
{
 "query" : {
  "simple_query_string" : {
   "query" : "crime punishment",
   "default_operator" : "or"
  }
 }
}
```

The query supports parameters such as `query`, `fields`, `default_operator`, `analyzer`, `lowercase_expanded_terms`, `locale`, `lenient`, and `minimum_should_match`, and can also be run against multiple fields using the `fields` property.

The identifiers query

This is a simple query that filters the returned documents to only those with the provided identifiers. It works on the internal `_uid` field, so it doesn't require the `_id` field to be enabled. The simplest version of such a query will look like the following:

```
{
  "query" : {
  "ids" : {
   "values" : [ "1", "2", "3" ]
  }
  }
}
```

This query will only return those documents that have one of the identifiers present in the values array. We can complicate the `identifiers` query a bit and also limit the documents on the basis of their type. For example, if we want to only include documents from the book types, we will send the following query:

```
{
 "query" : {
  "ids" : {
   "type" : "book",
   "values" : [ "1", "2", "3" ]
  }
  }
}
```

As you can see, we've added the `type` property to our query and we've set its value to the `type` we are interested in.

The prefix query

This query is similar to the `term` query in its configuration and to the `multi term` query when looking into its logic. The `prefix` query allows us to match documents that have the value in a certain field that starts with a given prefix. For example, if we want to find all the documents that have values starting with `cri` in the `title` field, we will run the following query:

```
{
  "query" : {
    "prefix" : {
      "title" : "cri"
    }
  }
}
```

Similar to the `term` query, you can also include the `boost` attribute to your prefix query which will affect the importance of the given prefix. For example, if we would like to change our previous query and give our query a `boost` of 3.0, we will send the following query:

```
{
  "query" : {
  "prefix" : {
    "title" : {
    "value" : "cri",
    "boost" : 3.0
    }
  }
  }
}
```

 Note that the prefix query is rewritten by Elasticsearch and because of that Elasticsearch allows us to pass an additional parameter, that is, controlling the rewrite method. However, for more details about that process, refer to the *Understanding the querying process* section in this chapter.

The fuzzy query

The `fuzzy` query allows us to find documents that have values similar to the ones we've provided in the query. The similarity of terms is calculated on the basis of the edit distance algorithm. The edit distance is calculated on the basis of terms we provide in the query and against the searched documents. This query can be expensive when it comes to CPU resources, but can help us when we need fuzzy matching; for example, when users make spelling mistakes. In our example, let's assume that instead of crime, our user enters the `crme` word into the search box and we would like to run the simplest form of `fuzzy` query. Such a query will look like this:

```
{
  "query" : {
    "fuzzy" : {
      "title" : "crme"
    }
  }
}
```

The response for such a query will be as follows:

```
{
  "took" : 81,
  "timed_out" : false,
  "_shards" : {
    "total" : 5,
    "successful" : 5,
    "failed" : 0
  },
  "hits" : {
    "total" : 1,
    "max_score" : 0.5,
    "hits" : [ {
      "_index" : "library",
      "_type" : "book",
      "_id" : "4",
      "_score" : 0.5,
      "_source" : {
        "title" : "Crime and Punishment",
        "otitle" : "Преступлéние и наказáние",
        "author" : "Fyodor Dostoevsky",
        "year" : 1886,
        "characters" : [ "Raskolnikov", "Sofia Semyonovna
          Marmeladova" ],
        "tags" : [ ],
        "copies" : 0,
        "available" : true
      }
    } ]
  }
}
```

Even though we made a typo, Elasticsearch managed to find the documents we were interested in.

We can control the `fuzzy` query behavior by using the following parameters:

- `value`: This specifies the actual query.
- `boost`: This specifies the boost value for the query. It defaults to `1.0`.
- `fuzziness`: This controls the behavior of the generated `fuzzy` query. Refer to the `match` query description for more information.

- `prefix_length`: This is the length of the common prefix of the differencing terms. It defaults to `0`.

- `max_expansions`: This specifies the maximum number of terms the query will be expanded to. The default value is unbounded.

The parameters should be wrapped in the name of the field we are running the query against. So if we would like to modify the previous query and add additional parameters, the query will look like the following code:

```
{
  "query" : {
   "fuzzy" : {
    "title" : {
     "value" : "crme",
     "fuzziness" : 2
    }
   }
  }
}
```

The wildcard query

A query that allows us to use * and ? wildcards in the values we search. Apart from that, the `wildcard` query is very similar to the term query in case of its body. To send a query that would match all the documents with the value of the `cr?me` term (? matching any character) we would send the following query:

```
{
  "query" : {
   "wildcard" : {
    "title" : "cr?me"
   }
  }
}
```

It will match the documents that have all the terms matching `cr?me` in the `title` field. However, you can also include the `boost` attribute to your `wildcard` query which will affect the importance of each term that matches the given value. For example, if we would like to change our previous query and give our term query a `boost` of `20.0`, we will send the following query:

```
{
  "query" : {
   "wildcard" : {
```

```
   "title" : {
     "value" : "cr?me",
     "boost" : 20.0
   }
  }
 }
}
```

> Note that wildcard queries are not very performance oriented queries and should be avoided if possible; especially avoid leading wildcards (terms starting with wildcards). The `wildcard` query is rewritten by Elasticsearch and because of that Elasticsearch allows us to pass an additional parameter, that is, controlling the rewrite method. For more details about this process, refer to the *Understanding the querying process* section in this chapter. Also remember that the `wildcard` query is not analyzed.

The range query

A query that allows us to find documents that have a field value within a certain range and which works for numerical fields as well as for string-based fields and date based fields (just maps to a different Apache Lucene query). The `range` query should be run against a single field and the query parameters should be wrapped in the field name. The following parameters are supported:

- `gte`: The query will match documents with the value greater than or equal to the one provided with this parameter

- `gt`: The query will match documents with the value greater than the one provided with this parameter

- `lte`: The query will match documents with the value lower than or equal to the one provided with this parameter

- `lt`: The query will match documents with the value lower than the one provided with this parameter

So for example, if we want to find all the books that have the value from `1700` to `1900` in the `year` field, we will run the following query:

```
{
 "query" : {
  "range" : {
   "year" : {
    "gte" : 1700,
```

```
        "lte" : 1900
      }
    }
  }
}
```

Regular expression query

Regular expression query allows us to use regular expressions as the `query` text. Remember that the performance of such queries depends on the chosen regular expression. If our regular expression would match many terms, the query will be slow. The general rule is that the more terms matched by the regular expression, the slower the query will be.

An example regular expression query looks like this:

```
{
  "query" : {
    "regexp" : {
      "title" : {
        "value" : "cr.m[ae]",
        "boost" : 10.0
      }
    }
  }
}
```

The preceding query will result in Elasticsearch rewriting the query. The rewritten query will have the number of term queries depending on the content of our index matching the given regular expression. The `boost` parameter seen in the query specifies the `boost` value for the generated queries.

The full regular expression syntax accepted by Elasticsearch can be found at `https://www.elastic.co/guide/en/elasticsearch/reference/current/query-dsl-regexp-query.html#regexp-syntax`.

The more like this query

One of the queries that got a major rework in Elasticsearch 2.0, the more like `this` query allows us to retrieve documents that are similar (or not similar) to the provided text or to the documents that were provided.

The more like this query allows us to get documents that are similar to the provided text. Elasticsearch supports a few parameters to define how the more like this query should work:

- `fields`: An array of fields that the query should be run against. It defaults to the `_all` field.

- `like`: This parameter comes in two flavors: it allows us to provide a text which the returned documents should be similar to or an array of documents that the returning document should be similar to.

- `unlike`: This is similar to the `like` parameter, but it allows us to define text or documents that our returning document should not be similar to.

- `min_term_freq`: The minimum term frequency (for the terms in the documents) below which terms will be ignored. It defaults to `2`.

- `max_query_terms`: The maximum number of terms that will be included in any generated query. It defaults to `25`. The higher value may mean higher precision, but lower performance.

- `stop_words`: An array of words that will be ignored when comparing documents and the query. It is empty by default.

- `min_doc_freq`: The minimum number of documents in which the term has to be present in order not to be ignored. It defaults to `5`, which means that a term needs to be present in at least five documents.

- `max_doc_freq`: The maximum number of documents in which the term may be present in order not to be ignored. By default, it is unbounded (set to `0`).

- `min_word_len`: The minimum length of a single word below which a word will be ignored. It defaults to `0`.

- `max_word_len`: The maximum length of a single word above which it will be ignored. It defaults to unbounded (which means setting the value to `0`).

- `boost_terms`: The `boost` value that will be used when boosting each term. It defaults to `0`.

- `boost`: The `boost` value that will be used when boosting the query. It defaults to `1`.

- `include`: This specifies if the input documents should be included in the results returned by the query. It defaults to `false`, which means that the input documents won't be included.

- `minimum_should_match`: This controls the number of terms that need to be matched in the resulting documents. By default, it is set to `30%`.

- `analyzer`: The name of the analyzer that will be used to analyze the text we provided.

An example for a more like this query looks like this:

```
{
 "query" : {
  "more_like_this" : {
   "fields" : [ "title", "otitle" ],
   "like" : "crime and punishment",
   "min_term_freq" : 1,
   "min_doc_freq" : 1
  }
 }
}
```

As we said earlier, the like property can also be used to show which documents the results should be similar to. For example, the following is the query that will use the like property to point to a given document (note that the following query won't return documents on our example data):

```
{
 "query" : {
 "more_like_this" : {
   "fields" : [ "title", "otitle" ],
   "min_term_freq" : 1,
   "min_doc_freq" : 1,
   "like" : [
    {
     "_index" : "library",
     "_type" : "book",
     "_id" : "4"
    }
   ]
  }
 }
}
```

We can also mix the documents and text together:

```
{
 "query" : {
 "more_like_this" : {
   "fields" : [ "title", "otitle" ],
   "min_term_freq" : 1,
   "min_doc_freq" : 1,
   "like" : [
    {
```

```
      "_index" : "library",
      "_type" : "book",
      "_id" : "4"
    },
    "crime and punishment"
    ]
  }
  }
}
```

Compound queries

In the *Basic queries* section of this chapter, we discussed the simplest queries exposed by Elasticsearch. We also talked about the position aware queries called span queries in the `Span queries` section. However, the simple ones and the span queries are not the only queries that Elasticsearch provides. The compound queries, as we call them, allow us to connect multiple queries together or alter the behavior of other queries. You may wonder if you need such functionality. Your deployment may not need it, but anything apart from a simple query will probably require compound queries. For example, combining a simple term query with a `match_phrase` query to get better search results may be a good candidate for compound queries usage.

The bool query

The `bool` query allows us to wrap a virtually unbounded number of queries and connect them with a logical value using one of the following sections:

- `should`: The query wrapped into this section may or may not match. The number of `should` sections that have to match is controlled by the `minimum_should_match` parameter

- `must`: The query wrapped into this section must match in order for the document to be returned.

- `must_not`: The query when wrapped into this section must not match in order for the document to be returned.

Each of the preceding mentioned sections can be present multiple times in a single `bool` query. This allows us to build very complex queries that have multiple levels of nesting (you can include the `bool` query in another `bool` query). Remember that the score of the resulting document will be calculated by taking a sum of all the wrapped queries that the document matched.

In addition to the preceding sections, we can add the following parameters to the query body to control its behavior:

- `filter`: This allows us to specify the part of the query that should be used as a filter. You can read more about filters in the *Filtering your results* section in *Chapter 4, Extending Your Querying Knowledge*.

- `boost`: This specifies the boost used in the query, defaulting to `1.0`. The higher the boost, the higher the score of the matching document.

- `minimum_should_match`: This describes the minimum number of should clauses that have to match in order for the checked document to be counted as a match. For example, it can be an integer value such as 2 or a percentage value such as 75%. For more information, refer to `https://www.elastic.co/guide/en/elasticsearch/reference/current/query-dsl-minimum-should-match.html`.

- `disable_coord`: A `Boolean` parameter (defaults to `false`), which allows us to enable or disable the score factor computation that is based on the fraction of all the query terms that a document contains. We should set it to `true` for less precise scoring, but slightly faster queries.

Imagine that we want to find all the documents that have the term `crime` in the title field. In addition, the documents may or may not have a range of `1900` to `2000` in the year field and may not have the `nothing` term in the `otitle` field. Such a query made with the `bool` query will look as follows:

```
{
  "query" : {
    "bool" : {
      "must" : {
        "term" : {
          "title" : "crime"
        }
      },
      "should" : {
        "range" : {
          "year" : {
            "from" : 1900,
            "to" : 2000
          }
        }
      },
      "must_not" : {
        "term" : {
```

```
        "otitle" : "nothing"
      }
    }
   }
  }
 }
```

 Note that the must, should, and must_not sections can contain a single query or an array of queries.

The dis_max query

The dis_max query is very useful as it generates a union of documents returned by all the sub queries and returns it as the result. The good thing about this query is the fact that we can control how the lower scoring sub queries affect the final score of the documents. For the dis_max query, we specify the queries using the queries property (query or an array of queries) and the tie breaker, with the tie_breaker property. We can also include additional boost by specifying the boost parameter.

The final document score is calculated as the sum of scores of the maximum scoring query and the sum of scores returned from the rest of the queries, multiplied by the value of the tie parameter. So, the tie_breaker parameter allows us to control how the lower scoring queries affect the final score. If we set the tie_breaker parameter to 1.0, we get the exact sum, while setting the tie parameter to 0.1 results in only 10 percent of the scores (of all the scores apart from the maximum scoring query) being added to the final score.

An example of the dis_max query is as follows:

```
{
  "query" : {
    "dis_max" : {
      "tie_breaker" : 0.99,
      "boost" : 10.0,
      "queries" : [
        {
          "match" : {
            "title" : "crime"
          }
        },
        {
          "match" : {
```

```
                    "author" : "fyodor"
                 }
              }
           ]
        }
     }
  }
```

As you can see, we included the `tie_breaker` and `boost` parameters. In addition to that, we specified the `queries` parameter that holds the array of queries that will be run and used to generate the union of documents for results.

The boosting query

The `boosting` query wraps around two queries and lowers the score of the documents returned by one of the queries. There are three sections of the boosting query that need to be defined: the `positive` section that holds the query whose document score will be left unchanged, the `negative` section whose resulting documents will have their score lowered, and the `negative_boost` section that holds the `boost` value that will be used to lower the second section's query score. The advantage of the `boosting` query is that the results of both the queries (the negative and the positive ones) will be present in the results, although the scores of some queries will be lowered. For comparison, if we were to use the `bool` query with the `must_not` section, we wouldn't get the results for such a query.

Let's assume that we want to have the results of a simple term query for the term `crime` in the `title` field and want the score of such documents to not be changed. However, we also want to have the documents that range from `1800` to `1900` in the year field, and the scores of documents returned by such a query to have an additional boost of `0.5`. Such a query will look like the following:

```
{
   "query" : {
      "boosting" : {
         "positive" : {
            "term" : {
               "title" : "crime"
            }
         },
         "negative" : {
            "range" : {
               "year" : {
                  "from" : 1800,
                  "to" : 1900
```

```
        }
      }
    },
    "negative_boost" : 0.5
  }
 }
}
```

The constant_score query

The `constant_score` query wraps another query and returns a constant score for each document returned by the wrapped query. We specify the score that should be given to the documents by using the `boost` property, which defaults to `1.0`. It allows us to strictly control the score value assigned for a document matched by a query. For example, if we want to have a score of `2.0` for all the documents that have the term `crime` in the `title` field, we send the following query to Elasticsearch:

```
{
   "query" : {
     "constant_score" : {
       "query" : {
         "term" : {
           "title" : "crime"
         }
       },
       "boost" : 2.0
     }
   }
}
```

The indices query

The `indices` query is useful when executing a query against multiple indices. It allows us to provide an array of indices (the `indices` property) and two queries, one that will be executed if we query the index from the list (the `query` property) and the second that will be executed on all the other indices (the `no_match_query` property). For example, assume we have an alias named books, holding two indices: library and users. What we want to do is use this alias. However, we want to run different queries depending on which index is used for searching. An example query following this logic will look as follows:

```
{
   "query" : {
```

```
"indices" : {
  "indices" : [ "library" ],
  "query" : {
    "term" : {
      "title" : "crime"
    }
  },
  "no_match_query" : {
    "term" : {
      "user" : "crime"
    }
  }
}
}
}
```

In the preceding query, the query described in the `query` property was run against the library index and the query defined in the `no_match_query` section was run against all the other indices present in the cluster, which for our hypothetical alias means the users index.

The `no_match_query` property can also have a string value instead of a query. This string value can either be all or none, but it defaults to all. If the `no_match_query` property is set to all, the documents from the indices that don't match will be returned. Setting the `no_match_query` property to none will result in no documents from the indices that don't match the query from that section.

Using span queries

Elasticsearch leverages Lucene span queries, which allow us to make queries when some tokens or phrases are near other tokens or phrases. Basically, we can call them position aware queries. When using the standard non span queries, we are not able to make queries that are position aware; to some extent, the `phrase` queries allow that, but only to some extent. So, for Elasticsearch and the underlying Lucene, it doesn't matter if the term is in the beginning of the sentence or at the end or near another term. When using span queries, it does matter.

The following span queries are exposed in Elasticsearch:

- span term query
- span first query
- span near query

- span or query
- span not query
- span within query
- span containing query
- span multi query

Before we continue with the description, let's index a document to a completely new index that we will use to show how span queries work. To do this, we use the following command:

```
curl -XPUT 'localhost:9200/spans/book/1' -d '{
 "title" : "Test book",
 "author" : "Test author",
 "description" : "The world breaks everyone, and afterward, some are
strong at the broken places"
}'
```

A span

A span, in our context, is a starting and ending token position in a field. For example, in our case, the world breaks everyone could be a single span, a world can be a single span too. As you may know, during analysis, Lucene, in addition to token, includes some additional parameters, such as position in the token stream. Position information combined with the terms allows us to construct spans using Elasticsearch span queries (which are mapped to Lucene span queries). In the next few pages, we will learn how to construct spans using different span queries and how to control which documents are matched.

Span term query

The span_term query is a builder for the other span queries. A span_term query is a query similar to the already discussed term query. On its own, it works just like the mentioned term query – it matches a term. Its definition is simple and looks as follows (we omitted some parts of the queries on purpose, because we will discuss it later):

```
{
  "query" : {
  ...
    "span_term" : {
    "description" : {
```

```
        "value" : "world",
        "boost" : 5.0
      }
    }
  }
}
```

As you can see, it is very similar to the standard term query. The above query is run against the description field and we want to have the documents that have the `world` term returned. We also specified the boost, which is also allowed.

One thing to remember is that the `span_term` query, similar to the standard term query, is not analyzed.

Span first query

The `span first` query allows us to match documents that have matches only in the first positions of the field. In order to define a span first query, we need to nest inside of it any other span query; for example, a span term query we already know. So, let's find the document that has the term `world` in the first two positions in the `description` field. We do that by sending the following query:

```
{
  "query" : {
    "span_first" : {
      "match" : {
        "span_term" : { "description" : "world" }
      },
      "end" : 2
    }
  }
}
```

In the results, we will get the document that we had indexed in the beginning of this section. In the `match` section of the span first query, we should include at least a single span query that should be matched at the maximum position specified by the `end` parameter.

So, to understand everything well, if we set the `end` parameter to 1, we shouldn't get our document with the previous query. So, let's check it by sending the following query:

```
{
  "query" : {
    "span_first" : {
```

```
      "match" : {
       "span_term" : { "description" : "world" }
      },
      "end" : 1
     }
    }
  }
```

The response to the preceding query will be as follows:

```
{
   "took" : 1,
   "timed_out" : false,
   "_shards" : {
     "total" : 5,
     "successful" : 5,
     "failed" : 0
   },
   "hits" : {
     "total" : 0,
     "max_score" : null,
     "hits" : [ ]
   }
}
```

So it is working as expected. This is because the first term in our index will be the term the and not the term world which we searched for.

Span near query

The span near query allows us to match documents that have other spans near each other and we can call this query a compound query as it wraps another span query. For example, if we want to find documents that have the term world near the term everyone, we will run the following query:

```
{
  "query" : {
   "span_near" : {
    "clauses" : [
      { "span_term" : { "description" : "world" } },
      { "span_term" : { "description" : "everyone" } }
    ],
    "slop" : 0,
    "in_order" : true
   }
  }
}
```

As you can see, we specify our queries in the `clauses` section of the `span near` query. It is an array of other span queries. The `slop` parameter defines the allowed number of terms between the spans. The `in_order` parameter can be used to limit the matches only to those documents that match our queries in the same order that they were defined in. So, in our case, we will get documents that have `world everyone`, but not `everyone world` in the description field.

So let's get back to our query, right now it would return 0 results. If you look at our example document, you will notice that between the terms world and everyone, an additional term is present and we set the slop parameter to 0 (slop was discussed during the `phrase` query description). If we increase it to 1, we will get our result. To test it, let's send the following query:

```
{
  "query" : {
    "span_near" : {
      "clauses" : [
        { "span_term" : { "description" : "world" } },
        { "span_term" : { "description" : "everyone" } }
      ],
      "slop" : 1,
      "in_order" : true
    }
  }
}
```

The results returned by Elasticsearch are as follows:

```
{
  "took" : 6,
  "timed_out" : false,
  "_shards" : {
    "total" : 5,
    "successful" : 5,
    "failed" : 0
  },
  "hits" : {
    "total" : 1,
    "max_score" : 0.10848885,
    "hits" : [ {
      "_index" : "spans",
      "_type" : "book",
      "_id" : "1",
      "_score" : 0.10848885,
      "_source" : {
        "title" : "Test book",
        "author" : "Test author",
```

```
          "description" : "The world breaks everyone, and afterward,
            some are strong at the broken places"
        }
      } ]
    }
  }
}
```

As we can see, the altered query successfully returned our indexed document.

Span or query

The span or query allows us to wrap other span queries and aggregate matches of all those that we've wrapped. Similar to the span_near query, the span_or query uses the array of clauses to specify other span queries. For example, if we want to get the documents that have the term world in the first two positions of the description field, or the ones that have the term world not further than a single position from the term everyone, we will send the following query to Elasticsearch:

```
{
  "query" : {
   "span_or" : {
    "clauses" : [
      {
       "span_first" : {
        "match" : {
         "span_term" : { "description" : "world" }
        },
        "end" : 2
       }
      },
      {
       "span_near" : {
        "clauses" : [
         { "span_term" : { "description" : "world" } },
         { "span_term" : { "description" : "everyone" } }
        ],
        "slop" : 1,
        "in_order" : true
       }
      }
    ]
   }
  }
}
```

The result of the preceding query will return our indexed document.

Span not query

The span not query allows us to specify two sections of queries. The first is the include section which specifies which span queries should be matched and the second section is the exclude one which specifies the span queries which shouldn't be overlapping the first ones. To keep it simple, if a query from the exclude one matches the same span (or a part of it) as the query from the include section, such a document won't be returned as a match for such a span not query. Each of these sections can contain multiple span queries.

So, to illustrate that query, let's make a query that will return all the documents that have the span constructed from a single term and which have the term breaks in the description field. Let's also exclude the documents that have a span which matches the terms world and everyone at the maximum of a single position from each other, when such a span overlaps the one defined in the first span query.

```
{
  "query" : {
  "span_not" : {
   "include" : {
    "span_term" : { "description" : "breaks" }
   },
   "exclude" : {
    "span_near" : {
      "clauses" : [
        { "span_term" : { "description" : "world" } },
        { "span_term" : { "description" : "everyone" } }
      ],
      "slop" : 1
    }
   }
  }
 }
}
```

The following is the result:

```
{
  "took" : 1,
  "timed_out" : false,
  "_shards" : {
    "total" : 5,
    "successful" : 5,
    "failed" : 0
  },
```

```
    "hits" : {
      "total" : 0,
      "max_score" : null,
      "hits" : [ ]
    }
  }
}
```

As you would have noticed, the result of the query is as we would have expected. Our document wasn't found because the span query from the exclude section was overlapping the span from the include section.

Span within query

The span_within query allows us to find documents that have a span enclosed in another span. We define two sections in the span_within query: the little and the big. The little section defines a span query that needs to be enclosed by the span query defined using the big section.

For example, if we would like to find a document that has the term world near the term breaks and those terms should be inside a span that is bound by the terms world and afterward not more than 10terms from each other, the query that does that will look as follows:

```
{
  "query" : {
    "span_within" : {
      "little" : {
        "span_near" : {
          "clauses" : [
            { "span_term" : { "description" : "world" } },
            { "span_term" : { "description" : "breaks" } }
          ],
          "slop" : 0,
          "in_order" : false
        }
      },
      "big" : {
        "span_near" : {
          "clauses" : [
            { "span_term" : { "description" : "world" } },
            { "span_term" : { "description" : "afterward" } }
          ],
          "slop" : 10,
```

```
        "in_order" : false
      }
    }
  }
 }
}
```

Span containing query

The span_contaning query can be seen as the opposite of the span_within query we just discussed. It allows us to match spans that overlap other spans. Again, we use two sections with the span queries: the little and the big. The little section defines a span query that needs to be enclosed by the span query defined using the big section.

We can use the same example. If we would like to find a document that has the term world near the term breaks, and those terms should be inside a span that is bound by the terms world and afterward not more than 10 terms from each other, the query that does that will look as follows:

```
{
 "query" : {
  "span_containing" : {
   "little" : {
    "span_near" : {
     "clauses" : [
       { "span_term" : { "description" : "world" } },
       { "span_term" : { "description" : "breaks" } }
     ],
     "slop" : 0,
     "in_order" : false
    }
   },
   "big" : {
    "span_near" : {
     "clauses" : [
       { "span_term" : { "description" : "world" } },
       { "span_term" : { "description" : "afterward" } }
     ],
     "slop" : 10,
     "in_order" : false
    }
   }
  }
 }
}
```

Span multi query

The last type of span query that Elasticsearch supports is the `span_multi` query. It allows us to wrap any multi term query that we've discussed (the `term` query, the `range` query, the `wildcard` query, the `regex` query, the `fuzzy` query, or the `prefix` query) as a `span` query.

For example, if we want to find documents that have the term starting with the prefix `wor` in the first two positions in the description field, we can do that by sending the following query:

```
{
  "query" : {
   "span_multi" : {
    "match" : {
     "prefix" : {
      "description" : { "value" : "wor" }
     }
    }
   }
  }
}
```

There is one thing to remember – the multi term query that we want to use needs to be enclosed in the match section of the `span_multi` query.

Performance considerations

A few words at the end of discussing span queries. Remember that they are costlier when it comes to processing power, because not only do the terms have to be matched but also positions have to be calculated and checked. This means that Lucene and thus Elasticsearch will need more CPU cycles to calculate all the needed information to find matching documents. You can expect span queries to be slower than the queries that don't take positions into account.

Choosing the right query

By now we've seen what queries are available in Elasticsearch, both the simple ones and the ones that can group other queries as well. Before continuing with more complicated topics, we would like to discuss which of the queries should be used for which use case. Of course, one could dedicate the whole book to showing different queries use cases, so we will only show a few of them to help you see what you can expect and which query to use.

The use cases

As you already know which queries can be used to find which data, what we would like to show you are example use cases using the data we indexed in *Chapter 2, Indexing Your Data*. To do this, we will start with a few guiding lines on how to chose the query and then we will show you example use cases and discuss why those queries could be used.

Limiting results to given tags

One of the simplest examples of querying Elasticsearch is the search for exact terms. By exact we mean character to character comparison of a term that is indexed and written into Lucene inverted index. To run such a query, we can use the `term` query provided by Elasticsearch. This is because its content is not analyzed by Elasticsearch. For example, let's assume that we would like to search for all the books with the value **novel** in the `tags` field, which as we know from the mappings is not analyzed. To do that, we would run the following command:

```
curl -XGET 'localhost:9200/library/_search?pretty' -d '{
  "query" : {
    "term" : {
      "tags" : "novel"
  }
  }
}'
```

Searching for values in a range

One of the simplest queries that can be run is a query matching documents in a given range of values. Usually such queries are a part of a larger query or a filter. For example, a query that would return books with the number of copies from 1 to 3 inclusive, would look as follows:

```
curl -XGET 'localhost:9200/library/_search?pretty' -d '{
 "query" : {
  "range" : {
   "copies" : {
    "gte" : 1,
    "lte" : 3
   }
  }
 }
}'
```

Boosting some of the matched documents

There are many common examples of using the `bool` query. For example, very simple ones like finding documents having a list of terms. What we would like to show you is how to use the `bool` query to boost some of the documents. For example, if we want to find all the documents that have one or more copy and have the ones that are published after `1950`, we will run the following query:

```
curl -XGET 'localhost:9200/library/_search?pretty' -d '{
  "query" : {
  "bool" : {
    "must" : [
    {
     "range" : {
      "copies" : {
       "gte" : 1
      }
     }
    }
    ],
    "should" : [
    {
     "range" : {
      "year" : {
       "gt" : 1950
      }
     }
    }
    ]
  }
  }
}'
```

Ignoring lower scoring partial queries

The dis_max query, as we discussed, allows us to control how influential the lower scoring partial queries are. For example, if we would only want to assign the score of the highest scoring partial query for the documents matching crime punishment in the title field or raskolnikov in the characters field, we would run the following query:

```
curl -XGET 'localhost:9200/library/_search?pretty' -d '{
  "fields" : ["_id", "_score"],
  "query" : {
  "dis_max" : {
    "tie_breaker" : 0.0,
    "queries" : [
    {
     "match" : {
      "title" : "crime punishment"
     }
    },
    {
     "match" : {
      "characters" : "raskolnikov"
     }
    }
    ]
   }
  }
}'
```

The result for the preceding query will look as follows:

```
{
  "took" : 2,
  "timed_out" : false,
  "_shards" : {
    "total" : 5,
    "successful" : 5,
    "failed" : 0
  },
  "hits" : {
```

```
    "total" : 1,
    "max_score" : 0.70710677,
    "hits" : [ {
      "_index" : "library",
      "_type" : "book",
      "_id" : "4",
      "_score" : 0.70710677
    } ]
  }
}
```

Now let's see the score of the partial queries alone. To do that, we will run the partial queries using the following commands:

```
curl -XGET 'localhost:9200/library/_search?pretty' -d '{
 "fields" : [ "_id", "_score" ],
 "query" : {
  "match" : {
   "title" : "crime punishment"
  }
 }
}'
```

The response for the preceding query is as follows:

```
{
  "took" : 4,
  "timed_out" : false,
  "_shards" : {
    "total" : 5,
    "successful" : 5,
    "failed" : 0
  },
  "hits" : {
    "total" : 1,
    "max_score" : 0.70710677,
    "hits" : [ {
      "_index" : "library",
      "_type" : "book",
      "_id" : "4",
      "_score" : 0.70710677
    } ]
  }
}
```

The following is the next command:

```
curl -XGET 'localhost:9200/library/_search?pretty' -d '{
 "fields" : [ "_id", "_score" ],
 "query" : {
  "match" : {
   "characters" : "raskolnikov"
  }
 }
}'
```

The response is as follows:

```
{
    "took" : 2,
    "timed_out" : false,
    "_shards" : {
       "total" : 5,
       "successful" : 5,
       "failed" : 0
    },
    "hits" : {
       "total" : 1,
       "max_score" : 0.5,
       "hits" : [ {
          "_index" : "library",
          "_type" : "book",
          "_id" : "4",
          "_score" : 0.5
       } ]
    }
}
```

As you can see, the score of the document returned by our dis_max query is equal to the score of the highest scoring partial query (the first partial query). That is because we set the tie_breaker property to 0.0.

Using Lucene query syntax in queries

Having a simple search syntax is very useful for users and we already have such – the Lucene query syntax. Using the `query_string` query is an example where we can leverage that by allowing the users to type in queries with additional control characters. For example, if we would like to find books having the terms `crime` and `punishment` in their title and the `fyodor dostoevsky` phrase in the `author` field, and not being published between `2000` (exclusive) and `2015` (inclusive), we would use the following command:

```
curl -XGET 'localhost:9200/library/_search?pretty' -d '{
  "query" : {
  "query_string" : {
   "query" : "+title:crime +title:punishment +author:\"fyodor
dostoevsky\" -copies:{2000 TO 2015]"
  }
  }
}'
```

As you can see, we used the Lucene query syntax to pass all the matching requirements and we let the query parser construct the appropriate query.

Handling user queries without errors

Using the `query_string` query is very handy, but it is not error tolerant. If our user provides incorrect Lucene syntax, the query will return an error. Because of that, Elasticsearch exposes a second query that supports analysis and full Lucene query syntax – the `simple_query_string` query. Using such a query allows us to run the user queries and not care about the parsing errors at all. For example, let's look at the following query:

```
curl -XGET 'localhost:9200/library/_search?pretty' -d '{
  "query" : {
    "query_string" : {
      "query" : "+crime +punishment \"",
      "default_field" : "title"
    }
  }
}'
```

The response will contain:

```
{
  "error" : {
    "root_cause" : [ {
      "type" : "query_parsing_exception",
      "reason" : "Failed to parse query [+crime +punishment \"]",
      "index" : "library",
      "line" : 6,
      "col" : 3
    } ],
    "type" : "search_phase_execution_exception",
    "reason" : "all shards failed",
    "phase" : "query",
    "grouped" : true,
    "failed_shards" : [ {
      "shard" : 0,
      "index" : "library",
      "node" : "7jznW07BRrqjG-aJ7iKeaQ",
      "reason" : {
        "type" : "query_parsing_exception",
        "reason" : "Failed to parse query [+crime +punishment
          \"]",
        "index" : "library",
        "line" : 6,
        "col" : 3,
        "caused_by" : {
          "type" : "parse_exception",
          "reason" : "Cannot parse '+crime +punishment \"':
            Lexical error at line 1, column 21.  Encountered:
              <EOF> after : \"\"",
          "caused_by" : {
            "type" : "token_mgr_error",
            "reason" : "Lexical error at line 1, column 21.
              Encountered: <EOF> after : \"\""
          }
        }
      }
    } ]
  },
  "status" : 400
}
```

This means that the query was not properly constructed and a parse error happened. That's why the `simple_query_string` query was introduced. It uses a query parser that tries to handle user mistakes and tries to guess how the query should look. Our query using that parser will look as follows:

```
curl -XGET 'localhost:9200/library/_search?pretty' -d '{
  "query" : {
    "simple_query_string" : {
      "query" : "+crime +punishment \"",
      "fields" : ["title"]
    }
  }
}'
```

If you run the preceding query, you will see that the proper document is returned by Elasticsearch even though the query is not properly constructed.

Autocomplete using prefixes

A very common use case is to provide autocomplete functionality on the indexed data. As we know, the prefix query is not analyzed and works on the basis of terms indexed in the field. So the actual functionality depends on which tokens are produced during indexing. For example, let's assume that we would like to provide autocomplete functionality on any token in the `title` field and the user provided `wes` prefix. A query that would match such a requirement looks as follows:

```
curl -XGET 'localhost:9200/library/_search?pretty' -d '{
  "query" : {
    "prefix" : {
      "title" : "wes"
    }
  }
}'
```

Finding terms similar to a given one

A very simple example is using the `fuzzy` query to find documents having a term similar to a given one. For example, if we want to find all the documents having a value similar to `crimea`, we will run the following query:

```
curl -XGET 'localhost:9200/library/_search?pretty' -d '{
 "query" : {
  "fuzzy" : {
   "title" : {
    "value" : "crimea",
    "fuzziness" : 2,
    "max_expansions" : 50
   }
  }
 }
}'
```

Matching phrases

The simplest position aware query, the `phrase` query allows us to find documents not with a term but terms positioned one after another – ones that form a phrase. For example, a query that would only match documents that have the `westen nichts neues` phrase in the `otitle` field would look as follows:

```
curl -XGET 'localhost:9200/library/_search?pretty' -d '{
 "query" : {
  "match_phrase" : {
   "otitle" : "westen nichts neues"
  }
 }
}'
```

Spans, spans everywhere

The last use case we would like to discuss is a more complicated example of position aware queries called span queries. Imagine that we would like to run a query to find documents that have the `western front` phrase not more than three positions after the term `quiet` and all that just after the `all` term? This can be done with span queries and the following command shows how such query will look:

```
curl -XGET 'localhost:9200/library/_search?pretty' -d '{
  "query": {
  "span_near": {
```

```
    "clauses": [
      {
    "span_term": {
      "title": "all"
      }
    },
      {
      "span_near": {
        "clauses": [
         {
      "span_term": {
        "title": "quiet"
       }
      },
        {
      "span_near": {
         "clauses": [
           {
      "span_term": {
       "title": "western"
       }
      },
          {
      "span_term": {
       "title": "front"
       }
      }
         ],
         "slop": 0,
         "in_order": true
        }
      }
       ],
       "slop": 3,
       "in_order": true
```

```
      }
    }
  ],
  "slop": 0,
  "in_order": true
  }
  }
}'
```

Note that the span queries are not analyzed. We can see that by looking at the response of the Explain API. To see that response, we should run the same request body (our query) to the `/library/book/1/_explain` REST end-point. The interesting part of the output looks as follows:

```
"description" : "weight(spanNear([title:all, spanNear([title:quiet,
spanNear([title:western, title:front], 0, true)], 3, true)], 0, true) in
0) [PerFieldSimilarity], result of:",
```

Summary

This chapter has been all about the querying process. We started by looking at how to query Elasticsearch and what Elasticsearch does when it needs to handle the query. We also learned about the basic and compound queries, so we are now able to use both simple queries as well as the ones that group multiple small queries together. Finally, we discussed how to choose the right query for a given use case.

In the next chapter, we will extend our query knowledge. We will start with filtering our queries and move to highlighting possibilities and a way to validate our queries using Elasticsearch API. We will discuss sorting of search results and query rewrite which will show us what happens to some queries in Elasticsearch internals.

4
Extending Your Querying Knowledge

In the previous chapter, we dived into Elasticsearch querying capabilities. We discussed how to query Elasticsearch in detail and we learned how Elasticsearch querying works. We now know the basic and compound queries of this great search engine and what are the configuration options for each query type. We also got to know when to use our queries and we discussed a few use cases and which queries can be used to handle them. This chapter is dedicated to extending our querying knowledge. By the end of this chapter, you will have learned the following topics:

- What filtering is and how to use it
- What highlighting is and how to use it
- What are the highlighter types and what benefits they bring
- How to validate your queries
- How to sort your query results
- What query rewrite is and how to control it

Filtering your results

In the previous chapter, we talked about various types of queries. The common part was that we always wanted to get the best results first. This is the main difference from the standard database approach where every document matches the query or not. In the database world, we do not ask how good the document is; our only interest lies in the results returned. When talking about full text search engines this is different – we are interested not only in the results, we are also interested in their quality. The reason is obvious, we are searching in unstructured data, using text fields that use language analysis, stemming, and so on. Because of that, the initial results of our queries, in most cases, give results that are far from optimal. This is why when we talk about searching, we talk about precision and document recall.

On the other hand, sometimes we want to limit the whole subset of documents to a chosen part. For example, in a library, we may want to search only the available books, the rest being unimportant. Sometimes the score, busily calculated for the given fields, only interferes with the overall score and has no meaning in terms of accuracy. In such cases, filters should be used to limit the results of the query, but not interfere with the calculated score.

Prior to Elasticsearch 2.0, filters were independent entities from queries. In practice, almost every query had its own counterpart in filters. There was the `term` query and the `term` filter, the `bool` query and the `bool` filter, the `range` query and the `range` filter, and so on. From the user point of view, the most important difference between the queries and the filters was scoring. The filter didn't calculate score, which resulted in the filter being easily cached and more efficient. But this difference was very inconvenient for users. With the release of Elasticsearch 2.0 and its usage of Lucene 5.3, filter queries were deprecated along with some types of queries that allowed us to use filters. Let's discuss how filtering works now and what we can do to achieve the same or better performance as before in Elasticsearch 2.0.

The context is the key

In Elasticsearch 2.0, queries can calculate score or omit it by choosing more efficient way of execution. This behavior, in many cases, is done automatically based on the context where the query is used. This is about the queries that include filter sections, which remove the documents based on some criteria. These documents are unnecessary in the returned results and should be skipped as quickly as possible without affecting the overall score. Thanks to this, after discarding some documents we can focus only on the rest of the documents, calculating their scores, and sorting them before returning. The example of this case can be the `must_not` clause of a Boolean query. The document that matches the `must_not` clause will be removed from the returned result set, so calculating the score for the documents matched by this part of the `bool` query would be an additional, unnecessary, and performance ineffective work.

The best thing about all the changes is that we don't need to care about if we want to use filtering or not. Elasticsearch and the underlying Apache Lucene library take care of choosing the right execution method for us.

Explicit filtering with bool query

As we mentioned in the *Compound queries* section in *Chapter 3, Searching Your Data,* the `bool` query in Elasticsearch 2.0 allows us to add a filter explicitly by adding the `filter` section and including a query in that section. This is very convenient if we want to have a part of the query that needs to match, but we are not interested in the score for those documents.

Let's look at the following query:

```
curl -XGET 'localhost:9200/library/book/_search?pretty' -d '{
  "query" : {
    "term" : {
      "available" : true
    }
  }
}'
```

We see a simple query that should return all the books in our library available for borrowing, which means the documents with the available field set to true. Now let's compare it with the following query:

```
curl -XGET 'localhost:9200/library/book/_search?pretty' -d '{
  "query" : {
    "bool" : {
      "must" : {
        "match_all" : { }
      },
      "filter" : {
        "term" : {
          "available" : true
        }
      }
    }
  }
}'
```

This query returns all the books, but it also contains the filter section, which tells Elasticsearch that we are only interested in the available books. The query will return the same results as the previous query we've seen, of course when looking only at the number of documents and which documents are returned. The difference is the score. For our example data, both the queries return two books. The results returned for the first query look as follows:

```
{
  "took" : 2,
  "timed_out" : false,
  "_shards" : {
    "total" : 5,
    "successful" : 5,
    "failed" : 0
  },
  "hits" : {
    "total" : 2,
    "max_score" : 1.0,
    "hits" : [ {
      "_index" : "library",
      "_type" : "book",
      "_id" : "4",
      "_score" : 1.0,
```

```
      "_source" : {
        "title" : "Crime and Punishment",
        "otitle" : "Преступление и наказание",
        "author" : "Fyodor Dostoevsky",
        "year" : 1886,
        "characters" : [ "Raskolnikov", "Sofia Semyonovna
          Marmeladova" ],
        "tags" : [ ],
        "copies" : 0,
        "available" : true
      }
    }, {
      "_index" : "library",
      "_type" : "book",
      "_id" : "1",
      "_score" : 0.30685282,
      "_source" : {
        "title" : "All Quiet on the Western Front",
        "otitle" : "Im Westen nichts Neues",
        "author" : "Erich Maria Remarque",
        "year" : 1929,
        "characters" : [ "Paul Bäumer", "Albert Kropp", "Haie
          Westhus", "Fredrich Müller", "Stanislaus Katczinsky",
            "Tjaden" ],
        "tags" : [ "novel" ],
        "copies" : 1,
        "available" : true,
        "section" : 3
      }
    } ]
  }
}
```

The results for the second query look as follows:

```
{
  "took" : 2,
  "timed_out" : false,
  "_shards" : {
    "total" : 5,
    "successful" : 5,
    "failed" : 0
  },
  "hits" : {
    "total" : 2,
```

```
        "max_score" : 1.0,
        "hits" : [ {
          "_index" : "library",
          "_type" : "book",
          "_id" : "4",
          "_score" : 1.0,
          "_source" : {
            "title" : "Crime and Punishment",
            "otitle" : "Преступлéние и наказáние",
            "author" : "Fyodor Dostoevsky",
            "year" : 1886,
            "characters" : [ "Raskolnikov", "Sofia Semyonovna
              Marmeladova" ],
            "tags" : [ ],
            "copies" : 0,
            "available" : true
          }
        }, {
          "_index" : "library",
          "_type" : "book",
          "_id" : "1",
          "_score" : 1.0,
          "_source" : {
            "title" : "All Quiet on the Western Front",
            "otitle" : "Im Westen nichts Neues",
            "author" : "Erich Maria Remarque",
            "year" : 1929,
            "characters" : [ "Paul Bäumer", "Albert Kropp", "Haie
              Westhus", "Fredrich Müller", "Stanislaus Katczinsky",
                "Tjaden" ],
            "tags" : [ "novel" ],
            "copies" : 1,
            "available" : true,
            "section" : 3
          }
        } ]
      }
    }
```

If you look at the score for the documents in each query, you'll notice the difference. In the simple `term` query, Elasticsearch (the Lucene library, in fact) has a score of `1.0` for the first document and a score of `0.30685282` for the second one. This is not a perfect solution because the availability check is more or less binary and we don't want it to interfere with the score. That's why the second query is better in this case. With the `bool` query and filtering, the score for the `filter` element is not calculated and the score for both the documents is the same, that is `1.0`.

Highlighting

You have probably heard of *highlighting* or seen it. You may not even know that you are actually using highlighting when you are using the bigger and smaller public search engines on the World Wide Web (WWW). When we talk about highlighting in context of full text search, we usually mean showing which words or phrases from the query were matched in the resulting documents. For example, if we use Google and search for the word **lucene,** we would see that word bolded in the search results:

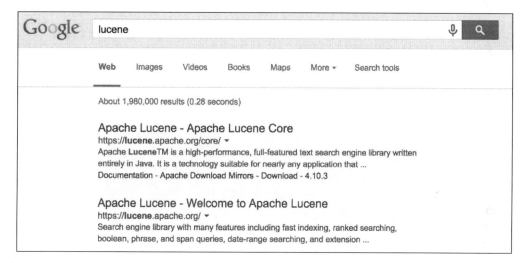

It is even more visible on the Microsoft Bing search engine:

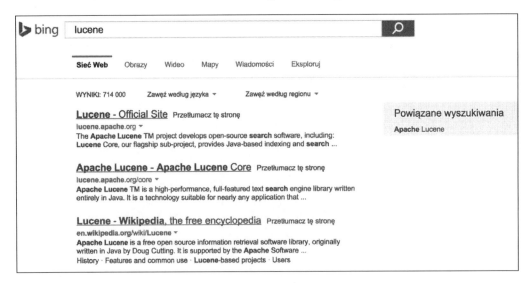

In this chapter, we will see how to use Elasticsearch highlighting capabilities to enhance our application with highlighted results.

Getting started with highlighting

There is no better way of showing how highlighting works other than making a query and looking at the results returned by Elasticsearch. So let's do that. We assume that we would like to highlight the terms that are matched in the `title` field of our documents to increase the search experience of our users. By now you know the example data from top to bottom, so let's again reuse the same data set. We want to match the term `crime` in the `title` field and we want to get highlighting results. One of the simplest queries that can achieve this looks as follows:

```
curl -XGET 'localhost:9200/library/book/_search?pretty' -d '{
  "query" : {
   "match" : {
    "title" : "crime"
   }
  },
  "highlight" : {
   "fields" : {
    "title" : {}
   }
  }
}'
```

The response for the preceding query is as follows:

```
{
  "took" : 16,
  "timed_out" : false,
  "_shards" : {
    "total" : 5,
    "successful" : 5,
    "failed" : 0
  },
  "hits" : {
    "total" : 1,
    "max_score" : 0.5,
    "hits" : [ {
      "_index" : "library",
      "_type" : "book",
      "_id" : "4",
      "_score" : 0.5,
      "_source" : {
        "title" : "Crime and Punishment",
        "otitle" : "Преступление и наказáние",
        "author" : "Fyodor Dostoevsky",
        "year" : 1886,
        "characters" : [ "Raskolnikov", "Sofia Semyonovna
          Marmeladova" ],
        "tags" : [ ],
        "copies" : 0,
        "available" : true
      },
      "highlight" : {
        "title" : [ "<em>Crime</em> and Punishment" ]
      }
    } ]
  }
}
```

As you can see, apart from the standard information about the documents that matched the query, we got a new section called highlight. Elasticsearch used the <em> HTML tag as the beginning of the highlighting section and its closing counterpart to close the highlighted section. This is the default behavior of Elasticsearch, but we will learn how to change that.

Field configuration

In order to perform highlighting, the original content of the field needs to be present. We have to set the fields we will use for highlighting. This is done by either marking a field to be stored or using the `_source` field with those fields included. If the field is set to be stored in the mappings, the stored version will be used, otherwise Elasticsearch will try to use the `_source` field and extract the field that needs to be highlighted.

Under the hood

Elasticsearch uses Apache Lucene under the hood and highlighting is one of the features of that library. Lucene provides three types of highlighting implementation: the standard one, which we just used; the second one called `FastVectorHighlighter` (`https://lucene.apache.org/core/5_4_0/highlighter/org/apache/lucene/search/vectorhighlight/FastVectorHighlighter.html`), which needs term vectors and positions to be able to work; and the third one called `PostingsHighlighter` (`http://lucene.apache.org/core/5_4_0/highlighter/org/apache/lucene/search/postingshighlight/PostingsHighlighter.html`). Elasticsearch chooses the right highlighter implementation automatically. If the field is configured with the `term_vector` property set to `with_positions_offsets`, `FastVectorHighlighter` will be used. If the field is configured with the `index_options` property set to `offsets`, `PostingsHighlighter` will be used. Otherwise, the standard highlighter will be used by Elasticsearch.

Which highlighter to use depends on your data, your queries, and the needed performance. The standard highlighter is a general use case one. However, if you want to highlight fields with lots of data, `FastVectorHighlighter` is the recommended one. The thing to remember about it is that it requires term vectors to be present and that will make your index slightly larger. Finally, the fastest highlighter, that is also recommended for natural language highlighting, is `PostingsHighlighter`. However, the thing to remember is that `PostingsHighlighter` doesn't support complex queries such as the `match_phrase_prefix` query and in such cases highlighting won't be returned.

Forcing highlighter type

While Elasticsearch chooses the highlighter type for us, we can also enforce the highlighting type if we really want to. To do that, we need to set the `type` property to one of the following values:

- `plain`: When this value is set, Elasticsearch will use the standard highlighter

- `fvh`: When this value is set, Elasticsearch will try using `FastVectorHighlighter`. It will require term vectors to be turned on for the field used for highlighting.

- `postings`: When this value is set, Elasticsearch will try using `PostingsHighlighter`. It will require offsets to be turned on for the field used for highlighting

For example, to use the standard highlighter, we will run the following query:

```
curl -XGET 'localhost:9200/library/book/_search?pretty' -d '{
 "query" : {
  "term" : {
   "title" : "crime"
  }
 },
 "highlight" : {
  "fields" : {
   "title" : { "type" : "plain" }
  }
 }
}'
```

Configuring HTML tags

The default behavior of highlighting mechanism may not be suited for everyone – not all of us would like to have the `<em>` and `</em>` tags to be used for highlighting. Because of that, Elasticsearch allows us to change the default behavior and change the tags that are used for that purpose. To do that, we should set the `pre_tags` and `post_tags` properties to the code snippets we want the highlighting to start from and end at; for example, by `<b>` and `</b>`. The `pre_tags` and `post_tags` properties are arrays and because of that we can provide more than a single opening and closing tag and Elasticsearch will use each of the defined tags to highlight different words. For example, if we want to use `<b>` as the opening tag and `</b>` as the closing tag, our query will look like this:

```
curl -XGET 'localhost:9200/library/book/_search?pretty' -d '{
 "query" : {
  "term" : {
   "title" : "crime"
  }
 },
 "highlight" : {
```

```
  "pre_tags" : [ "<b>" ],
  "post_tags" : [ "</b>" ],
  "fields" : {
   "title" : {}
  }
 }
}'
```

The result returned by Elasticsearch to the preceding query will be as follows:

```
{
    "took" : 3,
    "timed_out" : false,
    "_shards" : {
      "total" : 5,
      "successful" : 5,
      "failed" : 0
    },
    "hits" : {
      "total" : 1,
      "max_score" : 0.5,
      "hits" : [ {
        "_index" : "library",
        "_type" : "book",
        "_id" : "4",
        "_score" : 0.5,
        "_source" : {
          "title" : "Crime and Punishment",
          "otitle" : "Преступление и наказание",
          "author" : "Fyodor Dostoevsky",
          "year" : 1886,
          "characters" : [ "Raskolnikov", "Sofia Semyonovna
            Marmeladova" ],
          "tags" : [ ],
          "copies" : 0,
          "available" : true
        },
        "highlight" : {
          "title" : [ "<b>Crime</b> and Punishment" ]
        }
      } ]
    }
  }
}
```

As you can see, the term `Crime` in the `title` field was surrounded by the tags of our choice.

Controlling highlighted fragments

Elasticsearch allows us to control the number of highlighted fragments returned and their sizes by exposing two properties. The first one is `number_of_fragments`, which defines the number of fragments returned by Elasticsearch (defaults to 5). Setting this property to 0 causes the whole field to be returned, which can be handy for short fields but expensive for longer fields. The second property is `fragment_size` which lets us specify the maximum length of the highlighted fragments in characters and defaults to 100.

An example query using these properties will look as follows:

```
curl -XGET 'localhost:9200/library/book/_search?pretty' -d '{
 "query" : {
  "term" : {
   "title" : "crime"
  }
 },
 "highlight" : {
  "fields" : {
   "title" : { "fragment_size" : 200, "number_of_fragments" : 0 }
  }
 }
}'
```

Global and local settings

The highlighting properties we discussed previously can be set both on a global basis and per field basis. The global ones will be used for all the fields that don't overwrite them and should be placed on the same level as the `fields` section of your highlighting, for example, like this:

```
curl -XGET 'localhost:9200/library/book/_search?pretty' -d '{
 "query" : {
  "term" : {
   "title" : "crime"
  }
```

```
  },
 "highlight" : {
  "pre_tags" : [ "<b>" ],
  "post_tags" : [ "</b>" ],
  "fields" : {
   "title" : {}
  }
 }
}'
```

You can also set the properties for each field. For example, if we would like to keep the default behavior for all the fields except our `title` field, we would do the following:

```
curl -XGET 'localhost:9200/library/book/_search?pretty' -d '{
 "query" : {
  "term" : {
   "title" : "crime"
  }
 },
 "highlight" : {
  "fields" : {
   "title" : { "pre_tags" : [ "<b>" ], "post_tags" : [ "</b>" ] }
  }
 }
}'
```

As you can see, instead of placing the properties on the same level as the `fields` section, we placed it inside the empty JSON object that specifies the title `field` behavior. Of course, each field can be configured using different properties.

Require matching

Sometimes there may be a need (especially when using multiple highlighted fields) to show only the fields that matched our query. In order to have such behavior, we need to set the `require_field_match` property to `true`. Setting this property to `false` will cause all the terms to be highlighted even if a field didn't match the query.

To see how that works, let's create a new index called `users` and let's index a single document there. We will do that by sending the following command:

```
curl -XPUT 'http://localhost:9200/users/user/1' -d '{
 "name" : "Test user",
 "description" : "Test document"
}'
```

So, let's assume we want to highlight the hits in both of the preceding fields. Our command sending the query to our new index will look like this:

```
curl -XGET 'localhost:9200/users/_search?pretty' -d '{
 "query" : {
  "term" : {
   "name" : "test"
  }
 },
 "highlight" : {
  "fields" : {
   "name" : { "pre_tags" : ["<b>"], "post_tags" : ["</b>"] },
   "description" : { "pre_tags" : ["<b>"], "post_tags" : ["</b>"] }
  }
 }
}'
```

The result of the preceding query will be as follows:

```
{
   "took" : 3,
   "timed_out" : false,
   "_shards" : {
     "total" : 5,
     "successful" : 5,
     "failed" : 0
   },
   "hits" : {
     "total" : 1,
     "max_score" : 0.19178301,
     "hits" : [ {
       "_index" : "users",
       "_type" : "user",
       "_id" : "1",
```

```
      "_score" : 0.19178301,
      "_source":{
        "name" : "Test user",
        "description" : "Test document"
      },
      "highlight" : {
        "name" : [ "<b>Test</b> user" ]
      }
    } ]
  }
}
```

Note that we only got highlighting on the name field. This is because our query matched only that field. Let's see what will happen if we set the require_field_match property to false and use a command similar to the following one:

```
curl -XGET 'localhost:9200/users/_search?pretty' -d '{
 "query" : {
  "term" : {
   "name" : "test"
  }
 },
 "highlight" : {
  "require_field_match" : false,
  "fields" : {
   "name" : { "pre_tags" : ["<b>"], "post_tags" : ["</b>"] },
   "description" : { "pre_tags" : ["<b>"], "post_tags" : ["</b>"] }
  }
 }
}'
```

Now let's look at the modified query results:

```
{
    "took" : 2,
    "timed_out" : false,
    "_shards" : {
      "total" : 5,
      "successful" : 5,
      "failed" : 0
    },
    "hits" : {
```

```
        "total" : 1,
        "max_score" : 0.19178301,
        "hits" : [ {
          "_index" : "users",
          "_type" : "user",
          "_id" : "1",
          "_score" : 0.19178301,
          "_source":{
            "name" : "Test user",
            "description" : "Test document"
          },
          "highlight" : {
            "name" : [ "<b>Test</b> user" ],
            "description" : [ "<b>Test</b> document" ]
          }
        } ]
      }
    }
```

As you can see, Elasticsearch returned highlighting in both the fields now.

Custom highlighting query

There are use cases where your queries are complicated and not really suitable for highlighting, but you still want to use highlighting functionality. In such cases, Elasticsearch allows us to highlight results on the basis of a different query provided using the highlight_query property. An example of using a different highlighting query looks as follows:

```
curl -XGET 'localhost:9200/library/book/_search?pretty' -d '{
  "query" : {
    "term" : {
      "title" : "crime"
    }
  },
  "highlight" : {
    "fields" : {
      "title" : {
        "highlight_query" : {
          "term" : {
            "title" : "punishment"
          }
```

```
      }
     }
    }
   }
}'
```

The preceding query will result in highlighting the term punishment in the title field, instead of the crime one.

The Postings highlighter

It is time to talk about the third available highlighter. It was added in Elasticsearch 0.90.6 and is slightly different from the previous ones. PostingsHighlighter is automatically used when the field definition has index_options set to offsets. To illustrate how PostingsHighlighter works, we will create a simple index with proper configuration that allows that highlighter to work. We will do that by using the following commands:

```
curl -XPUT 'localhost:9200/hl_test'
curl -XPOST 'localhost:9200/hl_test/doc/_mapping' -d '{
  "doc" : {
   "properties" : {
    "contents" : {
     "type" : "string",
     "fields" : {
      "ps" : { "type" : "string", "index_options" : "offsets" }
     }
    }
   }
  }
}'
```

If everything goes well, we should have a new index and the mappings. The mappings have two fields defined: one named contents and the second one named contents.ps. In this second case, we turned on the offsets by using the index_options property. This means that Elasticsearch will use the standard highlighter for the contents field and the postings highlighter for the contents.ps field.

To see the difference, we will index a single document with a fragment from Wikipedia describing the history of Birmingham. We do that by running the following command:

```
curl -XPUT localhost:9200/hl_test/doc/1 -d '{
   "contents" : "Birmingham''s early history is that of a remote and
marginal area. The main centres of population, power and wealth in
the pre-industrial English Midlands lay in the fertile and accessible
river valleys of the Trent, the Severn and the Avon. The area of modern
Birmingham lay in between, on the upland Birmingham Plateau and within
the densely wooded and sparsely populated Forest of Arden."
}'
```

The last step is to send a query using both the highlighters. We can do it in a single request by using the following command:

```
curl 'localhost:9200/hl_test/_search?pretty' -d '{
 "query": {
  "term": {
   "contents.ps": "modern"
  }
 },
 "highlight": {
  "require_field_match" : false,
  "fields": {
   "contents": {},
   "contents.ps" : {}
  }
 }
}'
```

If everything goes well, you will find the following snippet in the response returned by Elasticsearch:

```
    "highlight" : {
     "contents" : [ " valleys of the Trent, the Severn and the Avon.
    The area of <em>modern</em> Birmingham lay in between, on the upland"
    ],
     "contents.ps" : [ "The area of <em>modern</em> Birmingham lay in
    between, on the upland Birmingham Plateau and within the densely
    wooded and sparsely populated Forest of Arden." ]
    }
```

As you see, both the highlighters found the occurrence of the desired word. The difference is that the postings highlighter returns the smarter snippet – it checks for the sentence boundaries.

Let's try one more query:

```
curl 'localhost:9200/hl_test/_search?pretty' -d '{
 "query": {
  "match_phrase": {
   "contents.ps": "centres of"
  }
 },
 "highlight": {
  "require_field_match" : false,
  "fields": {
   "contents": {},
   "contents.ps": {}
  }
 }
}'
```

We searched for the phrase centres of. As you may expect, the results for the two highlighters will differ. For the standard highlighter, run on the contents field, we will find the following phrase in the response:

> "Birminghams early history is that of a remote and marginal area. The main centres of population"

As you can clearly see, the standard highlighter divided the given phrase and highlighted individual terms. Also, not all occurrences of the terms centres and of were highlighted, but only the ones that formed the phrase.

On the other hand, the PostingsHighlighter returned the following highlighted fragment:

> "Birminghams early history is that of a remote and marginal area.", "The main centres of population, power and wealth in the pre-industrial English Midlands lay in the fertile and accessible river valleys of the Trent, the Severn and the Avon.", "The area of modern Birmingham lay in between, on the upland Birmingham Plateau and within the densely wooded and sparsely populated Forest of Arden."

This is the significant difference. The PostingsHighlighter highlighted all the terms matching the query and not only those that formed the phrase, and returned whole sentences. This is a very nice feature, especially when you want to display the highlighting results for the user in the UI of your application.

Validating your queries

There are times when you are not in total control of the queries that you send to Elasticsearch. The queries can be generated from multiple criteria making them a monster or even worse. They can be generated by some kind of a wizard which makes it hard to troubleshoot and find the part that is faulty and making the query fail. Because of such use cases, Elasticsearch exposes the Validate API, which helps us validate our queries and diagnose potential problems.

Using the Validate API

The usage of the Validate API is very simple. Instead of sending the query to the _search REST endpoint, we send it to the _validate/query one. And that's it. Let's look at the following command:

```
curl -XGET 'localhost:9200/library/_validate/query?pretty' --data-binary
'{
 "query" : {
  "bool" : {
    "must" : {
      "term" : {
        "title" : "crime"
      }
    },
    "should" : {
      "range : {
        "year" : {
          "from" : 1900,
          "to" : 2000
        }
      }
    },
    "must_not" : {
      "term" : {
        "otitle" : "nothing"
      }
    }
  }
 }
}'
```

A similar query was already used in this book in *Chapter 3, Searching Your Data*. The preceding command will tell Elasticsearch to validate it and return the information about its validity. The response of Elasticsearch to the preceding command will be similar to the following one:

```
{
   "valid" : false,
   "_shards" : {
      "total" : 1,
      "successful" : 1,
      "failed" : 0
   }
}
```

Look at the valid attribute. It is set to false. Something went wrong. Let's execute the query validation once again with the explain parameter added in the query:

```
curl -XGET 'localhost:9200/library/_validate/query?pretty&explain'
--data-binary '{
 "query" : {
  "bool" : {
    "must" : {
      "term" : {
        "title" : "crime"
      }
    },
    "should" : {
      "range : {
        "year" : {
          "from" : 1900,
          "to" : 2000
        }
      }
    },
    "must_not" : {
      "term" : {
        "otitle" : "nothing"
      }
    }
   }
  }
}'
```

Now the result returned from Elasticsearch is more verbose:

```
{
  "valid" : false,
  "_shards" : {
    "total" : 1,
    "successful" : 1,
    "failed" : 0
  },
  "explanations" : [ {
    "index" : "library",
    "valid" : false,
    "error" : "[library] QueryParsingException[Failed to parse];
nested: JsonParseException[Illegal unquoted character ((CTRL-CHAR,
code 10)): has to be escaped using backslash to be included in
name\n at [Source:
org.elasticsearch.transport.netty.ChannelBufferStreamInput@1110d090;
line: 10, column: 18]];;
com.fasterxml.jackson.core.JsonParseException: Illegal unquoted
character ((CTRL-CHAR, code 10)): has to be escaped using
backslash to be included in name\n at [Source:
org.elasticsearch.transport.netty.ChannelBufferStreamInput@1110d090;
line: 10, column: 18]"
  } ]
}
```

Now everything is clear. In our example, we have improperly quoted the range attribute.

You may wonder why in our curl query we used the --data-binary parameter. This parameter properly preserves the new line character when sending a query to Elasticsearch. This means that the line and the column number remain intact and it's easier to find errors. In the other cases, the –d parameter is more convenient because it's shorter.

The Validate API can also detect other errors, for example, incorrect format of a number or other mapping-related issues. Unfortunately, for our application, it is not easy to detect what the problem is because of a lack of structure in the error messages.

The Validate API supports most of the parameters that are supported by standard Elasticsearch queries, which include: `explain`, `ignore_unavailable`, `allow_no_indices`, `expand_wildcards`, `operation_threading`, `analyzer`, `analyze_wildcard`, `default_operator`, `df`, `lenient`, `lowercase_expanded_terms`, and `rewrite`.

Sorting data

So far we've run our queries and got the results in the order determined by the score of each document. However, it is not enough for all the use cases. It is really handy to be able to sort our results on the basis of the field values. For example, when you are searching logs or time-based data in general, you probably want to have the most recent data first. In addition to that, Elasticsearch allows us to control how the document such be sorted not only using field values, but also using more sophisticated sorting like ones that use scripts or sorting on fields that have multiple values. We will cover all that in this section.

Default sorting

Let's look at the following query that returns all the books with at least one of the specified words:

```
curl -XGET 'localhost:9200/library/book/_search?pretty' -d '{
  "query" : {
    "terms" : {
      "title" : [ "crime", "front", "punishment" ]
    }
  }
}'
```

Under the hood, we can imagine that Elasticsearch sees the preceding query as follows:

```
curl -XGET 'localhost:9200/library/book/_search?pretty' -d '{
  "query" : {
   "terms" : {
     "title" : [ "crime", "front", "punishment" ]
   }
  },
  "sort" : { "_score" : "desc" }
}'
```

Look at the highlighted section in the preceding query. This is the default sorting used by Elasticsearch. For better visibility, we can change the formatting slightly and show the highlighted fragment as follows:

```
"sort" : [
  { "_score" : "desc" }
]
```

The preceding section defines how the documents should be sorted in the results list. In this case, Elasticsearch will show the documents with the highest score on top of the results list. The simplest modification is to reverse the ordering by changing the sort section to the following one:

```
"sort" : [
  { "_score" : "asc" }
]
```

Selecting fields used for sorting

Default sorting is boring, isn't it? So, let's change it to sort on the basis of the values of the fields present in the documents. Let's choose the title field, which means that the sort section of our query will look as follows:

```
"sort" : [
  { "title" : "asc" }
]
```

Unfortunately, this doesn't work as expected. Although Elasticsearch sorted the documents, the ordering is somewhat strange. Look closely at the response. With every document, Elasticsearch returns information about the sorting; for example, for the Crime and Punishment book, the returned document looks like the following code:

```
{
  "_index" : "library",
  "_type" : "book",
  "_id" : "4",
  "_score" : null,
  "_source" : {
    "title" : "Crime and Punishment",
    "otitle" : "Преступле́ние и наказа́ние",
    "author" : "Fyodor Dostoevsky",
    "year" : 1886,
    "characters" : [ "Raskolnikov", "Sofia Semyonovna
      Marmeladova" ],
    "tags" : [ ],
```

```
        "copies" : 0,
        "available" : true
    },
    "sort" : [ "punishment" ]
}
```

If you compare the `title` field and the returned sorting information, everything should be clear. Elasticsearch, during the analysis process, splits the field into several tokens. Since sorting is done using a single token, Elasticsearch chooses one of the produced tokens. It does the best that it can by sorting these tokens alphabetically and choosing the first one. This is the reason why, in the sorting value, we find only a single word instead of the whole content of the `title` field. If you would like to see how Elasticsearch behaves when using different fields for sorting, you can try fields such as `copies`:

```
curl -XGET 'localhost:9200/library/book/_search?pretty' -d '{
 "query" : {
  "terms" : {
   "title" : [ "crime", "front", "punishment" ]
  }
 },
 "sort" : [
  { "copies" : "asc" }
 ]
}'
```

In general, it is a good idea to have a not analyzed field for sorting. We can use fields with multiple values for sorting, but, in most cases, it doesn't make much sense and has limited usage.

As an example of using two different fields, one for sorting and another for searching, let's change our `title` field. The changed `title` field definition will look as follows:

```
    "title" : {
      "type": "string",
      "fields": {
        "sort": { "type" : "string", "index": "not_analyzed" }
      }
    }
```

After changing the `title` field in the mappings (we've used the same mappings as in *Chapter 3, Searching Your Data*) and re-indexing the data, we can try sorting the `title.sort` field and see whether it works. To do this, we will need to send the following query:

```
{
  "query" : {
    "match_all" : { }
  },
  "sort" : [
    {"title.sort" : "asc" }
  ]
}
```

Now, it works properly. As you can see, we used the new field, the `title.sort` one. We set it as not to be analyzed, so there is a single token for that field in the index of Elasticsearch.

Sorting mode

In the response from Elasticsearch, every document contains information about the value used for sorting. For example, let's look at one of the documents returned by the query in which we used the `title` field for sorting:

```
{
  "_index" : "library",
  "_type" : "book",
  "_id" : "1",
  "_score" : null,
  "_source" : {
    "title" : "All Quiet on the Western Front",
    "otitle" : "Im Westen nichts Neues",
    "author" : "Erich Maria Remarque",
    "year" : 1929,
    "characters" : [ "Paul Bäumer", "Albert Kropp", "Haie
      Westhus", "Fredrich Müller", "Stanislaus Katczinsky",
        "Tjaden" ],
    "tags" : [ "novel" ],
    "copies" : 1,
    "available" : true,
    "section" : 3
  },
  "sort" : [ "all" ]
}
```

The sorting used in the query to get the preceding document, was as follows:

```
"sort" : [
  { "title" : "asc" }
]
```

However, because we are sorting on an analyzed field, which contains more than a single value, the sorting definition is in fact equivalent to the longer form, which looks as follows:

```
"sort" : [
  { "title" : { "order" : "asc", "mode" : "min" }
]
```

mode defines which token should be used for comparison when sorting on a field which has more than one value. The available values we can choose from are:

- min: Sorting will use the lowest value (or the first alphabetical value on the text based fields)

- max: Sorting will use the highest value (or the last alphabetical value on the text based fields)

- avg: Sorting will use the average value

- median: Sorting will use the median value

- sum: Sorting will use the sum of all the values in the field

 The modes such as median, avg, and sum are useful for numerical multivalued fields, but don't make much sense when it comes to text based fields.

Note that sort, in request and response, is given as an array. This suggests that we can use several different orderings. Elasticsearch will use the next element in the sorting definition list to determine ordering between the documents that have the same value of the previous sorting clause. So, if we have the same value in the title field, the documents will be sorted by the next field that we specify. For example, if we would like to get the documents that have the most copies and then sort by the title, we will run the following query:

```
curl -XGET 'localhost:9200/library/book/_search?pretty' -d '{
  "query" : {
    "terms" : {
      "title" : [ "crime", "front", "punishment" ]
    }
  },
  "sort" : [
    { "copies" : "desc" }, { "title" : "asc" }
  ]
}'
```

Specifying behavior for missing fields

What about when some of the documents that match the query don't have the field we want to sort on? By default, documents without the given field are returned first in the case of ascending order and last in the case of descending order. However, sometimes this is not exactly what we want to achieve.

When we use sorting on numeric fields, we can change the default Elasticsearch behavior for documents with missing fields. For example, let's take a look at the following query:

```
curl -XGET 'localhost:9200/library/book/_search?pretty' -d '{
    "query" : {
    "match_all" : { }
  },
  "sort" : [
    {
      "section" : {
        "order" : "asc",
        "missing" : "_last"
      }
    }
  ]
}'
```

Note the extended form of the `sort` section of our query. We've added the `missing` parameter to it. By setting the `missing` parameter to `_last`, Elasticsearch will place the documents without the given field at the bottom of the results list. Setting the `missing` parameter to `_first` will result in Elasticsearch placing documents without the given field at the top of the results list. It is worth mentioning that besides the `_last` and `_first` values, Elasticsearch also allows us to use any number. In such a case, a document without a defined field will be treated as the document with this given value.

Dynamic criteria

As we mentioned in the previous section, Elasticsearch allows us to sort using fields that have multiple values. We can control how the comparison is made using scripts. We do that by showing Elasticsearch how to calculate the value that should be used for sorting. Let's assume that we want to sort by the first value indexed in the `tags` field. Let's take a look at the following example query (note that running the following query requires the `script.inline` property set to `on` in the `elasticsearch.yml` file):

```
curl -XGET 'localhost:9200/library/book/_search?pretty' -d '{
   "query" : {
    "match_all" : { }
   },
   "sort" : {
     "_script" : {
        "script" : "doc[\"tags\"].values.size() > 0 ? doc[\"tags\"].
values[0] : \"\u19999\"",
        "type" : "string",
        "order" : "asc"
     }
   }
}'
```

In the preceding example, we replaced every nonexistent value with the Unicode code of a character that should be low enough in the list. The main idea of this code is to check if our array contains at least a single element. If it does, then the first value from the array is returned. If the array is empty, we return the Unicode character that should be placed at the bottom of the results list. Besides the `script` parameter, this option of sorting requires us to specify the `order` (ascending, in our case) and `type` parameters that will be used for the comparison (we return `string` from our script).

Calculate scoring when sorting

By default, Elasticsearch assumes that when you use sorting, the score is completely unimportant. Usually it is a good assumption; why do additional computations when the importance of the documents is given by the sorting formula. Sometimes, however, you want to know how good the document is in relation to the current query, even if the documents are presented in a different order. This is when the `track_scores` parameter should be used and set to `true`. An example query using it looks as follows:

```
curl -XGET 'localhost:9200/library/book/_search?pretty' -d '{
   "query" : {
    "match_all" : { }
   },
   "track_scores" : true,
   "sort" : [
     { "title" : { "order" : "asc" }}
   ]
}'
```

The preceding query calculates the score for every document. In fact, in our example, the score is boring and is always equal to 1.0 because of the match_all query which treats all the documents as equal.

Query rewrite

When debugging your queries, it is very valuable to know how all the queries are executed. Because of that, we decided to include the section on how query rewrite works in Elasticsearch, why it is used, and how to control it. If you have ever used queries, such as the prefix query and the wildcard query, basically any query that is said to be **multiterm** (a query that is built of multiple terms), you've used query rewriting even though you may not have known about it. Elasticsearch does rewrite for performance reasons. The rewrite process is about changing the original, expensive query into a set of queries that are far less expensive from an Apache Lucene point of view, thus speeding up the query execution.

Prefix query as an example

The best way to illustrate how the rewrite process is done internally is to look at an example and see which terms are used instead of the original query term. We will index three documents to our library_it index by using the following commands:

```
curl -XPOST 'localhost:9200/library_it/book/1' -d '{"title": "Solr 4
Cookbook"}'
curl -XPOST 'localhost:9200/library_it/book/2' -d '{"title": "Solr 3.1
Cookbook"}'
curl -XPOST 'localhost:9200/library_it/book/3' -d '{"title": "Mastering
Elasticsearch"}'
```

What we would like is to find all the documents that start with the letter s. Simple as that, we run the following query against our library_it index:

```
curl -XGET 'localhost:9200/library_it/_search?pretty' -d '{
  "query" : {
    "prefix" : {
      "title" : {
        "prefix" : "s",
        "rewrite" : "constant_score_boolean"
      }
    }
  }
}'
```

We've used a simple `prefix` query; we've said that we would like to find all the documents with the letter `s` in the `title` field. We've also used the `rewrite` property to specify the query `rewrite` method, but let's skip it for now as we will discuss the possible values of this parameter in the later part of this section.

As the response to the previous query, we get the following:

```
{
  "took" : 13,
  "timed_out" : false,
  "_shards" : {
    "total" : 5,
    "successful" : 5,
    "failed" : 0
  },
  "hits" : {
    "total" : 2,
    "max_score" : 1.0,
    "hits" : [ {
      "_index" : "library_it",
      "_type" : "book",
      "_id" : "2",
      "_score" : 1.0,
      "_source" : {
        "title" : "Solr 3.1 Cookbook"
      }
    }, {
      "_index" : "library_it",
      "_type" : "book",
      "_id" : "1",
      "_score" : 1.0,
      "_source" : {
        "title" : "Solr 4 Cookbook"
      }
    } ]
  }
}
```

As you can see, in response we got the two documents that had the contents of the `title` field starting with the desired character. We didn't specify the mappings explicitly, so we relied on Elasticsearch's ability to choose the mapping type for us. As we already know, for the text field, Elasticsearch uses the default analyzer. This means that the terms in our documents will be lowercased and, because of that, we used the lowercased letter in our `prefix` query (remember that the `prefix` query is not analyzed).

Getting back to Apache Lucene

Now let's take a step back and look at Apache Lucene again. If you recall what Lucene inverted index is built from, you can tell that it contains a term, count, and document pointer (if you don't recall, refer to the *Full text searching* section in *Chapter 1, Getting Started with Elasticsearch Cluster*). So, let's see how the simplified view of the index may look for the preceding data we've put to the `library_it` index:

Term	Count	Documents
1	1	<2>
3	1	<2>
4	1	<1>
cookbook	2	<1> <2>
elasticsearch	1	<3>
mastering	1	<3>
solr	2	<1> <2>

What you see in the column with the **Term** text is quite important. If you look at Elasticsearch and Apache Lucene internals, you can see that our `prefix` query was rewritten to the following Lucene query:

```
ConstantScore(title:solr)
```

We can check the portions of the rewrite using the Elasticsearch API. First of all, we can use the Explain API by running the following command:

```
curl -XGET 'localhost:9200/library_it/book/1/_explain?pretty' -d '{
  "query" : {
   "prefix" : {
    "title" : {
     "prefix" : "s",
     "rewrite" : "constant_score_boolean"
    }
   }
  }
}'
```

The result will be as follows:

```
{
  "_index" : "library_it",
  "_type" : "book",
  "_id" : "1",
  "matched" : true,
  "explanation" : {
    "value" : 1.0,
    "description" : "sum of:",
    "details" : [ {
      "value" : 1.0,
      "description" : "ConstantScore(title:solr), product of:",
      "details" : [ {
        "value" : 1.0,
        "description" : "boost",
        "details" : [ ]
      }, {
        "value" : 1.0,
        "description" : "queryNorm",
        "details" : [ ]
      } ]
    }, {
      "value" : 0.0,
      "description" : "match on required clause, product of:",
      "details" : [ {
        "value" : 0.0,
        "description" : "# clause",
        "details" : [ ]
      }, {
        "value" : 1.0,
        "description" : "_type:book, product of:",
        "details" : [ {
          "value" : 1.0,
          "description" : "boost",
          "details" : [ ]
        }, {
          "value" : 1.0,
          "description" : "queryNorm",
          "details" : [ ]
        } ]
      } ]
    } ]
  }
}
```

We can see that Elasticsearch used a constant score query with the term `solr` against the `title` field.

Query rewrite properties

We can control how the queries are rewritten internally. To do that, we place the `rewrite` parameter inside the JSON object responsible for the actual query. For example:

```
curl -XGET 'localhost:9200/library/book/_search?pretty' -d '{
   "query" : {
    "prefix" : {
      "title" : "s",
      "rewrite" : "constant_score_boolean"
    }
  }
}'
```

The `rewrite` property can take the following values:

- `scoring_boolean`: This rewrite method translates each generated term into a Boolean `should` clause in the Boolean query. This rewrite method causes the score to be calculated for each document. Because of that, this method may be CPU demanding. Please also note that, for queries that have many terms, it may exceed the Boolean query limit, which is set to `1024`. The default Boolean query limit can be changed by setting the `index.query.bool.max_clause_count` property in the `elasticsearch.yml` file. However, remember that the more Boolean queries produced, the lower the query performance may be.

- `constant_score`: This rewrite method chooses `constant_score_boolean` or `constant_score_filter` depending on the query and taking performance into consideration. This is also the default behavior when the rewrite property is not set at all.

- `constant_score_boolean`: This rewrite method is similar to the `scoring_boolean` rewrite method described previously, but less CPU demanding because the scoring is not computed and, instead of that, each term receives a score equal to the query boost (`one` by default, and which can be set using the `boost` property). Because this rewrite method also results in Boolean `should` clauses being created, similar to the `scoring_boolean` rewrite method, this method can also hit the maximum Boolean clauses limit.

- `top_terms_N`: A rewrite method that translates each generated term into a Boolean `should` clause in a Boolean query and keeps the scores as computed by the query. However, unlike the `scoring_boolean` rewrite method, it only keeps an N number of top scoring terms to avoid hitting the maximum Boolean clauses limit and increase the final query performance.

- `top_terms_blended_freqs_N`: A rewrite method that translates each term into a Boolean query and treat the terms as if they had the same term frequency.

- `top_terms_boost_N`: A rewrite method similar to the `top_terms_N` one, but the scores are not computed. Instead, the documents are given a score equal to the value of the `boost` property (one by default).

For example, if we would like our example query to use `top_terms_N` with N equal to 2, our query would look like this:

```
curl -XGET 'localhost:9200/library/book/_search?pretty' -d '{
  "query" : {
    "prefix" : {
     "title" : {
      "prefix" :"s",
      "rewrite" : "top_terms_2"
     }
    }
  }
}'
```

If you look at the results returned by Elasticsearch, you'll notice that, unlike our initial query, the documents were given a score different than the default 1.0:

```
{
   "took" : 4,
   "timed_out" : false,
   "_shards" : {
     "total" : 5,
     "successful" : 5,
     "failed" : 0
   },
   "hits" : {
     "total" : 1,
     "max_score" : 0.15342641,
     "hits" : [ {
       "_index" : "library",
```

```
            "_type" : "book",
            "_id" : "3",
            "_score" : 0.15342641,
            "_source" : {
                "title" : "The Complete Sherlock Holmes",
                "author" : "Arthur Conan Doyle",
                "year" : 1936,
                "characters" : [ "Sherlock Holmes", "Dr. Watson", "G.
                    Lestrade" ],
                "tags" : [ ],
                "copies" : 0,
                "available" : false,
                "section" : 12
            }
        } ]
    }
}
```

The score is different than the default `1.0` because we've used the `top_terms_N` rewrite type and this type of query rewrite keeps the score for *N* top scoring terms.

Before we finish the *Query rewrite* section of this chapter, we should ask ourselves one last question: when to use which rewrite type? The answer to this question greatly depends on your use case, but, to summarize, if you can live with lower precision and relevancy (but higher performance), you can go for the top *N* rewrite method. If you need high precision and thus more relevant queries (but lower performance), choose the Boolean approach.

Summary

The chapter you just finished was again focused on querying. We used filters and saw what highlighting is and how to use it. We learned what are the highlighter types and how they can help us. We validated our queries and we learned how Elasticsearch can help us when it comes to sorting our results. Finally, we discussed query rewriting, what that brings us, and how we can control it.

In the next chapter, we will get back to indexation topic. We will discuss indexing complex JSON objects such as tree-like structures and indexing data that is not flat. We will prepare Elasticsearch to handle relationships between documents and we will use the Elasticsearch API to update the structure of our indices.

5
Extending Your Index Structure

We started the previous chapter by learning how to deal with revised filtering in Elasticsearch 2.x and what to expect from it now. We also explored highlighting and how it can help us in improving the users' search experience. We discovered query validation in Elasticsearch and learned the ways of data sorting in Elasticsearch. Finally, we discussed query rewriting and how that affects our queries. By the end of this chapter, you will have learned the following topics:

- Indexing tree-like structures
- Indexing data that is not flat
- Handling document relationships by using nested object and parent–child features
- Modifying index structure by using Elasticsearch API

Indexing tree-like structures

Trees are everywhere. If you develop an e-commerce shop application, your products will probably be described with the use of categories. The thing about categories is that in most cases they are hierarchical. There are top categories, such as electronics, music, books, and so on. Each of the top level categories can have numerous children categories, such as fiction and science, and those can get even deeper into science fiction, romance, and so on. If you look at the file system, the files and directories are arranged in tree-like structures as well. This book can also be represented as a tree: chapters contain topics and topics are divided into subtopics. So the data around us is arranged into tree-like structures and as you can imagine, Elasticsearch is capable of indexing tree-like structures so that we can represent the data in an easier manner. Let's check how we can navigate through this type of data using `path_analyzer`.

Data structure

To begin with, let's create a simple index structure by using the following command:

```
curl -XPUT 'localhost:9200/path?pretty' -d '{
  "settings" : {
    "index" : {
      "analysis" : {
        "analyzer" : {
          "path_analyzer" : { "tokenizer" : "path_hierarchy" }
        }
      }
    }
  },
  "mappings" : {
    "category" : {
      "properties" : {
        "category" : {
          "type" : "string",
          "fields" : {
            "name" : { "type" : "string", "index" : "not_analyzed" },
            "path" : { "type" : "string", "analyzer" :
              "path_analyzer", "store" : true }
          }
        }
      }
    }
  }
}'
```

As you can see, we have a single type created – the category type. We will use it to store and index the information about the location of our document in the tree structure. The idea is simple – we can show the location of the document as a path, in the exact same manner as the files and directories are presented on your hard disk drive. For example, in an automotive shop, we can have /cars/passenger/sport, /cars/passenger/camper, or /cars/delivery_truck/. However, to achieve that, we need to index this path in two different ways. First of all, we will use an not analyzed field called name, to store and index paths name in its original form. We will also use a field called path, which will use the path_analyzer analyzer which we've defined to process the path so it is easier to search.

Analysis

Now, let's see what Elasticsearch will do with the category path during the analysis process. To see this, we will use the following command line, which uses the analysis API discussed in the *Understanding the explain information* section of *Chapter 6, Make Your Search Better*:

```
curl -XGET 'localhost:9200/path/_analyze?field=category.path&pretty' -d
'/cars/passenger/sport'
```

The following results will be returned by Elasticsearch:

```
{
  "tokens" : [ {
    "token" : "/cars",
    "start_offset" : 0,
    "end_offset" : 5,
    "type" : "word",
    "position" : 0
  }, {
    "token" : "/cars/passenger",
    "start_offset" : 0,
    "end_offset" : 15,
    "type" : "word",
    "position" : 0
  }, {
    "token" : "/cars/passenger/sport",
    "start_offset" : 0,
    "end_offset" : 21,
    "type" : "word",
    "position" : 0
  } ]
}
```

As we can see, our category path /cars/passenger/sport was processed by Elasticsearch and divided into three tokens. Thanks to this, we can simply find every document that belongs to a given category or its subcategories using the term filter. For the example to be complete, let's index a simple document by using the following command:

```
curl -XPUT 'localhost:9200/path/category/1' -d '{ "category" : "/cars/
passenger/sport" }'
```

An example of using filters is as follows:

```
curl -XGET 'localhost:9200/path/_search?pretty' -d '{
  "query" : {
    "bool" : {
      "filter" : {
        "term" : {
          "category.path" : "/cars"
        }
      }
    }
  }
}'
```

Note that we also have the original value indexed in the `category.name` field. This is handy when we want to find documents from a particular path, ignoring the documents that are deeper in the hierarchy.

Indexing data that is not flat

Not all data is flat like the examples we have used in the book until now. Most of the data you will encounter will have some structure and nested objects inside the root JSON object. Of course, if we are building our system that Elasticsearch will be a part of and we are in control of all the pieces of it, we can create a structure that is convenient for Elasticsearch. But even in such cases, flat data is not always an option. Thankfully, Elasticsearch allows us to index data that is not flat and this section will show us how to do that.

Data

Let's assume that we have the following data (we store it in the file called `structured_data.json`):

```
{
  "author" : {
    "name" : {
      "firstName" : "Fyodor",
      "lastName" : "Dostoevsky"
    }
  },
  "isbn" : "123456789",
  "englishTitle" : "Crime and Punishment",
  "year" : 1886,
```

```
    "characters" : [
      {
        "name" : "Raskolnikov"
      },
      {
        "name" : "Sofia"
      }
    ],
    "copies" : 0
  }
```

As you can see the data is not flat – it contains arrays and nested objects. If we want to create mappings and use the knowledge that we've got so far, we will have to flatten the data. However, as we already said, Elasticsearch allows some degree of structure and we should be able to create mappings that will work for the preceding example.

Objects

The preceding example data shows the structured JSON file. As you can see in the example, our root object has some additional, simple properties, such as englishTitle, isbn, year, and copies. These will be indexed as normal fields in the index and we already know how to deal with them (we discussed that in the *Mappings configuration* section of *Chapter 2, Indexing Your Data*). In addition to that, it has the characters array type and the author object. The author object has another object nested within it – the name object, which has two properties: firstName and lastName. So as you can see, we can have multiple nested objects inside each other.

Arrays

We have already used array type data, but we didn't talk about it. By default, all the fields in Lucene and thus in Elasticsearch are multivalued, which means that they can store multiple values. In order to send such fields to indexing to Elasticsearch, we use the JSON array type, which is nested within the opening and closing square brackets []. As you can see in the preceding example, we used the array type for the characters of our book.

Mappings

Let's now look at how our mappings would look like for the book object we showed earlier. We already said that to index arrays we don't need anything special. So, in our case, to index the characters data we will need to add fields definition similar to the following one:

```
"characters" : {
 "properties" : {
  "name" : {"type" : "string"}
 }
}
```

Nothing strange! We just nest the properties section inside the arrays name (which is characters in our case) and we define the fields there. As the result of the preceding mappings, we will get the characters.name multivalued field in the index.

We do similar thing for our author object. We call the section with the same name as it is present in the data. We have the author object, but it also has the name object nested in it, so we do the same – we just nest another object inside it. So, our mappings for the author field would look as follows:

```
"author" : {
 "properties" : {
  "name" : {
   "properties" : {
    "firstName" : {"type" : "string"},
    "lastName" : {"type" : "string"}
   }
  }
 }
}
```

The firstName and lastName fields appear in the index as author.name.firstName and author.name.lastName.

The rest of the fields are simple core types, so I'll skip discussing them as they were already discussed in the *Mappings configuration* section of *Chapter 2, Indexing Your Data*.

Final mappings

So our final mappings file, that we've called `structured_mapping.json`, looks like the following:

```
{
 "book" : {
  "properties" : {
   "author" : {
    "type" : "object",
    "properties" : {
     "name" : {
      "type" : "object",
      "properties" : {
       "firstName" : {"type" : "string"},
       "lastName" : {"type" : "string"}
      }
     }
    }
   },
   "isbn" : {"type" : "string"},
   "englishTitle" : {"type" : "string"},
   "year" : {"type" : "integer"},
   "characters" : {
    "properties" : {
     "name" : {"type" : "string"}
    }
   },
   "copies" : {"type" : "integer"}
  }
 }
}
```

Sending the mappings to Elasticsearch

Now that we have our mappings done, we would like to test if all the work we did actually works. This time we will use a slightly different technique of creating an index and putting the mappings. First, let's create the library index with the following command (you need to delete the library index if you already have it):

```
curl -XPUT 'localhost:9200/library'
```

Now, let's send our mappings for the book type:

```
curl -XPUT 'localhost:9200/library/book/_mapping' -d @structured_mapping.
json
```

Now we can index our example data:

```
curl -XPOST 'localhost:9200/library/book/1' -d @structured_data.json
```

To be or not to be dynamic

As we already know, Elasticsearch is schema-less, which means that it can index data without the need of creating the mappings upfront. What Elasticsearch will do in the background when a new field is encountered in the data is a mapping update – it will try to guess the field type and add it to the mappings. The dynamic behavior of Elasticsearch is turned on by default, but there may be situations where you may want to turn it off for some parts of your index. In order to do that, one should add the dynamic property to the given field and set it to false. This should be done on the same level of nesting as the type property for the object, which shouldn't be dynamic. For example, if we want our author and name objects to not be dynamic, we should modify the relevant part of the mappings file so that it looks as follows:

```
"author" : {
 "type" : "object",
 "dynamic" : false,
 "properties" : {
  "name" : {
   "type" : "object",
   "dynamic" : false,
   "properties" : {
    "firstName" : {"type" : "string", "index" : "analyzed"},
    "lastName" : {"type" : "string", "index" : "analyzed"}
   }
  }
 }
}
```

However, remember that in order to add new fields for such objects, we would have to update the mappings.

 You can also turn off the dynamic mappings functionality by adding the index.mapper.dynamic property to your elasticsearch.yml configuration file and setting it to false.

Disabling object indexing

There is one additional thing that we would like to mention when it comes to objects handling – we can disable indexing a particular object by using the `enabled` property and setting it to `false`. There may be various reasons for that, such as not wanting a field to be indexed or not wanting a whole JSON object to be indexed. For example, if we want to omit an object called information from our author object, we will have the author object definition look as follows:

```
"author" : {
 "type" : "object",
  "properties" : {
  "name" : {
   "type" : "object",
   "dynamic" : false,
   "properties" : {
    "firstName" : {"type" : "string", "index" : "analyzed"},
    "lastName" : {"type" : "string", "index" : "analyzed"},
    "information" : {"type" : "object", "enabled" : false}
   }
  }
 }
}
```

The `dynamic` parameter can also be set to `strict`. This means that new fields won't be added into the document when they appear and the indexing of such document will fail.

Using nested objects

Nested objects can come in handy in certain situations. Basically, with nested objects Elasticsearch allows us to connect multiple documents together – one main document and multiple dependent ones. The main document and the nested ones are indexed together and they are placed in the same segment of the index (actually, in the same block inside the segment, near each other), which guarantees the best performance we can get for such a data structure. The same goes for changing the document; unless you are using the update API, you need to index the parent document and all the other nested ones at the same time.

> If you would like to read more about how nested objects work on the Apache Lucene level, there is a very good blog post written by Mike McCandless at `http://blog.mikemccandless.com/2012/01/searching-relational-content-with.html`.

Now let's get on with our example use case. Imagine that we have a shop with clothes and we store the size and color of each t-shirt. Our standard, non-nested mappings will look like this (stored in `cloth.json`):

```
{
  "cloth" : {
   "properties" : {
    "name" : {"type" : "string"},
    "size" : {"type" : "string", "index" : "not_analyzed"},
    "color" : {"type" : "string", "index" : "not_analyzed"}
    }
   }
}
```

To create the shop index without cloth mapping, we run the following commands:

```
curl -XPOST 'localhost:9200/shop'
```

```
curl -XPUT 'localhost:9200/shop/cloth/_mapping' -d @cloth.json
```

Now imagine that we have a t-shirt in our shop that we only have in XXL size in red and in XL size in black. So our example document indexation command will look as follows:

```
curl -XPOST 'localhost:9200/shop/cloth/1' -d '{
 "name" : "Test shirt",
 "size" : [ "XXL", "XL" ],
 "color" : [ "red", "black" ]
}'
```

However, there is a problem with such a data structure. What if one of our clients searches our shop in order to find the XXL t-shirt in black? Let's check that by running the following query (we assume that we've used our mappings to create the index and we've indexed our example document):

```
curl -XGET 'localhost:9200/shop/cloth/_search?pretty=true' -d '{
  "query" : {
  "bool" : {
  "must" : [
    {
     "term" : { "size" : "XXL" }
    },
    {
     "term" : { "color" : "black" }
    }
    ]
  }
  }
 }'
```

We should get no results, right? But in fact Elasticsearch returned the following document:

```
{
   (...)
   "hits" : {
     "total" : 1,
     "max_score" : 0.4339554,
     "hits" : [ {
       "_index" : "shop",
       "_type" : "cloth",
       "_id" : "1",
       "_score" : 0.4339554,
       "_source" : {
         "name" : "Test shirt",
         "size" : [ "XXL", "XL" ],
         "color" : [ "red", "black" ]
       }
     } ]
   }
}
```

This is because the document was matched – we have the values we are searching for in the size field and in the color field. Of course, this is not what we would like to get.

So, let's modify our mappings to use the nested objects to separate color and size to different nested documents. The final mapping looks as follows (we store these mappings in the cloth_nested.json file):

```
{
  "cloth" : {
   "properties" : {
    "name" : {"type" : "string", "index" : "analyzed"},
    "variation" : {
     "type" : "nested",
     "properties" : {
      "size" : {"type" : "string", "index" : "not_analyzed"},
      "color" : {"type" : "string", "index" : "not_analyzed"}
     }
    }
   }
  }
}
```

Now, we will create a second index called `shop_nested` using our modified mappings by running the following commands:

```
curl -XPOST 'localhost:9200/shop_nested'
```

```
curl -XPUT 'localhost:9200/shop_nested/cloth/_mapping' -d @cloth_nested.json
```

As you can see, we've introduced a new object inside our cloth type – variation one, which is a nested one (the `type` property set to `nested`). It basically says that we will want to index the nested documents. Now, let's modify our document. We will add the variation object to it and that object will store the objects with two properties – size and color. So the `index` command for our modified example product will look like the following:

```
curl -XPOST 'localhost:9200/shop_nested/cloth/1' -d '{
  "name" : "Test shirt",
  "variation" : [
  { "size" : "XXL", "color" : "red" },
  { "size" : "XL", "color" : "black" }
  ]
}'
```

We've structured the document so that each size and its matching color is a separate document. However, if you run our previous query, it won't return any documents. This is because in order to query for nested documents, we need to use a specialized query. So now our query looks as follows:

```
curl -XGET 'localhost:9200/shop_nested/cloth/_search?pretty=true' -d '{
  "query" : {
  "nested" : {
   "path" : "variation",
   "query" : {
    "bool" : {
     "must" : [
      { "term" : { "variation.size" : "XXL" } },
      { "term" : { "variation.color" : "black" } }
     ]
    }
   }
  }
 }
}'
```

And now, the preceding query will not return the indexed document, because we don't have a nested document that has the size equal to XXL and color black.

Let's get back to the query for a second to discuss it briefly. As you can see, we used the nested query in order to search in the nested documents. The `path` property specifies the name of the nested object (yes, we can have multiple of them). We just included a standard query section under the nested type. Also note that we specified the full path for the field names in the nested objects, which is handy when you have multilevel nesting, which is also possible.

Scoring and nested queries

There is one additional property when it comes to handling nested documents during query. In addition to the `path` property, there is the `score_mode` property, which allows us to define how the scoring is calculated from the nested queries. Elasticsearch allows us to set the `score_mode` property to one of the following values:

- `avg`: This is the default value. Using it for the `score_mode` property will result in Elasticsearch taking the average value calculated from the scores of the defined nested queries. Calculated average will be included in the score of the main query.

- `sum`: Using this value for the `score_mode` property will result in Elasticsearch taking a sum of the scores for each nested query and including it in the score of the main query.

- `min`: Using this value for the `score_mode` property will result in Elasticsearch taking the score of the minimum scoring nested query and including it in the score of the main query.

- `max`: Using this value for the `score_mode` property will result in Elasticsearch taking the score of the maximum scoring nested query and including it in the score of the main query.

- `none`: Using this value for the `score_mode` property will result in no score being taken from the nested query.

Using the parent-child relationship

In the previous section, we discussed using Elasticsearch to index the nested documents along with the parent one. However, even though the nested documents are indexed as separate documents in the index, we can't change a single nested document (unless we use the update API). Elasticsearch allows us to have a real parent-child relationship and we will look at it in the following section.

Index structure and data indexing

Let's use the same example that we used when discussing the nested documents – the hypothetical cloth store. What we would like to have is the ability to update the sizes and colors without the need to index the whole parent document after each change. We will see how to achieve that using Elasticsearch parent-child functionality.

Child mappings

First we have to create a child index definition. To create child mappings, we need to add the `_parent` property with the name of the parent type, which will be cloth in our case. In the children documents, we want to have the size and the color of the cloth. So, the command that will create the shop index and the variation type will look as follows:

```
curl -XPOST 'localhost:9200/shop'
curl -XPUT 'localhost:9200/shop/variation/_mapping' -d '{
  "variation" : {
    "_parent" : { "type" : "cloth" },
    "properties" : {
      "size" : { "type" : "string", "index" : "not_analyzed" },
      "color" : { "type" : "string", "index" : "not_analyzed" }
    }
  }
}'
```

And that's all. You don't need to specify which field will be used to connect the child documents to the parent ones. By default, Elasticsearch will use the documents' unique identifier for that. If you remember from the previous chapters, the information about a unique identifier is present in the index by default.

Parent mappings

The only field we need to have in our parent document is name. We don't need anything more than that. So, in order to create our cloth type in the shop index, we will run the following commands:

```
curl -XPUT 'localhost:9200/shop/cloth/_mapping' -d '{
  "cloth" : {
    "properties" : {
```

```
    "name" : { "type" : "string" }
  }
 }
}'
```

The parent document

Now we are going to index our parent document. As we want to store the information about the size and the color in the child documents, the only thing we need to have in the parent documents is the name. Of course, there is one thing to remember – our parent documents need to be of type cloth, because of the _parent property value in the child mappings. The indexing command for our parent document is very simple and looks as follows:

```
curl -XPOST 'localhost:9200/shop/cloth/1' -d '{
  "name" : "Test shirt"
}'
```

If you look at the preceding command, you'll notice that our document will be given the identifier 1.

Child documents

To index the child documents, we need to provide information about the parent document with the use of the parent request parameter. The value of the parent parameter should point to the identifier of the parent document. So, to index two child documents to our parent document, we need to run the following command lines:

```
curl -XPOST 'localhost:9200/shop/variation/1000?parent=1' -d '{
  "color" : "red",
  "size" : "XXL"
}'
curl -XPOST 'localhost:9200/shop/variation/1001?parent=1' -d '{
  "color" : "black",
  "size" : "XL"
}'
```

And that's all. We've indexed two additional documents, which are of our variation type, but we've specified that our documents have a parent, the document with an identifier of 1.

Querying

We've indexed our data and now we need to use appropriate queries to match the documents with the data stored in their children. This is because, by default, Elasticsearch searches on the documents without looking at the parent-child relations. For example, the following query will match all three documents that we've indexed (two children and one parent):

```
curl -XGET 'localhost:9200/shop/_search?q=*&pretty'
```

This is not what we would like to achieve, at least in most cases. Usually, we are interested in parent documents that have children matching the query. Of course Elasticsearch provides such functionalities with specialized types of queries.

 The thing to remember though is that, when running queries against parents, the children documents won't be returned, and vice versa.

Querying data in the child documents

Imagine that we want to get clothes that are of the XXL size and are red. As you recall, the size and the color of the cloth are indexed in the child documents, so we need a specialized `has_child` query, to check which parent documents have children with the desired size and color. So an example query that matches our requirement looks as follows:

```
curl -XGET 'localhost:9200/shop/_search?pretty' -d '{
  "query" : {
    "has_child" : {
      "type" : "variation",
      "query" : {
        "bool" : {
          "must" : [
            { "term" : { "size" : "XXL" } },
            { "term" : { "color" : "red" } }
          ]
        }
      }
    }
  }
}'
```

The query is quite simple; it is of the `has_child` type, which tells Elasticsearch that we want to search in the child documents. In order to specify which type of children we are interested in, we specify the `type` property with the name of the child type. The query is provided using the `query` property. We've used a standard `bool` query, which we've already discussed. The result of the query will contain only those parent documents that have children matching our `bool` query. In our case, the single document returned looks as follows:

```
{
  "took" : 16,
  "timed_out" : false,
  "_shards" : {
    "total" : 5,
    "successful" : 5,
    "failed" : 0
  },
  "hits" : {
    "total" : 1,
    "max_score" : 1.0,
    "hits" : [ {
      "_index" : "shop",
      "_type" : "cloth",
      "_id" : "1",
      "_score" : 1.0,
      "_source" : {
        "name" : "Test shirt"
      }
    } ]
  }
}
```

The `has_child` query allows us to provide additional parameters to control its behavior. Every parent document found may be connected with one or more child documents. This means that every child document can influence the resulting score. By default, the query doesn't care about the children documents, how many of them matched, and what is their content – it only matters if they match the query or not. This can be changed by using the `score_mode` parameter, which controls the score calculation of the `has_child` query. The values this parameter can take are:

- none: The default one, the score generated by the relation is `1.0`
- min: The score is taken from the lowest scored child
- max: The score is taken from the highest scored child
- sum: The score is calculated as the sum of the child scores
- avg: The score is taken as the average of the child scores

Let's see an example:

```
curl -XGET 'localhost:9200/shop/_search?pretty' -d '{
  "query" : {
    "has_child" : {
      "type" : "variation",
      "score_mode" : "sum",
      "query" : {
        "bool" : {
          "must" : [
            { "term" : { "size" : "XXL" } },
            { "term" : { "color" : "red" } }
          ]
        }
      }
    }
  }
}'
```

We used sum as score_mode which results in children contributing to the final score of the parent document – the contribution is the sum of scores of every child document matching the query.

And finally, we can limit the number of children documents that need to be matched; we can specify both the maximum number of the children documents allowed to be matched (the max_children property) and the minimum number of children documents (the min_children property) that need to be matched. The query illustrating the usage of these parameters is as follows:

```
curl -XGET 'localhost:9200/shop/_search?pretty' -d '{
  "query" : {
    "has_child" : {
      "type" : "variation",
      "min_children" : 1,
      "max_children" : 3,
      "query" : {
        "bool" : {
          "must" : [
            { "term" : { "size" : "XXL" } },
```

```
        { "term" : { "color" : "red" } }
      ]
    }
  }
 }
}
}'
```

Querying data in the parent documents

Sometimes, we are not interested in the parent documents but in the children documents. If you would like to return the child documents that matches a given data in the parent document, Elasticsearch has a query for us – the has_parent query. It is similar to the has_child query; however, instead of the type property, we specify the parent_type property with the value of the parent document type. For example, the following query will return both the child documents that we've indexed, but not the parent document:

```
curl -XGET 'localhost:9200/shop/_search?pretty' -d '{
  "query" : {
    "has_parent" : {
      "parent_type" : "cloth",
      "query" : {
        "term" : { "name" : "test" }
      }
    }
  }
}'
```

The response from Elasticsearch will be similar to the following one:

```
{
  "took" : 3,
  "timed_out" : false,
  "_shards" : {
    "total" : 5,
    "successful" : 5,
    "failed" : 0
  },
  "hits" : {
    "total" : 2,
    "max_score" : 1.0,
```

```
    "hits" : [ {
      "_index" : "shop",
      "_type" : "variation",
      "_id" : "1000",
      "_score" : 1.0,
      "_routing" : "1",
      "_parent" : "1",
      "_source" : {
        "color" : "red",
        "size" : "XXL"
      }
    }, {
      "_index" : "shop",
      "_type" : "variation",
      "_id" : "1001",
      "_score" : 1.0,
      "_routing" : "1",
      "_parent" : "1",
      "_source" : {
        "color" : "black",
        "size" : "XL"
      }
    } ]
  }
}
```

Similar to the has_child query, the has_parent query also gives us the possibility of tuning the score calculation of the query. In this case, score_mode has only two options: none, the default one where the score calculated by the query is equal to 1.0, and score, which calculates the score of the document on the basis of the parent document contents. An example that uses score_mode in the has_parent query looks as follows:

```
curl -XGET 'localhost:9200/shop/_search?pretty' -d '{
  "query" : {
    "has_parent" : {
      "parent_type" : "cloth",
      "score_mode" : "score",
      "query" : {
        "term" : { "name" : "test" }
      }
    }
  }
}'
```

The one difference with the previous example is `score_mode`. If you check the results of these queries, you'll notice only a single difference. The score of all the documents from the first example is 1.0, while the score for the results returned by the preceding query is equal to 0.8784157. In this case, all the documents found have the same score, because they have a common parent document.

Performance considerations

When using Elasticsearch parent-child functionality, you have to be aware of the performance impact that it has. The first thing you need to remember is that the parent and the child documents need to be stored in the same shard in order for the queries to work. If you happen to have a high number of children for a single parent, you may end up with shards not having a similar number of documents. Because of that, your query performance can be lower on one of the nodes, resulting in the whole query being slower. Also, remember that parent-child queries will be slower than ones that run against the documents that don't have a relationship between them. There is a way of speeding up joins for the parent-child queries at the cost of memory by eagerly loading the so called global ordinals; however, we will discuss that method in the *Elasticsearch caches* section of *Chapter 9, Elasticsearch Cluster in Detail*.

Finally, the first query will preload and cache the document identifiers using the doc values. This takes time. In order to improve the performance of initial queries that use the parent-child relationship, Warmer API can be used. You can find more information about how to add warming queries to Elasticsearch in the *Warming up* section of *Chapter 10, Administrating Your Cluster*.

Modifying your index structure with the update API

In the previous chapters, we discussed how to create index mappings and index the data. But what if you already have the mappings created, and data indexed, but you want to modify the structure of the index? Of course one could say that we could just create a new index with new mappings, but that is not always a possibility, especially in a production environment. This is possible to some extent. For example, by default, if we index a document with a new field, Elasticsearch will add that field to the index structure. Let's now look at how to modify the index structure manually.

 For situations where mapping changes are needed and they are not possible because of conflicts with the current index structure, it is very good to use aliases – both read and write ones. We will discuss aliasing in the *Index aliasing* section of *Chapter 10, Administrating Your Cluster*.

The mappings

Let's assume that we have the following mappings for our users index stored in the user.json file:

```
{
  "user" : {
   "properties" : {
    "name" : {"type" : "string"}
   }
  }
}
```

As you can see, it is very simple. It just has a single property that will hold the user name. Now let's create an index called users and let's use the preceding mappings to create our type. To do that, we will run the following commands:

```
curl -XPOST 'localhost:9200/users'
curl -XPUT 'localhost:9200/users/user/_mapping' -d @user.json
```

If everything goes well, we will have our index (called users) and type (called user) created. So now let's try to add a new field to the mappings.

Adding a new field to the existing index

In order to illustrate how to add a new field to our mappings, we assume that we want to add a phone number to the data stored for each user. In order to do that, we need to send an HTTP PUT command to the /index_name/type_name/_mapping REST end point with the proper body that will include our new field. For example, to add the mentioned phone field, we will run the following command:

```
curl -XPUT 'http://localhost:9200/users/user/_mapping' -d '{
  "user" : {
   "properties" : {
    "phone" : {"type" : "string", index : "not_analyzed"}
   }
  }
}'
```

Similar to the previous command we ran, if everything goes well, we should have a new field added to our index structure.

Of course, Elasticsearch won't reindex our data or populate the newly added field automatically. It will just alter the mappings held by the master node and populate the mappings to all the other nodes in the cluster and that's all. Data reindexation must be done by us or the application that indexes the data in our environment. Until then, the old documents won't have the newly added field. This is crucial to remember. If you don't have the original documents, you can use the _source field to get the original data from Elasticsearch and index them once again.

To ensure everything is okay, we can run the GET HTTP request to the _mapping REST end point and Elasticsearch will return the appropriate mappings. An example command to get the mappings for our user type in the users index will look as follows:

```
curl -XGET 'localhost:9200/users/user/_mapping?pretty'
```

Modifying fields of an existing index

Our users index structure contains two fields: name and phone. Let's imagine that we indexed some data but after a while we decided that we want to search on the phone field and we would like to change its index property from not_analyzed to analyzed. Because we already know how to alter the index structure, we will run the following command:

```
curl -XPUT 'http://localhost:9200/users/user/_mapping?pretty' -d '{
  "user" : {
   "properties" : {
    "phone" : {"type" : "string", "store" : "yes", "index" : "analyzed"}
   }
  }
}'
```

What Elasticsearch will return is a response indicating an error, which looks as follows:

```
   {
     "error" : {
      "root_cause" : [ {
        "type" : "illegal_argument_exception",
```

```
        "reason" : "Mapper for [phone] conflicts with existing
          mapping in other types:\n[mapper [phone] has different
            [index] values, mapper [phone] has different [store]
              values, mapper [phone] has different [omit_norms]
                values, cannot change from disable to enabled,
                  mapper [phone] has different [analyzer]]"
    } ],
    "type" : "illegal_argument_exception",
    "reason" : "Mapper for [phone] conflicts with existing mapping
      in other types:\n[mapper [phone] has different [index]
        values, mapper [phone] has different [store] values,
          mapper [phone] has different [omit_norms] values, cannot
            change from disable to enabled, mapper [phone] has
              different [analyzer]]"
  },
  "status" : 400
}
```

This is because we can't change a field that was set to be `not_analyzed` to one that is `analyzed`. And not only that, in most cases you won't be able to update the fields mapping. This is a good thing, because if we would be allowed to change such settings, we would confuse Elasticsearch and Lucene. Imagine that we already have many documents with the phone field set to `not_analyzed` and we are allowed to change the mappings to analyzed. Elasticsearch wouldn't change the data that was already indexed, but the queries that are analyzed would be processed with a different logic and thus you wouldn't be able to properly find your data.

However, to give you some examples of what is prohibited and what is not, we decided to mention some of the operations for both the cases. For example, the following modification can be safely made:

- Adding a new type definition
- Adding a new field
- Adding a new analyzer

The following modifications are prohibited or will not work:

- Enabling norms for a field
- Changing a field to be stored or not stored
- Changing the type of the field (for example, from text to numeric)
- Changing a stored field to not stored and vice versa
- Changing the value of indexed property
- Changing the analyzer of an already indexed document

Remember that the preceding mentioned examples of allowed and not allowed updates do not mention all the possibilities of update API usage and you have to try for yourself if the update you are trying to do will work.

Summary

The chapter you just finished reading concentrated on indexing operations and handling data that is not flat or have relationships between the documents. We started with indexing tree-like structures and objects in Elasticsearch. We also used nested objects and learned when they can be used. We also used parent-child functionality and we learned how this approach is different compared to nested documents. Finally, we modified our indices structure with a call of an API and learned when this is possible.

In the next chapter, we will get back to querying related topics. We will learn how Lucene scoring works, how to use scripts in Elasticsearch, and how to handle multilingual data. We will affect scoring using boosts and we will use synonyms to improve users' search results. Finally, we will look at what we can do to see how our documents were scored.

6
Make Your Search Better

In the previous chapter, we were focused on indexing operations; we learned how to handle the structured data. We started with indexing tree-like structures and JSON objects. We used nested objects and indexed documents using parent-child functionality. Finally, at the end of the chapter, we used Elasticsearch API to modify our indices structures. By the end of this chapter, you will have learned the following topics:

- Understanding how Apache Lucene scoring works
- Using scripting
- Handling multilingual data
- Using boosting to affect document scoring
- Using synonyms
- Understanding how your documents were scored

Introduction to Apache Lucene scoring

When talking about queries and their relevance, we can't omit the information about the scoring and where it comes from. But what is a **score**? The score is a property that describes the relevance of a document in the context of a query. In the following section, we will talk about the default Apache Lucene scoring mechanism – the TF/IDF algorithm and how it affects the returned document.

 The TF/IDF is not the only available algorithm exposed by Elasticsearch. For more information about the available models, refer to the *Available similarity models* section in *Chapter 2, Indexing Your Data.* You can also refer to the books *Mastering Elasticsearch* and *Mastering Elasticsearch Second Edition* published by *Packt Publishing*.

When a document is matched

When a document is returned by Lucene, it means that it matched the query we sent to it. In most cases, each of the resulting documents in the response is given a score. The higher the score, the more relevant the document is from the search engine's point of view, of course, in the context of a given query. This means that the score factor calculated for the same document on two different queries will be different. Because of that, comparing scores between queries usually doesn't make much sense. However, let's get back to the scoring. To calculate the `score` property for a document, multiple factors are taken into account:

- `document boost`: The `boost` value given for a document during indexing.

- `field boost`: The `boost` value given for a field during querying and indexing.

- `coord`: The coordination factor that is based on the number of terms the document has. It is responsible for giving more value to the documents that contain more search terms compared to the other documents.

- `inverse document frequency`: The term based factor that tells the scoring formula how rarefor score property calculation:inverse document frequency" the given term is. The higher the inverse document frequency the less common the term is.

- `length norm`: The field based factor for normalization based on the number of terms the given field contains. The longer the field, the smaller boost this factor will give. It basically means that the shorter documents will be favored.

- `term frequency`: The term based factor describing how many times the given term occurs in a document. The higher the term frequency, the higher the score of the document will be.

- `query norm`: The query based normalization factor that is calculated as the sum of the squared weight of each of the query terms. Query norm is used to allow score comparison between queries, which we said is not always easy or possible.

Default scoring formula

The practical formula for the TF/IDF algorithm looks as follows:

$$score(q,d) = coord(q,d) * queryNorm(q) * \sum_{t\ in\ q} \left(tf(t\ in\ d) * idf(t)^2 * boost(t) * norm(t,d) \right)$$

To adjust your query relevance, you don't need to remember the details of the equation, but it is very important to know how it works – to at least be aware that there is an equation you can analyze. We can see that the score factor for the document is a function of query q and document d. There are also two factors that are not dependent directly on query terms: coord and queryNorm. These two elements of the formula are multiplied by the sum calculated for each term in the query. The sum on the other hand is calculated by multiplying the term frequency for the given term, its inverse document frequency, term boost, and the norm, which is the length norm we discussed previously.

 Note that the preceding formula is a practical one. You can find more information about the conceptual formula in Lucene Javadocs at http://lucene.apache.org/core/5_4_0/core/org/apache/lucene/search/similarities/TFIDFSimilarity.html.

The good thing about the preceding rules is that you don't need to remember all of that. What you should be aware of is what matters when it comes to the document score. Basically, there are a few rules which come from the preceding mentioned equation:

- The rarer the matched term is, the higher the score the document will have

- The shorter the document fields are (the less terms they have), the higher the score the document will have

- The higher the boost for the fields is, the higher the score the document will have

As we can see, Lucene gives a higher score for the documents that have many query terms matched and have shorter fields (less terms indexed) that were used for matching, and it also favors rarer terms instead of the common ones (of course, the ones that matched).

Relevancy matters

In most cases, we want to get the best matching documents. However, the most relevant documents don't always mean the same as the best matches. Some use cases define very strict rules on why a given document should be higher on the results list. For example, one could say that, in addition to the document being a perfect match in terms of TF/IDF similarity, we have paying customers to consider. Depending on the customer plan, we want to give more importance to such documents. In such cases, we could want the documents for the customers that pay the most to be on top of the search results. Of course, this is not relevant in TF/IDF.

The other example is yellow pages, where customers pay for more information describing the document. Such large documents may not be the most relevant ones according to TF/IDF, so you may want to adjust the scoring if you are working with such data.

These are very simple examples and Elasticsearch queries can become really complicated. We will talk about such queries in the *Influencing scores with query boosts* section in this chapter.

When working on search relevance, you should always remember that it is not a onetime process. Your data will change with time and your queries will need to be adjusted. In most cases, tuning the query relevancy will be constant work. You will need to react to your business rules and needs, to how the users behave, and so on. It is very important to remember that this process is not a single time one about which you can forget.

Scripting capabilities of Elasticsearch

Elasticsearch has a few functionalities where scripts can be used. You've already seen examples such as updating documents and searching. We will also use the scripting capabilities of Elasticsearch when we discuss aggregations. Even though scripts seem to be a rather advanced topic, we will look at the possibilities offered by Elasticsearch. That's because scripts are priceless in certain situations.

Elasticsearch can use several languages for scripting. When not explicitly declared, it assumes that Groovy (`http://www.groovy-lang.org/`) is used. Other languages available out of the box are Lucene expression language and Mustache (`https://mustache.github.io/`). Of course we can use plugins, which will make Elasticsearch understand additional scripting languages, such as JavaScript, MVEL, and Python. The thing worth mentioning is that independent from the scripting language that we choose, Elasticsearch exposes objects that we can use in our scripts. Let's start by briefly looking at what type of information we are allowed to use in our scripts.

Objects available during script execution

During different operations, Elasticsearch allows us to use different objects in our scripts. To develop a script that fits our use case, we should be familiar with these objects.

For example, during a search operation, the following objects are available:

- _doc (also available as doc): This is an instance of the org.elasticsearch. search.lookup.LeafDocLookup object. It gives us access to the current document found with the calculated score and field values.

- _source: This is an instance of the org.elasticsearch.search.lookup. SourceLookup object. It provides access to the source of the current document and the values defined in the source.

- _fields: This is an instance of the org.elasticsearch.search.lookup. LeafFieldsLookup object. It can be used to access the values of the document fields.

On the other hand, during a document update operation, the preceding mentioned variables are not accessible. Elasticsearch exposes only the ctx object with the _source property, which provides access to the document currently processed in the update request.

As we have previously seen, several methods are mentioned in the context of document fields and their values. Let's now look at examples of how to get the value for a particular field using the previously mentioned object available during the search operation. In the brackets after the script piece, you can see what Elasticsearch will return for one of our example documents from the library index (we will use the document with identifier 4):

- _doc.title.value (and)
- _source.title (crime and punishment)
- _fields.title.value (null)

A bit confusing, isn't it? During indexing, the original document is by default stored in the _source field. Of course, by default, all the fields are present in that _source field. In addition to that, the document is parsed and every field may be stored in an index if it is marked as stored (that is, if the store property is set to true; otherwise, by default, the fields are not stored). Finally, the field value may be configured as indexed. This means that the field value is analyzed and placed in the index. To sum up, one field may land in Elasticsearch index in the following ways:

- As a part of the _source document
- As a stored and unparsed original value
- As an indexed value that is processed by an analyzer

In scripts, we have access to all these field representations. The only exception is the update operation, which, as we've mentioned before, gives us only access to document _source as part of the ctx variable. You may wonder which version you should use. Well, if you want access to the processed form, the answer will be simple – use the _doc object. What about _source and _fields? In most cases, _source is a good choice. It is usually fast and needs less disk operations than reading the original field values from the index. This is especially true when you need to read the values of multiple fields in your scripts; fetching a single _source field is faster than fetching multiple independent fields from the index.

Script types

Elasticsearch allows us to use scripts in three different ways:

- **Inline scripts**: The source of the script is directly defined in the query
- **In file scripts**: The source is defined in the external file placed in the Elasticsearch config/scripts directory
- As a document in the dedicated index: The source of the script is defined as a document in a special index available by using the /_scripts API end-point

Choosing the way to define scripts depends on several factors. If you have scripts which you will use in many different queries, the file or the dedicated index seem to be the best solutions. The scripts in file is probably less convenient, but it is preferred from the security point of view; they can't be overwritten and injected into your query causing a security breach.

In file scripts

This is the only way to allow dynamic scripting if we don't want to enable query dynamic scripting in Elasticsearch. The idea is that every script used by the queries is defined in its own file placed in the config/scripts directory. We will now look at this method of using scripts. Let's create an example file called tag_sort.groovy and let's place it in the config/scripts directory of our Elasticsearch instance (or instances if we run a cluster). The content of the mentioned file should look like this:

```
_doc.tags.values.size() > 0 ? _doc.tags.values[0] : '\u19999'
```

After few seconds, Elasticsearch will automatically load a new file. You should see something like the following in the Elasticsearch logs:

```
[2015-08-30 13:14:33,005][INFO ][script                  ] [Alex Wilder]
compiling script file [/Users/negativ/Developer/ES/es-current/config/
scripts/tag_sort.groovy]
```

If you have multi-node cluster, you have to make sure that the script is available on every node.

Now we are ready to use this script in our queries. You may remember that we used exactly the same script in the *Sorting data* section in *Chapter 4, Extending Your Querying Knowledge*. Now the modified query that uses our script stored in the file looks as follows:

```
curl -XGET 'localhost:9200/library/_search?pretty' -d '{
  "query" : {
    "match_all" : { }
  },
  "sort" : {
    "_script" : {
      "script" : {
        "file" : "tag_sort"
      },
      "type" : "string",
      "order" : "asc"
    }
  }
}'
```

We will return to this, but first, the next possible way of defining inline scripts.

Inline scripts

Inline scripts are a more convenient way of using scripts, especially for constantly changing queries and for ad-hoc queries. The main drawback of such an approach is security. If we allow users to run any kind of query, including scripts, we can expose our Elasticsearch instance to attackers. Such attacks can execute arbitrary code on the server running Elasticsearch with rights equal to the ones given to the user running Elasticsearch. In the worst case scenario, the attacker could use security holes to gain super user rights. This is the reason why inline scripts are disabled by default. After careful consideration, you can enable them by adding:

```
script.inline: on
```

Add the preceding command line to the `elasticsearch.yml` file.

After allowing the inline script to be executed, we can run a query that looks as follows:

```
curl -XGET 'localhost:9200/library/_search?pretty' -d '{
  "query" : {
    "match_all" : { }
  },
  "sort" : {
    "_script" : {
      "script" : {
        "inline" : "_doc.tags.values.size() > 0 ? _doc.tags.values[0] :
\"\u19999\""
      },
      "type" : "string",
      "order" : "asc"
    }
  }
}'
```

Indexed scripts

The last option for defining scripts is storing them in the dedicated Elasticsearch index. For the same security reasons, dynamic execution of the indexed scripts is by default disabled. To enable the indexed scripts, we have to add a similar configuration option to the one we added to be able to use the inline scripts. We need to add the following line to the elasticsearch.yml file:

```
script.indexed: on
```

After adding the preceding property to all the nodes and restarting the cluster, we will be ready to start using the indexed scripts. Elasticsearch provides an additional, dedicated endpoint for this purpose. Let's store our script:

```
curl -XPOST 'localhost:9200/_scripts/groovy/tag_sort' -d '{
  "script" :  "_doc.tags.values.size() > 0 ? _doc.tags.values[0] : \"\
u19999\""
}'
```

The script is ready, but let's discuss what we just did. We sent an HTTP POST request to the special _scripts REST end-point. We also specified the language of the script (groovy in our case) and the name of the script (tag_sort). The body of the request is the script itself.

We can now move on to the query, which looks as follows:

```
curl -XGET 'localhost:9200/library/_search?pretty' -d '{
  "query" : {
    "match_all" : { }
  },
  "sort" : {
    "_script" : {
      "script" : {
        "id" : "tag_sort"
      },
      "type" : "string",
      "order" : "asc"
    }
  }
}'
```

As we see, the query is practically identical to the query used with the script defined in a file. The only difference is that we provided the identifier of the script using the id parameter instead of providing the file name.

Querying with scripts

If we look at any request made to Elasticsearch that uses scripts, we will notice some similar properties, which are as follows:

- script: This property wraps the script definition.
- inline: This property holds the code of the script itself.
- id: This property defines the identifier of the indexed script.
- file: The filename of the script without the extension.
- lang: This property defines the language of the script. If it is omitted, Elasticsearch assumes groovy.
- params: This object contains the parameters and their values. Every defined parameter can be used inside the script by specifying that parameter's name. The parameters allow us to write cleaner code which will be executed in a more efficient manner. Scripts using the parameters are executed faster than code with embedded constants because of caching.

Scripting with parameters

As our scripts become more and more complicated, the need for creating multiple, almost identical scripts can appear. These scripts usually differ in the values used, with the logic behind them being exactly the same. In our simple example, we used a hardcoded value used to mark documents with empty tags list. Let's change this to allow definition of the hardcoded value. Let's use in file script definition and create a `tag_sort_with_param.groovy` file with the following contents:

```
_doc.tags.values.size() > 0 ? _doc.tags.values[0] : tvalue
```

The only change we've made is the introduction of the parameter named `tvalue`, which can be set in the query in the following way:

```
curl -XGET 'localhost:9200/library/_search?pretty' -d '{
  "query" : {
    "match_all" : { }
  },
  "sort" : {
    "_script" : {
      "script" : {
        "file" : "tag_sort_with_param",
        "params" : {
          "tvalue" : "000"
        }
      },
      "type" : "string",
      "order" : "asc"
    }
  }
}'
```

The `params` section defines all the script parameters. In our simple example, we've only used a single parameter, but of course we can have multiple parameters in a single query.

Script languages

As we already said, the default language for scripting is Groovy. However, we are not limited to only a single scripting language when using Elasticsearch. In fact, if you would like to, you can even use Java to write your scripts. In addition to that, the community behind Elasticsearch provides additional languages support as plugins. So if you are willing to install plugins, you can extend the list of scripting languages that Elasticsearch supports even further. You may wonder why you would even consider using a scripting language other than the default Groovy. The first reason is your own preferences. If you are a python enthusiast, you are probably now thinking about how to use python for your Elasticsearch scripts. The other reason could be security. When we talked about the inline scripts, we told you that they are turned off by default. This is not exactly true for all the scripting languages available out of the box. The inline scripts are disabled by default when using Groovy, but you can use Lucene expressions and Mustache without any issues. This is because those languages are sandboxed, which means that the security sensitive functions are turned off. And of course, the last factor when choosing a language is performance. Theoretically, the native scripts (in Java) should have better performance than others, but you should remember that the difference can be insignificant. You should always consider the cost of development and measure performance.

Using other than embedded languages

Using Groovy for scripting is a simple and sufficient solution for most use cases. However, you may have a different preference and you may like to use something different, such as JavaScript, Python, or Mvel. Before using other languages, we must install an appropriate plugin. You can read more details about plugins in the *Elasticsearch plugins* section of *Chapter 9, Elasticsearch Cluster*. For now, we'll just run the following command from the `Elasticsearch` directory:

```
bin/plugin install lang-javascript
```

The preceding command will install a plugin that will allow the usage of JavaScript as the scripting language. The only change we should make in the request is to add the additional information about the language we are using for scripting and, of course, modify the script itself to correctly use the new language. Look at the following example:

```
curl -XGET 'localhost:9200/library/_search?pretty' -d '{
  "query" : {
    "match_all" : { }
  },
  "sort" : {
```

```
  "_script" : {
    "script" : {
      "inline" : "_doc.tags.values.length > 0 ? _doc.tags.values[0]
:\"\u19999\";",
      "lang" : "javascript"
    },
    "type" : "string",
    "order" : "asc"
  }
 }
}'
```

As you can see, we've used JavaScript for scripting instead of the default Groovy. The `lang` parameter informs Elasticsearch about the language being used.

Using native code

In case the scripts are too slow or you don't like scripting languages, Elasticsearch allows you to write Java classes and use them instead of scripts. There are two possible ways of adding native scripts: adding classes defining scripts to Elasticsearch classpath or adding script as a functionality provided by a plugin. We will describe this second solution as it is more elegant.

The factory implementation

We need to implement at least two classes to create a new native script. The first one is a factory for our script. For now, let's focus on it. The following sample code illustrates the factory for our script:

```
package pl.solr.elasticsearch.examples.scripts;

import java.util.Map;

import org.elasticsearch.common.Nullable;
import org.elasticsearch.script.ExecutableScript;
import org.elasticsearch.script.NativeScriptFactory;

public class HashCodeSortNativeScriptFactory implements
NativeScriptFactory {

    @Override
```

```
    public ExecutableScript newScript(@Nullable Map<String, Object>
params) {
        return new HashCodeSortScript(params);
    }

  @Override
  public boolean needsScores() {
    return false;
  }

}
```

The essential parts are highlighted in the code snippet. This class should implement the `org.elasticsearch.script.NativeScriptFactory` class. The interface forces us to implement two methods. The `newScript()` method takes the parameters defined in the API call and returns an instance of our script. Finally, `needsScores()` informs Elasticsearch if we want to use scoring and whether it should be calculated.

Implementing the native script

Now let's look at the implementation of our script. The idea is simple – our script will be used for sorting. Documents will be ordered by the `hashCode()` value of the chosen field. The documents without a value in the defined field will be first on the results list. We know the logic doesn't make too much sense, but it is good for presentation as it is simple. The source code for our native script looks as follows:

```
package pl.solr.elasticsearch.examples.scripts;

import java.util.Map;

import org.elasticsearch.script.AbstractSearchScript;

public class HashCodeSortScript extends AbstractSearchScript {
  private String field = "name";

  public HashCodeSortScript(Map<String, Object> params) {
    if (params != null && params.containsKey("field")) {
      this.field = params.get("field").toString();
    }
  }

  @Override
  public Object run() {
    Object value = source().get(field);
```

```
    if (value != null) {
      return value.hashCode();
    }
    return 0;
  }

}
```

First of all, our class inherits from the `org.elasticsearch.script.`
`AbstractSearchScript` class and implements the `run()` method. This is
where we get the appropriate values from the current document, process
it according to our strange logic, and return the result. You may notice the
`source()` call. It is exactly the same `_source` parameter that we used when
dealing with non-native scripts. The `doc()` and `fields()` methods are also
available and they follow the same logic we described earlier.

The thing worth looking at is how we've used the parameters. We assume that
a user can put the `field` parameter, telling us which document field will be
used for manipulation. We also provide a default value for this parameter.

The plugin definition

We said that we will install our script as a part of a plugin. This is why we
need additional files. The first file is the plugin initialization class where we
tell Elasticsearch about our new script:

```
package pl.solr.elasticsearch.examples.scripts;

import org.elasticsearch.plugins.Plugin;
import org.elasticsearch.script.ScriptModule;

public class ScriptPlugin extends Plugin {

  @Override
  public String description() {
    return "The example of native sort script";
  }

  @Override
  public String name() {
    return "naive-sort-plugin";
  }
```

```
    public void onModule(final ScriptModule module) {
        module.registerScript("native_sort",
    HashCodeSortNativeScriptFactory.class);

    }

}
```

The implementation is easy. The description() and name() methods are only for information, so let's focus on the onModule() method. In our case, we need access to the script module – Elasticsearch service with scripts and scripting languages. This is why we define onModule() with one ScriptModule argument. Thanks to Elasticsearch magic, we can use this module and register our script so it can be found by the engine. We have used the registerScript() method, which takes the script name and the previously defined factory class.

The second needed file is a plugin descriptor file: plugin-descriptor.properties. It defines the constants used by the Elasticsearch plugin subsystem. Without more thinking, let's look at the contents of this file:

```
jvm=true
classname=pl.solr.elasticsearch.examples.scripts.ScriptPlugin
elasticsearch.version=2.2.0
version=0.0.1-SNAPSHOT
name=native_script
description=Example Native Scripts
java.version=1.7
```

The appropriate lines have the following meaning:

- jvm: tells Elasticsearch that our file contains Java code
- classname: describes the main class with plugin definition
- elasticsearch.version and java.version: tells us about the Elasticsearch version that is supported by the plugin and the Java version that is needed
- name and description: Informative name and short description of our plugin

And that's it. We have all the files needed to run our script. Please note that you can have more than a single script packed as a single plugin.

Installing the plugin

Now it's time to install our native script embedded in the plugin. After packing the compiled classes as a JAR archive, we should put it in the Elasticsearch plugins/ native-script directory. The native-script part is a root directory for our plugin and you may name it as you wish. In this directory you also need the prepared plugin-descriptor.properties file. This makes our plugin visible to Elasicsearch.

Running the script

After restarting Elasticsearch (or the whole cluster if you run more than a single node), we can start sending the queries that use our native script. For example, we will send a query that uses our previously indexed data from the library index. This example query looks as follows:

```
curl -XGET 'localhost:9200/library/_search?pretty' -d '{
  "query" : {
    "match_all" : { }
  },
  "sort" : {
    "_script" : {
      "script" : {
        "script" : "native_sort",
        "lang" : "native",
        "params" : {
          "field" : "otitle"
        }
      },
      "type" : "string",
      "order" : "asc"
    }
  }
}'
```

Note the params part of the query. In this call, we want to sort on the otitle field. We provide the script name native_sort and the script language native. This is required. If everything goes well, we should see our results sorted by our custom sort logic. If we look at the response from Elasticsearch, we will see that the documents without the otitle field are at the first few positions of the results list and their sort value is 0.

Searching content in different languages

Until now, when discussing language analysis, we've talked mostly about theory. We didn't see an example regarding language analysis, handling multiple languages that our data can consist of, and so on. Now this will change, as this section is dedicated to information about how we can handle data in multiple languages.

Handling languages differently

As you already know, Elasticsearch allows us to choose different analyzers for our data. We can have our data divided on the basis of whitespaces, or have them lowercased, and so on. This can usually be done regardless of the language –the same tokenization on the basis of whitespaces will work for English, German, and Polish, although it won't work for Chinese. However, what if you want to find documents that contain words such as cat and cats by only sending the word cat to Elasticsearch? This is where language analysis comes into play with stemming algorithms for different languages, which allow the analyzed words to be reduced to their root forms. And now the worst part – we can't use one general stemming algorithm for all the languages in the world; we have to choose one appropriate language. The following sections in the chapter will help you with some parts of the language analysis process.

Handling multiple languages

There are a few ways of handling multiple languages in Elasticsearch and all of them have some pros and cons. We won't be discussing everything, but just for the purpose of giving you an idea, a few of those methods are as follows:

- Storing documents in different languages as different types
- Storing documents in different languages in separate indices
- Storing language data in different fields of a single document

For the purpose of the book, we will focus on a single method – the one that allows storing documents in different languages in a single index. We will focus on a problem where we have a single type of document, but each document may come from anywhere in the world and thus can be written in multiple languages. Also, we would like to enable our users to use all the analysis capabilities, such as stemming and stop words for different languages, not only for English.

Note that the stemming algorithms perform differently for different languages, both in terms of analysis performance and the resulting terms. For example, English stemmers are very good, but you can run into issues with European languages, such as German.

Detecting the language of the document

Before we continue with showing you how to solve our problem with handling multiple languages in Elasticsearch, we would like to tell you about one additional thing, that is language detection. There are situations where you just don't know what language your document or query are in. In such cases, language detection libraries may be a good choice, especially when using Java as your programming language of choice. Some of the libraries are as follows:

- Apache Tika (`http://tika.apache.org/`)
- Language detection (`https://github.com/shuyo/language-detection`)

The language detection library claims to have over 99 percent precision for 53 languages; that's a lot if you ask us.

You should remember, though, that data language detection will be more precise for longer text. Because the text of queries is usually short, you can expect to have some degree of error during query language identification.

Sample document

Let's start with introducing a sample document, which is as follows:

```
{
    "title" : "First test document",
    "content" : "This is a test document"
}
```

As you can see, the document is pretty simple; it contains the following two fields:

- `title`: This field holds the title of the document
- `content`: This field holds the actual content of the document

This document is quite simple, but, from the search point of view, the information about document language is missing. What we should do is enrich the document by adding the needed information. We can do that by using one of the previously mentioned libraries, which will try to detect the language.

After we have the language detected, we inform Elasticsearch which analyzer should be used and modify the document to directly show the language of each field. Each of the fields would have to be analyzed by a language analyzer dedicated to the detected language.

 A full list of these language analyzers can be found at https://www.elastic.co/guide/en/elasticsearch/reference/current/analysis-lang-analyzer.html).

If a document is written in a language that we are not supporting, we will just fall back to some default field with the default analyzer. For example, our processed and prepared for indexing document could look like this:

```
{
    "title_english" : "First test document",
    "content_english" : "This is a test document"
}
```

The thing is that all this processing we've mentioned would have to be done outside of Elasticsearch or in some kind of custom plugin that would implement the mentioned logic.

 In the previous versions of Elasticsearch, there was a possibility of choosing an analyzer based on the value of an additional field, which contained the analyzer name. This was a more convenient and elegant way but introduced some uncertainty about the field contents. You always had to deliver a proper analyzer when using the given field or strange things happened. The Elasticsearch team made the difficult decision and removed this feature.

There is also a simpler way: we can take our first document and index it in several ways independently from input language. Let's focus on this solution.

The mappings

To handle our solution, which will process the document using several defined languages, we need new mappings. Let's look at the mappings we've created to index our documents (we've stored them in the mappings.json file):

```
{
  "mappings" : {
    "doc" : {
      "properties" : {
        "title" : {
```

```
            "type" : "string",
            "index" : "analyzed",
            "fields" : {
              "english" : {
                "type" : "string",
                "index" : "analyzed",
                "analyzer" : "english"
              },
              "russian" : {
                "type" : "string",
                "index" : "analyzed",
                "analyzer" : "russian"
              },
              "german" : {
                "type" : "string",
                "index" : "analyzed",
                "analyzer" : "german"
              }
            }
          },
          "content" : {
            "type" : "string",
            "index" : "analyzed",
            "fields" : {
              "english" : {
                "type" : "string",
                "index" : "analyzed",
                "analyzer" : "english"
              },
              "russian" : {
                "type" : "string",
                "index" : "analyzed",
                "analyzer" : "russian"
              },
              "german" : {
                "type" : "string",
                "index" : "analyzed",
                "analyzer" : "german"
              }
            }
          }
        }
      }
    }
  }
}
```

In the preceding mappings, we've shown the definition for the `title` and `content` fields (if you are not familiar with any aspect of mappings definition, refer to the *Mappings configuration* section of *Chapter 2, Indexing Your Data*). We have used the multifield feature of Elasticsearch: each field can be indexed in several ways using various language analyzers (in our example, those analyzers are: English, Russian, and German).

In addition, the base field uses the default analyzer, which we may use at query time when the language is unknown. So, each field will actually have four fields – the default one and three language oriented fields.

In order to create a sample index called docs that uses our mappings, we will use the following command:

```
curl -XPUT 'localhost:9200/docs' -d @mappings.json
```

Querying

Now let's see how we can query our data to use the newly created language fields. We can divide the querying situation into two different cases. Of course, to start querying we need documents. Let's index our example document by running the following command:

```
curl -XPOST 'localhost:9200/docs/doc/1' -d '{"title" : "First test
document","content" : "This is a test document"}'
```

Queries with an identified language

The first case is when we have our query language identified. Let's assume that the identified language is English. In such cases, our query is as follows:

```
curl 'localhost:9200/docs/_search?pretty' -d '{
  "query" : {
    "match" : {
      "content.english" : "documents"
    }
  }
}'
```

The thing to put emphasis on in the preceding query is the field used for querying and the `query` type. The field used is `content.english`, which also indicates which analyzer we want to use. We used that field because we had identified our language before running the query. Thanks to this, the English analyzer can find our document even if we have the singular form of the word in the document. The response returned by Elasticsearch will be as follows:

```
{
  "took" : 2,
  "timed_out" : false,
  "_shards" : {
    "total" : 5,
    "successful" : 5,
    "failed" : 0
  },
  "hits" : {
    "total" : 1,
    "max_score" : 0.19178301,
    "hits" : [ {
      "_index" : "docs",
      "_type" : "doc",
      "_id" : "1",
      "_score" : 0.19178301,
      "_source": {
        "title" : "First test document",
        "content" : "This is a test document"
      }
    } ]
  }
}
```

The thing to note is also the query type – the `match` query. We used the match query because it analyzes its body with the analyzer used by the field that it is run against. We need that to properly match the data in the query and the data in the index.

Queries with an unknown language

Now let's look at the second situation – handling queries when we couldn't identify the language of the query. In such cases, we can't use the field name pointing to one of the languages, such as `content.german`. In such a case, we use the default field which uses the default analyzer and we send the query to the content field instead. The query will look as follows:

```
curl 'localhost:9200/docs/_search?pretty' -d '{
  "query" : {
```

```
    "match" : {
      "content" : "documents"
    }
  }
}'
```

However, we didn't get any results this time because the default analyzer can't deal with a singular form of a word when we are searching with a plural form.

Combining queries

To additionally boost the documents that perfectly match with our default analyzer, we can combine the two preceding queries with the `bool` query. Such a combined query will look as follows:

```
curl -XGET 'localhost:9200/docs/_search?pretty=true ' -d '{
  "query" : {
    "bool" : {
      "minimum_should_match" : 1,
      "should" : [
        {
          "match" : {
            "content.english" : "documents"
          }
        },
        {
          "match" : {
            "content" : "documents"
          }
        }
      ]
    }
  }
}'
```

For the document to be returned, at least one of the defined queries must match. If they both match, the document will have a higher score value and will be placed higher in the results.

There is one additional advantage of the preceding combined query. If our language analyzer doesn't find a document (for example, when the analysis is different from the one used during indexing), the second query has a chance to find the terms that are tokenized only by whitespace characters and lowercase.

Influencing scores with query boosts

In the beginning of this chapter, we learned what scoring is and how Elasticsearch uses the scoring formula. When an application grows, the need for improving the quality of search also increases - we call it search experience. We need to gain knowledge about what is more important to the user and we see how the users use the searches functionality. This leads to various conclusions; for example, we see that some parts of the documents are more important than others or that particular queries emphasize one field at the cost of others. We need to include such information in our data and queries so that both sides of the scoring equation are closer to our business needs. This is where boosting can be used.

The boost

Boost is an additional value used in the process of scoring. We already know it can be applied to:

- **Query**: When used, we inform the search engine that the given query is a part of a complex query and is more significant than the other parts.
- **Document**: When used during indexing, we tell Elasticsearch that a document is more important than the others in the index. For example, when indexing blog posts, we are probably more interested in the posts themselves than ping backs or comments.

Values assigned by us to a query or a document are not the only factors used when we calculate the resulting score and we know that. We will now look at a few examples of query boosting.

Adding the boost to queries

Let's imagine that our index has two documents and we've used the following commands to index them:

```
curl -XPOST 'localhost:9200/messages/email/1' -d '{
  "id" : 1,
  "to" : "John Smith",
  "from" : "David Jones",
```

```
    "subject" : "Top secret!"
}'

curl -XPOST 'localhost:9200/messages/email/2' -d '{
  "id" : 2,
  "to" : "David Jones",
  "from" : "John Smith",
  "subject" : "John, read this document"
}'
```

This data is trivial, but it should describe our problem very well. Now let's assume we have the following query:

```
curl -XGET 'localhost:9200/messages/_search?pretty' -d '{
  "query" : {
    "query_string" : {
      "query" : "john",
      "use_dis_max" : false
    }
  }
}'
```

In this case, Elasticsearch will create a query to the _all field and will find documents that contain the desired words. We also said that we don't want the disjunction query to be used by specifying the use_dis_max parameter to false (if you don't remember what a disjunction query is, refer to the *The dis_max query* section in *Chapter 3, Searching Your Data*). As we can easily guess, both our records will be returned. The record with identifier equal to 2 will be first because the word John occurs two times – once in the from field and once in the subject field. Let's check this out in the following result:

```
    "hits" : {
        "total" : 2,
        "max_score" : 0.13561106,
        "hits" : [ {
          "_index" : "messages",
          "_type" : "email",
          "_id" : "2",
          "_score" : 0.13561106,
          "_source" : {
            "id" : 2,
            "to" : "David Jones",
```

```
            "from" : "John Smith",
            "subject" : "John, read this document"
          }
        }, {
          "_index" : "messages",
          "_type" : "email",
          "_id" : "1",
          "_score" : 0.11506981,
          "_source" : {
            "id" : 1,
            "to" : "John Smith",
            "from" : "David Jones",
            "subject" : "Top secret!"
          }
        } ]
      }
```

Is everything all right? Technically, yes. But we think that the second document (the one with identifier 1) should be positioned as the first one in the result list, because when searching for something, the most important factor (in many cases) is matching people rather than the subject of the message. You can disagree, but this is exactly why full-text searching relevance is a difficult topic; sometimes it is hard to tell which ordering is better for a particular case. What can we do? First, let's rewrite our query to implicitly inform Elasticsearch what fields should be used for searching:

```
curl -XGET 'localhost:9200/messages/_search?pretty' -d '{
  "query" : {
    "query_string" : {
      "fields" : ["from", "to", "subject"],
      "query" : "john",
      "use_dis_max" : false
    }
  }
}'
```

This is not exactly the same query as the previous one. If we run it, we will get the same results (in our case). However, if you look carefully, you will notice differences in scoring. In the previous example, Elasticsearch only used one field, that is the default _all field. The query that we are using now is using three fields for matching. This means that several factors, such as field lengths, are changed. Anyway, this is not so important in our case. Elasticsearch under the hood generates a complex query made of three queries – one to each field. Of course, the score contributed by each query depends on the number of terms found in this field and the length of this field.

Let's introduce some differences between the fields and their importance. Compare the following query to the last one:

```
curl -XGET 'localhost:9200/messages/_search?pretty' -d '{
  "query" : {
    "query_string" : {
      "fields" : ["from^5", "to^10", "subject"],
      "query" : "john",
      "use_dis_max" : false
    }
  }
}'
```

Look at the highlighted parts (^5 and ^10). By using that notation (the ^ character followed by a number), we can inform Elasticsearch how important a given field is. We see that the most important field is the to field (because of the highest boost value). Next we have the from field, which is less important. The subject field has the default value for boost, which is 1.0 and is the least important field when it comes to score calculation. Always remember that this value is only one of the various factors. You may be wondering why we choose 5 and not 1000 or 1.23. Well, this value depends on the effect we want to achieve, what query we have, and, most importantly, what data we have in our index. Typically, when data changes in the meaningful parts, we should probably check and tune our relevance once again.

In the end, let's look at a similar example, but using the bool query:

```
curl -XGET 'localhost:9200/messages/_search?pretty' -d '{
 "query" : {
  "bool" : {
   "should" : [
    { "term" : { "from": { "value" : "john", "boost" : 5 }}},
    { "term" : { "to": { "value" : "john", "boost" : 10  }}},
    { "term" : { "subject": { "value" : "john" }}}
   ]
  }
 }
}'
```

The preceding query will yield the same results, which means that the first document on the results list will be the one with the identifier 1, but the scores will be slightly different. This is because the Lucene queries made from the last two examples are slightly different and thus the scores are different.

Modifying the score

The preceding example shows how to affect the result list by boosting particular query components – the fields. Another technique is to run a query and affect the score of the matched documents. In the following sections, we will summarize the possibilities offered by Elasticsearch. In the examples, we will use our library data that we have already used in the previous chapters.

Constant score query

A `constant_score` query allows us to take any query and explicitly set the value that should be used as the score that will be given for each matching document by using the `boost` parameter.

At first, this query doesn't seem to be practical. But when we think about building complex queries, this query allows us to set how many documents matching this query can affect the total score. Look at the following example:

```
curl -XGET 'localhost:9200/library/_search?pretty' -d '{
  "query" : {
    "constant_score" : {
      "query": {
        "query_string" : {
          "query" : "available:false author:heller"
        }
      }
    }
  }
}'
```

In our data, we have two documents with the available field set to `false`. One of these documents has an additional value in the author field. If we use a different query, the document with an additional value in the author field (a book with identifier 2) would be given a higher score, but, thanks to the constant score query, Elasticsearch will ignore that information during scoring. Both documents will be given a score equal to 1.0.

Boosting query

The next type of query that can be used with boosting is the boosting query. The idea is to allow us to define a part of query which will cause matched documents to have their scores lowered. The following example returns all the available books (available field set to true), but the books written by E. M. Remarque will have a negative boost of 0.1 (which means about ten times lower score):

```
curl -XGET 'localhost:9200/library/_search?pretty' -d '{
  "query" : {
    "boosting" : {
      "positive" : {
        "term" : {
          "available" : true
        }
      },
      "negative" : {
        "match" : {
          "author" : "remarque"
        }
      },
      "negative_boost" : 0.1
    }
  }
}'
```

The function score query

Till now we've seen two examples of queries that allowed us to alter the score of the returned documents. The third example we wanted to talk about, the function_score query, is way more complicated than the previously discussed queries. The function_score query is very useful when the score calculation is more complicated than giving a single boost to all the documents; boosting more recent documents is an example of a perfect use case for the function_score query.

Structure of the function query

The structure of the function query is quite simple and looks as follows:

```
{
 "query" : {
  "function_score" : {
   "query" : { ... },
   "functions" : [
     {
       "filter" : { ... },
       "FUNCTION" : { ... }
     }
   ],
   "boost_mode" : " ... ",
   "score_mode" : " ... ",
   "max_boost" : " ... ",
   "min_score" : " ... ",
   "boost" : " ... "
  }
 }
}
```

In general, the function score query can use a query, one of several functions, and additional parameters. Each function can have a filter defined to filter the results on which it will be applied. If no filter is given for a function, it will be applied to all the documents.

The logic behind the function score query is quite simple. First of all, the functions are matched against the documents and the score is calculated based on score_mode. After that, the query score for the document is combined with the score calculated for the functions and combined together on the basis of boost_mode.

Let's now discuss the parameters:

- Boost mode: The boost_mode parameter allows us to define how the score computed by the function queries will be combined with the score of the query. The following values are allowed:
  - multiply: The default behavior, which results in the query score being multiplied by the score computed from the functions
  - replace: The query score will be totally ignored and the document score will be equal to the score calculated by the functions
  - sum: The document score will be calculated as the sum of the query and the function scores

- ○ `avg`: The score of the document will be an average of the query score and the function score

- ○ `max`: The document will be given a maximum of query score and function score

- ○ `min`: The document will be given a minimum of query score and function score

- `Score mode`: The `score_mode` parameter defines how the score computed by the functions are combined together. The following `score_mode` parameter values are defined:

  - ○ `multiply`: The default behavior which results in the scores returned by the functions being multiplied

  - ○ `sum`: The scores returned by the defined functions are summed

  - ○ `avg`: The score returned by the functions is an average of all the scores of the matching functions

  - ○ `first`: The score of the first function with a filter matching the document is returned

  - ○ `max`: The maximum score of the functions is returned

  - ○ `min`: The minimum score of the functions is returned

There is one thing to remember – we can limit the maximum calculated score value by using the `max_boost` parameter in the function score query. By default, that parameter is set to `Float.MAX_VALUE`, which means the maximum `float` value.

The `boost` parameter allows us to set a query wide boost for the documents.

Of course, there is one thing we should remember – the score calculated doesn't affect which documents matched the query. Because of that, the `min_score` property has been introduced. It allows us to define the minimum score of the documents. Documents that have a score lower than the `min_score` property will be excluded from the results.

What we haven't talked about yet are the function scores that we can include in the functions section of our query. The currently available functions are:

- weight factor
- field value factor
- script score
- random
- decay

The weight factor function

The `weight factor` function allows us to multiply the score of the document by a given value. The value of the `weight` parameter is not normalized and is taken as is. An example using the weight function, where we multiply the score of the document by 20, looks as follows:

```
curl -XGET 'localhost:9200/library/_search?pretty' -d '{
 "query" : {
  "function_score" : {
   "query" : {
    "term" : {
     "available" : true
    }
   },
   "functions" : [
    { "weight" : 20 }
   ]
  }
 }
}'
```

Field value factor function

The `field_value_factor` function allows us to influence the score of the document by using a value of the field in that document. For example, to multiply the score of the document by the value of the year field, we run the following query:

```
curl -XGET 'localhost:9200/library/_search?pretty' -d '{
 "query" : {
  "function_score" : {
   "query" : {
    "term" : {
     "available" : true
    }
   },
   "functions" : [
    {
     "field_value_factor" : {
      "field" : "year",
```

```
      "missing" : 1
    }
  }
  ]
 }
}
}'
```

In addition to choosing the field whose value should be used, we can also control the behavior of the field value factor function by using the following properties:

- `factor`: The multiplication factor that will be used along with the field value. It defaults to 1.

- `modifier`: The modifier that will be applied to the `field` value. It defaults to none. It can take the value of `log`, `log1p`, `log2p`, `ln`, `ln1p`, `ln2p`, `square`, `sqrt`, and `reciprocal`.

- `missing`: The value that should be used when a document doesn't have any value in the field specified in the `field` property.

The script score function

The `script_score` function allows us to use a script to calculate the score that will be used as the score returned by a function (and thus will fall into behavior defined by the `boost_mode` parameter). An example of `script_score` usage is as follows (for the following example to work, inline scripting needs to be allowed, which means adding the `script.inline` property and setting it to on in `elasticsearch.yml`):

```
curl -XGET 'localhost:9200/library/_search?pretty' -d '{
  "query" : {
    "function_score" : {
      "query" : {
        "term" : {
          "available" : true
        }
      },
      "functions" : [
        {
          "script_score" : {
            "script" : {
            "inline" : "_score * _source.copies * parameter1",
```

```
      "params" : {
        "parameter1" : 12
      }
    }
  }
 }
]
}
}
}'
```

The random score function

By using the random_score function, we can generate a pseudo random score, by specifying a seed. In order to simulate randomness, we should specify a new seed every time. The random number will be generated by using the _uid field and the provided seed. If a seed is not provided, the current timestamp will be used. An example of using this is as follows:

```
curl -XGET 'localhost:9200/library/_search?pretty' -d '{
  "query" : {
    "function_score" : {
      "query" : {
        "term" : {
          "available" : true
        }
      },
      "functions" : [
        {
          "random_score" : {
            "seed" : 12345
          }
        }
      ]
    }
  }
}'
```

Decay functions

In addition to the earlier mentioned scoring functions, Elasticsearch exposes additional ones, called the `decay` functions. The difference from the previously described functions is that the score given by those functions lowers with distance. The distance is calculated on the basis of a single valued numeric field (such as a date, a geographical point, or a standard numeric field). The simplest example that comes to mind is boosting documents on the basis of distance from a given point or boosting on the basis of document date.

For example, let's assume that we have a point field that stores the location and we want our document's score to be affected by the distance from a point where the user stands (for example, our user sends a query from a mobile device). Assuming the user is at 52, 21, we could send the following query:

```
{
  "query" : {
   "function_score" : {
    "query" : {
     "term" : {
      "available" : true
     }
    },
    "functions" : [
     {
      "linear" : {
       "point" : {
        "origin" : "52, 21",
        "scale" : "1km",
        "offset" : 0,
        "decay" : 0.2
       }
      }
     }
    ]
   }
  }
}
```

In the preceding example, the linear is the name of the `decay` function. The value will decay linearly when using it. The other possible values are `gauss` and `exp`. We've chosen the linear decay function because of the fact that it sets the score to 0 when the field value exceeds the given origin value twice. This is useful when you want to lower the value of the documents that are too far away.

Note that the geographical searching capabilities of Elasticsearch will be discussed in the *Geo* section of *Chapter 8, Beyond Full-text Searching*.

Now let's discuss the rest of the query structure. The point is the name of the field we want to use for score calculation. If the document doesn't have a value in the defined field, it will be given a value of 1 for the time of calculation.

In addition to that, we've provided additional parameters. The `origin` and `scale` are required. The origin parameter is the central point from which the calculation will be done and the scale is the rate of decay. By default, the offset is set to 0. If defined, the decay function will only compute a score for the documents with value greater than the value of this parameter. The `decay` parameter tells Elasticsearch how much the score should be lowered and is set to 0.5 by default. In our case, we've said that, at the distance of 1 kilometer, the score should be reduced by 20% (0.2).

 We expect the `function_score` query to be modified and extended with the next versions of Elasticsearch (just as it was with Elasticsearch version 1.x). We suggest following the official documentation and the page dedicated to the `function_score` query at `https://www.elastic.co/guide/en/elasticsearch/reference/current/query-dsl-function-score-query.html`.

When does index-time boosting make sense?

In the previous section, we discussed boosting queries. This kind of approach to handling differences in the weight of documents is very handy, powerful, and easy to use. It is also sufficient in most situations. However, there are cases when a more convenient way of documents boosting is index-time boosting. One of such use case is the situation when we know which documents are important during the indexing phase. In such a case, we can prepare the document boost and include it as part of the document. We gain a boost that is independent from a query at the cost of reindexing the documents when the boost value is changed (because we need to apply the changed boost). In addition to that, the performance gets slightly better because some parts needed in the boosting process are already calculated at index time, which can matter when your indices have a large number of documents. Information about the boost is stored as a part of the normalization factor and because of that it is important to keep the norms turned on. This means that we can't set `norms.enabled` to `false` because we won't be able to use index time boosting.

Defining boosting in the mappings

It is also possible to directly define the field's boost in our mappings. This will result in Elasticsearch giving a boost for all the documents having a value in such a field. Of course, that will also happen during indexing time. The following example illustrates that:

```
{
    "mappings" : {
      "book" : {
        "properties" : {
          "title" : { "type" : "string" },
          "author" : { "type" : "string", "boost" : 10.0 }
        }
      }
    }
}
```

Thanks to the preceding boost, all queries will favor values found in the field named `author`. This also applies to queries using the `_all` field, because Elasticsearch will apply the boost to values copied between the fields.

Words with the same meaning

You may have heard about synonyms, words that have the same or similar meaning. Sometimes you would want to have some words matched when one of those words is entered into the search box. Let's recall our sample data from *Chapter 3, Searching Your Data*. There was a book called crime and punishment. What if we want that book to not only be matched when the words crime or punishment are used, but also when using the words such as criminality and abuse. At first glance, this may not sound like good behavior, but sometimes this is really needed, especially in use cases where there are multiple words meaning the same (like in medicine). To handle such use cases, we will use synonyms.

Synonym filter

Synonyms in Elasticsearch are handled on the analysis level – at both index and query time, by a dedicated synonyms filter. To use the synonym filter, we need to define our own analyzer. For example, let's define an analyzer that will be called synonym and will use the whitespace tokenizer and a single filter called `synonym`. Our filter's type property needs to be set to `synonym`, which tells Elasticsearch that this filter is a synonym filter.

In addition to that, we want to ignore case, so that the uppercased and lowercased synonyms are treated equally (set the `ignore_case` property to `true`). To define our custom synonym analyzer that uses a synonym filter when creating a new index, we would use the following command:

```
curl -XPOST 'localhost:9200/test' -d '{
  "index" : {
    "analysis" : {
      "analyzer" : {
        "synonym" : {
          "tokenizer" : "whitespace",
          "filter" : [
            "synonym"
          ]
        }
      },
      "filter" : {
        "synonym" : {
          "type" : "synonym",
          "ignore_case" : true,
          "synonyms" : [
            "crime => criminality"
          ]
        }
      }
    }
  }
}'
```

Synonyms in the mappings

In the definition you've just seen, we've specified the synonym rule in the mappings we send to Elasticsearch. To do that, we needed to add the synonyms property, which is an array of synonym rules. For example, the following part of the mappings definition defines a single synonym rule:

```
"synonyms" : [
  "crime => criminality"
]
```

The preceding rule tells Elasticsearch to change the crime term to the criminality term when the crime term is encountered during analysis.

Synonyms stored on the file system

Apart from storing the synonyms rules in the mappings, Elasticsearch allows us to use a file-based synonyms rule set. To use a file, we need to specify the `synonyms_path` property instead of the synonyms one. The `synonyms_path` property should be set to the name of the file that holds the synonym's definition and the specified file path is relative to the `Elasticsearch config` directory. So, if we store our synonyms in the `synonyms.txt` file and we save that file in the `config` directory, then, in order to use it, we should set `synonyms_path` to the value of `synonyms.txt`.

For example, this is how our synonym filter would look like if we want to use the synonyms stored in a file:

```
"filter" : {
  "synonym" : {
    "type" : "synonym",
    "synonyms_path" : "synonyms.txt"
  }
}
```

Defining synonym rules

So far we have discussed what we have to do in order to use synonym expansions in Elasticsearch. Now let's see what formats of synonyms are allowed.

Using Apache Solr synonyms

The most common synonym structure in the Apache Lucene world is probably the one used by Apache Solr (`http://lucene.apache.org/solr/`), the search engine built on top of Lucene, just like Elasticsearch is. This is the default way of handling synonyms in Elasticsearch and the possibilities of defining a new synonym are discussed in the following sections.

Explicit synonyms

A simple mapping allows us to map a list of words onto other words. So, in our case, if we want the word criminality to be mapped to crime and the word abuse to be mapped to punishment, we need to define the following entries:

```
criminality => crime
abuse => punishment
```

Of course, a single word can be mapped into multiple ones and multiple ones can be mapped into a single one. For example:

```
star wars, wars => starwars
```

The preceding example means that `star wars` and `wars` will be changed to `starwars` by the synonym filter.

Equivalent synonyms

In addition to the explicit mapping, Elasticsearch allows us to use equivalent synonyms. For example, the following definition will make all the words exchangeable so that you can use any of them to match a document that has one of them in its contents:

```
star, wars, star wars, starwars
```

Expanding synonyms

A synonym filter allows us to use one additional property when it comes to Apache Solr format synonyms – the `expand` property. When the `expand` property is set to `true` (by default it is set to `false`), all synonyms will be expanded by Elasticsearch to all equivalent forms. For example, let's say we have the following filter configuration:

```
"filter" : {
  "synonym" : {
    "type" : "synonym",
    "expand": false,
    "synonyms" : [
      "one, two, three"
    ]
  }
}
```

Elasticsearch will map the preceding synonym definition to the following:

```
one, two, three => one
```

This means that the words `one`, `two`, and `three` will be changed to `one`. However, if we set the expand property to `true`, the same synonym definition will be interpreted in the following way:

```
one, two, three => one, two, three
```

This basically means that each of the words from the left-side of the definition will be expanded to all the words on the right-side.

Using WordNet synonyms

If we want to use WordNet-structured (to learn more about WordNet, visit
`http://wordnet.princeton.edu/`) synonyms, we need to provide an additional
property for our synonym filter. The property name is `format` and we should set its
value to `wordnet` in order for Elasticsearch to understand that format.

Query or index-time synonym expansion

As with all the analyzers, one can wonder when to use the synonym filter – during
indexing, during querying, or maybe during indexing and querying. Of course,
it depends on your needs. However, remember that using index-time synonyms
requires data reindexing after each synonym change. That's because they need to
be reapplied to all the documents. If we use only the query-time synonyms, we can
update the synonym's lists and have them applied without data reindexation.

Understanding the explain information

Compared to databases, using systems capable of performing full-text search can
often be anything other than obvious. We can search in many fields simultaneously
and the data in the index can vary from the ones provided as the values of the
document fields (because of the analysis process, synonyms, abbreviations, and
others). It's even worse! By default, search engines sort data by relevance, which
means that each document is given a number indicating how similar the document
is to the query. The key point here is understanding the **how similar** phrase. As we
discussed in the beginning of the chapter, scoring takes many factors into account
– how many searched words were found in the document, how frequent the word
is, how many terms are in the field, and so on. This seems complicated and finding
out why a document was found and why another document is better is not easy.
Fortunately, Elasticsearch provides us with tools that can answer these questions
and we will look at them in this section.

Understanding field analysis

One of the common questions asked when analyzing the returned documents is why
a given document was not found. In many cases, the problem lies in the mappings
definition and the analysis process configuration. For debugging the analysis process,
Elasticsearch provides a dedicated REST API endpoint – the `_analyze` one.

Using it is very simple. Let's see how it is used by running a request to Elasticsearch to give us information on how the crime and punishment phrase is analyzed. To do that, we will run a command using HTTP GET to the _analyze REST end-point and we will provide the phrase as the request body. The following command does that:

```
curl -XGET 'localhost:9200/_analyze?pretty' -d 'Crime and Punishment'
```

In response, we get the following data:

```
{
  "tokens" : [ {
    "token" : "crime",
    "start_offset" : 0,
    "end_offset" : 5,
    "type" : "<ALPHANUM>",
    "position" : 0
  }, {
    "token" : "and",
    "start_offset" : 6,
    "end_offset" : 9,
    "type" : "<ALPHANUM>",
    "position" : 1
  }, {
    "token" : "punishment",
    "start_offset" : 10,
    "end_offset" : 20,
    "type" : "<ALPHANUM>",
    "position" : 2
  } ]
}
```

As we can see, Elasticsearch divided the input phrase into three tokens. During processing, the phrase was divided into tokens on the basis of whitespace characters and was lowercased. This shows us exactly what would be happening during the analysis process. We can also provide the name of the analyzer. For example, we can change the preceding command to something like this:

```
curl -XGET 'localhost:9200/_analyze?analyzer=standard&pretty' -d 'Crime and Punishment'
```

The preceding command will allow us to check how the standard analyzer analyzes the data.

It is worth noting that there is another form of analysis API available – one which allows us to provide tokenizers and filters. It is very handy when we want to experiment with configuration before creating the target mappings. Instead of specifying the analyzer parameter in the request, we provide the tokenizer and the filters parameters. We can provide a single tokenizer and a list of filters (separated by comma character). For example, to illustrate how tokenization using whitespace tokenizer works with lowercase and `kstem` filters we would run the following request:

```
curl -XGET 'localhost:9200/library/_analyze?tokenizer=whitespace&filters=
lowercase,kstem&pretty' -d 'John Smith'
```

As we can see, an analysis API can be very useful for tracking down bugs in the mapping configuration. It is also priceless when we want to solve problems with queries and matching. It can show us how our analyzers work, what terms they produce, and what the attributes of those terms are. With such information, analyzing the query problems will be easier to track down.

Explaining the query

In addition to looking at what happened during analysis, Elasticsearch allows us to explain how the score was calculated for a particular query and document. Let's look at the following example:

```
curl -XGET 'localhost:9200/library/book/1/_explain?pretty&q=quiet'
```

The preceding request specifies a document and a query to run. The document is specified in the URI and the query is passed using the q parameter. Using the _ explain endpoint, we ask Elasticsearch for an explanation about how the document was matched by Elasticsearch (or not matched). The response returned by Elasticsearch for the preceding request looks as follows:

```
{
   "_index" : "library",
   "_type" : "book",
   "_id" : "1",
   "matched" : true,
   "explanation" : {
     "value" : 0.057534903,
     "description" : "sum of:",
     "details" : [ {
       "value" : 0.057534903,
       "description" : "weight(_all:quiet in 0)
         [PerFieldSimilarity], result of:",
       "details" : [ {
```

```
            "value" : 0.057534903,
            "description" : "fieldWeight in 0, product of:",
            "details" : [ {
              "value" : 1.0,
              "description" : "tf(freq=1.0), with freq of:",
              "details" : [ {
                "value" : 1.0,
                "description" : "termFreq=1.0",
                "details" : [ ]
              } ]
            }, {
              "value" : 0.30685282,
              "description" : "idf(docFreq=1, maxDocs=1)",
              "details" : [ ]
            }, {
              "value" : 0.1875,
              "description" : "fieldNorm(doc=0)",
              "details" : [ ]
            } ]
          } ]
        }, {
          "value" : 0.0,
          "description" : "match on required clause, product of:",
          "details" : [ {
            "value" : 0.0,
            "description" : "# clause",
            "details" : [ ]
          }, {
            "value" : 3.2588913,
            "description" : "_type:book, product of:",
            "details" : [ {
              "value" : 1.0,
              "description" : "boost",
              "details" : [ ]
            }, {
              "value" : 3.2588913,
              "description" : "queryNorm",
              "details" : [ ]
            } ]
          } ]
        } ]
      }
    }
```

It can look slightly complicated and well, it is complicated. It is even worse if we realize that this is only a simple query! Elasticsearch, and more specifically the Lucene library, shows the internal information about the scoring process. We will only scratch the surface and will explain the most important things about the preceding response.

The first thing that you can notice is that for the particular query Elasticsearch provided the information if the document was a match or not. If the matched property is set to true, it means that the document was a match for the provided query.

The next important thing is the explanation object. It contains three properties: the value, the description, and the details. The value is the score calculated for the given part of the query. The description is the simplified text representation of the internal score calculation, and the details object contains detailed information about the score calculation. The nice thing is that the details object will again contain the same three properties and this is how Elasticsearch provides us with information on how the score is calculated.

For example, let's analyze the following part of the response:

```
"value" : 0.057534903,
"description" : "sum of:",
"details" : [ {
  "value" : 0.057534903,
  "description" : "weight(_all:quiet in 0)
    [PerFieldSimilarity], result of:",
  "details" : [ {
    "value" : 0.057534903,
    "description" : "fieldWeight in 0, product of:",
    "details" : [ {
      "value" : 1.0,
      "description" : "tf(freq=1.0), with freq of:",
      "details" : [ {
        "value" : 1.0,
        "description" : "termFreq=1.0",
        "details" : [ ]
      } ]
    }, {
      "value" : 0.30685282,
      "description" : "idf(docFreq=1, maxDocs=1)",
      "details" : [ ]
    }, {
      "value" : 0.1875,
      "description" : "fieldNorm(doc=0)",
      "details" : [ ]
    } ]
  } ]
} ]
```

The score of the element is `0.057534903` (the `value` property) and it is a sum of (we see that in the `description` property) all the inner elements. In the description on the first level of nesting of the preceding fragment, we can see that `PerFieldSimilarity` has been used and that the score of that element is the result of the inner elements – the second level of nesting.

On the second level of details nesting, we can see three elements. The first one shows us the score of the element, which is the product of the two scores of the elements below it. We can also see various internal statistics retrieved from the index: the term frequency which informs us how common the term is (`termFreq=1.0`), the inverted document frequency, which shows us how often the term appears in the documents (`idf(docFreq=1, maxDocs=1)`), and the field normalization factor (`fieldNorm(doc=0)`).

The Explain API supports the following parameters: `analyze_wildcard`, `analyzer`, `default_operator`, `df`, `fields`, `lenient`, `lowercase_expanded_terms`, `parent`, `preference`, `routing`, `_source`, `_source_exclude`, and `_source_include`. To learn more about all these parameters, refer to the official Elasticsearch documentation regarding **Explain API,** which is available at `https://www.elastic.co/guide/en/elasticsearch/reference/current/search-explain.html`.

Summary

The chapter we just finished was focused on querying; not about the matching part of it but mostly about scoring. We learned how Apache Lucene TF/IDF scoring works. We saw the scripting capabilities of Elasticsearch and we handled multilingual data. We used boosting to influence how the scores of the returned documents were calculated and we used synonyms. Finally, we used explain information to see how the document scores were calculated by the query.

In the next chapter, we will fully focus on Elasticsearch data analysis capabilities – the aggregations, their types, and how they can be used.

7
Aggregations for Data Analysis

In the previous chapter, we discussed the querying side of Elasticsearch again. We learned how the Lucene TF/IDF algorithm works and how to use Elasticsearch scripting capabilities. We handled multilingual data and influenced document scores with boosts. We used synonyms to match words that have the same meaning and we used Elasticsearch Explain API to see how document scores were calculated. By the end of this chapter, you will have learned the following topics:

- What are aggregations
- How the Elasticsearch aggregation engine works
- How to use metrics aggregations
- How to use buckets aggregations
- How to use pipeline aggregations

Aggregations

Introduced in Elasticsearch 1.0, aggregations are the heart of data analytics in Elasticsearch. Highly flexible and performant, aggregations brought Elasticsearch 1.0 to a new position as a full-featured analysis engine. Extended through the life of Elasticsearch 1.x, in 2.x they are yet more powerful, less memory demanding, and faster. With this framework, you can use Elasticsearch as the analysis engine for data extraction and visualization. Let's see how that functionality works and what we can achieve by using it.

General query structure

To use aggregations, we need to add an additional section in our query. In general, our queries with aggregations look like this:

```
{
    "query": { ... },
    "aggs" : {
      "aggregation_name" : {
        "aggregation_type" : {
           ...
        }
      }
    }
}
```

In the `aggs` property (you can use `aggregations` if you want; `aggs` is just an abbreviation), you can define any number of aggregations. Each aggregation is defined by its name and one of the types of aggregations that are provided by Elasticsearch. One thing to remember though is that the key defines the name of the aggregation (you will need it to distinguish particular aggregations in the server response). Let's take our `library` index and create the first query using use aggregations. A command sending such a query looks like this:

```
curl 'localhost:9200/library/_search?search_type=query_then_
fetch&size=0&pretty' -d '{
    "aggs": {
      "years": {
        "stats": {
           "field": "year"
        }
      },
      "words": {
        "terms": {
           "field": "copies"
        }
      }
    }
}'
```

This query defines two aggregations. The aggregation named `years` shows statistics for the `year` field. The `words` aggregation contains information about the terms used in a given field.

> In our examples we assumed that we perform aggregation in addition to searching. If we don't need found documents, a better idea is to use the `size` parameter and set it to 0. This omits some unnecessary work and is more efficient. In such a case, the endpoint should be `/library/_search?size=0`. You can read more about search types in *Chapter 3, Understanding the Querying Process*.

Let's now look at the response returned by Elasticsearch for the preceding query:

```
{
  "took" : 2,
  "timed_out" : false,
  "_shards" : {
    "total" : 5,
    "successful" : 5,
    "failed" : 0
  },
  "hits" : {
    "total" : 4,
    "max_score" : 0.0,
    "hits" : [ ]
  },
  "aggregations" : {
    "words" : {
      "doc_count_error_upper_bound" : 0,
      "sum_other_doc_count" : 0,
      "buckets" : [ {
        "key" : 0,
        "doc_count" : 2
      }, {
        "key" : 1,
        "doc_count" : 1
      }, {
        "key" : 6,
        "doc_count" : 1
      } ]
    },
    "years" : {
      "count" : 4,
      "min" : 1886.0,
      "max" : 1961.0,
```

```
        "avg" : 1928.0,
        "sum" : 7712.0
      }
    }
  }
}
```

As you see, both the aggregations (years and words) were returned. The first aggregation we defined in our query (years) returned general statistics for the given field gathered across all the documents that matched our query. The second of the defined aggregations (words) was a bit different. It created several sets called **buckets** that were calculated on the returned documents and each of the aggregated values was within one of these sets. As you can see, there are multiple aggregation types available and they return different results. We will see the differences in the later part of this section.

The great thing about the aggregation engine is that it allows you to have multiple aggregations and that aggregations can be nested. This means that you can have indefinite levels of nesting and any number of aggregations in general. The extended structure of the query is shown next:

```
{
   "query": { … },
   "aggs" : {
     "first_aggregation_name" : {
       "aggregation_type" : {
          ...
       },
     "aggregations" : {
         "first_nested_aggregation" : {
           ...
         },
         .
         .
         .
         "nth_nested_aggregation" : {
           ...
         }
       }
     },
     .
     .
     .
     "nth_aggregation_name" : {
       ...
     }
   }
}
```

Inside the aggregations engine

Aggregations work on the basis of results returned by the query. This is very handy as we get the information that we are interested in, both from the query as well as the data analysis perspective. So what does Elasticsearch do when we include the aggregation part of the query in the request that we send to Elasticsearch? First of all, the aggregation is executed on each relevant shard and the results are returned to the node that is responsible for running that query. That node waits for the partial results to be calculated; after it gets all the results, it merges the results, producing the final results.

This approach is nothing new when it comes to distributed systems and how they work and communicate, but can cause issues when it comes to the precision of the results. In most cases this is not a problem, but you should be aware about what to expect. Let's imagine the following example:

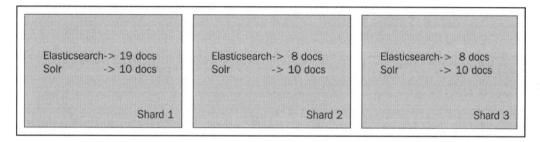

The preceding image shows a simplified view of three shards, each containing documents having only Elasticsearch and Solr terms in them. Now imagine that we are interested in a single term for our index. The terms aggregation when run using `size=1` would return a single `term`, that would be the one that is the most frequent (of course limited to the query we've run). So our aggregator node would see partial results telling us that `Elasticsearch` is present in 19 documents in **Shard 1** and the `Solr` term is present in 10 documents in **Shard 2** and **Shard 3**, which means that the top term is `Solr`, which is not true. This is an extreme case, but there are use cases (such as accounting) where precision is key and you should be aware about such situations.

 Compared to queries, aggregations are heavier for Elasticsearch in terms of both CPU cycles and memory consumption. We will discuss this in more detail in the *Caching Aggregations* section of this chapter.

Aggregation types

Elasticsearch 2.x allows us to use three types of aggregation: metrics, buckets, and pipeline. The metrics aggregations return a metric, just like the `stats` aggregation we used for the `stats` field. The bucket aggregations return buckets, the key and the number of documents sharing the same values, ranges, and so on, just like the `terms` aggregation we used for the `copies` field. Finally, the pipeline aggregations introduced in Elasticsearch 2.0 aggregate the output of the other aggregations and their metrics, which allows us to do even more sophisticated data analysis. Knowing all that, let's now look at all the aggregations we can use in Elasticsearch 2.x.

Metrics aggregations

We will start with the metrics aggregations, which can aggregate values from documents into a single metric. This is always the case with metrics aggregations – you can expect them to be a single metric on the basis of the data. Let's now take a look at the metrics aggregations available in Elasticsearch 2.x.

Minimum, maximum, average, and sum

The first group of metrics aggregations that we want to show you is the one that calculates the basic value from the given documents. These aggregations are:

- `min`: This calculates the minimum value from the given numeric field in the returned documents

- `max`: This calculates the maximum value from the given numeric field in the returned documents

- `avg`: This calculates an average from the given numeric field in the returned documents

- `sum`: This calculates the sum from the given numeric field in the returned documents

As you can see, the preceding mentioned aggregations are pretty self-explanatory. So, let's try to calculate the average value on our data. For example, let's assume that we want to calculate the average number of copies for our books. The query to do that will look as follows:

```
{
 "aggs" : {
  "avg_copies" : {
   "avg" : {
    "field" : "copies"
```

```
            }
          }
        }
      }
```

The results returned by Elasticsearch after running the preceding query will be as follows:

```
{
    "took" : 5,
    "timed_out" : false,
    "_shards" : {
      "total" : 5,
      "successful" : 5,
      "failed" : 0
    },
    "hits" : {
      "total" : 4,
      "max_score" : 0.0,
      "hits" : [ ]
    },
    "aggregations" : {
      "avg_copies" : {
        "value" : 1.75
      }
    }
}
```

So, we have an average of 1.75 copies per book. It is very easy to calculate – (6 + 0 + 1 + 0) / 4 is equal to 1.75. Seems that we got it right.

Missing values

The nice thing about the previously mentioned aggregations is that we can control what value Elasticsearch can use if the fields we've specified don't have any. For example, if we wanted Elasticsearch to use 0 as the value for the copies field in our previous example, we would add the missing property to our query and and set it to 0. For example:

```
{
  "aggs" : {
   "avg_copies" : {
    "avg" : {
     "field" : "copies",
     "missing" : 0
    }
   }
  }
}
```

Using scripts

The input values can also be generated by a script. For example, if we want to find the minimum value from all the values in the year field, but we want to subtract 1000 from those values, we will send an aggregation like the following one:

```
{
  "aggs": {
    "min_year": {
      "min": {
        "script": "doc['year'].value - 1000"
      }
    }
  }
}
```

> Note that the preceding query requires inline scripts to be allowed. This means that the query requires the script.inline property set to on in the elasticsearch.yml file.

In this case, the value the aggregations will use will be the original year field value reduced by 1000.

We can also use the value script capabilities of Elasticsearch. For example, to achieve the same as the previous script, we can use the following query:

```
{
  "aggs": {
    "min_year": {
      "min": {
        "field" : "year",
        "script" : {
          "inline" : "_value - factor",
          "params" : {
            "factor" : 1000
          }
        }
      }
    }
  }
}
```

If you are not familiar with Elasticsearch scripting capabilities, you can read more about it in the *Scripting capabilities of Elasticsearch* section of *Chapter 6, Make Your Search Better*.

One thing worth remembering is that using the command line may require proper escaping of the values in the doc array. For example, the command that executes the first scripted query would look as follows:

```
curl -XGET 'localhost:9200/library/_search?size=0&pretty' -d '{
 "aggs": {
  "min_year": {
   "min": {
    "script": "doc[\"year\"].value - 1000"
   }
  }
 }
}'
```

Field value statistics and extended statistics

The next aggregations we will discuss are the ones that provide us with the statistical information about the numeric field we are running the aggregation on: the stats and extended_stats aggregations.

For example, the following query provides extended statistics for the year field:

```
{
  "aggs" : {
   "extended_statistics" : {
    "extended_stats" : {
     "field" : "year"
    }
   }
  }
}
```

The response to the preceding query will be as follows:

```
{
  "took" : 1,
  "timed_out" : false,
  "_shards" : {
    "total" : 5,
```

```
      "successful" : 5,
      "failed" : 0
    },
    "hits" : {
      "total" : 4,
      "max_score" : 0.0,
      "hits" : [ ]
    },
    "aggregations" : {
      "extended_statistics" : {
        "count" : 4,
        "min" : 1886.0,
        "max" : 1961.0,
        "avg" : 1928.0,
        "sum" : 7712.0,
        "sum_of_squares" : 1.4871654E7,
        "variance" : 729.5,
        "std_deviation" : 27.00925767213901,
        "std_deviation_bounds" : {
          "upper" : 1982.018515344278,
          "lower" : 1873.981484655722
        }
      }
    }
  }
```

As you can see, in the response we got information about the number of documents with value in the year field, the minimum value, the maximum value, the average, and the sum. These are the values that we will get if we run the stats aggregation instead of extended_stats. The extended_stats aggregation provides additional information, such as the sum of squares, variance, and standard deviation. Elasticsearch provides two types of aggregations because extended_stats is slightly more expensive when it comes to processing power.

> The stats and extended_stats aggregations, similar to the min, max, avg, and sum aggregations, support scripting and allow us to specify which value should be used for the fields that don't have value in the specified field.

Value count

The `value_count` aggregation is a simple aggregation which allows counting values in aggregated documents. This is quite useful when used with nested aggregations. We are not focusing on that topic right now, but it is something to keep in mind. For example, to use the `value_count` aggregation on the copied field, we will run the following query:

```
{
  "aggs" : {
   "count" : {
    "value_count" : {
     "field" : "copies"
    }
   }
  }
}
```

 The `value_count` aggregation allows us to use scripts, discussed earlier in this chapter when we described the `min`, `max`, `avg`, and `sum` aggregations. Please refer to the beginning of Metrics aggregation section earlier in the current chapter for further reference.

Field cardinality

One of the aggregation that allows us to control how resource hungry the aggregation will be by controlling its precision, the `cardinality` aggregation calculates the count of distinct values in a given field. However, one thing needs to be remembered: the calculated count is an approximation, not the exact value. Elasticsearch uses the HyperLogLog++ algorithm (`http://static.googleusercontent.com/media/research.google.com/fr//pubs/archive/40671.pdf`) to calculate the value.

This aggregation has a wide variety of use cases, such as showing the number of distinct values in a field that is responsible for holding the status code for your indexed Apache access logs. One query, and you know the approximated count of the distinct values in that field.

For example, we can request the cardinality for our `title` field:

```
{
  "aggs" : {
   "card_title" : {
    "cardinality" : {
```

```
        "field" : "title"
      }
    }
  }
}
```

To control the precision of the cardinality calculation, we can specify the `precision_threshold` property – the higher the value, the more precise the aggregation will be and the more resources it will need. The current maximum `precision_threshold` value is `40000` and the default depends on the parent aggregation. An example query using the `precision_threshold` property looks as follows:

```
{
  "aggs" : {
    "card_title" : {
      "cardinality" : {
        "field" : "title",
        "precision_threshold" : 1000
      }
    }
  }
}
```

Percentiles

The percentiles aggregation is another example of aggregation in Elasticsearch. It uses an algorithmic approximation approach to provide us with results. It uses the T-Digest algorithm (`https://github.com/tdunning/t-digest/blob/master/docs/t-digest-paper/histo.pdf`) from Ted Dunning and Otmar Ertl and allows us to calculate percentiles: metrics that show us how many results are above a certain value. For example, the 99th percentile shows us the value that is greater than 99 percent of the other values.

Let's go into an example and look at a query that will calculate percentiles for the year field in our data:

```
{
  "aggs" : {
    "copies_percentiles" : {
      "percentiles" : {
        "field" : "year"
      }
    }
  }
}
```

The results returned by Elasticsearch for the preceding request will look as follows:

```
{
  "took" : 26,
  "timed_out" : false,
  "_shards" : {
    "total" : 5,
    "successful" : 5,
    "failed" : 0
  },
  "hits" : {
    "total" : 4,
    "max_score" : 0.0,
    "hits" : [ ]
  },
  "aggregations" : {
    "copies_percentiles" : {
      "values" : {
        "1.0" : 1887.2899999999997,
        "5.0" : 1892.4499999999998,
        "25.0" : 1918.25,
        "50.0" : 1932.5,
        "75.0" : 1942.25,
        "95.0" : 1957.25,
        "99.0" : 1960.25
      }
    }
  }
}
```

As you can see, the value that is higher than 99 percent of the values is `1960.25`.

You may wonder why such aggregation is important. It is very useful for performance metrics; for example, where we usually look at averages for some period of time. Imagine that the average response time of our queries for the last hour is 50 milliseconds, which is not bad. However, if the 95th percentile would show 2 seconds, that would mean that about 5 percent of the users had to wait two or more seconds for the search results, which is not that good.

By default, the `percentiles` aggregation calculates seven percentiles: 1, 5, 25, 50, 75, 95, and 99. We can control this by using the `percents` property and specify which percentiles we are interested in. For example, if we want to get only the 95th and the 99th percentile, we change our query to the following one:

```
{
  "aggs" : {
    "copies_percentiles" : {
      "percentiles" : {
```

```
    "field" : "year",
    "percents" : [ "95", "99" ]
   }
  }
 }
}
```

 Similar to the `min`, `max`, `avg`, and `sum` aggregations, the `percentiles` aggregation supports scripting and allows us to specify which value should be used for the fields that don't have value in the specified field.

We've mentioned earlier that the percentiles aggregation uses an algorithmic approach and is an approximation. As with all approximations, we can control the precision and memory usage of the algorithm. We do that by using the `compression` property, which defaults to `100`. It is an internal property of Elasticsearch and its implementation details may change between versions. It is worth knowing that setting the `compression` value to one higher than `100` can increase the algorithm precision at the cost of memory usage.

Percentile ranks

The `percentile_ranks` aggregation is similar to the `percentiles` one that we just discussed. It allows us to show which percentile a given value has. For example, to show us which percentile year `1932` and year `1960` are, we run the following query:

```
{
 "aggs" : {
  "copies_percentile_ranks" : {
   "percentile_ranks" : {
    "field" : "year",
    "values" : [ "1932", "1960" ]
   }
  }
 }
}
```

The response returned by Elasticsearch will be as follows:

```
{
  "took" : 2,
  "timed_out" : false,
  "_shards" : {
    "total" : 5,
```

```
      "successful" : 5,
      "failed" : 0
    },
    "hits" : {
      "total" : 4,
      "max_score" : 0.0,
      "hits" : [ ]
    },
    "aggregations" : {
      "copies_percentile_ranks" : {
        "values" : {
          "1932.0" : 49.5,
          "1960.0" : 61.5
        }
      }
    }
  }
}
```

Top hits aggregation

The top_hits aggregation keeps track of the most relevant document being aggregated. This doesn't sound very appealing, but it allows us to implement one of the most desired functionalities in Elasticsearch called document grouping, field collapsing, or document folding. Such functionality is very useful in some use cases—for example, when we want to show a book catalog but only one from a single publisher. To do that without the top_hits aggregation, we would have to run multiple queries. With the top_hits aggregation, we need only a single query.

The top_hits aggregation was introduced in Elasticsearch 1.3. In fact, the mentioned document folding is more or less a side effect and only one of the possible usage examples of the top_hits aggregation.

The idea behind the top_hits aggregation is simple. Every document that is assigned to a particular bucket can be also remembered. By default, only three documents per bucket are remembered.

> Note that, in order to show the full potential of the top_hits aggregation, we decided to use one of the bucketing aggregations as well and nest them to show the document grouping functionality implementation. The bucketing aggregations are described in detail later in this chapter.

To show you a potential use case that leverages the `top_hits` aggregation, we have decided to use a simple example. We would like to get the most relevant book published every 100 years. To do that we use the following query:

```
{
  "aggs": {
   "when": {
    "histogram": {
     "field": "year",
     "interval": 100
    },
     "aggs": {
      "book": {
       "top_hits": {
        "_source": {
         "include": [ "title", "available" ]
        },
        "size": 1
       }
      }
     }
    }
   }
  }
}
```

In the preceding example, we did the `histogram` aggregation on year ranges. Every bucket was created for every one hundred years. The nested `top_hits` aggregations remembers a single document with the greatest score from each bucket (because of the `size` property being set to 1). We added the `include` option only for simpler results, so that we only return the `title` and `available` fields for every aggregated document. The response returned by Elasticsearch will be as follows:

```
{
  "took" : 8,
  "timed_out" : false,
  "_shards" : {
    "total" : 5,
    "successful" : 5,
    "failed" : 0
  },
  "hits" : {
    "total" : 4,
    "max_score" : 0.0,
```

```
      "hits" : [ ]
    },
    "aggregations" : {
      "when" : {
        "buckets" : [ {
          "key" : 1800,
          "doc_count" : 1,
          "book" : {
            "hits" : {
              "total" : 1,
              "max_score" : 1.0,
              "hits" : [ {
                "_index" : "library",
                "_type" : "book",
                "_id" : "4",
                "_score" : 1.0,
                "_source" : {
                  "available" : true,
                  "title" : "Crime and Punishment"
                }
              } ]
            }
          }
        }, {
          "key" : 1900,
          "doc_count" : 3,
          "book" : {
            "hits" : {
              "total" : 3,
              "max_score" : 1.0,
              "hits" : [ {
                "_index" : "library",
                "_type" : "book",
                "_id" : "2",
                "_score" : 1.0,
                "_source" : {
                  "available" : false,
                  "title" : "Catch-22"
                }
              } ]
            }
          }
        } ]
      }
    }
  }
}
```

We can see that, because of the `top_hits` aggregation, we have the most scoring document (from each bucket) included in the response. In our particular case, the query was the `match_all` one and all the documents had the same score, so the top-scoring document for every bucket was more or less random. However, you need to remember that this is the default behavior. If we want to have custom sorting, this is not a problem for Elasticsearch. We just need to add the `sort` property for our `top_hits` aggregator. For example, we can return the first book from a given century:

```
{
 "aggs": {
  "when": {
   "histogram": {
    "field": "year",
    "interval": 100
   },
   "aggs": {
    "book": {
     "top_hits": {
      "sort": {
       "year": "asc"
      },
      "_source": {
       "include": [ "title", "available" ]
      },
      "size": 1
     }
    }
   }
  }
 }
}
```

We added sorting to the `top_hits` aggregation, so the results are sorted on the basis of the `year` field. This means that the first document will be the one with the lowest value in that field and this is the document that is going to be returned for each bucket.

Additional parameters

Sorting and field inclusion is not everything that we can we do inside the `top_hits` aggregation. Because this aggregation returns documents, we can also use functionalities such as:

- highlighting
- explain
- scripting

- fielddata field (uninverted representation of the fields)
- version

We just need to include an appropriate section in the `top_hits` aggregation body, similar to what we do when we construct a query. For example:

```
{
  "aggs": {
    "when": {
      "histogram": {
        "field": "year",
        "interval": 100
      },
      "aggs": {
        "book": {
          "top_hits": {
            "highlight": {
              "fields": {
              "title": {}
              }
            },
            "explain": true,
            "version": true,
            "_source": {
            "include": [ "title", "available" ]
            },
            "fielddata_fields" : ["title"],
            "script_fields": {
              "century": {
                "script": "(doc[\"year\"].value / 100).intValue()"
              }
            },
            "size": 1
          }
        }
      }
    }
  }
}
```

 Note that the preceding query requires the inline scripts to be allowed. This means that the query requires the `script.inline` property set to on in the `elasticsearch.yml` file.

Geo bounds aggregation

The `geo_bounds` aggregation is a simple aggregation that allows us to compute the bounding box that includes all the `geo_point` type field values from the aggregated documents.

 If you are interested in spatial searches, the section dedicated to it is called **Geo** and is included in *Chapter 8, Beyond Full-text Searching*.

We only need to provide the field (by using the field property; it needs to be of the `geo_point` type). We can also provide `wrap_longitude` (values `true` or `false`; it defaults to `true`) if the bounding box is allowed to overlap the international date line. In response, we get the latitude and longitude of the top-left and bottom-right corners of the bounding box. An example query using this aggregation looks as follows (using the hypothetical `location` field):

```
{
 "aggs" : {
  "box" : {
   "geo_bounds" : {
    "field" : "location"
   }
  }
 }
}
```

Scripted metrics aggregation

The last metric aggregation we want to discuss is the `scripted_metric` aggregation, which allows us to define our own aggregation calculation using scripts. For this aggregation, we can provide the following scripts (`map_script` is the only required one, the rest are optional):

- `init_script`: This script is run during initialization and allows us to set up an initial state of the calculation.

- `map_script`: This is the only required script. It is executed once for every document that needs to store the calculation in an object called `_agg`.

- `combine_script`: This script is executed once on each shard after Elasticsearch finishes document collection on that shard.

- `reduce_script`: This script is executed once on the node that is coordinating a particular query execution. This script has access to the `_aggs` variable, which is an array of the values returned by `combine_script`.

For example, we can use the `scripted_metric` aggregation to calculate all the copies of all the books we have in our library by running the following request (we show the whole request to show how the names are escaped):

```
curl -XGET 'localhost:9200/library/_search?size=0&pretty' -d '{
 "aggs" : {
  "all_copies" : {
   "scripted_metric" : {
    "init_script" : "_agg[\"all_copies\"] = 0",
    "map_script" : "_agg.all_copies += doc.copies.value",
    "combine_script" : "return _agg.all_copies",
    "reduce_script" : "sum = 0; for (number in _aggs) { sum += number
      }; return sum"
   }
  }
 }
}'
```

Of course, the preceding script is just a simple sum and we could use sum aggregation, but we just wanted to show you a simple example of what you can do with the `scripted_metric` aggregation.

 Note that the preceding query requires inline scripts to be allowed. This means that the query requires the `script.inline` property set to on in the `elasticsearch.yml` file.

As you can see, the `init_script` part of the aggregation is used to initialize the `all_copies` variable. Next, we have `map_script`, which is executed once for every document and we just add the value of the `copies` field to the earlier initialized variable. The `combine_script` part, executed once on each shard, tells Elasticsearch to return the calculated variable. Finally, the `reduce_script` part, executed once for the whole query on the aggregator node, will run a `for` loop, which will go through all the returned values that are stored in the `_aggs` array and return the sum of those. The final result returned by Elasticsearch for the preceding query looks as follows:

```
{
  "took" : 2,
  "timed_out" : false,
  "_shards" : {
    "total" : 5,
    "successful" : 5,
```

```
      "failed" : 0
    },
    "hits" : {
      "total" : 4,
      "max_score" : 0.0,
      "hits" : [ ]
    },
    "aggregations" : {
      "all_copies" : {
        "value" : 7
      }
    }
  }
}
```

Buckets aggregations

The second type of aggregations that we will discuss are the buckets aggregations. In comparison to metrics aggregations, bucket aggregation returns data not as a single metric but as a list of key value pairs called buckets. For example, the terms aggregation returns the number of documents associated with each term in a given field. The very powerful thing about buckets aggregations is that they can have sub-aggregations, which means that we can nest other aggregations inside the aggregations that return buckets (we will discuss this at the end of the buckets aggregation discussion). Let's look at the bucket aggregations that are provided by Elasticsearch now.

Filter aggregation

The filter aggregation is a simple bucketing aggregation that allows us to filter the results to a single bucket. For example, let's assume that we want to get a count and the average copies count of all the books that are novels, which means they have the term novel in the tags field. The query that will return such results looks as follows:

```
{
  "aggs" : {
    "novels_count" : {
      "filter" : {
        "term": {
          "tags": "novel"
        }
      },
      "aggs" : {
        "avg_copies" : {
```

```
      "avg" : {
        "field" : "copies"
      }
     }
    }
   }
  }
 }
}
```

As you can see, we defined the filter in the `filter` section of the aggregation definition and we defined a second nested aggregation. The nested aggregation is the one that will be run on the filtered documents.

The response returned by Elasticsearch looks as follows:

```
{
  "took" : 13,
  "timed_out" : false,
  "_shards" : {
    "total" : 5,
    "successful" : 5,
    "failed" : 0
  },
  "hits" : {
    "total" : 4,
    "max_score" : 0.0,
    "hits" : [ ]
  },
  "aggregations" : {
    "novels_count" : {
      "doc_count" : 2,
      "avg_copies" : {
        "value" : 3.5
      }
    }
  }
}
```

In the returned bucket, we have information about the number of documents (represented by the `doc_count` property) and the average number of copies, which is all we wanted.

Filters aggregation

The second bucket aggregation we want to show you is the `filters` aggregation. While the previously discussed `filter` aggregation resulted in a single bucket, the `filters` aggregation returns multiple buckets – one for each of the defined filters. Let's extend our previous example and assume that, in addition to the average number of copies for the novels, we also want to know the average number of copies for the books that are available. The query that will get us this information will use the `filters` aggregation and will look as follows:

```
{
  "aggs" : {
    "count" : {
      "filters" : {
        "filters" : {
          "novels" : {
            "term" : {
              "tags" : "novel"
            }
          },
          "available" : {
            "term" : {
              "available" : true
            }
          }
        }
      },
      "aggs" : {
        "avg_copies" : {
          "avg" : {
            "field" : "copies"
          }
        }
      }
    }
  }
}
```

Let's stop here and look at the definition of the aggregation. As you can see, we defined two filters using the `filters` section of the `filters` aggregation. Each filter has a name and the actual Elasticsearch filter; the first is called `novels` and the second is called `available`. Elasticsearch will use these names in the returned response. The thing to remember is that Elasticsearch will create a bucket for each defined filter and will calculate the nested aggregation that we defined – in our case, the one that calculates the average number of copies.

The filters aggregation allows us to return one more bucket in addition to the defined ones – a bucket with all the documents that didn't match the filters. In order to calculate such a bucket, we need to add the `other_bucket` property to the body of the aggregation and set it to `true`.

The results returned by Elasticsearch are as follows:

```
{
  "took" : 4,
  "timed_out" : false,
  "_shards" : {
    "total" : 5,
    "successful" : 5,
    "failed" : 0
  },
  "hits" : {
    "total" : 4,
    "max_score" : 0.0,
    "hits" : [ ]
  },
  "aggregations" : {
    "count" : {
      "buckets" : {
        "novels" : {
          "doc_count" : 2,
          "avg_copies" : {
            "value" : 3.5
          }
        },
        "available" : {
          "doc_count" : 2,
          "avg_copies" : {
            "value" : 0.5
          }
        }
      }
    }
  }
}
```

As you can see, we got two buckets, which is what we expected.

Terms aggregation

One of the most commonly used bucket aggregations is the `terms` aggregation. It allows us to get information about the terms and the count of documents having those terms. For example, one of the simplest uses is getting the count of the books that are available and not available. We can do that by running the following query:

```
{
  "aggs" : {
   "counts" : {
    "terms" : {
     "field" : "available"
    }
   }
  }
}
```

In the response, we will get two buckets (because the `Boolean` field can only have two values – `true` and `false`). Here, this will look as follows:

```
{
  "took" : 7,
  "timed_out" : false,
  "_shards" : {
    "total" : 5,
    "successful" : 5,
    "failed" : 0
  },
  "hits" : {
    "total" : 4,
    "max_score" : 0.0,
    "hits" : [ ]
  },
  "aggregations" : {
    "counts" : {
      "doc_count_error_upper_bound" : 0,
      "sum_other_doc_count" : 0,
      "buckets" : [ {
        "key" : 0,
        "key_as_string" : "false",
        "doc_count" : 2
      }, {
        "key" : 1,
        "key_as_string" : "true",
```

```
            "doc_count" : 2
        } ]
      }
    }
  }
}
```

By default, the data is sorted on the basis of document count, which means that the most common terms will be placed on top of the aggregation results. Of course, we can control this behavior by specifying the `order` property and providing the order just like we usually do when sorting by arbitrary field values. Elasticsearch allows us to sort by the document count (using the `_count` static value) and by the term (using the `_term` static value). For example, if we want to sort our preceding aggregation results by descending term, we can run the following query:

```
{
  "aggs" : {
    "counts" : {
      "terms" : {
        "field" : "available",
        "order" : { "_term" : "desc" }    }
    }
  }
}
```

However, that's not all when it comes to sorting. We can also sort by the results of the nested aggregations that were included in the query.

> `terms` aggregation, similar to the `min`, `max`, `avg`, and `sum` aggregations discussed in the metrics aggregation section of this chapter, supports scripting and allows us to specify which value should be used for the fields that don't have a value in the specified field.

Counts are approximate

The thing to remember when discussing `terms` aggregation is that the counts are approximate. This is because each shard provides its own counts and returns that aggregated information to the coordinating node. The coordinating node aggregates the information it got returning the final information to the client. Because of that, depending on the data and how it is distributed between the shards, some information about the counts may be lost and the counts will not be exact. Of course, when dealing with low cardinality fields, the approximation will be closer to exact numbers, but still this is something that should be considered when using the `terms` aggregation.

We can control how much information is returned from each of the shards to the coordinating node. We can do this by specifying the `size` and the `shard_size` properties. The `size` property specifies how many buckets will be returned at most. The higher the `size` property, the more accurate the calculation will be. However, that will cost us additional memory and CPU cycles, which means that the calculation will be more expensive and will put more pressure on the hardware. This is because the results returned to the coordinating node from each shard will be larger and the result merging process will be harder.

The `shard_size` property can be used to minimize the work that needs to be done by the coordinating node. When set, the coordinating node will fetch (from each shard) the number of buckets determined by the `shard_size` property. This allows us to increase the precision of the aggregation while avoiding the additional overhead on the coordinating node. Remember that the `shard_size` property cannot be smaller than the `size` property.

Finally, the `size` property can be set to 0, which will tell Elasticsearch not to limit the number of returned buckets. It is usually not wise to set the `size` property to 0 as it can result in high resource consumption. Also, avoid setting the `size` property to 0 for high cardinality fields as this will likely make your Elasticsearch cluster explode.

Minimum document count

Elasticsearch provides us with two additional properties, which can be useful in certain situations: `min_doc_count` and `shard_min_doc_count`. The `min_doc_count` property defaults to 1 and specifies how many documents must match a term to be included in the aggregation results. One thing to remember is that setting the `min_doc_count` property to 0 will result in returning all the terms, no matter if they have a matching document or not. This can result in a very large result set for aggregation results. For example, if we want to return terms matched by 5 or more documents, we will run the following query:

```
{
 "aggs" : {
  "counts" : {
   "terms" : {
    "field" : "available",
    "min_doc_count" : 5    }
  }
 }
}
```

The `shard_min_doc_count` property is very similar and defines how many documents must match a term to be included in the aggregation's results, but on the shard level.

Range aggregation

The `range` aggregation allows us to define one or more ranges and Elasticsearch calculates buckets for them. For example, if we want to check how many books were published in a given period of time, we create the following query:

```
{
  "aggs": {
   "years": {
    "range": {
     "field": "year",
     "ranges": [
       { "to" : 1850 },
       { "from": 1851, "to": 1900 },
       { "from": 1901, "to": 1950 },
       { "from": 1951, "to": 2000 },
       { "from": 2001 }
     ]
    }
   }
  }
}
```

We specify the field we want the aggregation to be calculated on and the array of ranges. Each range is defined by one or two properties: the `two` and `from` similar to the range queries which we already discussed.

The result returned by Elasticsearch for our data looks as follows:

```
{
  "took" : 23,
  "timed_out" : false,
  "_shards" : {
    "total" : 5,
    "successful" : 5,
    "failed" : 0
  },
  "hits" : {
    "total" : 4,
    "max_score" : 0.0,
    "hits" : [ ]
  },
  "aggregations" : {
    "years" : {
```

```
"buckets" : [ {
  "key" : "*-1850.0",
  "to" : 1850.0,
  "to_as_string" : "1850.0",
  "doc_count" : 0
}, {
  "key" : "1851.0-1900.0",
  "from" : 1851.0,
  "from_as_string" : "1851.0",
  "to" : 1900.0,
  "to_as_string" : "1900.0",
  "doc_count" : 1
}, {
  "key" : "1901.0-1950.0",
  "from" : 1901.0,
  "from_as_string" : "1901.0",
  "to" : 1950.0,
  "to_as_string" : "1950.0",
  "doc_count" : 2
}, {
  "key" : "1951.0-2000.0",
  "from" : 1951.0,
  "from_as_string" : "1951.0",
  "to" : 2000.0,
  "to_as_string" : "2000.0",
  "doc_count" : 1
}, {
  "key" : "2001.0-*",
  "from" : 2001.0,
  "from_as_string" : "2001.0",
  "doc_count" : 0
} ]
        }
      }
    }
```

For example, between 1901 and 1950 we had two books released.

> The range aggregation, similar to the min, max, avg, and sum aggregations discussed in the metrics aggregations section of this chapter, supports scripting and allows us to specify which value should be used for the fields that don't have a value in the specified field.

Keyed buckets

One thing that should mention when it comes to the range aggregation is that we can give the defined ranges names. For example, let's assume that we want to use the names Before 18th century for the books released before 1799, 18th century for the books released between 1800 and 1900, 19th century for the books released between 1900 and 1999, and After 19th century for the books released after 2000. We can do this by adding the key property to each defined range, giving it the name, and adding the keyed property set to true. Setting the keyed property to true will associate a unique string value to each bucket and the key property defines the name for the bucket that will be used as the unique name. A query that does that will look as follows:

```
{
  "aggs": {
    "years": {
      "range": {
        "field": "year",
        "keyed": true,
        "ranges": [
          { "key": "Before 18th century", "to": 1799 },
          { "key": "18th century", "from": 1800, "to": 1899 },
          { "key": "19th century", "from": 1900, "to": 1999 },
          { "key": "After 19th century", "from": 2000 }
        ]
      }
    }
  }
}
```

The response returned by Elasticsearch in such a case will look as follows:

```
{
  "took" : 2,
  "timed_out" : false,
  "_shards" : {
    "total" : 5,
    "successful" : 5,
    "failed" : 0
  },
  "hits" : {
    "total" : 4,
    "max_score" : 0.0,
```

```
        "hits" : [ ]
    },
    "aggregations" : {
        "years" : {
            "buckets" : {
                "Before 18th century" : {
                    "to" : 1799.0,
                    "to_as_string" : "1799.0",
                    "doc_count" : 0
                },
                "18th century" : {
                    "from" : 1800.0,
                    "from_as_string" : "1800.0",
                    "to" : 1899.0,
                    "to_as_string" : "1899.0",
                    "doc_count" : 1
                },
                "19th century" : {
                    "from" : 1900.0,
                    "from_as_string" : "1900.0",
                    "to" : 1999.0,
                    "to_as_string" : "1999.0",
                    "doc_count" : 3
                },
                "After 19th century" : {
                    "from" : 2000.0,
                    "from_as_string" : "2000.0",
                    "doc_count" : 0
                }
            }
        }
    }
}
```

 An important and quite useful point about the `range` aggregation is that the defined ranges need not be disjoint. In such cases, Elasticsearch will properly count the document for multiple buckets.

Date range aggregation

The date_range aggregation is similar to the previously discussed range aggregation but it is designed for fields that use date-based types. However, in the library index, the documents have years, but the field is a number, not a date. For the purpose of showing how this aggregation works, let's imagine that we want to extend our library index to support newspapers. To do this we will create a new index (called library2) by using the following command:

```
curl -XPOST localhost:9200/_bulk --data-binary '{ "index": {"_index":
"library2", "_type": "book", "_id": "1"}}
{ "title": "Fishing news", "published": "2010/12/03 10:00:00", "copies":
3, "available": true }
{ "index": {"_index": "library2", "_type": "book", "_id": "2"}}
{ "title": "Knitting magazine", "published": "2010/11/07 11:32:00",
"copies": 1, "available": true }
{ "index": {"_index": "library2", "_type": "book", "_id": "3"}}
{ "title": "The guardian", "published": "2009/07/13 04:33:00", "copies":
0, "available": false }
{ "index": {"_index": "library2", "_type": "book", "_id": "4"}}
{ "title": "Hadoop World", "published": "2012/01/01 04:00:00", "copies":
6, "available": true }
'
```

For the purpose of this example, we will leave the mappings definition for Elasticsearch – this is sufficient in this case. Let's start with the first query using the date_range aggregation:

```
{
  "aggs": {
   "years": {
    "date_range": {
     "field": "published",
     "ranges": [
      { "to" : "2009/12/31" },
      { "from": "2010/01/01", "to": "2010/12/31" },
      { "from": "2011/01/01" }
     ]
    }
   }
  }
}
```

Compared with the ordinary `range` aggregation, the only thing that changed is the aggregation type, which is now `date_range`. The dates can be passed as a string in a form recognized by Elasticsearch or as a number value (number of milliseconds since 1970-01-01). The response returned by Elasticsearch for the preceding query looks as follows:

```
{
    "took" : 5,
    "timed_out" : false,
    "_shards" : {
        "total" : 5,
        "successful" : 5,
        "failed" : 0
    },
    "hits" : {
        "total" : 4,
        "max_score" : 0.0,
        "hits" : [ ]
    },
    "aggregations" : {
        "years" : {
            "buckets" : [ {
                "key" : "*-2009/12/31 00:00:00",
                "to" : 1.2622176E12,
                "to_as_string" : "2009/12/31 00:00:00",
                "doc_count" : 1
            }, {
                "key" : "2010/01/01 00:00:00-2010/12/31 00:00:00",
                "from" : 1.262304E12,
                "from_as_string" : "2010/01/01 00:00:00",
                "to" : 1.2937536E12,
                "to_as_string" : "2010/12/31 00:00:00",
                "doc_count" : 2
            }, {
                "key" : "2011/01/01 00:00:00-*",
                "from" : 1.29384E12,
                "from_as_string" : "2011/01/01 00:00:00",
                "doc_count" : 1
            } ]
        }
    }
}
```

As you can see, the response is no different when compared to the response returned by the range aggregation. We have two attributes for each bucket - named `from` and `to` which represent the number of milliseconds from 1970-01-01. The properties `from_as_string` and `to_as_string` present the same information as `from` and `to`, but in a human-readable form. Of course the `keyed` parameter and `key` in the definition of date range work in the already described way.

Elasticsearch also allows us to define the format of presented dates using the `format` attribute. In our example, we presented the dates with year resolution, so the day and time parts were unnecessary. If we want to show the month names, we can send a query such as the following one:

```
{
  "aggs": {
   "years": {
    "date_range": {
     "field": "published",
     "format": "MMMM YYYY",
     "ranges": [
       { "to" : "December 2009" },
       { "from": "January 2010", "to": "December 2010" },
       { "from": "January 2011" }
     ]
    }
   }
  }
}
```

Note that the dates in the `to` and `from` parameters also need to be provided in the specified format. One of the returned ranges looks as follows:

```
{
  "key" : "January 2010-December 2010",
  "from" : 1.262304E12,
  "from_as_string" : "January 2010",
  "to" : 1.2911616E12,
  "to_as_string" : "December 2010",
  "doc_count" : 1
}
```

 The available formats we can use in `format` are defined in the Joda Time library. The full list is available at `http://joda-time.sourceforge.net/apidocs/org/joda/time/format/DateTimeFormat.html`.

There is one more thing about the `date_range` aggregation that we want to mention. Imagine that some time we may want to build an aggregation that can change with time. For example, we may want to see how many newspapers were published in the last 3, 6, 9, and 12 months. This is possible without the need to adjust the query every time, as we can use constants such as `now-9M`. The following example shows this:

```
{
 "aggs": {
  "years": {
   "date_range": {
    "field": "published",
    "format": "dd-MM-YYYY",
    "ranges": [
     { "to" : "now-9M/M"  },
     { "to" : "now-9M"  },
     { "from": "now-6M/M", "to": "now-9M/M" },
     { "from": "now-3M/M" }
    ]
   }
  }
 }
}
```

The key here is expressions such as `now-9M`. Elasticsearch does the math and generates the appropriate value. For example, you can use `y` (year), `M` (month), `w` (week), `d` (day), `h` (hour), `m` (minute), and `s` (second). For example, the expression `now+3d` means three days from now. The `/M` in our example takes only the date rounded to months. Thanks to such notation, we only count full months. The second advantage is that the calculated date is more cache-friendly without the rounding date changes every millisecond that make every cache based on the range irrelevant and basically useless in most cases.

IPv4 range aggregation

A very interesting aggregation is the `ip_range` one as it works on Internet addresses. It works on the fields defined with the `ip` type and allows defining ranges given by the IP range in CIDR notation (http://en.wikipedia.org/wiki/Classless_Inter-Domain_Routing). An example usage of the `ip_range` aggregation looks as follows:

```
{
 "aggs": {
  "access": {
   "ip_range": {
```

```
      "field": "ip",
      "ranges": [
        { "from": "192.168.0.1", "to": "192.168.0.254" },
        { "mask": "192.168.1.0/24" }
      ]
    }
   }
  }
 }
}
```

The response to the preceding query is as follows:

```
        "access": {
          "buckets": [
            {
              "from": 3232235521,
              "from_as_string": "192.168.0.1",
              "to": 3232235774,
              "to_as_string": "192.168.0.254",
              "doc_count": 0
            },
            {
              "key": "192.168.1.0/24",
              "from": 3232235776,
              "from_as_string": "192.168.1.0",
              "to": 3232236032,
              "to_as_string": "192.168.2.0",
              "doc_count": 4
            }
          ]
        }
```

Similar to the range aggregation, we define both ends of the brackets and the mask. The rest is done by Elasticsearch itself.

Missing aggregation

The missing aggregation allows us to create a bucket and see how many documents have no value in a specified field. For example, we can check how many of our books in the library index don't have the original title defined – the otitle field. To do this, we run the following query:

```
{
  "aggs": {
    "missing_original_title": {
```

```
      "missing": {
       "field": "otitle"
     }
    }
   }
  }
```

The response returned by Elasticsearch in this case will look as follows:

```
{
   "took" : 15,
   "timed_out" : false,
   "_shards" : {
     "total" : 5,
     "successful" : 5,
     "failed" : 0
   },
   "hits" : {
     "total" : 4,
     "max_score" : 0.0,
     "hits" : [ ]
   },
   "aggregations" : {
     "missing_original_title" : {
        "doc_count" : 2
     }
   }
}
```

As we can see, we have two documents without the `otitle` field.

Histogram aggregation

The `histogram` aggregation is an interesting one because of its automation. This aggregation defines buckets itself. We are only responsible for defining the field and the interval, and the rest is done automatically. The simplest form of a query that uses this aggregation looks as follows:

```
{
 "aggs": {
  "years": {
   "histogram": {
    "field" : "year",
    "interval": 100
   }
  }
 }
}
```

The new information we need to provide is `interval`, which defines the length of every range that will be used to create a bucket. We set the interval to `100`, which in our case will result in buckets that are 100 years wide. The aggregation part of the response to the preceding query that was sent to our `library` index is as follows:

```
{
  "took" : 13,
  "timed_out" : false,
  "_shards" : {
    "total" : 5,
    "successful" : 5,
    "failed" : 0
  },
  "hits" : {
    "total" : 4,
    "max_score" : 0.0,
    "hits" : [ ]
  },
  "aggregations" : {
    "years" : {
      "buckets" : [ {
        "key" : 1800,
        "doc_count" : 1
      }, {
        "key" : 1900,
        "doc_count" : 3
      } ]
    }
  }
}
```

Similar to the `range` aggregation, the `histogram` aggregation allows us to use the `keyed` property to define named buckets. The other available option is `min_doc_count`, which allows us to specify the minimum number of documents required to create a bucket. If we set the `min_doc_count` property to `zero`, Elasticsearch will also include buckets with the document count of zero. We can also use the `missing` property to specify the value Elasticsearch should use when a document doesn't have a value in the specified field.

Date histogram aggregation

As a `date_range` aggregation is a specialized form of the `range` aggregation, `date_histogram` is an extension of the `histogram` aggregation that works on dates. For the purpose of this example, we will again use the data we indexed when discussing the `date` aggregation. This means that we will run our queries against the index called `library2`. An example query using the `date_histogram` aggregation looks as follows:

```
{
 "aggs": {
  "years": {
   "date_histogram": {
    "field" : "published",
    "format" : "yyyy-MM-dd HH:mm",
    "interval" : "10d",
    "min_doc_count" : 1     }
   }
  }
 }
}
```

The difference between the `histogram` and `date_histogram` aggregations is the `interval` property. The value of this property is now a string describing the time interval, which in our case is 10 days. Of course we can set it to anything we want. It uses the same suffixes we discussed while talking about formats in the `date_range` aggregation. It is worth mentioning that the number can be a `float` value. For example, `1.5m` means that the length of the bucket will be one and a half minutes. The `format` attribute is the same as in the `date_range` aggregation. Thanks to it, Elasticsearch can add a human-readable date text according to the defined format. Of course the `format` attribute is not required but useful. In addition to that, similar to the other range aggregations, the `keyed` and `min_doc_count` attributes still work.

Time zones

Elasticsearch stores all the dates in the UTC time zone. You can define the time zone to be used by Elasticsearch by using the `time_zone` attribute. By setting this property, we basically tell Elasticsearch which time zone should be used to perform the calculations. There are three notations with which to set these attributes:

- We can set the hours offset; for example, `time_zone:5`
- We can use the time format; for example, `time_zone:"-04:30"`
- We can use the name of the time zone; for example, `time_zone:"Europe\ Warsaw"`

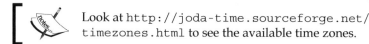
Look at http://joda-time.sourceforge.net/timezones.html to see the available time zones.

Geo distance aggregations

The next two aggregations are connected with maps and spatial searches. We will talk about geo types and queries in the *Elasticsearch spatial capabilities* section of *Chapter 8, Beyond Full-text Searching*, so feel free to skip these two topics now and return to them later.

Look at the following query:

```
{
  "aggs": {
    "neighborhood": {
      "geo_distance": {
        "field": "location",
        "origin": [-0.1275, 51.507222],
        "ranges": [
          { "to": 1200 },
          { "from": 1201 }
        ]
      }
    }
  }
}
```

You can see that the query is similar to the range aggregation. The preceding aggregation will calculate the number of documents that fall into two buckets: one closer than 1200 km and the second one further than 1200 km from the geographical point defined by the origin property (in the preceding case, the origin is London). The aggregation section of the response returned by Elasticsearch looks as follows:

```
"neighborhood": {
  "buckets": [
    {
      "key": "*-1200.0",
      "from": 0,
      "to": 1200,
      "doc_count": 1
    },
    {
      "key": "1201.0-*",
      "from": 1201,
```

```
                    "doc_count": 4
                }
            ]
        }
```

The `keyed` and the `key` attributes work in the `geo_distance` aggregation as well, so we can easily modify the response to our needs and create named buckets.

The `geo_distance` aggregation supports a few additional parameters that are shown in the following query:

```
{
 "aggs": {
  "neighborhood": {
   "geo_distance": {
    "field": "location",
    "origin": { "lon": -0.1275, "lat": 51.507222},
    "unit": "m",
    "distance_type" : "plane",
    "ranges": [
     { "to": 1200 },
     { "from": 1201 }
    ]
   }
  }
 }
}
```

We have highlighted three things in the preceding query. The first change is how we defined the `origin` point. This time we specified the location by providing the latitude and longitude explicitly.

The second change is the `unit` attribute. It defines the units used in the `ranges` array. The possible values are: km (the default, kilometers), mi (miles), in (inches), yd (yards), m (meters), cm (centimeters), and mm (millimeters).

The last attribute, `distance_type`, specifies how Elasticsearch calculates the distance. The possible values are (from the fastest but least accurate to the slowest but the most accurate): `plane`, `sloppy_arc` (the default), and `arc`.

Geohash grid aggregation

The second aggregation related to geographical analysis is based on grids and is called geohash_grid. It organizes areas into grids and assigns every location to a cell in such a grid. To do this efficiently, Elasticsearch uses **Geohash** (http://en.wikipedia.org/wiki/Geohash), which encodes the location into a string. The longer the string is, the more accurate the description of a particular location. For example, one letter is sufficient to declare a box of about five thousand square kilometers and 5 letters are enough to increase the accuracy to five square kilometers. Let's look at the following query:

```
{
  "aggs": {
    "neighborhood": {
      "geohash_grid": {
        "field": "location",
        "precision": 5
      }
    }
  }
}
```

We defined the geohash_grid aggregation with buckets that have a precision of five square kilometers (the precision attribute describes the number of letters used in the geohash string object). The table with resolutions versus the length of geohash can be found at https://www.elastic.co/guide/en/elasticsearch/reference/master/search-aggregations-bucket-geohashgrid-aggregation.html.

Of course, the more accurate we want the aggregation to be, the more resources Elasticsearch will consume, because of the number of buckets that the aggregation has to calculate. By default, Elasticsearch does not generate more than 10,000 buckets. You can change this behavior by using the size attribute, but keep in mind that the performance may suffer for very wide queries consisting of thousands of buckets.

Global aggregation

The global aggregation is an aggregation that defines a single bucket containing all the documents from a given index and type, and not influenced by the query itself. The thing that differentiates the global aggregation from all the others is that the global aggregation has an empty body. For example, look at the following query:

```
{
  "query" : {
    "term" : {
```

```
      "available" : "true"
    }
  },
  "aggs": {
   "all_books" : {
    "global" : {}
   }
  }
 }
}
```

In our `library` index, we only have two available books, but the response to the preceding query looks as follows:

```
{
   "took" : 1,
   "timed_out" : false,
   "_shards" : {
     "total" : 5,
     "successful" : 5,
     "failed" : 0
   },
   "hits" : {
     "total" : 3,
     "max_score" : 0.0,
     "hits" : [ ]
   },
   "aggregations" : {
     "all_books" : {
        "doc_count" : 4
     }
   }
}
```

As you can see, the `global` aggregation is not bound by the query. Because the result of the `global` aggregation is a single bucket containing all the documents (not narrowed down by the query itself), it is a perfect candidate for use as a top-level parent aggregation for nesting aggregations.

Significant terms aggregation

The `significant_terms` aggregation allows us to get the terms that are relevant and probably the most significant for a given query. The good thing is that it doesn't only show the top terms from the results of the given query, but also the one that seems to be the most important one.

The use cases for this aggregation type can vary from finding the most troublesome server working in your application environment, to suggesting nicknames from text. Whenever Elasticsearch sees a significant change in the popularity of a term, such a term is a candidate for being significant.

> Remember that the `significant_terms` aggregation is very expensive when it comes to resources and running against large indices. Work is being done to provide a lightweight version of that aggregation; as a result, the API for `significant_terms` aggregation may change in the future.

The best way to describe the `significant_terms` aggregation type is to use an example. Let's start with indexing 12 simple documents, which represent reviews of work done by interns:

```
curl -XPOST 'localhost:9200/interns/review/1' -d '{"intern" : "Richard",
"grade" : "bad", "type" : "grade"}'

curl -XPOST 'localhost:9200/interns/review/2' -d '{"intern" : "Ralf",
"grade" : "perfect", "type" : "grade"}'

curl -XPOST 'localhost:9200/interns/review/3' -d '{"intern" : "Richard",
"grade" : "bad", "type" : "grade"}'

curl -XPOST 'localhost:9200/interns/review/4' -d '{"intern" : "Richard",
"grade" : "bad", "type" : "review"}'

curl -XPOST 'localhost:9200/interns/review/5' -d '{"intern" : "Richard",
"grade" : "good", "type" : "grade"}'

curl -XPOST 'localhost:9200/interns/review/6' -d '{"intern" : "Ralf",
"grade" : "good", "type" : "grade"}'

curl -XPOST 'localhost:9200/interns/review/7' -d '{"intern" : "Ralf",
"grade" : "perfect", "type" : "review"}'

curl -XPOST 'localhost:9200/interns/review/8' -d '{"intern" : "Richard",
"grade" : "medium", "type" : "review"}'

curl -XPOST 'localhost:9200/interns/review/9' -d '{"intern" : "Monica",
"grade" : "medium", "type" : "grade"}'

curl -XPOST 'localhost:9200/interns/review/10' -d '{"intern" : "Monica",
"grade" : "medium", "type" : "grade"}'

curl -XPOST 'localhost:9200/interns/review/11' -d '{"intern" : "Ralf",
"grade" : "good", "type" : "grade"}'

curl -XPOST 'localhost:9200/interns/review/12' -d '{"intern" : "Ralf",
"grade" : "good", "type" : "grade"}'
```

Of course, to show the real power of the `significant_terms` aggregation, we should use a way larger data set. However, for the purpose of this book, we will concentrate on this example, so it is easier to illustrate how this aggregation works.

Now let's try finding the most significant grade for Richard. To do this we will use the following query:

```
curl -XGET 'localhost:9200/interns/_search?size=0&pretty' -d '{
 "query" : {
  "match" : {
   "intern" : "Richard"
  }
 },
 "aggregations" : {
  "description" : {
   "significant_terms" : {
    "field" : "grade"
   }
  }
 }
}'
```

The result of the preceding query looks as follows:

```
{
   "took" : 2,
   "timed_out" : false,
   "_shards" : {
     "total" : 5,
     "successful" : 5,
     "failed" : 0
   },
   "hits" : {
     "total" : 5,
     "max_score" : 0.0,
     "hits" : [ ]
   },
   "aggregations" : {
     "description" : {
       "doc_count" : 5,
       "buckets" : [ {
         "key" : "bad",
         "doc_count" : 3,
         "score" : 0.84,
         "bg_count" : 3
       } ]
     }
   }
}
```

As you can see, for our query Elasticsearch informed us that the most significant grade for Richard is bad. Maybe it wasn't the best internship for him; who knows.

Choosing significant terms

To calculate significant terms, Elasticsearch looks for data that reports a significant change in their popularity between two sets of data: the **foreground** set and the **background** set. The foreground set is the data returned by our query, while the background set is the data in our index (or indices, depending on how we run our queries). If a term exists in 10 documents out of one million indexed, but appears in 5 documents from the 10 returned, then such a term is definitely significant and worth concentrating on.

Let's get back to our preceding example now to analyze it a bit. Richard got three grades from the reviewers – **bad** three times, **medium** one time, and **good** one time. From these three, the bad value appeared in three out of the five documents matching the query. In general, the bad grade appeared in three documents (the `bg_count` property) out of the 12 documents in the index (this is our background set). This gives us 25 percent of the indexed documents. On the other hand, the bad grade appeared in three out of the five documents matching the query (this is our foreground set), which gives us 60 percent of the documents. As you can see, the change in popularity is significant for the `bad` grade and that's why Elasticsearch has returned it in the `significant_terms` aggregation results.

Multiple value analysis

The `significant_terms` aggregation can be nested and provide us with nice data analysis capabilities that connect two multiple sets of data. For example, let's try to find a significant grade for each of the interns that we have information about. To do this we will nest the `significant_terms` aggregation inside the `terms` aggregation. The query that does that looks as follows:

```
curl -XGET 'localhost:9200/interns/_search?size=0&pretty' -d '{
  "aggregations" : {
    "grades" : {
     "terms" : {
      "field" : "intern"
     },
     "aggregations" : {
      "significantGrades" : {
       "significant_terms" : {
        "field" : "grade"
       }
      }
     }
    }
   }
}'
```

The results returned by Elasticsearch for the preceding query are as follows:

```
{
  "took" : 2,
  "timed_out" : false,
  "_shards" : {
    "total" : 5,
    "successful" : 5,
    "failed" : 0
  },
  "hits" : {
    "total" : 12,
    "max_score" : 0.0,
    "hits" : [ ]
  },
  "aggregations" : {
    "grades" : {
      "doc_count_error_upper_bound" : 0,
      "sum_other_doc_count" : 0,
      "buckets" : [ {
        "key" : "ralf",
        "doc_count" : 5,
        "significantGrades" : {
          "doc_count" : 5,
          "buckets" : [ {
            "key" : "good",
            "doc_count" : 3,
            "score" : 0.48,
            "bg_count" : 4
          } ]
        }
      }, {
        "key" : "richard",
        "doc_count" : 5,
        "significantGrades" : {
          "doc_count" : 5,
          "buckets" : [ {
            "key" : "bad",
            "doc_count" : 3,
            "score" : 0.84,
            "bg_count" : 3
          } ]
        }
      }, {
```

```
        "key" : "monica",
        "doc_count" : 2,
        "significantGrades" : {
          "doc_count" : 2,
          "buckets" : [ ]
        }
    } ]
    }
  }
}
```

Sampler aggregation

The sampler aggregation is one of the experimental aggregations in Elasticsearch. It allows us to limit the sub aggregation processing to a sample of documents that are top-scoring ones. This allows filtering and potential removal of garbage in the data. It is a very nice candidate as a top-level aggregation to limit the amount of data the significant_terms aggregation runs on. The simplest example of using this aggregation is as follows:

```
{
  "aggs": {
    "sampler_example" : {
     "sampler" : {
      "field" : "tags",
      "max_docs_per_value" : 1,
      "shard_size" : 10
     },
     "aggs" : {
      "best_terms" : {
       "terms" : {
        "field" : "title"
       }
      }
     }
    }
  }
}
```

To see the real power of sampling, we will have to play with it on a larger data set, but for now we will discuss the preceding example. The `sampler` aggregation was defined with three properties: `field`, `max_docs_per_value`, and `shard_size`. The first two properties allow us to control the diversity of the sampling. We tell Elasticsearch how many documents at maximum (the value of the `max_doc_per_value` property) can be collected on a shard with the same value in the defined field (the value of the `field` property).

The `shard_size` property tells Elasticsearch how many documents (at most) to collect from each shard.

Children aggregation

The `children` aggregation is a single-bucket aggregation that creates a bucket with all the children of the specified type. Let's get back to the *Using the parent-child relationship* section in *Chapter 5, Extending Your Index Structure*, and let's use the created shop index. To create a bucket of all children documents with the variation type in the shop index, we run the following query:

```
{
 "aggs": {
  "variation_children" : {
   "children" : {
    "type" : "variation"
   }
  }
 }
}
```

The response returned by Elasticsearch is as follows:

```
{
   "took" : 4,
   "timed_out" : false,
   "_shards" : {
     "total" : 5,
     "successful" : 5,
     "failed" : 0
   },
   "hits" : {
     "total" : 3,
     "max_score" : 0.0,
     "hits" : [ ]
   },
```

```
    "aggregations" : {
      "variation_children" : {
        "doc_count" : 2
      }
    }
}
```

 Because the `children` aggregation uses parent–child functionality, it relies on the `_parent` field, which needs to be present.

Nested aggregation

In the *Using nested objects* section of *Chapter 5, Extending Your Index Structure,* we learned about nested documents. Let's use that data to look into the next type of aggregation – the nested one. Let's create the simplest working query, which looks like this (we use the `shop_nested` index created in the mentioned chapter):

```
{
  "aggs": {
    "variations": {
      "nested": {
        "path": "variation"
      }
    }
  }
}
```

The preceding query is similar in structure to any other aggregation. However, instead of providing the field name on which the aggregation should be calculated, it contains a single parameter `path`, which points to the nested document. In the response we get a number of nested documents:

```
{
  "took" : 4,
  "timed_out" : false,
  "_shards" : {
    "total" : 5,
    "successful" : 5,
    "failed" : 0
  },
  "hits" : {
    "total" : 1,
    "max_score" : 0.0,
```

```
      "hits" : [ ]
    },
    "aggregations" : {
      "variations" : {
        "doc_count" : 2
      }
    }
  }
}
```

The preceding response means that we have two nested documents in the index, with the provided type `variation`.

Reverse nested aggregation

The `reverse_nested` aggregation is a special, single-bucket aggregation that allows aggregation on parent documents from the nested documents. The `reverse_nested` aggregation doesn't have a body similar to global aggregation. Sounds quite complicated, but it is not. Let's look at the following query that we run against the `shop_nested` index created in *Chapter 5, Extending Your Index Structure* in the *Using nested objects* section:

```
{
 "aggs": {
  "variations": {
   "nested": {
    "path": "variation"
   },
   "aggs" : {
    "sizes" : {
     "terms" : {
      "field" : "variation.size"
     },
     "aggs" : {
      "product_name_terms" : {
       "reverse_nested" : {},
       "aggs" : {
        "product_name_terms_per_size" : {
         "terms" : {
          "field" : "name"
         }
        }
       }
      }
     }
    }
   }
  }
 }
}
```

```
        }
       }
      }
     }
    }
```

We start with the top level aggregation, which is the same `nested` aggregation that we used when discussing the `nested` aggregation. However, we include a sub-aggregation that uses `reverse_nested` to be able to show terms from the title for each size returned by the top-level nested aggregation. This is possible because, when the `reverse_nested` aggregation is used, Elasticsearch calculates the data on the basis of the parent documents instead of using the nested documents.

 Remember that the `reverse_nested` aggregation must be used inside the `nested` aggregation.

The response to the preceding query will look as follows:

```
{
   "took" : 7,
   "timed_out" : false,
   "_shards" : {
     "total" : 5,
     "successful" : 5,
     "failed" : 0
   },
   "hits" : {
     "total" : 1,
     "max_score" : 0.0,
     "hits" : [ ]
   },
   "aggregations" : {
     "variations" : {
       "doc_count" : 2,
       "sizes" : {
         "doc_count_error_upper_bound" : 0,
         "sum_other_doc_count" : 0,
         "buckets" : [ {
           "key" : "XL",
           "doc_count" : 1,
           "product_name_terms" : {
             "doc_count" : 1,
             "product_name_terms_per_size" : {
```

```
          "doc_count_error_upper_bound" : 0,
          "sum_other_doc_count" : 0,
          "buckets" : [ {
            "key" : "shirt",
            "doc_count" : 1
          }, {
            "key" : "test",
            "doc_count" : 1
          } ]
        }
      }
    }, {
      "key" : "XXL",
      "doc_count" : 1,
      "product_name_terms" : {
        "doc_count" : 1,
        "product_name_terms_per_size" : {
          "doc_count_error_upper_bound" : 0,
          "sum_other_doc_count" : 0,
          "buckets" : [ {
            "key" : "shirt",
            "doc_count" : 1
          }, {
            "key" : "test",
            "doc_count" : 1
          } ]
        }
      }
    } ]
  }
 }
}
}
```

Nesting aggregations and ordering buckets

When talking about bucket aggregations, we just need to get back to the topic of nesting aggregations. This is a very powerful technique, because it allows you to further process the data for documents in the buckets. For example, the `terms` aggregation will return a bucket for each term and the `stats` aggregation can show us the statistics for documents in each bucket. For example, let's look at the following query:

```
{
 "aggs": {
  "copies" : {
```

```
        "terms" : {
         "field" : "copies"
        },
        "aggs" : {
         "years" : {
          "stats" : {
           "field" : "year"
          }
         }
        }
       }
      }
     }
    }
```

This is an example of nested aggregations. The terms aggregation will return buckets for each term from the copies field (three buckets in the case of our data), and the stats aggregation will calculate statistics for the year field for the documents falling into each bucket returned by the top aggregation. The response from Elasticsearch for the preceding query looks as follows:

```
{
    "took" : 3,
    "timed_out" : false,
    "_shards" : {
      "total" : 5,
      "successful" : 5,
      "failed" : 0
    },
    "hits" : {
      "total" : 4,
      "max_score" : 0.0,
      "hits" : [ ]
    },
    "aggregations" : {
      "copies " : {
        "doc_count_error_upper_bound" : 0,
        "sum_other_doc_count" : 0,
        "buckets" : [ {
          "key" : 0,
          "doc_count" : 2,
          "years" : {
            "count" : 2,
            "min" : 1886.0,
            "max" : 1936.0,
```

```
            "avg"  :  1911.0,
            "sum"  :  3822.0
          }
        },  {
          "key"  :  1,
          "doc_count"  :  1,
          "years"  :  {
            "count"  :  1,
            "min"  :  1929.0,
            "max"  :  1929.0,
            "avg"  :  1929.0,
            "sum"  :  1929.0
          }
        },  {
          "key"  :  6,
          "doc_count"  :  1,
          "years"  :  {
            "count"  :  1,
            "min"  :  1961.0,
            "max"  :  1961.0,
            "avg"  :  1961.0,
            "sum"  :  1961.0
          }
        } ]
      }
    }
  }
```

This is a powerful feature and allows us to build very complex data processing pipelines. Of course, we are not limited to a single nested aggregation and we can nest multiple of them and even nest an aggregation inside a nested aggregation. For example:

```
{
  "aggs": {
    "popular_tags" : {
      "terms" : {
        "field" : "copies"
      },
      "aggs" : {
        "years" : {
          "terms" : {
            "field" : "year"
          },
```

```
    "aggs" : {
     "available_by_year" : {
      "stats" : {
       "field" : "available"
      }
     }
    }
   },
   "available" : {
    "stats" : {
     "field" : "available"
    }
   }
  }
 }
}
```

As you can see, the possibilities are almost unlimited, if you have enough memory and CPU power to handle very complicated aggregations.

Buckets ordering

There is one more feature about nested aggregations and the ordering of aggregation results. Elasticsearch can use values from the nested aggregations to sort the parent buckets. For example, let's look at the following query:

```
{
 "aggs": {
  "availability": {
   "terms": {
    "field": "copies",
    "order": { "numbers.avg": "desc" }
   },
   "aggs": {
    "numbers": { "stats" : {} }
   }
  }
 }
}
```

In the previous example, the order in the availability aggregation is based on the average value from the numbers aggregation. The notation numbers.avg is required in this case, because stats is a multivalued aggregation and provides multiple information and we were interested in the average. If it were the sum aggregation, the name of the aggregation would be sufficient.

Pipeline aggregations

The last type of aggregation we will discuss is pipeline aggregations. Till now we've learned about metrics aggregations and bucket aggregations. The first one returned metrics while the second type returned buckets. And both metrics and buckets aggregations worked on the basis of returned documents. Pipeline aggregations are different. They work on the output of the other aggregations and their metrics, allowing functionalities such as moving-average calculations (https://en.wikipedia.org/wiki/Moving_average).

 Remember that pipeline aggregations were introduced in Elasticsearch 2.0 and are considered experimental. This means that the API can change in the future, breaking backwards-compatibility.

Available types

There are two types of pipeline aggregation. The so called `parent` aggregations family works on the output of other aggregations. They are able to produce new buckets or new aggregations to add to existing buckets. The second type is called **sibling** aggregations and these aggregations are able to produce new aggregations on the same level.

Referencing other aggregations

Because of their nature, the pipeline aggregations need to be able to access the results of the other aggregations. We can do that via the `buckets_path` property, which is defined using a specified format. We can use a few keywords that allow us to tell Elasticsearch exactly which aggregation and metric we are interested in. The `>` separates the aggregations and the `.` character separates the aggregation from its metrics. For example, `my_sum.sum` means that we take the `sum` metric of an aggregation called `my_sum`. Another example is `popular_tags>my_sum.sum`, which means that we are interested in the `sum` metric of a sub aggregation called `my_sum`, which is nested inside the `popular_tags` aggregation. In addition to this, we can use a special path called `_count`. This can be used to calculate the pipeline aggregations on document count instead of specified metrics.

Gaps in the data

Our data can contain gaps – situations where the data doesn't exist. For such use cases, we have the ability to specify the `gap_policy` property and set it to `skip` or `insert_zeros`. The `skip` value tells Elasticsearch to ignore the missing data and continue from the next available value, while `insert_zeros` replaces the missing values with zero.

Pipeline aggregation types

Most of the aggregations we will show in this section are very similar to the ones we've already seen in the sections about metrics and buckets aggregations. Because of that, we won't discuss them in depth. There are also new, specific pipeline aggregations that we want to talk about in a little more data.

Min, max, sum, and average bucket aggregations

The `min_bucket`, `max_bucket`, `sum_bucket`, and `avg_bucket` aggregations are sibling aggregations, similar in what they return to the `min`, `max`, `sum`, and `avg` aggregations. However, instead of working on the data returned by the query, they work on the results of the other aggregations.

To show you a simple example of how this aggregation works, let's calculate the sum of all the buckets returned by the other aggregations. The query that will do that looks as follows:

```
{
  "aggs" : {
   "periods_histogram" : {
    "histogram" : {
     "field" : "year",
     "interval" : 100
    },
    "aggs" : {
     "copies_per_100_years" : {
      "sum" : {
       "field" : "copies"
      }
     }
    }
   },
   "sum_copies" : {
    "sum_bucket" : {
     "buckets_path" : "periods_histogram>copies_per_100_years"
    }
   }
  }
}
```

As you can see, we used the `histogram` aggregation and we included a nested aggregation that calculates the sum of the copies field. Our `sum_bucket` sibling aggregation is used outside the main aggregation and refers to it using the `buckets_path` property. It tells Elasticsearch that we are interested in summing the values of metrics returned by the `copies_per_100_years` aggregation. The result returned by Elasticsearch for this query looks as follows:

```
{
  "took" : 2,
  "timed_out" : false,
  "_shards" : {
    "total" : 5,
    "successful" : 5,
    "failed" : 0
  },
  "hits" : {
    "total" : 4,
    "max_score" : 0.0,
    "hits" : [ ]
  },
  "aggregations" : {
    "periods_histogram" : {
      "buckets" : [ {
        "key" : 1800,
        "doc_count" : 1,
        "copies_per_100_years" : {
          "value" : 0.0
        }
      }, {
        "key" : 1900,
        "doc_count" : 3,
        "copies_per_100_years" : {
          "value" : 7.0
        }
      } ]
    },
    "sum_copies" : {
      "value" : 7.0
    }
  }
}
```

As you can see, Elasticsearch added another bucket to the results, called `sum_copies`, which holds the value we were interested in.

Cumulative sum aggregation

The `cumulative_sum` aggregation is a parent pipeline aggregation that allows us to calculate the sum in the `histogram` or `date_histogram` aggregation. A simple example of the aggregation looks as follows:

```
{
 "aggs" : {
  "periods_histogram" : {
   "histogram" : {
    "field" : "year",
    "interval" : 100
   },
   "aggs" : {
    "copies_per_100_years" : {
     "sum" : {
      "field" : "copies"
     }
    },
    "cumulative_copies_sum" : {
     "cumulative_sum" : {
      "buckets_path" : "copies_per_100_years"
     }
    }
   }
  }
 }
}
```

Because this aggregation is a parent pipeline aggregation, it is defined in the sub aggregations. The returned result looks as follows:

```
{
  "took" : 2,
  "timed_out" : false,
  "_shards" : {
    "total" : 5,
    "successful" : 5,
    "failed" : 0
  },
  "hits" : {
    "total" : 4,
    "max_score" : 0.0,
    "hits" : [ ]
  },
```

```
"aggregations" : {
  "periods_histogram" : {
    "buckets" : [ {
      "key" : 1800,
      "doc_count" : 1,
      "copies_per_100_years" : {
        "value" : 0.0
      },
      "cumulative_copies_sum" : {
        "value" : 0.0
      }
    }, {
      "key" : 1900,
      "doc_count" : 3,
      "copies_per_100_years" : {
        "value" : 7.0
      },
      "cumulative_copies_sum" : {
        "value" : 7.0
      }
    } ]
  }
}
}
```

The first `cumulative_copies_sum` is 0 because of the sum defined in the bucket. The second is the sum of all the previous ones and the current bucket, which means 7. The next will be the sum of all the previous ones and the next bucket.

Bucket selector aggregation

The `bucket_selector` aggregation is another sibling parent aggregation. It allows using a script to decide if a bucket should be retained in the parent multi-bucket aggregation. For example, to keep only buckets that have more than one copy per period, we can run the following query (it needs the `script.inline` property to be set to `on` in the `elasticsearch.yml` file):

```
{
  "aggs" : {
    "periods_histogram" : {
      "histogram" : {
        "field" : "year",
        "interval" : 100
      },
      "aggs" : {
```

```
          "copies_per_100_years" : {
           "sum" : {
            "field" : "copies"
           }
          },
          "remove_empty_buckets" : {
           "bucket_selector" : {
            "buckets_path" : {
             "sum_copies" : "copies_per_100_years"
            },
            "script" : "sum_copies > 1"
           }
          }
         }
        }
       }
      }
```

There are two important things here. The first is the `buckets_path` property, which is different to what we've used so far. Now it uses a key and a value. The key is used to reference the value in the script. The second important thing is the `script` property, which defines the script that decides if the processed bucket should be retained. The results returned by Elasticsearch in this case are as follows:

```
{
  "took" : 330,
  "timed_out" : false,
  "_shards" : {
    "total" : 5,
    "successful" : 5,
    "failed" : 0
  },
  "hits" : {
    "total" : 4,
    "max_score" : 0.0,
    "hits" : [ ]
  },
  "aggregations" : {
    "periods_histogram" : {
      "buckets" : [ {
        "key" : 1900,
        "doc_count" : 3,
        "copies_per_100_years" : {
```

```
            "value" : 7.0
          }
      } ]
    }
  }
}
```

As we can see, the bucket with the `copies_per_100_years` value equal to `0` has been removed.

Bucket script aggregation

The `bucket_script` aggregation (sibling parent) allows us to define multiple bucket paths and use them inside a script. The used metrics must be the numeric type and the returned value also needs to be numeric. An example of using this aggregation follows (the following query needs the `script.inline` property to be set to `on` in the `elasticsearch.yml` file):

```
{
 "aggs" : {
  "periods_histogram" : {
   "histogram" : {
    "field" : "year",
    "interval" : 100
   },
   "aggs" : {
    "copies_per_100_years" : {
     "sum" : {
      "field" : "copies"
     }
    },
    "stats_per_100_years" : {
     "stats" : {
      "field" : "copies"
     }
    },
    "example_bucket_script" : {
     "bucket_script" : {
      "buckets_path" : {
       "sum_copies" : "copies_per_100_years",
       "count" : "stats_per_100_years.count"
      },
```

```
            "script" : "sum_copies / count * 1000"
          }
        }
      }
    }
  }
}
```

There are two things here. The first thing is that we've defined two entries in the buckets_path property. We are allowed to do that in the bucket_script aggregation. Each entry is a key and a value. The key is the name of the value that we can use in the script. The second is the path to the aggregation metric we are interested in. Of course, the script property defines the script that returns the value.

The returned results for the preceding query are as follows:

```
{
  "took" : 5,
  "timed_out" : false,
  "_shards" : {
    "total" : 5,
    "successful" : 5,
    "failed" : 0
  },
  "hits" : {
    "total" : 4,
    "max_score" : 0.0,
    "hits" : [ ]
  },
  "aggregations" : {
    "periods_histogram" : {
      "buckets" : [ {
        "key" : 1800,
        "doc_count" : 1,
        "copies_per_100_years" : {
          "value" : 0.0
        },
        "stats_per_100_years" : {
          "count" : 1,
          "min" : 0.0,
          "max" : 0.0,
          "avg" : 0.0,
          "sum" : 0.0
        },
```

```
        "example_bucket_script" : {
          "value" : 0.0
        }
      }, {
        "key" : 1900,
        "doc_count" : 3,
        "copies_per_100_years" : {
          "value" : 7.0
        },
        "stats_per_100_years" : {
          "count" : 3,
          "min" : 0.0,
          "max" : 6.0,
          "avg" : 2.3333333333333335,
          "sum" : 7.0
        },
        "example_bucket_script" : {
          "value" : 2333.3333333333335
        }
      } ]
    }
  }
}
```

Serial differencing aggregation

The `serial_diff` aggregation is a parent pipeline aggregation that implements a technique where the values in time series data (such as a histogram or date histogram) are subtracted from themselves at different time periods. This technique allows drawing the data changes between time periods instead of drawing the whole value. You know that the population of a city grows with time. If we use the serial differencing aggregation with the period of one day, we can see the daily growth.

To calculate the `serial_diff` aggregation, we need the parent aggregation, which is a `histogram` or a `date_histogram`, and we need to provide it with `buckets_path`, which points to the metric we are interested in, and `lag` (a positive, non-zero integer value), which tells which previous bucket to subtract from the current one. We can omit `lag`, in which case Elasticsearch will set it to 1.

Let's now look at a simple query that uses the discussed aggregation:

```
{
  "aggs" : {
    "periods_histogram" : {
      "histogram" : {
```

```
    "field" : "year",
    "interval" : 100
   },
   "aggs" : {
    "copies_per_100_years" : {
     "sum" : {
      "field" : "copies"
     }
    },
    "first_difference" : {
     "serial_diff" : {
      "buckets_path" : "copies_per_100_years",
      "lag" : 1
     }
    }
   }
  }
 }
}
```

The response to the preceding query looks as follows:

```
{
  "took" : 68,
  "timed_out" : false,
  "_shards" : {
    "total" : 5,
    "successful" : 5,
    "failed" : 0
  },
  "hits" : {
    "total" : 4,
    "max_score" : 0.0,
    "hits" : [ ]
  },
  "aggregations" : {
    "periods_histogram" : {
      "buckets" : [ {
        "key" : 1800,
        "doc_count" : 1,
        "copies_per_100_years" : {
          "value" : 0.0
        }
      }, {
```

```
        "key" : 1900,
        "doc_count" : 3,
        "copies_per_100_years" : {
          "value" : 7.0
        },
        "first_difference" : {
          "value" : 7.0
        }
      } ]
    }
  }
}
```

As you can see, with the second bucket we got our aggregation (we will get it with every bucket after that as well). The calculated value is 7 because the current value of copies_per_100_years is 7 and the previous is 0. Subtracting 0 from 7 gives us 7.

Derivative aggregation

The derivative aggregation is another example of parent pipeline aggregation. As its name suggests, it calculates a derivative (https://en.wikipedia.org/wiki/Derivative) of a given metric from a histogram or date histogram. The only thing we need to provide is buckets_path, which points to the metric we are interested in. An example query using this aggregation looks as follows:

```
{
  "aggs" : {
    "periods_histogram" : {
      "histogram" : {
        "field" : "year",
        "interval" : 100
      },
      "aggs" : {
        "copies_per_100_years" : {
          "sum" : {
            "field" : "copies"
          }
        },
        "derivative_example" : {
          "derivative" : {
            "buckets_path" : "copies_per_100_years"
          }
        }
      }
    }
  }
}
```

Moving avg aggregation

The last pipeline aggregation that we want to discuss is the `moving_avg` one. It calculates the moving average metric (https://en.wikipedia.org/wiki/Moving_average) over the buckets of the parent aggregation (yes, this is a parent pipeline aggregation). Similar to the few previously discussed aggregations, it needs to be run on the parent histogram or date histogram aggregation.

When calculating the moving average, Elasticsearch will take the window (specified by the `window` property and set to 5 by default), calculate the average for buckets in the window, move the window one bucket further, and repeat. Of course we also need to provide `buckets_path`, which points to the metric that the moving average should be calculated for.

An example of using this aggregation looks as follows:

```
{
  "aggs" : {
   "periods_histogram" : {
    "histogram" : {
     "field" : "year",
     "interval" : 10
    },
    "aggs" : {
     "copies_per_10_years" : {
      "sum" : {
       "field" : "copies"
      }
     },
     "moving_avg_example" : {
      "moving_avg" : {
       "buckets_path" : "copies_per_10_years"
      }
     }
    }
   }
  }
}
```

We will omit including the response for the preceding query as it is quite large.

Predicting future buckets

The very nice thing about moving average aggregation is that it supports predictions; it can attempt to extrapolate the data it has and create future buckets. To force the aggregation to predict buckets, we just need to add the `predict` property to any moving average aggregation and set it to the number of predictions we want to get. For example, if we want to add five predictions to the preceding query, we will change it to look as follows:

```
{
 "aggs" : {
  "periods_histogram" : {
   "histogram" : {
    "field" : "year",
    "interval" : 10
   },
   "aggs" : {
    "copies_per_10_years" : {
     "sum" : {
      "field" : "copies"
     }
    },
    "moving_avg_example" : {
     "moving_avg" : {
      "buckets_path" : "copies_per_10_years",
      "predict" : 5
     }
    }
   }
  }
 }
}
```

If you look at the results and compare the response returned for the previous query with the one with predictions, you will notice that the last bucket in the previous query ends on the key property equal to 1960, while the query with predictions ends on the key property equal to 2010, which is exactly what we wanted to achieve.

The models

By default, Elasticsearch uses the simplest model for calculating the moving averages aggregation, but we can control that by specifying the `model` property; this property holds the name of the model and the settings object, which we can use to provide model properties.

The possible models are: `simple`, `linear`, `ewma`, `holt`, and `holt_winters`. Discussing each of the models in detail is beyond the scope of the book, so if you are interested in details about the different models, refer to the official Elasticsearch documentation regarding the moving averages aggregation available at `https://www.elastic.co/guide/en/elasticsearch/reference/master/search-aggregations-pipeline-movavg-aggregation.html`.

An example query using different model looks as follows:

```
{
  "aggs" : {
   "periods_histogram" : {
    "histogram" : {
     "field" : "year",
     "interval" : 10    },
    "aggs" : {
     "copies_per_10_years" : {
       "sum" : {
         "field" : "copies"
             } },
   "moving_avg_example" : {
    "moving_avg" : {
     "buckets_path" : "copies_per_10_years",
     "model" : "holt",
     "settings" : {
      "alpha" : 0.6,
      "beta" : 0.4
     }
    }
   }
   }
   }
   }
  }
}
```

Summary

The chapter we just finished was all about data analysis in Elasticsearch: the aggregations engine. We learned what the aggregations are and how they work. We used metrics, buckets, and newly introduced pipeline aggregations, and learned what we can do with them.

In the next chapter, we'll go beyond full text searching. We will use suggesters to build efficient autocomplete functionality and correct the users' spelling mistakes. We will see what percolation is and how to use it in our application. We will use the geospatial abilities of Elasticsearch and we'll learn how to efficiently fetch large amount of data from Elasticsearch.

Beyond Full-text Searching

8

The previous chapter was fully dedicated to data analysis and how we can perform it with Elasticsearch. We learned how to use aggregations, what types of aggregation are available, and what aggregations are available within each type and how to use them. In this chapter, we will get back to query related topics. By the end of this chapter, you will have learned the following topics:

- What is percolator and how to use it
- What are the geospatial capabilities of Elasticsearch
- How to use and build functionalities using Elasticsearch suggesters
- How to use the Scroll API to efficiently fetch large numbers of results

Percolator

Have you ever wondered what would happen if we reverse the traditional model of using queries to find documents in Elasticsearch? Does it make sense to have a document and search for queries matching it? It is not surprising that there is a whole range of solutions where this model is very useful. Whenever you operate on an unbounded stream of input data, where you search for the occurrences of particular events, you can use this approach. This can be used for the detection of failures in a monitoring system or for the "Tell me when a product with the defined criteria will be available in this shop" functionality. In this section, we will look at how an Elasticsearch percolator works and how we can use it to implement one of the aforementioned use cases.

The index

In all the examples to be used when discussing percolator functionality, we will use an index called `notifier`. The mentioned index is created by using the following command:

```
curl -XPOST 'localhost:9200/notifier' -d '{
  "mappings": {
    "book" : {
      "properties" : {
        "title" : {
          "type" : "string"
        },
        "otitle" : {
          "type" : "string"
        },
        "year" : {
          "type" : "integer"
        },
        "available" : {
          "type" : "boolean"
        },
        "tags" : {
          "type" : "string",
          "index" : "not_analyzed"
        }
      }
    }
  }
}'
```

It is quite simple. It contains a single type and five fields, which will be used during our journey through the world.

Percolator preparation

Elasticsearch exposes a special type called `.percolator` that is treated differently. This means that we can store any documents and also search them like an ordinary type in any index. If you look at any Elasticsearch query, you will notice that each is a valid JSON document, which means that we can index and store it as a document as well. The thing is that percolator allows us to inverse the search logic and search for queries which match a given document. This is possible because of the two just discussed features: the special `.percolator` type and the fact that queries in Elasticsearch are valid JSON documents.

Let's get back to the `library` example from *Chapter 2, Indexing Your Data*, and try to index one of the queries in the percolator. We assume that our users need to be informed when any book matching the criteria defined by the query is available.

Look at the following `query1.json` file that contains an example query generated by the user:

```
{
  "query" : {
    "bool" : {
      "must" : {
        "term" : {
          "title" : "crime"
        }
      },
      "should" : {
        "range" : {
          "year" : {
            "gt" : 1900,
            "lt" : 2000
          }
        }
      },
      "must_not" : {
        "term" : {
          "otitle" : "nothing"
        }
      }
    }
  }
}
```

To enhance the example, we also assume that our users are allowed to define filters using our hypothetical user interface. For example, our user may be interested in the available books that were written before the year 2010. An example query that could have been constructed by such a user interface would look as follows (the query was written to the query2.json file):

```
{
  "query" : {
    "bool": {
      "must" : {
        "range" : {
          "year" : {
            "lt" : 2010
          }
        }
      },
      "filter" : {
        "term" : {
          "available" : true
        }
      }
    }
  }
}
```

Now, let's register both queries in the percolator (note that we are registering the queries and haven't indexed any documents). In order to do this, we will run the following commands:

```
curl -XPUT 'localhost:9200/notifier/.percolator/1' -d @query1.json
curl -XPUT 'localhost:9200/notifier/.percolator/old_books' -d @query2.json
```

In the preceding examples, we used two completely different identifiers. We did that in order to show that we can use an identifier that best describes the query. It is up to us to decide under which name we would like the query to be registered.

We are now ready to use our percolator. Our application will provide documents to the percolator and check if any of the already registered queries match the document. This is exactly what a percolator allows us to do - to reverse the search logic. Instead of indexing the documents and running queries against them, we store the queries and send the documents to find the matching queries.

Let's use an example document that will match both stored queries; it will have the required title and the release date, and will mention whether it is currently available. The command to send such a document to the percolator looks as follows:

```
curl -XGET 'localhost:9200/notifier/book/_percolate?pretty' -d '{
  "doc" : {
    "title": "Crime and Punishment",
    "otitle": "Преступлéние и наказáние",
    "author": "Fyodor Dostoevsky",
    "year": 1886,
    "characters": ["Raskolnikov", "Sofia Semyonovna Marmeladova"],
      "tags": [],
    "copies": 0,
    "available" : true
  }
}'
```

As we expected, both queries matched and the Elasticsearch response includes the identifiers of the matching queries. Such a response looks as follows:

```
{
  "took" : 36,
  "_shards" : {
    "total" : 5,
    "successful" : 5,
    "failed" : 0
  },
  "total" : 2,
  "matches" : [ {
    "_index" : "notifier",
    "_id" : "old_books"
  }, {
    "_index" : "notifier",
    "_id" : "1"
  } ]
}
```

This works like a charm. One very important thing to note is the endpoint used in this query: _percolate. Using this endpoint is required when we want to use the percolator. The index name corresponds to the index where the queries were stored, and the type is equal to the type defined in the mappings.

The response format contains information about the index and the query identifier. This information is included for cases when we search against multiple indices at once. When using a single index, adding an additional query parameter, `percolate_format=ids`, will change the response as follows:

```
"matches" : [ "old_books", "1" ]
```

Getting deeper

Because the queries registered in a percolator are in fact documents, we can use a normal query sent to Elasticsearch in order to choose which queries stored in the `.percolator` type should be used in the percolation process. This may sound weird, but it really gives a lot of possibilities. In our library, we can have several groups of users. Let's assume that some of them have permissions to borrow very rare books, or that we have several branches in the city and the user can declare where he or she would like to get the book from.

Let's see how such use cases can be implemented by using the percolator. To do this, we will need to update our mapping and include the branch information. We do that by running the following command:

```
curl -XPOST 'localhost:9200/notifier/.percolator/_mapping' -d '{
  ".percolator" : {
    "properties" : {
      "branches" : {
        "type" : "string",
        "index" : "not_analyzed"
      }
    }
  }
}'
```

Now, in order to register a query, we use the following command:

```
curl -XPUT 'localhost:9200/notifier/.percolator/3' -d '{
  "query" : {
    "term" : {
      "title" : "crime"
    }
  },
  "branches" : ["brA", "brB", "brD"]
}'
```

In the preceding example, we registered a query that shows a user's interest. Our hypothetical user is interested in any book with the term crime in the title field (the term query is responsible for this). He or she wants to borrow this book from one of the three listed branches. When specifying the mappings, we defined that the branches field is a non-analyzed string field. We can now include a query along with the document we sent previously. Let's look at how to do this.

Our book system just got the book, and it is ready to report the book and check whether the book is of interest to anyone. To check this, we send the document that describes the book and add an additional query to such a request - the query that will limit the users to only the ones interested in the brB branch. Such a request looks as follows:

```
curl -XGET 'localhost:9200/notifier/book/_percolate?pretty' -d '{
  "doc" : {
    "title": "Crime and Punishment",
    "otitle": "Преступление и наказание",
    "author": "Fyodor Dostoevsky",
    "year": 1886,
    "characters": ["Raskolnikov", "Sofia Semyonovna Marmeladova"],
      "tags": [],
    "copies": 0,
    "available" : true
  },
  "size" : 10,
  "filter" : {
    "term" : {
      "branches" : "brB"
    }
  }
}'
```

If everything was executed correctly, the response returned by Elasticsearch should look as follows (we indexed our query with 3 as an identifier):

```
{
  "took" : 27,
  "_shards" : {
    "total" : 5,
    "successful" : 5,
    "failed" : 0
```

```
  },
  "total" : 1,
  "matches" : [ {
    "_index" : "notifier",
    "_id" : "3"
  } ]
}
```

Controlling the size of returned results

The size of the results when it comes to percolator makes the difference. The more queries a single document matches, the more results will be returned and more memory will be needed by Elasticsearch. Because of this, there is one additional thing to note - the `size` parameter. It allows us to limit the number of matches returned.

Percolator and score calculation

In the previous examples, we filtered our queries using a single term query, but we didn't think about the scoring process at all. Elasticsearch allows us to calculate the score when using the percolator. Let's change the previously used document sent to the percolator and adjust it so that scoring is used:

```
curl -XGET 'localhost:9200/notifier/book/_percolate?pretty' -d '{
  "doc" : {
    "title": "Crime and Punishment",
    "otitle": "Преступлéние и наказáние",
    "author": "Fyodor Dostoevsky",
    "year": 1886,
    "characters": ["Raskolnikov", "Sofia Semyonovna Marmeladova"],
    "tags": [],
    "copies": 0,
    "available" : true
  },
  "size" : 10,
  "query" : {
    "term" : {
      "branches" : "brB"
    }
  },
  "track_scores" : true,
  "sort" : {
    "_score" : "desc"
  }
}'
```

As you can see, we used the `query` section and included an additional `track_scores` attribute set to `true`. This is needed, because by default Elasticsearch won't calculate the score for the documents because of performance. If we need scores in the percolation process, we should be aware that such queries will be slightly more demanding when it comes to CPU processing power than the ones that omit calculating the score.

> In the preceding example, we told Elasticsearch to sort our result on the basis of the score in descending order. This is the default behavior when `track_scores` is turned on, so we can omit sort declaration. At the time of writing, sorting on score in descending direction is the only available option.

Combining percolators with other functionalities

If we are allowed to use queries along with the documents sent for percolation, why can we not use other Elasticsearch functionalities? Of course, this is possible. For example, the following document is sent along with an aggregation and the results will include the aggregation calculation:

```
curl -XGET 'localhost:9200/notifier/book/_percolate?pretty' -d '{
  "doc": {
    "title": "Crime and Punishment",
    "available": true
  },
  "aggs" : {
    "test" : {
      "terms" : {
        "field" : "branches"
      }
    }
  }
}'
```

As we can see, percolator allows us to run both query and aggregations. Look at the following example document:

```
curl -XGET 'localhost:9200/notifier/book/_percolate?pretty' -d '{
  "doc": {
    "title": "Crime and Punishment",
```

```
    "year": 1886,
    "available": true
  },
  "size" : 10,
  "highlight": {
    "fields": {
      "title": {}
    }
  }
}'
```

As you can see, it contains a highlighting section. A fragment of the response returned by Elasticsearch looks as follows:

```
{
  "_index" : "notifier",
  "_id" : "3",
  "highlight" : {
    "title" : [ "<em>Crime</em> and Punishment" ]
  }
}
```

> Note that there are some limitations when it comes to the query types supported by the percolator functionality. In the current implementation, parent-child relations are not available in the percolator, so you can't use queries such as has_child, top_children, and has_parent.

Getting the number of matching queries

Sometimes you don't care about the matched queries and you only want the number of matched queries. In such cases, sending a document against the standard percolator endpoint is not efficient. Elasticsearch exposes the _percolate/count endpoint to handle such cases in an efficient way. An example of such a command follows:

```
curl -XGET 'localhost:9200/notifier/book/_percolate/count?pretty' -d '{
  "doc" : { ... }
}'
```

Indexed document percolation

In the final, closing paragraph of the percolation section, we want to show you one more thing – the possibility of percolating a document that is already indexed. To do this, we need to use the GET operation on the document and provide information about which percolator index should be used. Let's look at the following command:

```
curl -XGET 'localhost:9200/library/book/1/_percolate?percolate_
index=notifier'
```

This command checks the document with the 1 identifier from our library index against the percolator index defined by the percolate_index parameter. Remember that, by default, Elasticsearch will use the percolator in the same index as the document; that's why we've specified the percolate_index parameter.

Elasticsearch spatial capabilities

The search servers such as Elasticsearch are usually looked at from the perspective of full-text searching. Elasticsearch, because of its marketing as being part of ELK (Elasticsearch, Logstash, and Kibana), is also highly known for being able to handle large amount of time series data. However, this is only a part of the whole view. Sometimes both of the mentioned use cases are not enough. Imagine searching for local services. For the end user, the most important thing is the accuracy of the results. By accuracy, we not only mean the proper results of the full-text search, but also the results being as near as they can in terms of location. In several cases, this is the same as a text search on geographical names such as cities or streets, but in other cases we can find it very useful to be able to search on the basis of the geographical coordinates of our indexed documents. And this is also a functionality that Elasticsearch is capable of handling.

With the release of Elasticsearch 2.2, the geo_point type received a lot of changes, especially internally where all the optimizations were done. Prior to 2.2, the geo_point type was stored in the index as a two not analyzed string values and this changed. With the release of Elasticsearch 2.2, the geo_point type got all the great improvements from Apache Lucene library and is now more efficient.

Mapping preparation for spatial searches

In order to discuss the spatial search functionality, let's prepare an index with a list of cities. This will be a very simple index with one type named `poi` (which stands for the point of interest), the name of the city, and its coordinates. The mappings are as follows:

```
{
  "mappings" : {
    "poi" : {
      "properties" : {
        "name" : { "type" : "string" },
        "location" : { "type" : "geo_point" }
      }
    }
  }
}
```

Assuming that we put this definition into the `mapping1.json` file, we can create an index by running the following command:

```
curl -XPUT localhost:9200/map -d @mapping1.json
```

The only new thing in the preceding mappings is the `geo_point` type, which is used for the `location` field. By using it, we can store the geographical position of our city and use spatial-based functionalities.

Example data

Our example `documents1.json` file with documents looks as follows:

```
{ "index" : { "_index" : "map", "_type" : "poi", "_id" : 1 }}
{ "name" : "New York", "location" : "40.664167, -73.938611" }
{ "index" : { "_index" : "map", "_type" : "poi", "_id" : 2 }}
{ "name" : "London", "location" : [-0.1275, 51.507222] }
{ "index" : { "_index" : "map", "_type" : "poi", "_id" : 3 }}
{ "name" : "Moscow", "location" : { "lat" : 55.75, "lon" : 37.616667
}}
{ "index" : { "_index" : "map", "_type" : "poi", "_id" : 4 }}
{ "name" : "Sydney", "location" : "-33.859972, 151.211111" }
{ "index" : { "_index" : "map", "_type" : "poi", "_id" : 5 }}
{ "name" : "Lisbon", "location" : "eycs0p8ukc7v" }
```

In order to perform a bulk request, we added information about the index name, type, and unique identifiers of our documents; so, we can now easily import this data using the following command:

```
curl -XPOST localhost:9200/_bulk --data-binary @documents1.json
```

One thing that we should take a closer look at is the location field. We can use various notations for coordination. We can provide the latitude and longitude values as a string, as a pair of numbers, or as an object. Note that the string and array methods of providing the geographical location have different orders for the latitude and longitude parameters. The last record shows that there is also a possibility to give coordination as a Geohash value (the notation is described in detail at http://en.wikipedia.org/wiki/Geohash).

Additional geo_field properties

With the release of Elasticsearch 2.2, the number of parameters that the geo_point type can accept has been reduced and is as follows:

- geohash: Boolean parameter telling Elasticsearch whether the .geohash field should be created. Defaults to false unless geohash_prefix is used.

- geohash_precision: Maximum size of geohash and geohash_prefix.

- geohash_prefix: Boolean parameter telling Elasticsearch to index the geohash and its prefixes. Defaults to false.

- ignore_malformed: Boolean parameter telling Elasticsearch to ignore a badly written geo_field point instead of rejecting the whole document. Defaults to false, which means that the badly formatted geo_field data will result in an indexation error for the whole document.

- lat_lon: Boolean parameter telling Elasticsearch to index the spatial data in two separate fields called .lat and .lon. Defaults to false.

- precision_step: Parameter allowing control over how our numeric geographical points will be indexed.

Keep in mind that the geohash field related and lat_lon field related properties were not removed for backward-compatibility reasons. The users can still use them. However, the queries will not use them but will instead use the highly optimized data structure that is built during indexing by the geo_point type.

Sample queries

Now let's look at several examples of using coordinates and solving common requirements in modern applications that require geographical data searching along with full-text searching.

 If you are interested in all the geospatial queries that are available for Elasticsearch users, refer to the official documentation available at https://www.elastic.co/guide/en/elasticsearch/reference/current/geo-queries.html.

Distance-based sorting

Let's start with a very common requirement: sorting the returned results by distance from a given point. In our example, we want to get all the cities and sort them by their distances from the capital of France, Paris. To do this, we send the following query to Elasticsearch:

```
curl -XGET localhost:9200/map/_search?pretty -d '{
  "query" : {
    "match_all" : {}
  },
  "sort" : [{
    "_geo_distance" : {
      "location" : "48.8567, 2.3508",
      "unit" : "km"
    }
  }]
}'
```

If you remember the *Sorting data* section from *Chapter 4, Extending Your Querying Knowledge*, you'll notice that the format is slightly different. We are using the `_geo_distance` key to indicate sorting by distance. We must give the base location (the `location` attribute, which holds the information of the location of Paris in our case), and we need to specify the units that can be used in the results. The available values are `km` and `mi`, which stand for kilometers and miles, respectively. The result of such a query will be as follows:

```
{
  "took" : 5,
  "timed_out" : false,
```

```
"_shards" : {
  "total" : 5,
  "successful" : 5,
  "failed" : 0
},
"hits" : {
  "total" : 5,
  "max_score" : null,
  "hits" : [ {
    "_index" : "map",
    "_type" : "poi",
    "_id" : "2",
    "_score" : null,
    "_source" : {
      "name" : "London",
      "location" : [ -0.1275, 51.507222 ]
    },
    "sort" : [ 343.17487356850313 ]
  }, {
    "_index" : "map",
    "_type" : "poi",
    "_id" : "5",
    "_score" : null,
    "_source" : {
      "name" : "Lisbon",
      "location" : "eycs0p8ukc7v"
    },
    "sort" : [ 1452.9506736367805 ]
  }, {
    "_index" : "map",
    "_type" : "poi",
    "_id" : "3",
    "_score" : null,
    "_source" : {
      "name" : "Moscow",
      "location" : {
        "lat" : 55.75,
        "lon" : 37.616667
      }
    },
    "sort" : [ 2483.837565935267 ]
  }, {
    "_index" : "map",
```

```
          "_type" : "poi",
          "_id" : "1",
          "_score" : null,
          "_source" : {
            "name" : "New York",
            "location" : "40.664167, -73.938611"
          },
          "sort" : [ 5832.645958617513 ]
        }, {
          "_index" : "map",
          "_type" : "poi",
          "_id" : "4",
          "_score" : null,
          "_source" : {
            "name" : "Sydney",
            "location" : "-33.859972, 151.211111"
          },
          "sort" : [ 16978.094780773998 ]
        } ]
      }
    }
```

As with the other examples of sorting, Elasticsearch shows information about the value used for sorting. Let's look at the highlighted record. As we can see, the distance between Paris and London is about 343 km, and if you check a traditional map, you will see that this is true.

Bounding box filtering

The next example that we want to show is narrowing down the results to a selected area that is bounded by a given rectangle. This is very handy if we want to show results on the map or when we allow a user to mark the map area for searching. You already read about filters in the *Filtering your results* section of *Chapter 4, Extending Your Querying Knowledge,* but there we didn't mention spatial filters. The following query shows how we can filter by using the bounding box:

```
curl -XGET localhost:9200/map/_search?pretty -d '{
  "query" : {
    "bool" : {
      "must" : { "match_all": {}},
      "filter" : {
```

```
  "geo_bounding_box" : {
    "location" : {
      "top_left" : "52.4796, -1.903",
      "bottom_right" : "48.8567, 2.3508"
    }
  }
}
}
}'
```

In the preceding example, we selected a map fragment between Birmingham and Paris by providing the top-left and bottom-right corner coordinates. These two corners are enough to specify any rectangle we want, and Elasticsearch will do the rest of the calculation for us. The following screenshot shows the specified rectangle on the map:

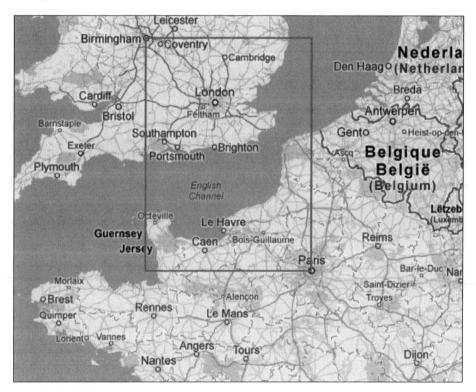

As we can see, the only city from our data that meets the criteria is London. So, let's check whether Elasticsearch knows this by running the preceding query. Let's now look at the returned results:

```
{
  "took" : 38,
  "timed_out" : false,
  "_shards" : {
    "total" : 5,
    "successful" : 5,
    "failed" : 0
  },
  "hits" : {
    "total" : 1,
    "max_score" : 1.0,
    "hits" : [ {
      "_index" : "map",
      "_type" : "poi",
      "_id" : "2",
      "_score" : 1.0,
      "_source" : {
        "name" : "London",
        "location" : [ -0.1275, 51.507222 ]
      }
    } ]
  }
}
```

As you can see, again Elasticsearch agrees with the map.

Limiting the distance

The last example shows the next common requirement: limiting the results to the places that are located no further than the defined distance from a given point. For example, if we want to limit our results to all the cities within the 500km radius from Paris, we can use the following query:

```
curl -XGET localhost:9200/map/_search?pretty -d '{
  "query" : {
    "bool" : {
      "must" : { "match_all": {}},
      "filter" : {
        "geo_distance" : {
          "location" : "48.8567, 2.3508",
          "distance" : "500km"
        }
```

```
        }
      }
    }
  }
}'
```

If everything goes well, Elasticsearch should only return a single record for the preceding query, and the record should be London again. However, we will leave it for you as a reader to check.

Arbitrary geo shapes

Sometimes, using a single geographical point or a single rectangle is just not enough. In such cases something more sophisticated is needed, and Elasticsearch addresses this by giving you the possibility to define shapes. In order to show you how we can leverage custom shape-limiting in Elasticsearch, we need to modify our index or create a new one and introduce the geo_shape type. Our new mapping looks as follows (we will use this to create an index called map2):

```
{
  "mappings" : {
    "poi" : {
      "properties" : {
        "name" : { "type" : "string", "index": "not_analyzed" },
        "location" : { "type" : "geo_shape" }
      }
    }
  }
}
```

Assuming we wrote the preceding mapping definition to the mapping2.json file, we can create an index by using the following command:

```
curl -XPUT localhost:9200/map2 -d @mapping2.json
```

 Elasticsearch allows us to set several attributes for the geo_shape type. The most commonly used is the precision parameter. During indexing, the shapes have to be converted to a set of terms. The more accuracy required, the more terms should be generated, which is directly reflected in the index size and performance. Precision can be defined in the following units: in, inch, yd, yard, mi, miles, km, kilometers, m, meters, cm, centimeters, or mm, millimeters. By default, the precision is set to 50m.

Next, let's change our example data to match our new index structure and create the documents2.json file with the following contents:

```
{ "index" : { "_index" : "map2", "_type" : "poi", "_id" : 1 }}
{ "name" : "New York", "location" : { "type": "point", "coordinates":
[-73.938611, 40.664167] }}
{ "index" : { "_index" : "map2", "_type" : "poi", "_id" : 2 }}
{ "name" : "London", "location" : { "type": "point", "coordinates":
[-0.1275, 51.507222] }}
{ "index" : { "_index" : "map2", "_type" : "poi", "_id" : 3 }}
{ "name" : "Moscow", "location" : { "type": "point", "coordinates": [
37.616667, 55.75]}}
{ "index" : { "_index" : "map2", "_type" : "poi", "_id" : 4 }}
{ "name" : "Sydney", "location" : { "type": "point", "coordinates":
[151.211111, -33.865143]}}
{ "index" : { "_index" : "map2", "_type" : "poi", "_id" : 5 }}
{ "name" : "Lisbon", "location" : { "type": "point",
"coordinates": [-9.142685, 38.736946] }}
```

The structure of the field of the geo_shape type is different from geo_point. It is syntactically called GeoJSON (http://en.wikipedia.org/wiki/GeoJSON). It allows us to define various geographical types. Now it's time to index our data:

```
curl -XPOST localhost:9200/_bulk --data-binary @documents2.json
```

Let's sum up the types that we can use during querying, at least the ones that we think are the most useful ones.

Point

A point is defined by the table when the first element is the longitude and the second is the latitude. An example of such a shape is as follows:

```
{
  "type": "point",
  "coordinates": [-0.1275, 51.507222]
}
```

Envelope

An envelope defines a box given by the coordinates of the upper-left and bottom-right corners of the box. An example of such a shape is as follows:

```
{
  "type": "envelope",
  "coordinates": [[ -0.087890625, 51.50874245880332 ], [
2.4169921875, 48.80686346108517 ]]
}
```

Polygon

A polygon defines a list of points that are connected to create our polygon. The first and the last point in the array must be the same so that the shape is closed. An example of such a shape is as follows:

```
{
  "type": "polygon",
  "coordinates": [[
    [-5.756836, 49.991408],
    [-7.250977, 55.124723],
    [1.845703, 51.500194],
    [-5.756836, 49.991408]
  ]]
}
```

If you look closely at the shape definition, you will find a supplementary level of tables. Thanks to this, you can define more than a single polygon. In such a case, the first polygon defines the base shape and the rest of the polygons are the shapes that will be excluded from the base shape.

Multipolygon

The multipolygon shape allows us to create a shape that consists of multiple polygons. An example of such a shape is as follows:

```
{
  "type": "multipolygon",
  "coordinates": [
    [[
        [-5.756836, 49.991408],
        [-7.250977, 55.124723],
        [1.845703, 51.500194],
        [-5.756836, 49.991408]
    ]], [[
        [-0.087890625, 51.50874245880332],
        [2.4169921875, 48.80686346108517],
        [3.88916015625, 51.01375465718826],
        [-0.087890625, 51.50874245880332]
    ]] ]
}
```

The multipolygon shape contains multiple polygons and falls into the same rules as the polygon type. So, we can have multiple polygons and, in addition to this, we can include multiple exclusion shapes.

An example usage

Now that we have our index with the geo_shape fields, we can check which cities are located in the UK. The query that will allow us to do this looks as follows:

```
curl -XGET localhost:9200/map2/_search?pretty -d '{
  "query" : {
    "bool" : {
      "must" : { "match_all": {}},
      "filter": {
        "geo_shape": {
          "location": {
            "shape": {
              "type": "polygon",
              "coordinates": [[
                [-5.756836, 49.991408], [-7.250977, 55.124723],
                [-3.955078, 59.352096], [1.845703, 51.500194],
                [-5.756836, 49.991408]
              ]]
            }
          }
        }
      }
    }
  }
}'
```

The polygon type defines the boundaries of the UK (in a very, very imprecise way), and Elasticsearch's response is as follows:

```
{
  "took" : 7,
  "timed_out" : false,
  "_shards" : {
    "total" : 5,
    "successful" : 5,
    "failed" : 0
  },
  "hits" : {
    "total" : 1,
```

```
    "max_score" : 1.0,
    "hits" : [ {
      "_index" : "map2",
      "_type" : "poi",
      "_id" : "2",
      "_score" : 1.0,
      "_source" : {
        "name" : "London",
        "location" : {
          "type" : "point",
          "coordinates" : [ -0.1275, 51.507222 ]
        }
      }
    } ]
  }
}
```

As far as we know, the response is correct.

Storing shapes in the index

Usually, shape definitions are complex, and the defined areas don't change too often (for example, the boundaries of the UK). In such cases, it is convenient to define the shapes in the index and use them in queries. This is possible, and we will now discuss how to do it. As usual, we will start with the appropriate mapping, which is as follows:

```
{
  "mappings" : {
    "country": {
      "properties": {
        "name": { "type": "string", "index": "not_analyzed" },
        "area": { "type": "geo_shape" }
      }
    }
  }
}
```

This mapping is similar to the mapping used previously. We have only changed the field name and saved it in the `mapping3.json` file. Let's create a new index by running the following command:

```
curl -XPUT localhost:9200/countries -d @mapping3.json
```

The example data that we will use looks as follows (stored in the file called documents3.json):

```
{"index": { "_index": "countries", "_type": "country", "_id": 1 }}
{"name": "UK", "area": {"type": "polygon", "coordinates": [[
[-5.756836, 49.991408], [-7.250977, 55.124723], [-3.955078,
59.352096], [1.845703, 51.500194], [-5.756836, 49.991408] ]]}}
{"index": { "_index": "countries", "_type": "country", "_id": 2 }}
{"name": "France", "area": { "type":"polygon", "coordinates": [ [
[ 3.1640625, 42.09822241118974 ], [ -1.7578125, 43.32517767999296
], [ -4.21875, 48.22467264956519 ], [ 2.4609375, 50.90303283111257
], [ 7.998046875, 48.980216985374994 ], [ 7.470703125,
44.08758502824516 ], [ 3.1640625, 42.09822241118974 ] ] ] }}
{"index": { "_index": "countries", "_type": "country", "_id": 3 }}
{"name": "Spain", "area": { "type": "polygon", "coordinates": [ [
[ 3.33984375, 42.22851735620852 ], [ -1.845703125,
43.32517767999296 ], [ -9.404296875, 43.19716728250127 ], [
-6.6796875, 41.57436130598913 ], [ -7.3828125, 36.87962060502676 ],
[ -2.109375, 36.52729481454624 ], [ 3.33984375, 42.22851735620852
] ] ] }}
```

To index the data, we just need to run the following command:

```
curl -XPOST localhost:9200/_bulk --data-binary @documents3.json
```

As you can see in the data, each document contains a polygon type. The polygons define the area of the given countries (again, it is far from being accurate). If you remember, the first point of a shape needs to be the same as the last one so that the shape is closed. Now, let's change our query to include the shapes from the index. Our new query looks as follows:

```
curl -XGET localhost:9200/map2/_search?pretty -d '{
  "query" : {
    "bool" : {
      "must" : { "match_all": {}},
      "filter": {
        "geo_shape": {
          "location": {
            "indexed_shape": {
              "index": "countries",
              "type": "country",
              "path": "area",
              "id": "1"
            }
          }
        }
      }
    }
```

```
        }
      }
    }
  }
}'
```

When comparing these two queries, we can note that the `shape` object changed to `indexed_shape`. We need to tell Elasticsearch where to look for this shape. We can do this by defining the index (the `index` property, which defaults to `shape`), the type (the `type` property), and the path (the `path` property, which defaults to `shape`). The one item lacking is an `id` property of the shape. In our case, this is `1`. However, if you want to index more shapes, we advise you to index the shapes with their name as their identifier.

Using suggesters

A long time ago, starting from Elasticsearch 0.90 (which was released on April 29, 2013), we got the ability to use so-called suggesters. We can define a **suggester** as a functionality allowing us to correct the user's spelling mistakes and build autocomplete functionality keeping performance in mind. This section is dedicated to these functionalities and will help you learn about them. We will discuss each available suggester type and show the most common properties that allow us to control them. However, keep in mind that this section is not a comprehensive guide describing each and every property. Description of all the details about suggesters are a very broad topic and is out of the scope of this book. If you want to dig into their functionality, refer to the official Elasticsearch documentation (`https://www.elastic.co/guide/en/elasticsearch/reference/current/search-suggesters.html`) or to the *Mastering Elasticsearch Second Edition* book published by Packt Publishing.

Available suggester types

These have changed since the initial introduction of the Suggest API to Elasticsearch. We are now able to use four type of suggesters:

- `term`: A suggester returning corrections for each word passed to it. Useful for suggestions that are not phrases, such as single term queries.

- `phrase`: A suggester working on phrases, returning a proper phrase.

- `completion`: A suggester designed to provide fast and efficient autocomplete results.

- `context`: Extension to the Suggest API of Elasticsearch. Allows us to handle parts of the `suggest` queries in memory and thus very effective in terms of performance.

Including suggestions

Let's now try getting suggestions along with the query results. For example, let's use a `match_all` query and try getting a suggestion for a `serlock holnes` phrase, which has two terms spelled incorrectly. To do this, we run the following command:

```
curl -XGET 'localhost:9200/library/_search?pretty' -d '{
 "query" : {
  "match_all" : {}
 },
 "suggest" : {
  "first_suggestion" : {
   "text" : "serlock holnes",
   "term" : {
    "field" : "_all"
   }
  }
 }
}'
```

As you can see, we've introduced a new section to our query – the `suggest` one. We've specified the text we want to get the correction for by using the `text` property. We've specified the suggester we want to use (the term one) and configured it specifying the name of the field that should be used for building suggestions using the `field` property. `first_suggestion` is the name we give to our suggester; we need to do this because there can be multiple ones used. This is how you send a request for suggestion in general.

If we want to get multiple suggestions for the same text, we can embed our suggestions in the `suggest` object and place the `text` property as the `suggest` object option. For example, if we want to get suggestions for the `serlock holnes` text for the `title` field and for the `_all` field, we run the following command:

```
curl -XGET 'localhost:9200/library/_search?pretty' -d '{
 "query" : {
  "match_all" : {}
 },
 "suggest" : {
  "text" : "serlock holnes",
  "first_suggestion" : {
```

```
  "term" : {
   "field" : "_all"
  }
 },
 "second_suggestion" : {
  "term" : {
   "field" : "title"
  }
 }
}
}'
```

Suggester response

Now let's look at the response of the first query we sent. As you can guess, the response includes both the query results and the suggestions:

```
{
    "took" : 10,
    "timed_out" : false,
    "_shards" : {
      "total" : 5,
      "successful" : 5,
      "failed" : 0
    },
    "hits" : {
      "total" : 4,
      "max_score" : 1.0,
      "hits" : [ ... ]
    },
    "suggest" : {
      "first_suggestion" : [ {
        "text" : "serlock",
        "offset" : 0,
        "length" : 7,
        "options" : [ {
          "text" : "sherlock",
          "score" : 0.85714287,
          "freq" : 1
        } ]
      }, {
```

```
        "text" : "holnes",
        "offset" : 8,
        "length" : 6,
        "options" : [ {
          "text" : "holmes",
          "score" : 0.8333333,
          "freq" : 1
        } ]
      } ]
    }
  }
```

We can see that we got both the search results and the suggestions (we've omitted the results to make the example more readable) in the response. The term suggester returned a list of possible suggestions for each term that was present in the `text` parameter. For each term, the term suggester returns an array of possible suggestions. Looking at the data returned for the `serlock` term, we can see the original word (the `text` parameter), its offset in the original `text` parameter (the `offset` parameter), and its length (the `length` parameter).

The `options` array contains suggestions for the given word and will be empty if Elasticsearch doesn't find any suggestions. Each entry in this array is a suggestion and described by the following properties:

- `text`: Text of the suggestion.

- `score`: Suggestion score; the higher the score, the better the suggestion.

- `freq`: Frequency of the suggestion. The frequency represents how many times the word appears in the documents in the index we are running the suggestion query against.

Term suggester

The term suggester works on the basis of string edit distance. This means that the suggestion with the fewest characters that need to be changed, added, or removed to make the suggestion look as the original word, is the best one. For example, let's take the words `worl` and `work`. To change the `worl` term to `work`, we need to change the `l` letter to `k`, so it means a distance of 1. The text provided to the suggester is of course analyzed and then terms are chosen to be suggested.

Term suggester configuration options

The common and most used term suggester options can be used for all the suggester implementations that are based on the term one. Currently, these are the phrase suggester and of course the base term one. The available options are:

- `text`: The text we want to get the suggestions for. This parameter is required in order for the suggester to work.

- `field`: Another required parameter that we need to provide. The `field` parameter allows us to set which field the suggestions should be generated for.

- `analyzer`: The name of the analyzer which should be used to analyze the text provided in the `text` parameter. If not set, Elasticsearch utilizes the analyzer used for the field provided by the `field` parameter.

- `size`: Defaults to 5 and specifies the maximum number of suggestions allowed to be returned by each term provided in the `text` parameter.

- `suggest_mode`: Controls which suggestions will be included and for what terms the suggestions will be returned. The possible options are: `missing` – the default behavior, which means that the suggester will only provide suggestions for terms that are not present in the index; `popular` – means that the suggestions will only be returned when they are more frequent than the provided term; and finally `always` means that suggestions will be returned every time.

- `sort`: Allows us to specify how the suggestions are sorted in the result returned by Elasticsearch. By default, it is set to `score`, which tells Elasticsearch that the suggestions should be sorted by the suggestion score first, the suggestion document frequency next, and finally by the term. The second possible value is `frequency`, which means that the results are first sorted by the document frequency, then by the score, and finally by the term.

Additional term suggester options

In addition to the preceding common term suggest options, Elasticsearch allows us to use additional ones that only make sense for the term suggester itself. Some of these options are as follows:

- `lowercase_terms`: When set to `true`, it tells Elasticsearch to lowercase all the terms that are produced from the `text` field after analysis.

- `max_edits`: It defaults to 2 and specifies the maximum edit distance that the suggestion can have to be returned as a term suggestion. Elasticsearch allows us to set this value to 1 or 2.

- `prefix_len`: By default, it is set to 1. If we are struggling with suggester performance, increasing this value will improve the overall performance, because fewer suggestions will need to be processed.

- `min_word_len`: It defaults to 4 and specifies the minimum number of characters a suggestion must have in order to be returned on the suggestions list.

- `shard_size`: It defaults to the value specified by the `size` parameter and allows us to set the maximum number of suggestions that should be read from each shard. Setting this property to values higher than the `size` parameter can result in more accurate document frequency at the cost of degradation in suggester performance.

> The provided list of parameters does not contain all the options that are available for the `term` suggester. Refer to the official Elasticsearch documentation for reference, at `https://www.elastic.co/guide/en/elasticsearch/reference/current/search-suggesters-term.html`.

Phrase suggester

The term suggester provides a great way to correct user spelling mistakes on per term basis, but it is not great for phrases. That's why the phrase suggester was introduced. It is built on top of the term suggester, but adds additional phrase calculation logic to it.

Let's start with an example of how to use the phrase suggester. This time we will omit the `query` section in our query. We do that by running the following command:

```
curl -XGET 'localhost:9200/library/_search?pretty' -d '{
 "suggest" : {
  "text" : "sherlock holnes",
  "our_suggestion" : {
   "phrase" : { "field" : "_all" }
  }
 }
}'
```

As you can see in the preceding command, it is almost the same as we sent when using the term suggester, but instead of specifying the term suggester type we've specified the phrase type. The response to the preceding command is as follows:

```
{
    "took" : 24,
    "timed_out" : false,
    "_shards" : {
        "total" : 5,
        "successful" : 5,
        "failed" : 0
    },
    "hits" : {
        "total" : 4,
        "max_score" : 1.0,
        "hits" : [ ... ]
    },
    "suggest" : {
        "our_suggestion" : [ {
            "text" : "sherlock holnes",
            "offset" : 0,
            "length" : 15,
            "options" : [ {
                "text" : "sherlock holmes",
                "score" : 0.12227806
            } ]
        } ]
    }
}
```

As you can see, the response is very similar to the one returned by the term suggester but, instead of a single word being returned, it is already combined and returned as a phrase.

Configuration

Because the phrase suggester is based on the term suggester, it can also use some of the configuration options provided by it. Those options are: `text`, `size`, `analyzer`, and `shard_size`. In addition to the mentioned properties, the phrase suggester exposes additional options. Some of these options are:

- `max_errors`: Specifies the maximum number (or percentage) of terms that can be erroneous in order to create a correction using it. The value of this property can be either an integer number, such as `1`, or a float between `0` and `1` which will be treated as a percentage value. By default, it is set to `1`, which means that at most a single term can be misspelled in a given correction.

- `separator`: Defaults to a whitespace character and specifies the separator that will be used to divide the terms in the resulting bigram field.

> The provided list of parameters does not contain all the options that are available for the phrase suggester. In fact, the list is way more extensive than what we've provided. Refer to the official Elasticsearch documentation for reference, at `https://www.elastic.co/guide/en/elasticsearch/reference/current/search-suggesters-phrase.html`, or to *Mastering Elasticsearch Second Edition* published by Packt Publishing.

Completion suggester

The completion suggester allows us to create autocomplete functionality in a very performance-effective way, because of storing complicated structures in the index instead of calculating them during query time. We need to prepare Elasticsearch for that by using a dedicated field type called completion. Let's assume that we want to create an autocomplete feature to allow us to show book authors. In addition to author's name we want to return the identifiers of the books she/he wrote. We start with creating the authors index by running the following command:

```
curl -XPOST 'localhost:9200/authors' -d '{
  "mappings" : {
   "author" : {
    "properties" : {
     "name" : { "type" : "string" },
     "ac" : {
      "type" : "completion",
      "payloads" : true,
      "analyzer" : "standard",
```

```
    "search_analyzer" : "standard"
      }
    }
  }
 }
}'
```

Our index will contain a single type called `author`. Each document will have two fields: the `name` and the `ac` field, which is the field we will use for autocomplete. We've defined the `ac` field using the `completion` type. In addition to that, we've used the `standard` analyzer for both the index and the query time. The last thing is the payload - the additional, optional information we will return along with the suggestion - in our case it will be an array of book identifiers.

Indexing data

To index the data, we need to provide some additional information along with the ones we usually provide during indexing. Let's look at the following commands that index two documents describing the authors:

```
curl -XPOST 'localhost:9200/authors/author/1' -d '{
 "name" : "Fyodor Dostoevsky",
 "ac" : {
  "input" : [ "fyodor", "dostoevsky" ],
  "output" : "Fyodor Dostoevsky",
  "payload" : { "books" : [ "123456", "123457" ] }
 }
}'
curl -XPOST 'localhost:9200/authors/author/2' -d '{
 "name" : "Joseph Conrad",
 "ac" : {
  "input" : [ "joseph", "conrad" ],
  "output" : "Joseph Conrad",
  "payload" : { "books" : [ "121211" ] }
 }
}'
```

Note the structure of the data for the ac field. We have provided the `input`, `output`, and `payload` properties. The optional `payload` property is used to provide the additional information that will be returned. The `input` property is used to provide the input information that will be used for building the completion used by the suggester. It will be used for user input matching. The optional `output` property is used to tell the suggester which data should be returned for the document.

We can also omit the additional parameters section and index data in the way we are used to, just like in the following example:

```
curl -XPOST 'localhost:9200/authors/author/1' -d '{
 "name" : "Fyodor Dostoevsky",
 "ac" : "Fyodor Dostoevsky"
}'
```

However, because the completion suggester uses FST under the hood, we won't be able to find the preceding document by starting with the second part of the ac field. That's why we think that indexing the data in the way we showed first is more convenient, because we can explicitly control what we want to match and what we want to show as an output.

Querying indexed completion suggester data

If we want to find documents that have authors starting with `fyo`, we run the following command:

```
curl -XGET 'localhost:9200/authors/_suggest?pretty' -d '{
 "authorsAutocomplete" : {
  "text" : "fyo",
  "completion" : {
   "field" : "ac"
  }
 }
}'
```

Before we look at the results, let's discuss the query. As you can see, we've run the command to the _suggest endpoint, because we don't want to run a standard query; we are just interested in the autocomplete results. The query is quite simple. We set its name to `authorsAutocomplete`, we set the text we want to get the completion for (the `text` property), and we added the `completion` object with the configuration in it. The result of the preceding command looks as follows:

```
{
  "_shards" : {
    "total" : 5,
```

```
      "successful" : 5,
      "failed" : 0
    },
    "authorsAutocomplete" : [ {
      "text" : "fyo",
      "offset" : 0,
      "length" : 3,
      "options" : [ {
        "text" : "Fyodor Dostoevsky",
        "score" : 1.0,
        "payload" : {
          "books" : [ "123456", "123457" ]
        }
      } ]
    } ]
}
```

As you can see in the response, we get the document we were looking for along with the payload information, if it is available (for the preceding response, it is not).

We can also use fuzzy searches, which allow us to tolerate spelling mistakes. We do that by including the additional fuzzy section in our query. For example, to enable fuzzy matching in the completion suggester and set the maximum edit distance to 2 (which means that a maximum of two errors are allowed), we send the following query:

```
curl -XGET 'localhost:9200/authors/_suggest?pretty' -d '{
 "authorsAutocomplete" : {
  "text" : "fio",
  "completion" : {
   "field" : "ac",
   "fuzzy" : {
    "edit_distance" : 2
   }
  }
 }
}'
```

Although we've made a spelling mistake, we will still get the same results as we got earlier.

Custom weights

By default, the term frequency is used to determine the weight of the document returned by the prefix suggester. However, this may not be the best solution. In such cases, it is useful to define the weight of the suggestion by specifying the `weight` property for the field defined as `completion`. The `weight` property should be set to an integer value. The higher the `weight` property value, the more important the suggestion. For example, if we want to specify a weight for the first document in our example, we run the following command:

```
curl -XPOST 'localhost:9200/authors/author/1' -d '{
 "name" : "Fyodor Dostoevsky",
 "ac" : {
  "input" : [ "fyodor", "dostoevsky" ],
  "output" : "Fyodor Dostoevsky",
  "payload" : { "books" : [ "123456", "123457" ] },
  "weight" : 30
 }
}'
```

Now if we run our example query, the results will be as follows:

```
{
  ...
  "authorsAutocomplete" : [ {
    "text" : "fyo",
    "offset" : 0,
    "length" : 3,
    "options" : [ {
      "text" : "Fyodor Dostoevsky",
      "score" : 30.0,
      "payload":{
        "books":["123456","123457"]
      }
    } ]
  } ]
}
```

Look how the score of the result changed. In our initial example, it was `1.0` and now it is `30.0`. This is so because we set the weight parameter to `30` during indexing.

Context suggester

The context suggester is an extension to the Elasticsearch Suggest API for Elasticsearch 2.1 and older versions that we just discussed. When describing the completion suggester for Elasticsearch 2.1, we mentioned that this suggester allows us to handle suggester-related searches entirely in memory. Using this suggester, we can define the so called *context* for the query that will limit the suggestions to a subset of documents. Because we define the context in the mappings, it is calculated during indexation, which makes query time calculations easier and less demanding in terms of performance.

> Remember that this section is related to Elasticsearch 2.1. Contexts in Elasticsearch 2.2 are handled differently and were discussed when discussing the completion suggester.

Context types

Elasticsearch 2.1 supports two types of context: `category` and `geo`. The `category` type of context allows us to assign a document to one or more categories during the index time. Later, during the query time, we can tell Elasticsearch which category we are interested in and Elasticsearch will limit the suggestions to those categories. The `geo` context allows us to limit the documents returned by the suggesters to a given location or to a certain distance from a point. The nice thing about context is that we can have multiple contexts. For example, we can have both the `category` context and the `geo` context for the same document. Let's now see what we need to do to use context in suggestions.

Using context

Using the `geo` and `category` context is very similar – they just differ in parameters. We will show you how to use contexts in an example using the simpler `category` context and later we will get back to the `geo` context and show you what we need to provide.

The first step when using context suggester is creating a proper mapping. Let's get back to our author mapping, but this time let's assume that each author can be given one or more category – the `brand` of books she/he is writing. This will be our context. The mappings using the context look as follows:

```
curl -XPOST 'localhost:9200/authors_geo_context' -d '{
  "mappings" : {
    "author" : {
      "properties" : {
        "name" : { "type" : "string" },
```

```
  "ac" : {
   "type" : "completion",
   "analyzer" : "simple",
   "search_analyzer" : "simple",
   "context" : {
    "brand" : {
     "type" : "category",
     "default" : [ "none" ]
    }
   }
  }
 }
 }
 }
}'
```

We've introduced a new section in our `ac` field definition: `context`. Each context is given a name, which is `brand` in our case, and inside that object we provide configuration. We need to provide the type using the `type` property – we will be using the `category` context suggester now. In addition to that, we've set the `default` array, which provides us with the value or values that should be used as the default context. If we want, we can also provide the `path` property, which will point Elasticsearch to a field in the documents from which the context value should be taken.

We can now index a single author by modifying the commands we used earlier, because we need to provide the context:

```
curl -XPOST 'localhost:9200/authors_context/author/1' -d '{
 "name" : "Fyodor Dostoevsky",
 "ac" : {
  "input" : "Fyodor Dostoevsky",
  "context" : {
   "brand" : "drama"
  }
 }
}'
```

As you can see, the `ac` field definition is a bit different now; it is an object. The `input` property is used to provide the value for autocomplete and the `context` object is used to provide the values for each of the contexts defined in the mappings.

Finally, we can query the data. As you could imagine, we will again provide the context we are interested in. The query that does that looks as follows:

```
curl -XGET 'localhost:9200/authors_context/_suggest?pretty' -d '{
 "authorsAutocomplete" : {
  "text" : "fyo",
  "completion" : {
   "field" : "ac",
   "context" : {
    "brand" : "drama"
   }
  }
 }
}'
```

As you can see, we've included the context object in the query inside the completion section and we've set the context we are interested in using the context name. The response returned by Elasticsearch is as follows:

```
{
   "_shards" : {
     "total" : 5,
     "successful" : 5,
     "failed" : 0
   },
   "authorsAutocomplete" : [ {
     "text" : "fyo",
     "offset" : 0,
     "length" : 3,
     "options" : [ {
       "text" : "Fyodor Dostoevsky",
       "score" : 1.0
     } ]
   } ]
}
```

However, if we change the brand context to comedy, for example, Elasticsearch will return no results, because we don't have authors with such a context. Let's test it by running the following query:

```
curl -XGET 'localhost:9200/authors_context/_suggest?pretty' -d '{
 "authorsAutocomplete" : {
```

```
  "text" : "fyo",
  "completion" : {
   "field" : "ac",
   "context" : {
    "brand" : "comedy"
   }
  }
 }
}'
```

This time Elasticsearch returns the following response:

```
{
  "_shards" : {
    "total" : 5,
    "successful" : 5,
    "failed" : 0
  },
  "authorsAutocomplete" : [ {
    "text" : "fyo",
    "offset" : 0,
    "length" : 3,
    "options" : [ ]
  } ]
}
```

This is because no author with the brand context and the value of comedy is present in the authors_context index.

Using the geo location context

The geo context is similar to the category context when it comes to using it. However, instead of filtering by terms, we filter using geographical points and distances. When we use the geo context, we need to provide precision, which defines the precision of the calculated geohash. The second property that we provide is the neighbors one, which can be set to true or false. By default, it is set to true, which means that the neighboring geohashes will be included in the context.

In addition to that, similar to the category context, we can provide path, which specifies which field to use as the lookup for the geographical point, and the default property, specifying the default geopoint for the documents.

For example, let's assume that we want to filter on the birth place of our authors. The mappings for such a suggester will look as follows:

```
curl -XPOST 'localhost:9200/authors_geo_context' -d '{
 "mappings" : {
  "author" : {
   "properties" : {
    "name" : { "type" : "string" },
    "ac" : {
     "type" : "completion",
     "analyzer" : "simple",
     "search_analyzer" : "simple",
     "context" : {
      "birth_location" : {
       "type" : "geo",
       "precision" : [ "1000km" ],
       "neighbors" : true,
       "default" : {
        "lat" : 0.0,
        "lon" : 0.0
       }
      }
     }
    }
   }
  }
 }
}'
```

Now we can index the documents and provide the birth location. For our example author, it will look as follows (the centre of Moscow):

```
curl -XPOST 'localhost:9200/authors_geo_context/author/1' -d '{
 "name" : "Fyodor Dostoevsky",
 "ac" : {
  "input" : "Fyodor Dostoevsky",
  "context" : {
   "birth_location" : {
```

```
    "lat" : 55.75,
   "lon" : 37.61
  }
 }
}
}'
```

As you can see, we've provided the `birth_location` context for our author.

Now during query time, we need to provide the context that we are interested in and we can (but we are not obligated to) provide the precision as the subset of the precision values provided in the mappings. We've defined the precision to 1000 km, so let's find all the authors starting with `fyo` that were born in Kazan, which is about 800 km from Moscow. We should find our example author.

The query that does that looks as follows:

```
curl -XGET 'localhost:9200/authors_geo_context/_suggest?pretty' -d '{
 "authorsAutocomplete" : {
  "text" : "fyo",
  "completion" : {
   "field" : "ac",
   "context" : {
    "birth_location" : {
     "lat" : 55.45,
     "lon" : 49.8
    }
   }
  }
 }
}'
```

The response returned by Elasticsearch looks as follows:

```
    {
      "_shards" : {
        "total" : 5,
        "successful" : 5,
        "failed" : 0
      },
      "authorsAutocomplete" : [ {
```

```
          "text" : "fyo",
          "offset" : 0,
          "length" : 3,
          "options" : [ {
            "text" : "Fyodor Dostoevsky",
            "score" : 1.0
          } ]
        } ]
    }
```

However, if we run the same query but point to the North Pole, we will get no results:

```
curl -XGET 'localhost:9200/authors_geo_context/_suggest?pretty' -d '{
 "authorsAutocomplete" : {
  "text" : "fyo",
  "completion" : {
   "field" : "ac",
   "context" : {
    "birth_location" : {
     "lat" : 0.0,
     "lon" : 0.0
    }
   }
  }
 }
}'
```

The following is the response from Elasticsearch in this case:

```
    {
      "_shards" : {
        "total" : 5,
        "successful" : 5,
        "failed" : 0
      },
      "authorsAutocomplete" : [ {
        "text" : "fyo",
        "offset" : 0,
        "length" : 3,
        "options" : [ ]
      } ]
    }
```

The Scroll API

Let's imagine that we have an index with several million documents. We already know how to build our query and so on. However, when trying to fetch a large number of documents, you see that when getting further and further with pages of the results, the queries slow down and finally timeout or result in memory issues.

The reason for this is that full-text search engines, especially those that are distributed, don't handle paging very well. Of course, getting a few hundred pages of results is not a problem for Elasticsearch, but for going through all the indexed documents or through large result set, a specialized API has been introduced.

Problem definition

When Elasticsearch generates a response, it must determine the order of the documents that form the result. If we are on the first page, this is not a big problem. Elasticsearch just finds the set of documents and collects the first ones; let's say, 20 documents. But if we are on the tenth page, Elasticsearch has to take all the documents from pages one to ten and then discard the ones that are on pages one to nine. This is even more complicated if we have a distributed environment, because we don't know from which nodes the results will come. Because of that, each node needs to build the response and keep it in memory for some time. The problem is not Elasticsearch-specific; a similar situation can be found in the database systems, for example, generally, in every system that uses the so-called priority queue.

Scrolling to the rescue

The solution is simple. Since Elasticsearch has to do some operations (determine the documents for the previous pages) for each request, we can ask Elasticsearch to store this information for subsequent queries. The drawback is that we cannot store this information forever due to limited resources. Elasticsearch assumes that we can declare how long we need this information to be available. Let's see how it works in practice.

First of all, we query Elasticsearch as we usually do. However, in addition to all the known parameters, we add one more: the parameter with the information that we want to use scrolling with and how long we suggest that Elasticsearch should keep the information about the results. We can do this by sending a query as follows:

```
curl 'localhost:9200/library/_search?pretty&scroll=5m' -d '{
  "size" : 1,
  "query" : {
```

```
    "match_all" : { }
  }
}'
```

The content of this query is irrelevant. The important thing is how Elasticsearch modifies the response. Look at the following first few lines of the response returned by Elasticsearch:

```
{
  "_scroll_id" :
"cXVlcnlUaGVuRmV0Y2g7NTsxNjo1RDNrYnlfb1JTeU1sX20yS0NRSUZ3OzE3OjVEM2ti
eV9vUlN5TWxfbTJLQ1FJRnc7MTg6NUQza2J5X29SU31NbF9tMktDUUlGdzsxOTo1RDNrY
nlfb1JTeU1sX20yS0NRSUZ3OzIwOjVEM2tieV9vUlN5TWxfbTJLQ1FJRnc7MDs=",
  "took" : 3,
  "timed_out" : false,
  "_shards" : {
    "total" : 5,
    "successful" : 5,
    "failed" : 0
  },
  "hits" : {
    "total" : 4,
    ...
```

The new part is the `_scroll_id` section. This is a handle that we will use in the queries that follow. Elasticsearch has a special endpoint for this: the `_search/scroll` endpoint. Let's look at the following example:

```
curl -XGET 'localhost:9200/_search/scroll?pretty' -d '{
  "scroll" : "5m",
  "scroll_id" :
"cXVlcnlUaGVuRmV0Y2g7NTsyNjo1RDNrYnlfb1JTeU1sX20yS0NRSUZ3OzI3OjVEM2tie
V9vUlN5TWxfbTJLQ1FJRnc7Mjg6NUQza2J5X29SU31NbF9tMktDUUlGdzsyOTo1RDNrYnl
fb1JTeU1sX20yS0NRSUZ3OzMwOjVEM2tieV9vUlN5TWxfbTJLQ1FJRnc7MDs="
}'
```

Now every call to this endpoint with `scroll_id` returns the next page of results. Remember that this handle is only valid for the defined time of inactivity.

Of course, this solution is not ideal, and it is not very appropriate when there are many requests to random pages of various results or when the time between the requests is difficult to determine. However, you can use this successfully for use cases where you want to get larger result sets, such as transferring data between several systems.

Summary

In the chapter that we just finished, we learned about some functionalities of Elasticsearch that we won't probably use everyday or at least not everyone of us will use them. We discussed percolator – an upside down search functionality that allows us to index queries and find which documents match them. We learned about the spatial capabilities of Elasticsearch and we used suggesters to correct user spelling mistakes and build a highly efficient autocomplete functionality. We also used the Scroll API to efficiently fetch large number of results from our Elasticsearch indices.

 In the next chapter, we will focus on clusters and its configuration. We will discuss node discovery, gateway, and recovery modules – what they are responsible for and how to configure them to match our needs. We will use templates and dynamic templates, and we will see how to install plugins extending Elasticsearch's out-of-the box functionalities. We will learn what are the caches of Elasticsearch caches are and how to configure them efficiently to make the most out of them. Finally, we will use the update settings API to update Elasticsearch configuration on live and running clusters.

Elasticsearch Cluster in Detail

9

The previous chapter was fully dedicated to search functionalities that are not only about full text searching. We learned how to use percolator – an inversed search that allows us to build altering functionalities on top of Elasticsearch. We learned to use spatial functionalities of Elasticsearch and we used the suggest API that allowed us to correct user's spelling mistakes as well as build very efficient autocomplete functionalities. But let's now focus on running and administering Elasticsearch. By the end of this chapter, you will have learned the following topics:

- How does Elasticsearch find new nodes that should join the cluster
- What are the gateway and recovery modules
- How do templates work
- How to use dynamic templates
- How to use the Elasticsearch plugin mechanism
- What are the caches in Elasticsearch and how to tune them
- How to use the Update Settings API to update Elasticsearch settings on running clusters

Understanding node discovery

When starting your Elasticsearch node, one of the first things that happens is looking for a master node that has the same cluster name and is visible. If a master is found, the node gets joined into an already formed cluster. If no master is found, then the node itself is selected as a master (of course if the configuration allows such behavior). The process of forming a cluster and finding nodes is called discovery. The module responsible for discovery has two main purposes: electing a master and discovering new nodes within a cluster. In this section, we will discuss how we can configure and tune the discovery module.

Discovery types

By default, without installing additional plugins, Elasticsearch allows us to use Zen discovery, which provides us with unicast discovery. Unicast (`http://en.wikipedia.org/wiki/Unicast`) allows transmission of a single message over the network to a single host at once. Elasticsearch node sends the message to the nodes defined in the configuration and waits for a response. When the node is accepted into the cluster, the recovery module kicks in and starts the recovery process if needed, or the master election process if the master is still not elected.

> Prior to Elasticsearch 2.0, the Zen discovery module allowed us to use multicast discovery. On a multicast capable network, Elasticsearch was able to automatically discover nodes without specifying any IP addresses of other Elasticsearch servers sharing the same cluster name. This was very mistake prone and not advised for production use and thus it was deprecated and removed to a plugin.

Elasticsearch architecture is designed to be peer to peer. When running operations such as indexing or searching, the master node doesn't take part in communication and the relevant nodes communicate with each other directly.

Node roles

Elasticsearch nodes can be configured to work in one of the following roles:

- **Master**: The node responsible for maintaining the global cluster state, changing it depending on the needs, and handling the addition and removal of nodes. There can only be a single master node active in a single cluster.

- **Data**: The node responsible for holding the data and executing data related operations (indexation and searching) on the shards that are present locally for the node.

- **Client**: The node responsible for handling requests. For the indexing requests, the client node forwards the request to the appropriate primary shard and, for the search requests, it sends it to all the relevant shards and aggregates the results.

By default, each node can work as master, data, or client. It can be a data and a client at the same time for example. On large and highly loaded clusters, it is very important to divide the roles of the nodes in the cluster and have the nodes do only a single role at a time. When dealing with such clusters, you will often see at least three master nodes, multiple data nodes, and a few client only nodes as part of the whole cluster.

Master node

It is the most important node type from Elasticsearch cluster's point of view. It handles the cluster state, changes it, manages the nodes joining and leaving the cluster, checks the health of the other nodes in the cluster (by running ping requests), and manages the shard relocation operations. If the master is somehow disconnected from the cluster, the remaining nodes will select a new master from each other. All these processes are done automatically on the basis of the configuration values we provide. You usually want the master nodes to only communicate with the other Elasticsearch nodes, using the internal Java communication. To avoid hitting the master nodes by mistake, it is advised to turn off the HTTP module for them in the configuration.

Data node

The data node is responsible for holding the data in the indices. The data nodes are the ones that need the most disk space because of being loaded with data indexation requests and running searches on the data they have locally. The data nodes, similar to the master nodes can have the HTTP module disabled.

Client node

The client nodes are in most cases nodes that don't have any data and are not master nodes. The client nodes are the ones that communicate with the outside world and with all the nodes in the cluster. They forward the data to the appropriate shards and aggregate the search and aggregations results from all the other nodes.

Keep in mind that client nodes can have data as well, but in such a case they will run both the indexing requests and the search requests for the local data and will aggregate the data from the other nodes, which in large clusters may be too much work for a single node.

Configuring node roles

By default, Elasticsearch allows every node to be a master node, a data node, or a client node. However, as we already mentioned, in certain situations you may want to have nodes that only hold data, client nodes that are only used to process requests, and master hosts to manage the cluster. One such situation is when massive amounts of data needs to be handled, where the data nodes should be as performant as possible. To tell Elasticsearch what role it should take, we use three Boolean properties set in the `elasticsearch.yml` configuration file:

- `node.master`: When set to `true`, we tell Elasticsearch that the node is master eligible, which means that it can take the role of a master. However, note that the master will be automatically marked as not master eligible as soon as it is assigned a client role.

- `node.data`: When set to `true`, we tell Elasticsearch that the node can be used to hold data.

- `node.client`: When set to `true`, we tell Elasticsearch that the node should be used as a client.

So, to set a node to only hold data, we should add the following properties to the `elasticsearch.yml` configuration file:

```
node.master: false
node.data: true
node.client: false
```

To set the node to not hold data and only be a master node, we need to instruct Elasticsearch that we don't want the node to hold data. In order to do this, we add the following properties to the `elasticsearch.yml` configuration file:

```
node.master: true
node.data: false
node.client: false
```

Setting the cluster's name

If we don't set the `cluster.name` property in our `elasticsearch.yml` file, Elasticsearch uses the `elasticsearch` default value. This is not a good thing, because each new Elasticsearch node will have the same cluster name and you may want to have multiple clusters in the same network. In such a case, connecting the wrong nodes together is just a matter of time. Because of that, we suggest setting the `cluster.name` property to some other value of your choice. Usually, it is a good idea to adjust cluster names based on cluster responsibilities.

Zen discovery

The default discovery method used by Elasticsearch and one that is commonly used in the Elasticsearch world is called Zen discovery. It supports unicast discovery and allows adjusting various parts of its configuration.

 Note that there are additional discovery types available as plugins, such as Amazon EC2 discovery, Microsoft Azure discovery, and Google Compute Engine discovery.

Master election configuration

Imagine that you have a cluster that is built of 10 nodes. Everything is working fine until one day when your network fails and 3 of your nodes are disconnected from the cluster, but they still see each other. Because of the Zen discovery and master election process, the nodes that got disconnected elect a new master and you end up with two clusters with the same name, with two master nodes. Such a situation is called a split-brain and you must avoid it as much as possible. When split-brain happens, you end up with two (or more) clusters that won't join each other until the network (or any other) problems are fixed. The thing to remember is that split-brain may result in not recoverable errors, such as data conflicts in which you end up with data corruption or partial data loss. That's why it is important to avoid such situations at all costs.

In order to prevent split-brain situations, Elasticsearch provides a `discovery.zen.minimum_master_nodes` property. This property defines the minimum amount of master eligible nodes that should be connected to each other in order to form a cluster. So now let's get back to our cluster; if we set the `discovery.zen.minimum_master_nodes` property to 50 percent of the total nodes available + 1 (which is 6 in our case), we will end up with a single cluster. Why is that? Before the network failure, we had 10 nodes, which is more than six nodes, and those nodes formed a cluster. After the disconnection of the three nodes, we would still have the first cluster up and running. However, because only three nodes got disconnected and three is less than six, these three nodes wouldn't be allowed to elect a new master and they would wait for reconnection with the original cluster.

Of course this is also not a perfect scenario. It is advised to have a dedicated master eligible nodes only, that don't work as data or client nodes. To have a quorum in such a case, we need at least three dedicated master eligible nodes, because that will allow us to have a single master offline and still keep the quorum. This is usually enough to keep the clusters in a good shape when it comes to master related features and to be split-brain proof. Of course, in such a case, the `discovery.zen.minimum_master_nodes` property should be set to 2 and we should have the three master nodes up and running.

Furthermore, Elasticsearch allows us to additionally specify two additional Boolean properties: `discover.zen.master_election.filter_client` and `discover.zen.master_election.filter_data`. They allow us to tell Elasticsearch to ignore ping requests from the client and data nodes during master election. By default, the first mentioned property is set to `true` and the second is set to `false`. This allows Elasticsearch to focus on the master election and not be overloaded with ping requests from the nodes that are not master eligible.

In addition to the mentioned properties, Elasticsearch allows configuring timeouts related to the master election process. `discovery.zen.ping_timeout`, which defaults to 3s (three seconds), allows configuring timeout for slow networks – the higher the value, the lesser the chance of failure, but the election process can take longer. The second property is called `discover.zen.join_timeout` and specifies the timeout for the join request to the master. It defaults to 20 times the `discovery.zen.ping_timeout` property.

Configuring unicast

Because of the way unicast works, we need to specify at least a host that the unicast message should be sent to. To do this, we should add the `discovery.zen.ping.unicast.hosts` property to our `elasticsearch.yml` configuration file. Basically, we should specify all the hosts that form the cluster in the `discovery.zen.ping.unicast.hosts` property (we don't have to specify all the hosts, we just need to provide enough so that we are sure that a single one will work). For example, if we want the hosts `192.168.2.1`, `192.168.2.2` and `192.168.2.3` for our host, we should specify the preceding property in the following way:

```
discovery.zen.ping.unicast.hosts: 192.168.2.1:9300, 192.168.2.2:9300,
192.168.2.3:9300
```

One can also define a range of the ports Elasticsearch can use. For example, to say that ports from `9300` to `9399` can be used, we specify the following:

```
discovery.zen.ping.unicast.hosts: 192.168.2.1:[9300-9399],
192.168.2.2:[9300-9399], 192.168.2.3:[9300-9399]
```

Note that the hosts are separated with a comma character and we've specified the port on which we expect unicast messages.

Fault detection ping settings

In addition to the settings discussed previously, we can also control or alter the default ping configuration. Ping is a signal sent between the nodes to check if they are running and responsive. The master node pings all the other nodes in the cluster and each of the other nodes in the cluster pings the master node. The following properties can be set:

- `discovery.zen.fd.ping_interval`: This defaults to `1s` (one second) and specifies how often the nodes ping each other

- `discovery.zen.fd.ping_timeout`: This defaults to `30s` (30 seconds) and defines how long a node will wait for the response to its ping message before considering a node as unresponsive

- `discovery.zen.fd.ping_retries`: This defaults to `3` and specifies how many retries should be taken before considering a node as not working

If you experience some problems with your network, or you know that your nodes need more time to see the ping response, you can adjust the preceding values to the ones that are good for your deployment.

Cluster state updates control

As we have already discussed, the master node is the one responsible for handling the changes of the cluster state and Elasticsearch allows us to control that process. For most use cases, the default settings are more than enough, but you may run into situations where changing the settings is required.

The master node processes a single cluster state command at a time. First the master node propagates the changes to other nodes and then it waits for response. Each cluster state change is not considered finished until enough nodes respond to the master with acknoledgment. The number of nodes that need to respond is specified by `discovery.zen.minimum_master_nodes`, which we are already aware of. The maximum time an Elasticsearch node waits for the nodes to respond is `30s` by default and is specified by the `discovery.zen.commit_timeout` property. If not enough nodes respond to the master, the cluster state change is rejected.

Once enough nodes respond to the master publish message, the cluster state change is accepted on the master and the cluster state is changed. Once that is done, the master sends a message to all the nodes saying that the change can be applied. The timeout of this message is again set to `30 seconds` and is controlled using the `discovery.zen.publish_timeout` property.

Dealing with master unavailability

If a cluster has no master node, whatever the reason may be, it is not fully operational. By default, we can't change the metadata, cluster wide commands will not be working, and so on. Elasticsearch allows us to configure the behavior of the nodes when the master node is not elected. To do that, we can use the `discovery.zen.no_master_block` property which the settings of `all` and `write`. Setting this property to `all` means that all the operations on the node will be rejected, that is, the search operations, the write related operations, and the cluster wide operations such as health or mappings retrieval. Setting this property to `write` means that only the write operation will be rejected – this is the default behavior of Elasticsearch.

Adjusting HTTP transport settings

While discussing the node discovery module and process, we mentioned the HTTP module a few times. We would like to get back to that topic now and discuss a few useful properties when discussing and using Elasticsearch.

Disabling HTTP

The first thing is disabling the HTTP completely. This is useful to ensure that the master and data nodes won't accept any queries or requests in general from users. To disable the HTTP transport completely, we just need to add the `http.enabled` property and set it to false in our `elasticsearch.yml` file.

HTTP port

Elasticsearch allows us to define the port on which it will be listening to HTTP requests. This is done by using the `http.port` property. It defaults to 9200-9300, which means that Elasticsearch will start from `9200` port and increase if the port is not available (so the next instance will use `9201` port, and so on). There is also `http.publish_port`, which is very useful when running Elasticsearch behind a firewall and when the HTTP port is not directly accessible. It defines which port should be used by the clients connecting to Elasticsearch and defaults to the same value as the `http.port` property.

HTTP host

We can also define the host to which Elasticsearch will bind. To specify it, we need to define the `http.host` property. The default value is the one set by the network module. If needed, we can set the publish host and the bind host separately using the `http.publish_host` and `http.bind_host` properties. You usually don't have to specify these properties unless your nodes have non standard host names or multiple names and you want Elasticsearch to bind to a single one only.

You can find the full list of properties allowed for the HTTP module in Elasticsearch official documentation available at `https://www.elastic.co/guide/en/elasticsearch/reference/2.2/modules-http.html`.

The gateway and recovery modules

Apart from our indices and the data indexed inside them, Elasticsearch needs to hold the metadata, such as the type mappings, the index level settings, and so on. This information needs to be persisted somewhere so it can be read during cluster recovery. Of course, it could be stored in memory, but full cluster restart or a fatal failure would result in this information being lost, which is not something that we want. This is why Elasticsearch introduced the gateway module. You can think about it as a safe heaven for your cluster data and metadata. Each time you start your cluster, all the needed data is read from the gateway and, when you make a change to your cluster, it is persisted using the gateway module.

The gateway

In order to set the type of gateway we want to use, we need to add the `gateway.type` property to the `elasticsearch.yml` configuration file and set it to the local value. Currently, Elasticsearch recommends using the local gateway type (`gateway.type` set to `local`), which is the default one and the only one available without additional plugins.

The default local gateway type stores the indices and their metadata in the local file system. Compared to the other gateways, the write operation to this gateway is not performed in an asynchronous way, so, whenever a write succeeds, you can be sure that the data was written into the gateway (so basically indexed or stored in the transaction log).

Recovery control

In addition to choosing the gateway type, Elasticsearch allows us to configure when to start the initial recovery process. The recovery is a process of initializing all the shards and replicas, reading all the data from the transaction log, and applying them on the shards. Basically, it's a process needed to start Elasticsearch.

For example, let's imagine that we have a cluster that consists of 10 Elasticsearch nodes. We should inform Elasticsearch about the number of nodes by setting `gateway.expected_nodes` to that value, so 10 in our case. We inform Elasticsearch about the number of expected nodes that are eligible to hold the data and eligible to be selected as a master. Elasticsearch will start the recovery process immediately if the number of nodes in the cluster is equal to that property.

We would also like to start the recovery after six nodes are together. To do this, we should set the `gateway.recover_after_nodes` property to `6`. This property should be set to a value that ensures that the newest version of the cluster state snapshot will be available, which usually means that you should start recovery when most of your nodes are available.

There is also one more thing. We would like the gateway recovery process to start 5 minutes after the `gateway.recover_after_nodes` condition is met. To do this, we set the `gateway.recover_after_time` property to `5m`. This property tells the gateway module how long to wait with the recovery process after the number of nodes reached the minimum specified by the `gateway.recovery_after_nodes` property. We may want to do this because we know that our network is quite slow and we want the nodes communication to be stable. Note that Elasticsearch won't delay the recovery if the number of master and data eligible nodes that formed the cluster is equal to the value of the `gateway.expected_nodes` property.

The preceding property values should be set in the `elasticsearch.yml` configuration file. For example: if we would like to have the previously discussed value in the mentioned file, we would end up with the following section in the file:

```
gateway.recover_after_nodes: 6
gateway.recover_after_time: 5m
gateway.expected_nodes: 10
```

Additional gateway recovery options

In addition to the mentioned options, Elasticsearch allows us some additional degree of control. These additional options are:

- `gateway.recover_after_master_nodes`: This is similar to the `gateway_recover_after_nodes` property, but instead of taking into consideration all the nodes, it allows us to specify how many master eligible nodes should be present in the cluster before recovery starts

- `gateway.recover_after_data_nodes`: This is also similar to the `gateway_recover_after_nodes` property, but it allows specifying how many data nodes should be present in the cluster before recovery starts

- `gateway.expected_master_nodes`: This is similar to the `gateway.expected_nodes` property, but instead of specifying the number of all the nodes that we expect in the cluster, it allows specifying how many master eligible nodes we expect to be present

- `gateway.expected_master_nodes`: This is similar to the `gateway.expected_nodes` property, but allows specifying how many master nodes we expect to be present

- `gateway.expected_data_nodes`: This is also similar to the `gateway.expected_nodes` property, but allows specifying how many data nodes we expect to be present

Indices recovery API

There is also one other thing when it comes to the recovery process – the indices recovery API. It allows us to see the process of index or indices recovery. To use it, we just need to specify the indices and use the `_recovery` end-point. For example, to check the recovery process of the `library` index, we will run the following command:

```
curl -XGET 'localhost:9200/library/_recovery?pretty'
```

The response for the preceding command can be large and depends on the number of shards in the index and of course the amount of indices we want to get information for. In our case, the response looks as follows (we left information about a single shard to make it less extensive):

```
{
  "library" : {
    "shards" : [ {
      "id" : 0,
      "type" : "STORE",
      "stage" : "DONE",
```

```
"primary" : true,
"start_time_in_millis" : 1444030695956,
"stop_time_in_millis" : 1444030695962,
"total_time_in_millis" : 5,
"source" : {
  "id" : "Brt5ejEVSVCkIfvY9iDMRQ",
  "host" : "127.0.0.1",
  "transport_address" : "127.0.0.1:9300",
  "ip" : "127.0.0.1",
  "name" : "Puff Adder"
},
"target" : {
  "id" : "Brt5ejEVSVCkIfvY9iDMRQ",
  "host" : "127.0.0.1",
  "transport_address" : "127.0.0.1:9300",
  "ip" : "127.0.0.1",
  "name" : "Puff Adder"
},
"index" : {
  "size" : {
    "total_in_bytes" : 157,
    "reused_in_bytes" : 157,
    "recovered_in_bytes" : 0,
    "percent" : "100.0%"
  },
  "files" : {
    "total" : 1,
    "reused" : 1,
    "recovered" : 0,
    "percent" : "100.0%"
  },
  "total_time_in_millis" : 1,
  "source_throttle_time_in_millis" : 0,
  "target_throttle_time_in_millis" : 0
},
"translog" : {
  "recovered" : 0,
  "total" : -1,
  "percent" : "-1.0%",
  "total_on_start" : -1,
  "total_time_in_millis" : 4
},
"verify_index" : {
```

```
            "check_index_time_in_millis" : 0,
            "total_time_in_millis" : 0
          }
       },
       ...
       ]
    }
  }
}
```

As you can see in the response, we see the information about each shard. For each shard, we see the type of the operation (the `type` property), the stage (the `stage` property) describing what part of the recovery process is in progress, and whether it is a primary shard (the `primary` property). In addition to this, we see sections about the source shard, the target shard, the index the shard is part of, the information about the transaction log, and finally information about the index verification. All of this allows us to see what is the status of the recovery of our indices.

Delayed allocation

We already discussed that by default Elasticsearch tries to balance the shards in the cluster accordingly to the number of nodes in that cluster. Because of that, when a node drops off the cluster (or multiple nodes do) or when nodes join the cluster, Elasticsearch starts rebalancing the cluster, moving the shards and the replicas around. This is usually very expensive – new primary shards may be promoted out of the available replicas, large amount of data may be copied between the new primary and its replicas, and so on. And this may be happening because a single node was just restarted for 30 seconds maintenance.

To avoid such situations, Elasticsearch provides us with the possibility to control how long to wait before beginning allocation of shards that are in unassigned state. We can control the delay by using the `index.unassigned.node_left.delayed_timeout` property and setting it on per index basis. For example, to configure the allocation timeout for the `library` index to 10 minutes, we run the following command:

```
curl -XPUT 'localhost:9200/library/_settings' -d '{
 "settings": {
  "index.unassigned.node_left.delayed_timeout": "10m"
 }
}'
```

We can also configure the allocation timeout for all the indices by running the following command:

```
curl -XPUT 'localhost:9200/_all/_settings' -d '{
 "settings": {
  "index.unassigned.node_left.delayed_timeout": "10m"
 }
}'
```

Index recovery prioritization

Elasticsearch 2.2 exposes one more feature when it comes to the indices recovery process that allows us to define which indices should be prioritized when it comes to recovery. By specifying the `index.priority` property in the index settings and assigning it a positive integer value, we define the order in which Elasticsearch should recover the indices; the ones with the higher `index.priority` property will be started first.

For example, let's assume that we have two indices, `library` and `map`, and we want the `library` index to be recovered before the `map` index. To do this, we will run the following commands:

```
curl -XPUT 'localhost:9200/library/_settings' -d '{
 "settings": {
  "index.priority": 10
 }
}'
curl -XPUT 'localhost:9200/map/_settings' -d '{
 "settings": {
  "index.priority": 1
 }
}'
```

We assigned higher priority to the `library` index and, because of that, it will be recovered faster.

Templates and dynamic templates

In the *Mappings configuration* section of Chapter 2, *Indexing Your Data*, we discussed mappings, how they are created, and how the type-determining mechanism works. Now we will get into more advanced topics. We will show you how to dynamically create mappings for new indices and how to apply some logic to the templates, so that new indices are already created with predefined mappings.

Templates

In various parts of the book, when discussing index configuration and its structure, we've seen that this can become complicated, especially when we have sophisticated data structures that we want to index, search, and aggregate. Especially if you have a lot of similar indices, taking care of the mappings in each of them can be a very painful process – each new index has to be created with appropriate mappings. Elasticsearch creators predicted this and implemented a feature called index templates. Each template defines a pattern, which is compared to a newly created index name. When both of them match, the values defined in the template are copied to the index structure definition. When multiple templates match the name of the newly created index, all of them are applied and the values from the templates that are applied later override the values defined in the previously applied templates. This is very convenient because we can define a few common settings in the general templates and change them in the more specialized ones. In addition, there is an order parameter that lets us force the desired template ordering. You can think of templates as dynamic mappings that can be applied not to the types in documents but to the indices.

An example of a template

Let's see a real example of a template. Imagine that we want to create many indices in which we don't want to store the source of the documents so that our indices are smaller. We also don't need any replicas. We can create a template that matches our need by using the Elasticsearch REST API and the `/_template` end point, by sending the following command:

```
curl -XPUT http://localhost:9200/_template/main_template?pretty -d '{
  "template" : "*",
    "order" : 1,
    "settings" : {
    "index.number_of_replicas" : 0
  },
  "mappings" : {
```

```
    "_default_" : {
      "_source" : {
        "enabled" : false
      }
    }
  }
}'
```

From now on, all the created indices will have no replicas and no source stored. This is because the template parameter value is set to *, which matches all the names of the indices. Note the `_default_` type name in our example. This is a special type name which indicates that the current rule should be applied to every document type. The second interesting thing is the order parameter. Let's define a second template by using the following command:

```
curl -XPUT http://localhost:9200/_template/ha_template?pretty -d '{
  "template" : "ha_*",
  "order" : 10,
  "settings" : {
    "index.number_of_replicas" : 5
  }
}'
```

After running the preceding command, all the new indices will behave as earlier except the ones with names beginning with ha_. In case of these indices, both the templates are applied. First, the template with the lower order value is used and then the next template overwrites the replica's setting. So, the indices whose names start with ha_ will have five replicas and disabled sources stored.

 Before version 2.0, Elasticsearch templates could also be stored in files. Starting with Elasticsearch 2.0, this feature is no longer available.

Dynamic templates

Sometimes we want to have the possibility of defining type that is dependent on the field name and the type. This is where dynamic templates can help. Dynamic templates are similar to the usual mappings, but each template has its pattern defined, which is applied to a document's field name. If a field name matches the pattern, the template is used.

Let's have a look at the following example:

```
curl -XPOST 'localhost:9200/news' -d '{
  "mappings" : {
    "article" : {
      "dynamic_templates" : [
        {
          "template_test": {
            "match" : "*",
            "mapping" : {
              "index" : "analyzed",
              "fields" : {
                "str": {
                  "type": "{dynamic_type}",
                  "index": "not_analyzed"
                }
              }
            }
          }
        }
      ]
    }
  }
}'
```

In the preceding example, we defined the mapping for the article type. In this mapping, we have only one dynamic template named `template_test`. This template is applied for every field in the input document because of the single asterisk pattern in the `match` property. Each field will be treated as a multifield, consisting of a field named as the original field (for example, `title`) and the second field with a name suffixed with `str` (for example, `title.str`). The first field will have its type determined by Elasticsearch (with the `{dynamic_type}` type), and the second field will be a string (because of the `string` type).

The matching pattern

We have two ways of defining the matching pattern. They are as follows:

- `match`: This template is used if the name of the field matches the pattern (this pattern type was used in our example)

- `unmatch`: This template is used if the name of the field doesn't match the pattern

By default, the pattern is very simple and uses glob patterns. This can be changed by using `match_pattern=regexp`. After adding this property, we can use all the magic provided by regular expressions to match and `unmatch` the patterns. There are variations such as `path_match` and `path_unmatch` that can be used to match the names in nested documents (by providing path, similar to queries).

Field definitions

When writing a target field definition, the following variables can be used:

- `{name}`: The name of the original field found in the input document

- `{dynamic_type}`: The type determined from the original document

> Note that Elasticsearch checks the templates in the order of their definitions and the first matching template is applied. This means that the most generic templates (for example, with `"match"`: `"*"`) must be defined at the end.

Elasticsearch plugins

At various places in this book, we have used different plugins that have been able to extend the core functionality of Elasticsearch. You probably remember the additional programming languages used in scripts described in the *Scripting capabilities of Elasticsearch* section of *Chapter 6, Make Your Search Better*. In this section, we will look at how the plugins work and how to install them.

The basics

By default, Elasticsearch plugins are located in their own subdirectory in the plugins subdirectory of the search engine home directory. If you have downloaded a new plugin manually, you can just create a new directory with the plugin name and unpack that plugin archive to this directory. There is also a more convenient way to install plugins: by using the `plugin` script. We have used it several times in this book without talking about it, so this time let's take the time and describe this tool.

Elasticsearch has two main types of plugins. These two types can be categorized based on the content of the `plugin-descriptor.properties` file: Java plugins and site plugins. Let's start with the site plugins. They usually contain sets of HTML, CSS, and JavaScript files and add additional UI components to Elasticsearch. Elasticsearch treats the site plugins as a file set that should be served by the built-in HTTP server under the `/_plugin/plugin_name/` URL (for example, `/_plugin/bigdesk/`). This type of plugin doesn't change anything in core Elasticsearch functionality.

The Java plugins are the ones that add or modify the core Elasticsearch features. They usually contain the JAR files. The `plugin-descriptor.properties` file contains information about the main class that should be used by Elasticsearch as an entry point to configure plugins and allow them to extend the Elasticsearch functionality. The nice thing about the Java plugins is that they can contain the site part as well. The site part of the plugin needs to be placed in the `_site` directory if we are unpacking the plugin manually.

Installing plugins

Plugins can be downloaded from three source types. The first is the official repository located at `https://download.elastic.co`. All plugins from this source can be installed by referring to the plugin name. For example:

```
bin/plugin install lang-javascript
```

The preceding command results in installation of a plugin that allows us to use an additional scripting language, JavaScript. Elasticsearch automatically tries to find a plugin version that is the same as the version of Elasticsearch we are using. Sometimes, like in the following example, a plugin may ask for additional permissions during installation.

Just so we know what to expect, this is an example result of running the preceding command:

```
-> Installing lang-javascript...
Trying https://download.elastic.co/elasticsearch/release/org/
elasticsearch/plugin/lang-javascript/2.2.0/lang-javascript-2.2.0.zip ...
Downloading ................................................................
..............DONE
Verifying https://download.elastic.co/elasticsearch/release/org/
elasticsearch/plugin/lang-javascript/2.2.0/lang-javascript-2.2.0.zip
checksums if available ...
Downloading .DONE
@@@@@@@@@@@@@@@@@@@@@@@@@@@@@@@@@@@@@@@@@@@@@@@@@@@@@@@@@@@@@@@
@        WARNING: plugin requires additional permissions        @
@@@@@@@@@@@@@@@@@@@@@@@@@@@@@@@@@@@@@@@@@@@@@@@@@@@@@@@@@@@@@@@
* java.lang.RuntimePermission createClassLoader
* org.elasticsearch.script.ClassPermission <<STANDARD>>
* org.elasticsearch.script.ClassPermission org.mozilla.javascript.
ContextFactory
* org.elasticsearch.script.ClassPermission org.mozilla.javascript.
Callable
* org.elasticsearch.script.ClassPermission org.mozilla.javascript.
NativeFunction
* org.elasticsearch.script.ClassPermission org.mozilla.javascript.Script
* org.elasticsearch.script.ClassPermission org.mozilla.javascript.
ScriptRuntime
* org.elasticsearch.script.ClassPermission org.mozilla.javascript.
Undefined
* org.elasticsearch.script.ClassPermission org.mozilla.javascript.
optimizer.OptRuntime
See http://docs.oracle.com/javase/8/docs/technotes/guides/security/
permissions.html
for descriptions of what these permissions allow and the associated
risks.


Continue with installation? [y/N]y
Installed lang-javascript into /Users/someplace/elasticsearch-2.2.0/
plugins/lang-javascript
Installed lang-javascript into /Users/negativ/Developer/Elastic/
elasticsearch-2.2.0/plugins/lang-javascript
```

If the plugin is not available at the first location, it can be placed in one of the Apache Maven repositories: Maven Central (`https://search.maven.org/`) or Maven Sonatype (`https://oss.sonatype.org/`). In this case, the `plugin` name for installation should be equal to `groupId/artifactId/version`, just as every library for Maven (`http://maven.apache.org/`). For example:

```
bin/plugin install org.elasticsearch/elasticsearch-mapper-
attachments/3.0.1
```

The third source are the GitHub (`https://github.com/`) repositories. The plugin tool assumes that the given plugin address contains the organization name followed by the plugin name and, optionally, the version number. Let's look at the following command example:

```
bin/plugin install mobz/elasticsearch-head
```

If you write your own plugin and you have no access to the earlier-mentioned sites, there is no problem. The `plugin` tool accepts the `url` property from where the `plugin` should be downloaded (instead of specifying the name of the `plugin`). This option allows us to set any location for the plugins, including the local file system (using the `file://` prefix) or remote file (using the `http://` prefix). For example, the following command will result in the installation of a plugin archived on the local file system in the `/tmp/elasticsearch-lang-javascript-3.0.0.RC1.zip` directory:

```
bin/plugin install file:///tmp/elasticsearch-lang-javascript-3.0.0.RC1.zip
```

Removing plugins

Removing a plugin is as simple as removing its directory. You can also do this by using the `plugin` tool. For example, to remove the previously installed JavaScript plugin, we run a command as follows:

```
bin/plugin remove lang-javascript
```

The output from the command just confirms that the plugin was removed:

```
-> Removing lang-javascript...
Removed lang-javascript
```

 You need to restart the Elasticsearch node for the plugin installation or removal to take effect.

Elasticsearch caches

Until now we haven't mentioned Elasticsearch caches much in the book. However, as most common systems Elasticsearch users a variety of caches to perform more complicated operations or to speed up performance of heavy data retrieval from disk based Lucene indices. In this section, we will look at the most common caches of Elasticsearch, what they are used for, what are the performance implications of using them, and how to configure them.

Fielddata cache

In the beginning of the book, we discussed that Elasticsearch uses the so called inverted index data structure to quickly and efficiently search through the documents. This is very good when searching and filtering the data, but for features such as aggregations, sorting, or script usage, Elasticsearch needs an un-inverted data structure, because these functions rely on per document data information.

Because of the need for uninverted data, when Elasticsearch was first released it contained and still contains an in memory data structure called fielddata. Fielddata is used to store all the values of a given field to memory to provide very fast document based lookup. However, the cost of using fielddata is memory and increased garbage collection. Because of memory and performance cost, starting from Elasticsearch 2.0, each indexed, not analyzed field uses `doc` values by default. Other fields, such as analyzed text fields, still use fielddata and because of that it is good to know how to handle fielddata.

Fielddata size

Elasticsearch allows us to control how much memory the fielddata cache uses. By default, the cache is unbounded, which is very dangerous. If you have large indices, you may run into memory issues, where the fielddata cache will eat most of the memory given to Elasticsearch and will result in node failure. We are allowed to configure the size of the fielddata cache by using the static `indices.fielddata.cache.size` property set to an explicit value (like `10GB`) or to a percentage of the whole memory given to Elasticsearch (like `20%`).

Remember that the fielddata cache is very expensive to build as it needs to load all the values of a given field to memory. This can take a lot of time resulting in degradation in the performance of the queries. Because of this, it is advised to have enough memory to keep the needed cache permanently in Elasticsearch memory. However, we understand that this is not always possible because of hardware costs.

Circuit breakers

The nice thing about Elasticsearch is that it allows us to achieve a similar thing in multiple ways and we have the same situation when it comes to fielddata and limiting the memory usage. Elasticsearch allows us to use a functionality called circuit breakers, which can estimate how much memory a request or a query will use, and if it is above a defined threshold, it won't be executed at all, resulting in no memory usage and an exception thrown. This is very nice when we don't want to limit the size of the fielddata cache but we also don't want a single query to cause memory issues and make the cluster unstable. There are two main circuit breakers: the field data circuit breaker and the request circuit breaker.

The first circuit breaker, the field data one, estimates the amount of memory that will need to be used to load data to the `fielddata` cache for a given query. We can configure the limit by using the `indices.breaker.fielddata.limit` property, which is by default set to `60%`, which means that a fielddata cache for a single query can't use more than 60 percent of the memory given to Elasticsearch.

The second circuit breaker, the request one, estimates the memory used by per request data structures and prevents them from using more than the amount specified by the `indices.breaker.request.limit` property. By default, the mentioned property is set to `40%`, which means that single request data structures, such as the ones used for aggregation calculation, can't use more than 40% of the memory given to Elasticsearch.

Finally, there is one more circuit breaker that is defined by the `indices.breaker.limit.total` property (by default set to `70%`). This circuit breaker defines the total amount of memory that can be used by both the per request data structures and fielddata.

Remember that the settings for circuit breakers are dynamic and can be updated using cluster update settings.

Fielddata and doc values

As we already discussed, instead of fielddata cache, `doc` values can be used. Of course, this is only true for not analyzed fields and ones using numeric data types and not multivalued ones. This will save memory and should be faster than the fielddata cache during query time, at the cost of slight indexing speed degradations (very small) and a slightly larger index. If you can use doc values, do that – it will help your Elasticsearch cluster to maintain stability and respond to queries quickly.

Shard request cache

The first of the caches that operates on the queries. The shard request cache caches the aggregations and suggestions resulted by the query, but, when writing this book, it was not caching query hits. When Elasticsearch executes the query, this cache can save the resource consuming aggregations for the query and speed up the subsequent queries by retrieving the aggregations or suggestions from memory.

 During the writing of this book, the shard request cache was only used when the `size=0` parameter was set for the query. This means that only the total number of hits, aggregation results, and suggestions will be cached. Remember that when running queries with dates and using the `now` constant, the shard query cache won't also be used.

The shard request cache, as its name says, caches the results of the queries on each shard, before they are returned to the node that aggregates the results. This can be very good when your aggregations are heavy, like the ones that do a lot of computation on the data returned by the query. If you run a lot of aggregations with your queries and the queries can be repeated, think about using the shard request cache as it should help you with queries latency.

Enabling and configuring the shard request cache

The shard request cache is disabled by default, but can be easily enabled. To enable it, we should set the `index.requests.cache.enable` property to `true` when creating the index. For example, to enable the shard request cache for an index called `new_library`, we use the following command:

```
curl -XPUT 'localhost:9200/new_library' -d '{
 "settings": {
  "index.requests.cache.enable": true
 }
}'
```

One thing to remember is that the mentioned setting is not dynamically updatable. We need to include it in the index creation command or we can update it when the index is closed.

The maximum size of the cache is specified using the `indices.requests.cache.size` property and is set to 1% by default (which means 1% of the total memory given to Elasticsearch). We can also specify how long each entry should be kept by using the `indices.requests.cache.expire` property, but it is not set by default. Also, the cache is invalidated once the index is refreshed (during index searcher reopening), which makes the setting useless most of the time.

> Note that in the earlier versions of Elasticsearch, for example in the 1.x branch, to enable or disable this cache, the `index.cache.query.enable` property was used. This may be important when migrating from older Elasticsearch versions.

Per request shard request cache disabling

Elasticsearch allows us to control the request shard cache used on a per request basis. If we have the mentioned cache enabled, we can still force the search engine to omit caching for such requests. This is done by using the `request_cache` parameter. If set to `true`, the request will be cached and, if set to `false`, the request won't be cached. This is especially useful when we want to cache our requests in general but omit caching for some queries that are rare and not used often. It is also wise for requests that use non-deterministic scripts and time ranges to not be cached.

Shard request cache usage monitoring

If we don't use any monitoring software that allows monitoring the caches usage, we can use Elasticsearch API to check the metrics around the shard request cache. This can be done both at the indices level or at the nodes level.

To check the metrics for the shard request cache for all the indices, we should use the indices stats API and run the following command:

```
curl 'localhost:9200/_stats/request_cache?pretty'
```

To check the request cache metrics, but in per node view, we run the following command:

```
curl 'localhost:9200/_nodes/stats/indices/request_cache?pretty'
```

Node query cache

The node query cache is responsible for holding the results of queries for the whole node. Its size is defined using `indices.queries.cache.size`, defaulting to 10%, and is sharable across all the shards present on the node. We can set it both to the percentage of the heap memory given to Elasticsearch, like the default one, or to an explicit value, like `1024mb`. One thing to remember about the cache is that its configuration is static, it can't be updated dynamically and should be set in the `elasticsearch.yml` file. The node query cache uses the least recent used eviction policy, which means that, when full, it removes the data that was used the least.

This cache is very useful when you run queries that are repetetive and heavy, such as the ones used to generate category pages or the main page in an e-commerce application.

Indexing buffers

The last cache we want to discuss is the indexing buffer that allows us to improve indexing throughput. The indexing buffer is divided between all the shards on the node and is used to store newly indexed documents. Once the cache fills up, Elasticsearch flushes the data from the cache to disk, creating a new Lucene segment in the index.

There are four static properties that allow us to configure the indexing buffer size. They need to be set in the `elasticsearch.yml` file and can't be changed dynamically using the Settings API. These properties are:

- `indices.memory.index_buffer_size`: This property defines the amount of memory used by a node for the indexing buffer. It accepts both a percentage value as well as an explicit value in bytes. It defaults to `10%`, which means that `10%` of the heap memory given to a node will be used as the indexing buffer.
- `indices.memory.min_index_buffer_size`: This property defaults to `48mb` and specifies the minimum memory that will be used by the indexing buffer. It is useful when `indices.memory.index_buffer_size` is defined as a percentage value, so that the indexing buffer is never smaller than the value defined by this property.
- `indices.memory.max_index_buffer_size`: This property specifies the maximum memory that will be used by the indexing buffer. It is useful when `indices.memory.index_buffer_size` is defined as a percentage value, so that the indexing buffer never crosses a certain amount of memory usage.

- `indices.memory.min_shard_index_buffer_size`: This property defaults to `4mb` and sets the hard minimum limit of the indexing buffer that is given to each shard on a node. The indexing buffer for each shard will not be lower than the value set by this property.

When it comes to indexing performance, if you need higher indexing throughput, consider setting the indexing buffer size to a value higher than the default size. It will allow Elasticsearch to flush the data to disk less often and create fewer segments. This will result in less merges, thus less I/O and CPU intensive operations. Because of that, Elasticsearch will be able to use more resources for indexing purposes.

When caches should be avoided

The usual question that may be asked by users is if they should really cache all their requests. The answer is obvious – of course, caches are not the tool for everyone. Using caching is not free – it requires memory and additional operations to put the data to cache or get the data out of there.

What's more, you should remember that Elasticsearch round robins queries between primary shards are replicas, so, if you have replicas, not every request after the first one will use the cache. Imagine that you have an index which has a single primary shard and two replicas. When the first request comes, it will hit a random shard, but the next request, even with the same query, will hit another shard, not the same one (unless routing is used). You should take this into consideration when using caches, because if your queries are not repeated, you may have them running longer because of a cache being used.

So to answer the question if you should use caching or not, we would advise taking your data, taking your queries, and running performance tests using tools such as JMeter (`http://jmeter.apache.org`). This will let you see how your cluster behaves with real data under a test load and see if the queries are actually faster with or without the caches.

The update settings API

Elasticsearch lets us tune itself by specifying the various parameters in the `elasticsearch.yml` file. But you should treat this file as the set of default values that can be changed in the runtime using the Elasticsearch REST API. We can change both the per index setting and the cluster wide settings. However, you should remember that not all properties can be dynamically changed. If you try to alter these parameters, Elasticsearch will respond with a proper error.

The cluster settings API

In order to set one of the cluster properties, we need to use the HTTP PUT method and send a proper request to the _cluster/settings URI. However, we have two options: adding the changes as transient or permanent.

The first one, transient, will set the property only until the first restart. In order to do this, we send the following command:

```
curl -XPUT 'localhost:9200/_cluster/settings' -d '{
  "transient" : {
    "PROPERTY_NAME" : "PROPERTY_VALUE"
  }
}'
```

As you can see, in the preceding command, we used the object named transient and we added our property definition there. This means that the property will be valid only until the restart. If we want our property settings to persist between restarts, instead of using the object named transient, we use the one named persistent.

At any moment, you can fetch these settings using the following command:

```
curl -XGET localhost:9200/_cluster/settings
```

The indices settings API

To change the indices related settings, Elasticsearch provides the /_settings endpoint for changing the parameters for all the indices and the /index_name/_settings endpoint for modifying the settings of a single index. When compared to the cluster wide settings, all the changes done to indices using the API are always persistent and valid after Elasticsearch restarts. To change the settings for all the indices, we send the following command:

```
curl -XPUT 'localhost:9200/_settings' -d '{
  "index" : {
    "PROPERTY_NAME" : "PROPERTY_VALUE"
  }
}'
```

The current settings for all the indices can be listed using the following command:

```
curl -XGET localhost:9200/_settings
```

To set a property for a single index, we run the following command:

```
curl -XPUT 'localhost:9200/index_name/_settings' -d '{
  "index" : {
    "PROPERTY_NAME" : "PROPERTY_VALUE"
  }
}'
```

The get the settings for the `library` index, we run the following command:

```
curl -XGET localhost:9200/library/_settings
```

Summary

In the chapter we just finished, we learned a few very important things about Elasticsearch. First of all, we learned how we can configure the node discovery mechanism. In addition to that, we learned to control what happens after the cluster is initially formed using the recovery and gateway modules. We used dynamic and non-dynamic templates to handle our indices more easily, and we learned what type of caches Elasticsearch has and how to control them. Finally, we used the update settings API to update the various Elasticsearch configuration variables on an already live cluster.

In the next chapter, we will focus on cluster administration. We will start with learning how to backup our data and how to monitor the key cluster metrics. We'll see the way to control cluster rebalancing and shard allocation, and we will use a human friendly Cat API that allows us to get varied information about the cluster. Finally, we will learn about warming up our indices and aliasing.

10
Administrating Your Cluster

In the previous chapter, we focused on Elasticsearch nodes and cluster configuration. We started by discussing the node discovery process, what it is and how to configure it. We've discussed gateway and recovery modules and tuned them to match our needs. We've used templates and dynamic templates to manage data structure easily and learned how to install plugins to extend the functionalities of Elasticsearch. Finally, we've learned about the caches of Elasticsearch and how to update indices and cluster settings using a dedicated API. By the end of this chapter, you will have learned the following topics:

- Backing up your indices in Elasticsearch
- Monitoring your clusters
- Controlling shards and rebalancing replicas
- Controlling shards and allocating replicas
- Using CAT API to learn about cluster state
- Warming up
- Aliasing

Elasticsearch time machine

A good piece of software is a one that can manage exceptional situations such as hardware failure or human error. Even though a cluster of a few servers is less dependent on hardware problems, bad things can still happen. For example, let's imagine that you need to restore your indices. One possible solution is to reindex all your data from a primary data store such as a SQL database. But what will you do if it takes too long or, even worse, the only data store is Elasticsearch? Before Elasticsearch 1.0, creating backups of indices was not easy. The procedure included stopping indexation, flushing the data to disk, shutting down the cluster, and, finally, copying the data to a backup device.

Fortunately, now we can take snapshots and this section will guide you and show how this functionality works.

Creating a snapshot repository

A snapshot keeps all the data related to the cluster from the time the snapshot creation starts and it includes information about the cluster state and indices. Before we create snapshots, at least the first one, a snapshot repository must be created. Each repository is recognized by its name and should define the following aspects:

- name: A unique name of the repository; we will need it later.
- type: The type of the repository. The possible values are fs (a repository on a shared file system) and url (a read-only repository available via URL)
- settings: Additional information needed depending on the repository type

Now, let's create a file system repository. Before this, we have to make sure that the directory for our backups fulfils two requirements. The first is related to security. Every repository has to be placed in the path defined in the Elasticsearch configuration file as path.repo. For example, our elasticsearch.yml includes a line similar to the following one:

```
path.repo: ["/tmp/es_backup_folder", "/tmp/backup/es"]
```

The second requirement says that every node in the cluster should be able to access the directory we set for the repository.

So now, let's create a new file system repository by running the following command:

```
curl -XPUT localhost:9200/_snapshot/backup -d '{
  "type": "fs",
  "settings": {
    "location": "/tmp/es_backup_folder/cluster1"
  }
}'
```

The preceding command creates a repository named backup, which stores the backup files in the directory given by the location attribute. Elasticsearch responds with the following information:

```
{"acknowledged":true}
```

At the same time, es_backup_folder on the local file system is created — without any content yet.

You can also set a relative path with the location parameter. In this case, Elasticsearch determines the absolute path by first getting the directory defined in path.repo.

As we said, the second repository type is url. It requires a url parameter instead of the location, which points to the address where the repository resides, for example, the HTTP address. As in the previous case, the address should be defined in the repositories.url.allowed_urls parameter in the Elasticsearch configuration. The parameter allows the use of wildcards in the address.

 Note that file:// addresses are checked against the paths defined in the path.repo parameter.

You can also store snapshots in Amazon S3, HDFS, or Azure using the additional plugins available. To learn about these, please visit the following pages:

- https://github.com/elastic/elasticsearch-cloud-aws#s3-repository

- https://github.com/elastic/elasticsearch-hadoop/tree/master/repository-hdfs

- https://github.com/elastic/elasticsearch-cloud-azure#azure-repository

Now that we have our first repository, we can see its definition using the following command:

```
curl -XGET localhost:9200/_snapshot/backup?pretty
```

We can also check all the repositories by running a command like the following:

```
curl -XGET localhost:9200/_snapshot/_all?pretty
```

Or simply, we can use this:

```
curl -XGET localhost:9200/_snapshot/?pretty
```

If you want to delete a snapshot repository, the standard DELETE command helps:

```
curl -XDELETE localhost:9200/_snapshot/backup?pretty
```

Creating snapshots

By default, Elasticsearch takes all the indices and cluster settings (except the transient ones) when creating snapshots. You can create any number of snapshots and each will hold information available right from the time when the snapshot was created. The snapshots are created in a smart way; only new information is copied. This means that Elasticsearch knows which segments are already stored in the repository and doesn't have to save them again.

To create a new snapshot, we need to choose a unique name and use the following command:

```
curl -XPUT 'localhost:9200/_snapshot/backup/bckp1'
```

The preceding command defines a new snapshot named bckp1 (you can only have one snapshot with a given name; Elasticsearch will check its uniqueness) and data is stored in the previously defined backup repository. The command returns an immediate response, which looks as follows:

```
{"accepted":true}
```

The preceding response means that the process of snapshot-ing has started and continues in the background. If you would like the response to be returned only when the actual snapshot is created, you can add the wait_for_completion=true parameter as shown in the following example:

```
curl -XPUT 'localhost:9200/_snapshot/backup/bckp2?wait_for_completion=true&pretty'
```

The response to the preceding command shows the status of a created snapshot:

```
{
  "snapshot" : {
    "snapshot" : "bckp2",
    "version_id" : 2000099,
    "version" : "2.2.0",
    "indices" : [ "news" ],
    "state" : "SUCCESS",
    "start_time" : "2016-01-07T21:21:43.740Z",
    "start_time_in_millis" : 1446931303740,
    "end_time" : "2016-01-07T21:21:44.750Z",
    "end_time_in_millis" : 1446931304750,
    "duration_in_millis" : 1010,
    "failures" : [ ],
    "shards" : {
      "total" : 5,
```

```
        "failed" : 0,
        "successful" : 5
      }
    }
  }
```

As you can see, Elasticsearch presents information about the time taken by the snapshot-ing process, its status, and the indices affected.

Additional parameters

The snapshot command also accepts the following additional parameters:

- `indices`: The names of the indices of which we want to take snapshots.

- `ignore_unavailable`: When this is set to `false` (the default), Elasticsearch will return an error if any index listed using the indices parameter is missing. When set to true, Elasticsearch will just ignore the missing indices during backup.

- `include_global_state`: When this is set to `true` (the default), the cluster state is also written to the snapshot (except for the transient settings).

- `partial`: The snapshot operation success depends on the availability of all the shards. If any of the shards is not available, the snapshot operation will fail. Setting partial to true causes Elasticsearch to save only the available shards and omit the lost ones.

An example of using additional parameters can look as follows:

```
curl -XPUT 'localhost:9200/_snapshot/backup/bckp3?wait_for_completion=true&pretty' -d '{
  "indices": "b*",
  "include_global_state": "false"
}'
```

Restoring a snapshot

Now that we have our snapshots done, we will also learn how to restore data from a given snapshot. As we said earlier, a snapshot can be addressed by its name. We can list all the snapshots using the following command:

```
curl -XGET 'localhost:9200/_snapshot/backup/_all?pretty'
```

The response returned by Elasticsearch to the preceding command shows the list of all available backups. Every list item is similar to the following:

```
{
  "snapshot" : {
    "snapshot" : "bckp2",
    "version_id" : 2000099,
    "version" : "2.2.0",
    "indices" : [ "news" ],
    "state" : "SUCCESS",
    "start_time" : "2016-01-07T21:21:43.740Z",
    "start_time_in_millis" : 1446931303740,
    "end_time" : "2016-01-07T21:21:44.750Z",
    "end_time_in_millis" : 1446931304750,
    "duration_in_millis" : 1010,
    "failures" : [ ],
    "shards" : {
      "total" : 5,
      "failed" : 0,
      "successful" : 5
    }
  }
}
```

The repository we created earlier is called backup. To restore a snapshot named bckp1 from our snapshot repository, run the following command:

```
curl -XPOST 'localhost:9200/_snapshot/backup/bckp1/_restore'
```

During the execution of this command, Elasticsearch takes the indices defined in the snapshot and creates them with the data from the snapshot. However, if the index already exists and is not closed, the command will fail. In this case, you may find it convenient to only restore certain indices, for example:

```
curl -XPOST 'localhost:9200/_snapshot/backup/bckp1/_restore?pretty' -d '{
"indices": "c*"}'
```

The preceding command restores only the indices that begin with the letter c. The other available parameters are as follows:

- ignore_unavailable: This parameter when set to false (the default behavior), will cause Elasticsearch to fail the restore process if any of the expected indices is not available.

- include_global_state: This parameter when set to true will cause Elasticsearch to restore the global state included in the snapshot, which is also the default behavior.

- `rename_pattern`: This parameter allows the renaming of the index during a restore operation. Thanks to this, the restored index will have a different name. The value of this parameter is a regular expression that defines the source index name. If a pattern matches the name of the index, name substitution will occur. In the pattern, you should use groups limited by parentheses used in the `rename_replacement` parameter.

- `rename_replacement`: This parameter along with `rename_pattern` defines the target index name. Using the dollar sign and number, you can recall the appropriate group from `rename_pattern`.

For example, due to `rename_pattern=products_(.*)`, only the indices with names that begin with `products_` will be restored. The rest of the index name will be used during replacement. `rename_pattern=products_(.*)` together with `rename_replacement=items_$1` causes the `products_cars` index to be restored to an index called `items_cars`.

Cleaning up – deleting old snapshots

Elasticsearch leaves snapshot repository management up to you. Currently, there is no automatic clean-up process. But don't worry; this is simple. For example, let's remove our previously taken snapshot:

```
curl -XDELETE 'localhost:9200/_snapshot/backup/bckp1?pretty'
```

And that's all. The command causes the snapshot named `bckp1` from the `backup` repository to be deleted.

Monitoring your cluster's state and health

Monitoring is essential when it comes to handling your cluster and ensuring it is in a healthy state. It allows administrators and develops to detect possible problems and prevent them before they occur or to act as soon as they start showing. In the worst case, monitoring allows us to do a post mortem analysis of what happened to the application—in this case, our Elasticsearch cluster and each of the nodes.

Elasticsearch provides very detailed information that allows us to check and monitor our nodes or the cluster as a whole. This includes statistics and information about the servers, nodes, indices, and shards. Of course, we are also able to get information about the entire cluster state. Before we get into the details about the mentioned API, please remember that the API is complex and we are only describing the basics. We will try to show you where to start so you'll be able to know what to look for when you need very detailed information.

Cluster health API

One of the most basic APIs is the cluster health API, which allows us to get information about the entire cluster state with a single HTTP command. For example, let's run the following command:

```
curl -XGET 'localhost:9200/_cluster/health?pretty'
```

A sample response returned by Elasticsearch for the preceding command looks as follows:

```
{
  "cluster_name" : "elasticsearch",
  "status" : "yellow",
  "timed_out" : false,
  "number_of_nodes" : 1,
  "number_of_data_nodes" : 1,
  "active_primary_shards" : 11,
  "active_shards" : 11,
  "relocating_shards" : 0,
  "initializing_shards" : 0,
  "unassigned_shards" : 11,
  "delayed_unassigned_shards" : 0,
  "number_of_pending_tasks" : 0,
  "number_of_in_flight_fetch" : 0,
  "task_max_waiting_in_queue_millis" : 0,
  "active_shards_percent_as_number" : 50.0
}
```

The most important information is about the status of the cluster. In our example, we see that the cluster is in yellow status. This means that all the primary shards have been allocated properly, but the replicas were not (because of a single node in the cluster, but that doesn't matter for now).

Of course, apart from the cluster name and status, we can see how the request was timed out, how many nodes there are, how many data nodes, primary shards, initializing shards, unassigned ones, and so on.

Let's stop here and talk about the cluster and when the cluster, as a whole, is fully operational. Cluster is fully operational when Elasticsearch is able to allocate all the shards and replicas according to the configuration. This is when the cluster is in the green state. The yellow state means that we are ready to handle requests because the primary shards are allocated, but some (or all) replicas are not. The last state, the red one, means that at least one primary shard was not allocated and because of this, the cluster is not ready yet. That means that the queries may return errors or not complete results.

The preceding command can also be executed to check the health state of certain indices. For example, if we would like to check the health of the `library` and `map` indices, we would run the following command:

```
curl -XGET 'localhost:9200/_cluster/health/library,map/?pretty'
```

Controlling information details

Elasticsearch allows us to specify a special `level` parameter, which can take the value of `cluster` (default), `indices`, or `shards`. This allows us to control the details of information returned by the health API. We've already seen the default behavior. When setting the `level` parameter to `indices`, apart from the cluster information, we will also get per index health. Setting the mentioned parameter to `shards` tells Elasticsearch to return per shard information in addition to what we've seen in the example.

Additional parameters

In addition to the `level` parameter, we have a few additional parameters that can control the behavior of the health API.

The first of the mentioned parameters is `timeout` and allows us to control how long at the most, the command execution will wait when one of the following parameters is used: `wait_for_status`, `wait_for_nodes`, `wait_for_relocating_shards`, and `wait_for_active_shards`. By default, it is set to `30s` and means that the health command will wait 30 seconds maximum and return the response by then.

The `wait_for_status` parameter allows us to tell Elasticsearch which health status the cluster should be at to return the command. It can take the values of `green`, `yellow`, and `red`. For example, when set to `green`, the health API call will return the results until the green status or timeout is reached.

The `wait_for_nodes` parameter allows us to set the required number of nodes available to return the health command response (or until a defined timeout is reached). It can be set to an integer number like `3` or to a simple equation like `>=3` (means, greater than or equal to three nodes) or `<=3` (means less than or equal to three nodes).

The `wait_for_active_shards` parameter means that Elasticsearch will wait for a specified number of active shards to be present before returning the response.

The last parameter is the `wait_for_relocating_shard`, which is by default not specified. It allows us to tell Elasticsearch how many relocating shards it should wait for (or until the timeout is reached). Setting this parameter to `0` means that Elasticsearch should wait for all the relocating shards.

An example usage of the health command with some of the mentioned parameters is as follows:

```
curl -XGET 'localhost:9200/_cluster/health?wait_for_status=green&wait_
for_nodes=>=3&timeout=100s'
```

Indices stats API

Elasticsearch index is the place where our data lives and it is a crucial part for most deployments. With the use of the indices stats API available using the `_stats` endpoint, we can get a lot of information about the indices living inside our cluster. Of course, as with most of the API's in Elasticsearch, we can send a command to get the information about all the indices (using the pure `_stats` endpoint), about one particular index (for example `library/_stats`) or several indices at the same time (for example `library,map/_stats`). For example, to check the statistics for the `map` and `library` indices we've used in the book, we could run the following command:

```
curl -XGET 'localhost:9200/library,map/_stats?pretty'
```

The response to the preceding command has more than 700 lines, so we only describe its structure omitting the response itself. Apart from the information about the response status and the response time, we can see three objects named `primaries`, `total` (in `_all` object), and `indices`. The `indices` object contains information about the `library` and `map` indices. The `primaries` object contains information about the primary shards allocated to the current node, and the `total` object contains information about all the shards including replicas. All these objects can contain objects describing a particular statistic such as the following: `docs`, `store`, `indexing`, `get`, `search`, `merges`, `refresh`, `flush`, `warmer`, `query_cache`, `fielddata`, `percolate`, `completion`, `segments`, `translog`, `suggest`, `request_cache`, and `recovery`.

We can limit the amount of information that we get from the indices stats API by providing the type of data we are interested in using the names of the statistics mentioned previously. For example, if we want to get information about indexing and searching, we can run the following command:

```
curl -XGET 'localhost:9200/library,map/_stats/indexing,search?pretty'
```

Let's discuss the information stored in those objects.

Docs

The docs section of the response shows information about indexed documents. For example, it could look as follows:

```
"docs" : {
 "count" : 4,
 "deleted" : 0
}
```

The main information is the count, indicating the number of documents in the described index. When we delete documents from the index, Elasticsearch doesn't remove these documents immediately and only marks them as deleted. Documents are physically deleted during the segment merge process. The number of documents marked as deleted is presented by the deleted attribute and should be 0 right after the merge.

Store

The next statistic, the store one, provides information regarding storage. For example, such a section could look as follows:

```
"store" : {
 "size_in_bytes" : 6003,
 "throttle_time_in_millis" : 0
}
```

The main information is about the index (or indices) size. We can also look at throttling statistics. This information is useful when the system has problems with the I/O performance and has configured limits on an internal operation during segment merging.

Indexing, get, and search

The indexing, get, and search sections of the response provide information about data manipulation indexing with delete operations, using real-time get and searching. Let's look at the following example returned by Elasticsearch:

```
"indexing" : {
 "index_total" : 0,
 "index_time_in_millis" : 0,
 "index_current" : 0,
 "delete_total" : 0,
 "delete_time_in_millis" : 0,
 "delete_current" : 0,
```

```
    "noop_update_total" : 0,
    "is_throttled" : false,
    "throttle_time_in_millis" : 0
},
"get" : {
    "total" : 0,
    "time_in_millis" : 0,
    "exists_total" : 0,
    "exists_time_in_millis" : 0,
    "missing_total" : 0,
    "missing_time_in_millis" : 0,
    "current" : 0
},
"search" : {
    "open_contexts" : 0,
    "query_total" : 0,
    "query_time_in_millis" : 0,
    "query_current" : 0,
    "fetch_total" : 0,
    "fetch_time_in_millis" : 0,
    "fetch_current" : 0,
    "scroll_total" : 0,
    "scroll_time_in_millis" : 0,
    "scroll_current" : 0
}
```

As you can see, all of these statistics have similar structures. We can read the total time spent in various request types (in milliseconds), the number of requests (which with the total time allows us to calculate the average time of a single query). In the case of get requests, valuable information is how many fetches were unsuccessful (missing documents); an indexing request has information about throttling, and search includes information regarding scrolling.

Additional information

In addition to the previously described section, Elasticsearch provides the following information:

- merges: This section contains information about Lucene segment merges
- refresh: This section contains information about the refresh operation
- flush: This section contains information about flushes
- warmer: This section contains information about warmers and for how long they were executed

- `query_cache`: This query caches statistics
- `fielddata`: This field data caches statistics
- `percolate`: This section contains information about the percolator usage
- `completion`: This section contains information about the completion suggester
- `segments`: This section contains information about Lucene segments
- `translog`: This section contains information about the transaction logs count and size
- `suggest`: This section contains suggesters-related statistics
- `request_cache`: This contains shard request caches statistics
- `recovery`: This contains shards recovery information

Nodes info API

The nodes info API provides us with information about the nodes in the cluster. To get information from this API, we need to send the request to the _nodes REST endpoints. The simplest command to retrieve nodes related information from Elasticsearch would be as follows:

```
curl -XGET 'localhost:9200/_nodes?pretty'
```

This API can be used to fetch information about particular nodes or a single node using the following:

- **Node name**: If we would like to get information about the node named `Pulse`, we could run a command to the following REST endpoint: `_nodes/Pulse`

- **Node identifier**: If we would like to get information about the node with an identifier equal to `ny4hftjNQtuKMyEvpUdQWg`, we could run a command to the following REST endpoint: `_nodes/ny4hftjNQtuKMyEvpUdQWg`

- **IP address**: We can use IP addresses to get information about the nodes. For example, if we would like to get information about the node with an IP address equal to `192.168.1.103`, we could run a command to the following REST endpoint: `_nodes/192.168.1.103`

- **Parameters from the Elasticsearch configuration**: If we would like to get information about all the nodes with the `node.rack` property set to `2`, we could run a command to the following REST endpoint: `/_nodes/rack:2`

This API also allows us to get information about several nodes at once using these:

- Patterns, for example: `_nodes/192.168.1.*` or `_nodes/P*`
- Nodes enumeration, for example: `_nodes/Pulse,Slab`
- Both patterns and enumerations, for example: `/_nodes/P*,S*`

Returned information

By default, the nodes API will return extensive information about each node along with the name, identifier, and addresses. This extensive information includes the following:

- `settings`: The Elasticsearch configuration
- `os`: Information about the server such as processor, RAM, and swap space
- `process`: Process identifier and refresh interval
- `jvm`: Information about Java Virtual Machine such as memory limits, memory pools, and garbage collectors
- `thread_pool`: The configuration of thread pools for various operations
- `transport`: Listening addresses for the transport protocol
- `http`: Information about listening addresses for an HTTP-based API
- `plugins`: Information about the plugins installed by the user
- `modules`: Information about the built-in plugins

An example usage of this API can be illustrated by the following command:

```
curl 'localhost:9200/_nodes/Pulse/os,jvm,plugins'
```

The preceding command will return the basic information about the node named `Pulse` and, in addition to this, it will include the operating system information, java virtual machine information, and plugins-related information.

Nodes stats API

The nodes stats API is similar to the nodes info API described in the preceding section. The main difference is that the previous API provided information about the environment in which the node is running, while the one we are currently discussing tells us about what happened with the cluster during its work. To use the nodes stats API, you need to send a command to the `/_nodes/stats` REST endpoint. However, similar to the nodes info API, we can also retrieve information about specific nodes (for example: `_nodes/Pulse/stats`).

The simplest command to retrieve nodes related information from Elasticsearch would be as follows:

```
curl -XGET 'localhost:9200/_nodes/stats?pretty'
```

By default, Elasticsearch returns all the available statistics but we can limit the ones we are interested in. The available options are as follows:

- `indices`: Information about the indices including size, document count, indexing related statistics, search and get time, caches, segment merges, and so on
- `os`: Operating system related information such as free disk space, memory, swap usage, and so on
- `process`: Memory, CPU, and file handler usage related to the Elasticsearch process
- `jvm`: Java virtual machine memory and garbage collector statistics
- `transport`: Information about data sent and received by the transport module
- `http`: Information about `http` connections
- `fs`: Information about available disk space and I/O operations statistics
- `thread_pool`: Information about the state of the threads assigned to various operations
- `breakers`: Information about circuit breakers
- `script`: Scripting engine related information

An example usage of this API can be illustrated by the following command:

```
curl 'localhost:9200/_nodes/Pulse/stats/os,jvm,breaker'
```

Cluster state API

Another API provided by Elasticsearch is the cluster state API. As its name suggests, it allows us to get information about the entire cluster (we can also limit the returned information to a local node by adding the `local=true` parameter to the request). The basic command used to get all the information returned by this API looks as follows:

```
curl -XGET 'localhost:9200/_cluster/state?pretty'
```

We can also limit the provided information to the given metrics in comma–separated form, specified after the `_cluster/state` part of the REST call. For example:

```
curl -XGET 'localhost:9200/_cluster/state/version,nodes?pretty'
```

We can also limit the information to the given metrics and indices. For example, if we would like to get the metadata for the `library` index, we could run the following command:

```
curl -XGET 'localhost:9200/_cluster/state/metadata/library?pretty'
```

The following metrics are allowed to be used:

- `version`: This returns information about the cluster state version.
- `master_node`: This returns information about the elected master node.
- `nodes`: This returns nodes information.
- `routing_table`: This returns routing related information.
- `metadata`: This returns metadata related information. When specifying retrieving the metadata metric we can also include an additional parameter such as `index_templates=true`, which will result in including the defined index templates.
- `blocks`: This returns the `blocks` part of the response.

Cluster stats API

The cluster stats API allows us to get statistics about the indices and nodes from the cluster wide perspective. To use this API, we need to run the GET request to the `/_cluster/stats` REST endpoint, for example:

```
curl -XGET 'localhost:9200/_cluster/stats?pretty'
```

The response size depends on the number of shards, indices, and nodes in the cluster. It will include basic indices information such as shards, their state, recovery information, caches information, and node related information.

Pending tasks API

One of the API's that helps us in seeing what Elasticsearch is doing; it allows us to check which tasks are waiting to be executed. To retrieve this information, we need to send a request to the `/_cluster/pending_tasks` REST endpoint. In this response, we will see an array of tasks with information about them, such as task priority and time in queue.

Indices recovery API

The recovery API gives us insight about the recovery status of the shards that are building indices in our cluster (learn more about recovery in *The gateway and recovery modules* section of *Chapter 9, Elasticsearch Cluster in Detail*).

The simplest command that would return the information about the recovery of all the shards in the cluster would look as follows:

```
curl -XGET 'http://localhost:9200/_recovery?pretty'
```

We can also get information about recovery for particular indices, such as the library index for example:

```
curl -XGET 'http://localhost:9200/library/_recovery?pretty'
```

The response returned by Elasticsearch is divided by indices and shards. A response for a single shard could look as follows:

```
{
 "id" : 2,
 "type" : "STORE",
 "stage" : "DONE",
 "primary" : true,
 "start_time_in_millis" : 1446132761730,
 "stop_time_in_millis" : 1446132761734,
 "total_time_in_millis" : 4,
 "source" : {
  "id" : "DboTibRlT1KJSQYnDPxwZQ",
  "host" : "127.0.0.1",
  "transport_address" : "127.0.0.1:9300",
  "ip" : "127.0.0.1",
  "name" : "Plague"
 },
 "target" : {
  "id" : "DboTibRlT1KJSQYnDPxwZQ",
  "host" : "127.0.0.1",
  "transport_address" : "127.0.0.1:9300",
  "ip" : "127.0.0.1",
  "name" : "Plague"
 },
 "index" : {
  "size" : {
   "total_in_bytes" : 156,
   "reused_in_bytes" : 156,
   "recovered_in_bytes" : 0,
```

```
     "percent" : "100.0%"
    },
    "files" : {
     "total" : 1,
     "reused" : 1,
     "recovered" : 0,
     "percent" : "100.0%"
    },
    "total_time_in_millis" : 0,
    "source_throttle_time_in_millis" : 0,
    "target_throttle_time_in_millis" : 0
   },
   "translog" : {
    "recovered" : 0,
    "total" : -1,
    "percent" : "-1.0%",
    "total_on_start" : -1,
    "total_time_in_millis" : 3
   },
   "verify_index" : {
    "check_index_time_in_millis" : 0,
    "total_time_in_millis" : 0
   }
  }
}
```

In the preceding response, we can see information about the shard identifier, the stage of recovery, information whether the shard is a primary or a replica, the timestamps of the start and end of recovery, and the total time the recovery process took. We can see the source node, target node, and information about the shard's physical statistics, such as size, number of files, transaction log-related statistics, and index verification time.

It is worth knowing the information about the stages of recovery and types. When it comes to the types of recovery (the type attribute in the response), we can expect the following: the STORE, SNAPSHOT, REPLICA, and RELOCATING values. When it comes to the stage of recovery (the stage attribute in the response), we can expect values such as INIT (recovery has not started), INDEX (Elasticsearch copies metadata information and data from source to destination), START (Elasticsearch is opening the shard for use), FINALIZE (final stage, which cleans up garbage), and DONE (recovery has ended).

We can limit the response returned by the indices recovery API to only the shards that are currently in active recovery by including the active_only=true parameter in the request. Finally, we can request more detailed information by adding the detailed=true parameter in the API call.

Indices shard stores API

The indices shard stores API gives us information about the store for the shards of our indices. We use this API by running a simple command to the /_shard_stores REST endpoint and providing or not providing the comma-separated indices names.

For example, to get information about all the indices, we would run the following command:

```
curl -XGET 'http://localhost:9200/_shard_stores?pretty'
```

We can also get information about particular indices, such as the library and map ones:

```
curl -XGET 'http://localhost:9200/library,map/_shard_stores?pretty'
```

The response returned by Elasticsearch contains information about the store for each shard. For example, this is what Elasticsearch returned for one of the shards of the library index:

```
"0" : {
 "stores" : [ {
  "DboTibRlT1KJSQYnDPxwZQ" : {
   "name" : "Plague",
   "transport_address" : "127.0.0.1:9300",
   "attributes" : { }
  },
  "version" : 6,
  "allocation" : "primary"
 } ]
}
```

We can see information about the node in the stores arrays. Each entry contains node related information (the node where the shard is physically located), the version of the store copy, and the allocation, which can take the values of primary (for primary shards), replica (for replicas), and unused (for unassigned shards).

Indices segments API

The last API we want to mention is the Lucene segments API that can be availed by using the /_segments endpoint. We can either run it for the entire cluster, for example like this:

```
curl -XGET 'localhost:9200/_segments?pretty'
```

We can also run the command for individual indices. For example, if we would like to get segments related information for the map and library indices, we would use the following command:

```
curl -XGET 'localhost:9200/library,map/_segments?pretty'
```

This API provides information about shards, their placements, and information about segments connected with the physical index managed by the Apache Lucene library.

Controlling the shard and replica allocation

The indices that live inside your Elasticsearch cluster can be built from many shards and each shard can have many replicas. The ability to divide a single index into multiple shards gives us the possibility of dividing the data into multiple physical instances. The reasons why we want to do this may be different. We may want to parallelize indexing to get more throughput, or we may want to have smaller shards so that our queries are faster. Of course, we may have too many documents to fit them on a single machine and we may want a shard because of this. With replicas, we can parallelize the query load by having multiple physical copies of each shard. We can say that, using shards and replicas, we can scale out Elasticsearch. However, Elasticsearch has to figure out where in the cluster it should place shards and replicas. It needs to figure out on which server/nodes each shard or replica should be placed.

Explicitly controlling allocation

One of the most common use cases that use explicit controlling of shards and replicas allocation in Elasticsearch is time-based data, that is, logs. Each log event has a timestamp associated with it; however, the amount of logs in most organizations is just enormous. The thing is that you need a lot of processing power to index them, but you don't usually search historical data. Of course, you may want to do that, but it will be done less frequently than the queries for the most recent data.

Because of this, we can divide the cluster into so called two tiers—the cold and the hot tier. The hot tier contains more powerful nodes, ones that have very fast disks, lots of CPU processing power, and memory. These nodes will handle both a lot of indexing as well as queries for recent data. The cold tier, on the other hand, will contain nodes that have very large disks, but are not very fast. We won't be indexing into the cold tier; we will only store our historical indices here and search them from time to time. With the default Elasticsearch behavior, we can't be sure where the shards and replicas will be placed, but luckily Elasticsearch allows us to control this.

The main assumption when it comes to time series data is that once they are indexed, they are not being updated. This is true for log indexing use cases and we assume we create Elasticsearch deployment for such a use case.

The idea is to create the indices that index today's data on the hot nodes and, when we stop using it (when another day starts), we update the index settings so that it is moved to the tier called cold. Let's now see how we can do this.

Specifying node parameters

So let's divide our cluster into two tiers. We say tiers, but they can be any name you want, we just like the term "tier" and it is commonly used. We assume that we have six nodes. We want our more powerful nodes numbered 1 and 2 to be placed in the tier called `hot` and the nodes numbered 3, 4, 5, and 6, which are smaller in terms of CPU and memory, but very large in terms of disk space, to be placed in a tier called `cold`.

Configuration

To configure, we add the following property to the `elasticsearch.yml` configuration file on nodes 1 and 2 (the ones that are more powerful):

```
node.tier: hot
```

Of course, we will add a similar property to the `elasticsearch.yml` configuration file on nodes 3, 4, 5, and 6 (the less powerful ones):

```
node.tier: cold
```

Index creation

Now let's create our daily index for today's data, one called `logs_2015-12-10`. As we said earlier, we want this to be placed on the nodes in the hot tier. We do this by running the following commands:

```
curl -XPUT 'http://localhost:9200/logs_2015-12-10' -d '{
 "settings" : {
  "index" : {
   "routing.allocation.include.tier" : "hot"
  }
 }
}'
```

The preceding command will result in the creation of the `logs_2015-12-10` index and specification of the `index.routing.allocation.include.tier` property to it. We set this property to the `hot` value, which means that we want to place the `logs_2015-12-10` index on the nodes that have the `node.tier` property set to `hot`.

Now, when the day ends and we need to create a new index, we again put it on the hot nodes. We do this by running the following command:

```
curl -XPUT 'http://localhost:9200/logs_2015-12-11' -d '{
  "settings" : {
   "index" : {
    "routing.allocation.include.tier" : "hot"
   }
  }
}'
```

Finally, we need to tell Elasticsearch to move the index holding the data for the previous day to the cold tier. We do this by updating the index settings and setting the `index.routing.allocation.include.tier` property to `cold`. This is done using the following command:

```
curl -XPUT 'http://localhost:9200/logs_2015-12-10/_settings' -d '{
  "index.routing.allocation.include.tier" : "cold"
}'
```

After running the preceding command, Elasticsearch will start relocating the index called `logs_2015-12-10` to the nodes that have the `node.tier` property set to `cold` in the `elasticsearch.yml` file without any manual work needed from us.

Excluding nodes from allocation

In the same manner as we specified on which nodes the index should be placed, we can also exclude nodes from index allocation. Referring to the previously shown example. if we want the index called `logs_2015-12-10` to not be placed on the nodes with the `node.tier` property set to `cold`, we would run the following command:

```
curl -XPUT 'localhost:9200/logs_2015-12-10/_settings' -d '{
  "index.routing.allocation.exclude.tier" : "cold"
}'
```

Notice that instead of the `index.routing.allocation.include.tier` property, we've used the `index.routing.allocation.exclude.tier` property.

Requiring node attributes

In addition to inclusion and exclusion rules, we can also specify the rules that must match in order for a shard to be allocated to a given node. The difference is that when using the `index.routing.allocation.include` property, the index will be placed on any node that matches at least one of the provided property values. Using `index.routing.allocation.require`, Elasticsearch will place the index on a node that has all the defined values. For example, let's assume that we've set the following settings for the `logs_2015-12-10` index:

```
curl -XPUT 'localhost:9200/logs_2015-12-10/_settings' -d '{
 "index.routing.allocation.require.tier" : "hot",
 "index.routing.allocation.require.disk_type" : "ssd"
}'
```

After running the preceding command, Elasticsearch would only place the shards of the `logs_2015-12-10` index on a node with the `node.tier` property set to `hot` and the `node.disk_type` property set to `ssd`.

Using the IP address for shard allocation

Instead of adding a special parameter to the nodes configuration, we are allowed to use IP addresses to specify which nodes we want to include or exclude from the shards and replicas allocation. In order to do this, instead of using the `tier` part of the `index.routing.allocation.include.tier` or `index.routing.allocation.exclude.tier` properties, we should use the `_ip`. For example, if we would like our `logs_2015-12-10` index to be placed only on the nodes with the `10.1.2.10` and `10.1.2.11` IP addresses, we would run the following command:

```
curl -XPUT 'localhost:9200/logs_2015-12-10/_settings' -d '{
 "index.routing.allocation.include._ip" : "10.1.2.10,10.1.2.11"
}'
```

 In addition to `_ip`, Elasticsearch also allows us to use `_name` to specify allocation rules using node names and `_host` to specify allocation rules using host names.

Disk-based shard allocation

In addition to the already described allocation filtering methods, Elasticsearch gives us disk-based shard allocation rules. It allows us to set allocation rules based on the nodes' disk usage.

Configuring disk based shard allocation

There are four properties that control the behavior of a disk-based shard allocation. All of them can be updated dynamically or set in the `elasticsearch.yml` configuration file.

The first of these is `cluster.info.update.interval`, which is by default set to 30 seconds and defines how often Elasticsearch updates information about disk usage on nodes.

The second property is the `cluster.routing.allocation.disk.watermark.low`, which is by default set to `0.85`. This means that Elasticsearch will not allocate new shards to a node that uses more than 85% of its disk space.

The third property is the `cluster.routing.allocation.disk.watermark.high`, which controls when Elasticsearch will start relocating shards from a given node. It defaults to `0.90` and means that Elasticsearch will start reallocating shards when the disk usage on a given node is equal to or more than 90%.

Both the `cluster.routing.allocation.disk.watermark.low` and `cluster.routing.allocation.disk.watermark.high` properties can be set to a percentage value (such as `0.60`, meaning 60%) and to an absolute value (such as `600mb`, meaning 600 megabytes).

Finally, the last property is `cluster.routing.allocation.disk.include_relocations`, which by default is set to `true`. It tells Elasticsearch to take into account the shards that are not yet copied to the node but Elasticsearch is in the process of doing that. Having this behavior turned on by default means that the disk-based allocation mechanism will be more pessimistic when it comes to available disk spaces (when shards are relocating), but we won't run into situations where shards can't be relocated because the assumptions about disk space were wrong.

Disabling disk based shard allocation

The disk based shard allocation is enabled by default. We can disable it by specifying the `cluster.routing.allocation.disk.threshold_enabled` property and setting it to `false`. We can do this in the `elasticsearch.yml` file or dynamically using the cluster settings API:

```
curl -XPUT localhost:9200/_cluster/settings -d '{
 "transient" : {
  "cluster.routing.allocation.disk.threshold_enabled" : false
 }
}'
```

The number of shards and replicas per node

In addition to specifying shards and replicas allocation, we are also allowed to specify the maximum number of shards that can be placed on a single node for a single index. For example, if we would like our `logs_2015-12-10` index to have only a single shard per node, we would run the following command:

```
curl -XPUT 'localhost:9200/logs_2015-12-10/_settings' -d '{
  "index.routing.allocation.total_shards_per_node" : 1
}'
```

This property can be placed in the `elasticsearch.yml` file or can be updated on live indices using the preceding command. Please remember that your cluster can stay in the red state if Elasticsearch won't be able to allocate all the primary shards.

Allocation throttling

The Elasticsearch allocation mechanism can be throttled, which means that we can control how much resources Elasticsearch will use during the shard allocation and recovery process. We are given five properties to control, which are as follows:

- `cluster.routing.allocation.node_concurrent_recoveries`: This property defines how many concurrent shard recoveries may be happening at the same time on a node. This defaults to 2 and should be increased if you would like more shards to be recovered at the same time on a single node. However, increasing this value will result in more resource consumption during recovery. Also, please remember that during the replica recovery process, data will be copied from the other nodes over the network, which can be slow.

- `cluster.routing.allocation.node_initial_primaries_recoveries`: This property defaults to 4 and defines how many primary shards are recovered at the same time on a given node. Because primary shard recovery uses data from local disks, this process should be very fast.

- `cluster.routing.allocation.same_shard.host`: A `Boolean` property that defaults to `false` and is applicable only when multiple Elasticsearch nodes are started on the same machine. When set to true, this will force Elasticsearch to check whether physical copies of the same shard are present on a single physical machine. The default `false` value means no check is done.

- `indices.recovery.concurrent_streams`: This is the number of network streams used to copy data from other nodes that can be used concurrently on a single node. The more the streams, the faster the data will be copied, but this will result in more resource consumption. This property defaults to 3.

- `indices.recovery.concurrent_small_file_streams`: This is similar to the `indices.recovery.concurrent_streams` property, but defines how many concurrent data streams Elasticsearch will use to copy small files (ones that are under `5mb` in size). This property defaults to `2`.

This allows us to perform a check to prevent the allocation of multiple instances of the same shard on a single host, based on host name and host address. This defaults to `false`, meaning that no check is performed by default. This setting only applies if multiple nodes are started on the same machine.

Cluster-wide allocation

In addition to the per indices allocation settings, Elasticsearch also allows us to control shard and indices allocation on a cluster-wide basis—so called shard allocation awareness. This is especially useful when we have nodes in different physical racks and we would like to place shards and replicas in different physical nodes.

Let's start with a simple example. We assume that we have a cluster built of four nodes. Each node in a different physical rack. The simple graphic that illustrates this is as follows:

```
IP address: 192.168.2.1
node.tag: node1
node.group: groupA



                                    Elasticsearch
```

```
IP address: 192.168.2.2
node.tag: node2
node.group: groupA



                                    Elasticsearch
```

```
IP address: 192.168.3.1
node.tag: node3
node.group: groupB



                                    Elasticsearch
```

```
IP address: 192.168.3.2
node.tag: node4
node.group: groupB



                                    Elasticsearch
```

As you can see, our cluster is built from four nodes. Each node was bound to a specific IP address and each node was given the `tag` property and a `group` property (added to `elasticsearch.yml` as the `node.tag` and `node.group` properties). This cluster will serve the purpose of showing how shard allocation filtering works. The `group` and `tag` properties can be given whatever names you want, you just need to prefix your desired property name with the `node` name, for example, if you would like to use a `party` property name, you would just add `node.party: party1` to your `elasticsearch.yml`.

Allocation awareness

Allocation awareness allows us to configure shards and their replicas allocation with the use of generic parameters. In order to illustrate how allocation awareness works, we will use our example cluster. For the example to work, we should add the following property to the `elasticsearch.yml` file:

```
cluster.routing.allocation.awareness.attributes: group
```

This will tell Elasticsearch to use the `node.group` property as the awareness parameter.

> You can specify multiple attributes when setting the `cluster.routing.allocation.awareness.attributes` property. For example:
> ```
> cluster.routing.allocation.awareness.attributes: group, node
> ```

After this, let's start the first two nodes, the ones with the `node.group` parameter equal to `groupA`, and let's create an index by running the following command:

```
curl -XPOST 'localhost:9200/awarness' -d '{
 "settings" : {
  "index" : {
   "number_of_shards" : 1,
   "number_of_replicas" : 1
  }
 }
}'
```

After this command, our two-node cluster will look more or less like this:

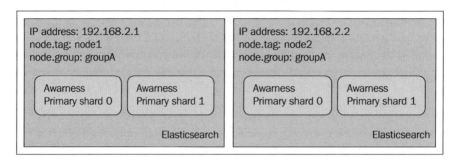

As you can see, the index was divided between the two nodes evenly. Now let's see what happens when we launch the rest of the nodes (the ones with `node.group` set to `groupB`):

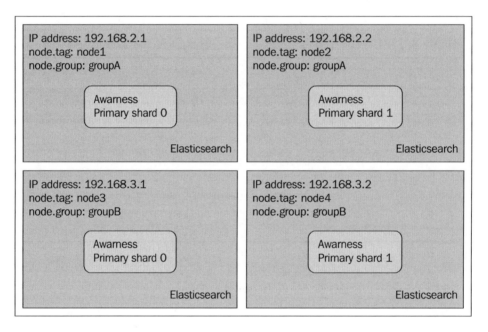

Notice the difference—the primary shards were not moved from their original allocation nodes, but the replica shards were moved to the nodes with a different `node.group` value. That's exactly right; when using shard allocation awareness, Elasticsearch won't allocate the primary shards and replicas of the same index to the nodes with the same value of the property used to determine the allocation awareness (which in our case is the `node.group`).

Please remember that when using allocation awareness, shards will not be allocated to the node that doesn't have the expected attributes set. So in our example, a node without the node.group property set will not be taken into consideration by the allocation mechanism.

Forcing allocation awareness

Forcing allocation awareness can come in handy when we know, in advance, how many values our awareness attributes can take and we don't want more replicas than needed to be allocated in our cluster, for example, not to overload our cluster with too many replicas. For this, we can force the allocation awareness to be active only for certain attributes. We can specify these values using the `cluster.routing.allocation.awareness.force.zone.values` property and providing a list of comma-separated values to it. For example, if we would like the allocation awareness to use only the `groupA` and `groupB` values of the `node.group` property, we would add the following to the `elasticsearch.yml` file:

```
cluster.routing.allocation.awareness.attributes: group
cluster.routing.allocation.awareness.force.zone.values: groupA, groupB
```

Filtering

Elasticsearch allows us to configure allocation for the entire cluster or for the index level. In the case of cluster allocation, we can use the properties prefixes:

- `cluster.routing.allocation.include`
- `cluster.routing.allocation.require`
- `cluster.routing.allocation.exclude`

When it comes to index-specific allocation, we can use the following properties prefixes:

- `index.routing.allocation.include`
- `index.routing.allocation.require`
- `index.routing.allocation.exclude`

The previously mentioned prefixes can be used with the properties that we've defined in the `elasticsearch.yml` file (our `tag` and `group` properties) and with a special property called `_ip` that allows us to match or exclude the use of the nodes' IP addresses, for example, like this:

```
cluster.routing.allocation.include._ip: 192.168.2.1
```

If we would like to include nodes with a `group` property matching the `groupA` value, we would set the following property:

```
cluster.routing.allocation.include.group: groupA
```

Notice that we've used the `cluster.routing.allocation.include` prefix and we've concatenated it with the name of the property, which is `group` in our case.

What do include, exclude, and require mean

If you look closely at the preceding parameters, you will notice that there are three kinds:

- `include`: This type will result in including all the nodes with this parameter defined. If multiple `include` conditions are visible than all the nodes that match at least a one of these conditions will be taken into consideration when allocating shards. For example, if we add two `cluster.routing.allocation.include.tag` parameters to our configuration, one with a property with the value of `node1` and second with the `node2` value, we would end up with indices (actually their shards) being allocated to the first and second node (counting from left to right). To sum up the nodes that have the `include allocation` parameter type will be taken into consideration by Elasticsearch when choosing the nodes to place shards on, but this doesn't mean that Elasticsearch will put shards in them.

- `require`: This parameter, which was introduced in the Elasticsearch 0.90 type of allocation filter, requires all the nodes to have a value that matches the value of this property. For example, if we add one `cluster.routing.allocation.require.tag` parameter to our configuration with the value of `node1` and a `cluster.routing.allocation.require.group` parameter with the value of `groupA`, we would end up with shards allocated only to the first node (the one with an IP address of `192.168.2.1`).

- `exclude`: This parameter allows us to exclude nodes with given properties from the allocation process. For example, if we set `cluster.routing.allocation.include.tag` to `groupA`, we would end up with indices being allocated only to the nodes with IP addresses `192.168.3.1` and `192.168.3.2` (the third and fourth nodes in our example).

> The property value can use simple wildcard characters. For example, if we want to include all the nodes that have the `group` parameter value beginning with group, we could set the `cluster.routing.allocation.include.group` property to `group*`. In the example cluster case, this would result in matching nodes with the `groupA` and `groupB` group parameter values.

Manually moving shards and replicas

The last thing we wanted to discuss is the ability to manually move shards between nodes. Elasticsearch exposes the _cluster/reroute REST end-point, which allows us to control that. The following operations are available:

- Moving a shard from node to node
- Cancelling shard allocation
- Forcing shard allocation

Now let's look closely at all of the preceding operations.

Moving shards

Let's say we have two nodes called es_node_one and es_node_two, and we have two shards of the shop index placed by Elasticsearch on the first node and we would like to move the second shard to the second node. In order to do this, we can run the following command:

```
curl -XPOST 'localhost:9200/_cluster/reroute' -d '{
  "commands" : [ {
   "move" : {
    "index" : "shop",
    "shard" : 1,
    "from_node" : "es_node_one",
    "to_node" : "es_node_two"
   }
  } ]
}'
```

We've specified the move command, which allows us to move shards (and replicas) of the index specified by the index property. The shard property is the number of shards we want to move. And, finally, the from_node property specifies the name of the node we want to move the shard from and the to_node property specifies the name of the node we want the shard to be placed on.

Canceling shard allocation

If we would like to cancel an on-going allocation process, we can run the `cancel` command and specify the index, node, and shard we want to cancel the allocation for. For example:

```
curl -XPOST 'localhost:9200/_cluster/reroute' -d '{
 "commands" : [ {
  "cancel" : {
   "index" : "shop",
   "shard" : 0,
   "node" : "es_node_one"
  }
 } ]
}'
```

The preceding command would cancel the allocation of shard 0 of the shop index on the es_node_one node.

Forcing shard allocation

In addition to cancelling and moving shards and replicas, we are also allowed to allocate an unallocated shard to a specific node. For example, if we have an unallocated shard numbered 0 for the users index and we would like it to be allocated to es_node_two by Elasticsearch, we would run the following command:

```
curl -XPOST 'localhost:9200/_cluster/reroute' -d '{
 "commands" : [ {
  "allocate" : {
   "index" : "users",
   "shard" : 0,
   "node" : "es_node_two"
  }
 } ]
}'
```

Multiple commands per HTTP request

We can, of course, include multiple commands in a single HTTP request. For example:

```
curl -XPOST 'localhost:9200/_cluster/reroute' -d '{
 "commands" : [
  {"move" : {"index" : "shop", "shard" : 1, "from_node" : "es_node_one",
"to_node" : "es_node_two"}},
  {"cancel" : {"index" : "shop", "shard" : 0, "node" : "es_node_one"}}
 ]
}'
```

Allowing operations on primary shards

The `cancel` and `allocate` commands accept an additional `allow_primary` parameter. If set to `true`, it tells Elasticsearch that the operation can be performed on the primary shard. Please be advised that operations with the `allow_primary` parameter set to `true` may result in data loss.

Handling rolling restarts

There is one more thing that we would like to discuss when it comes to shard and replica allocation—handling rolling restarts. When Elasticsearch is restarted, it may take some time to get it back to the cluster. During this time, the rest of the cluster may decide to do rebalancing and move shards around. When we know we are doing rolling restarts, for example, to update Elasticsearch to a new version or install a plugin, we may want to tell this to Elasticsearch. The procedure for restarting each node should be as follows:

First, before you do any maintenance, you should stop the allocation by sending the following command:

```
curl -XPUT 'localhost:9200/_cluster/settings' -d '{
 "transient" : {
  "cluster.routing.allocation.enable" : "none"
 }
}'
```

This will tell Elasticsearch to stop allocation. After this, we will stop the node we want to do maintenance on and start it again. After it joins the cluster, we can enable the allocation again by running the following:

```
curl -XPUT 'localhost:9200/_cluster/settings' -d '{
 "transient" : {
  "cluster.routing.allocation.enable" : "all"
 }
}'
```

This will enable the allocation again. This procedure should be repeated for each node we want to perform maintenance on.

Controlling cluster rebalancing

By default, Elasticsearch tries to keep the shards and their replicas evenly balanced across the cluster. Such behavior is good in most cases, but there are times when we want to control this behavior—for example, during rolling restarts. We don't want to rebalance the entire cluster when one or two nodes are restarted. In this section, we will look at how to avoid cluster rebalance and control this process' behavior in depth.

Imagine a situation where you know that your network can handle very high amounts of traffic or the opposite of this— your network is used extensively and you want to avoid too much load on it. The other example is that you may want to decrease the pressure that is put on your I/O subsystem after a full-cluster restart and you want to have less shards and replicas being initialized at the same time. These are only two examples where rebalance control may be handy.

Understanding rebalance

Rebalancing is the process of moving shards between different nodes in our cluster. As we have already mentioned, it is fine in most situations, but sometimes you may want to completely avoid this. For example, if we define how our shards are placed and we want to keep it this way, we may want to avoid rebalancing. However, by default, Elasticsearch will try to rebalance the cluster whenever the cluster state changes and Elasticsearch thinks a rebalance is needed (and the delayed timeout has passed as discussed in *The gateway and recovery modules* section of *Chapter 9, Elasticsearch Cluster in Detail*).

Cluster being ready

We already know that our indices are built from shards and replicas. Primary shards or just shards are the ones that get the data first. The replicas are physical copies of the primaries and get the data from them. You can think of the cluster as being ready to be used when all the primary shards are assigned to their nodes in your cluster – as soon as the yellow health state is achieved. However, Elasticsearch may still initialize other shards – the replicas. However, you can use your cluster and be sure that you can search your entire data set and send index change commands. Then the commands will be processed properly.

The cluster rebalance settings

Elasticsearch lets us control the rebalance process with the use of a few properties that can be set in the `elasticsearch.yml` file or by using the Elasticsearch REST API (as described in *The update settings API* section of *Chapter 9, Elasticsearch Cluster in Detail*).

Controlling when rebalancing will be allowed

The `cluster.routing.allocation.allow_rebalance` property allows us to specify when rebalancing is allowed. This property can take the following values:

- `always`: Rebalancing will be allowed as soon as it's needed
- `indices_primaries_active`: Rebalancing will be allowed when all the primary shards are initialized
- `indices_all_active`: The default one, which means that rebalancing will be allowed when all the shards and replicas are initialized

The `cluster.routing.allocation.allow_rebalance` property can be set in the `elasticsearch.yml` configuration file and updated dynamically as well.

Controlling the number of shards being moved between nodes concurrently

The `cluster.routing.allocation.cluster_concurrent_rebalance` property allows us to specify how many shards can be moved between nodes at once in the entire cluster. If you have a cluster that is built from many nodes, you can increase this value. This value defaults to 2. You can increase the default value if you would like the rebalancing to be performed faster, but this will put more pressure on your cluster resources and will affect indexing and querying. The `cluster.routing.allocation.cluster_concurrent_rebalance` property can be set in the `elasticsearch.yml` configuration file and updated dynamically as well.

Controlling which shards may be rebalanced

The `cluster.routing.allocation.enable` property allows us to specify when which shards will be allowed to be rebalanced by Elasticsearch. This property can take the following values:

- `all`: The default behavior, which tells Elasticsearch to rebalance all the shards in the cluster
- `primaries`: This value allows the rebalancing of the primary shards only
- `replicas`: This value allows the rebalancing of the replica shards only
- `none`: This value disables the rebalancing of all type of shards for all indices in the cluster

The `cluster.routing.allocation.enable` property can be set in the `elasticsearch.yml` configuration file and updated dynamically as well.

The Cat API

The Elasticsearch Admin API is quite extensive and covers almost every part of Elasticsearch architecture: from low-level information about Lucene to high-level ones about the cluster nodes and their health. All this information is available using the Elasticsearch Java API as well as the REST API. However, the returned data, even though it is a JSON document, is not very readable by a user, at least when it comes to the amount of information given.

Because of this, Elasticsearch provides us with a more human-friendly API – the Cat API. The special Cat API returns data in a simple text, tabular format and what's more – it provides aggregated data that is usually usable without any further processing.

The basics

The base endpoint for the Cat API is quite obvious: it is `/_cat`. Without any parameters, it shows all the available endpoints for this API. We can check this by running the following command:

```
curl -XGET 'localhost:9200/_cat'
```

The response returned by Elasticsearch should be similar or identical (depending on your Elasticsearch version) to the following one:

```
=^.^=
/_cat/allocation
```

```
/_cat/shards
/_cat/shards/{index}
/_cat/master
/_cat/nodes
/_cat/indices
/_cat/indices/{index}
/_cat/segments
/_cat/segments/{index}
/_cat/count
/_cat/count/{index}
/_cat/recovery
/_cat/recovery/{index}
/_cat/health
/_cat/pending_tasks
/_cat/aliases
/_cat/aliases/{alias}
/_cat/thread_pool
/_cat/plugins
/_cat/fielddata
/_cat/fielddata/{fields}
/_cat/nodeattrs
/_cat/repositories
/_cat/snapshots/{repository}
```

So looking from the top Elasticsearch allows us to get the following information using the Cat API:

- Shard allocation-related information
- All shards-related information (also one limited to a given index)
- Information about the master node
- Nodes information
- Indices statistics (also one limited to a given index)
- Segments statistics (also one limited to a given index)
- Documents count (also one limited to a given index)
- Recovery information (also one limited to a given index)
- Cluster health
- Tasks pending for execution
- Index aliases and indices for a given alias
- Thread pool configuration
- Plugins installed on each node

- Field data cache size and field data cache sizes for individual fields
- Node attributes information
- Defined backup repositories
- Snapshots created in the backup repository

Using Cat API

Using the Cat API is as simple as running the GET request to the one of the previously mentioned REST end-points. For example, to get information about the cluster state, we could run the following command:

```
curl -XGET 'localhost:9200/_cat/health'
```

The response returned by Elasticsearch for the preceding command should be similar to the following one, but, of course, will be dependent on your cluster:

```
1446292041 12:47:21 elasticsearch yellow 1 1 21 21 0 0 21 0 - 50.0%
```

This is clean and nice. Because it is in tabular format, it is also easy to use the response in tools such as grep, awk, or sed – a standard set of tools for every administrator. It is also more readable once you know what it is all about.

To add a header describing each column purpose, we just need to add an additional v parameter, just like this:

```
curl -XGET 'localhost:9200/_cat/health?v'
```

Common arguments

Every Cat API endpoint has its own arguments, but there are a few common options that are shared among all of them:

- v: This adds a header line to the response with the names of presented items.
- h: This allows us to show only the chosen columns, for example h=status,node.total,shards,pri.
- help: This lists all the possible columns that this particular endpoint is able to show. The command shows the name of the parameter, its abbreviation, and description.

- bytes: This is the format for the information representing the values in bytes. As we said earlier, the Cat API is designed to be used by humans and because of this, by default, these values are represented in human-readable form, for example: 3.5kB or 40GB. The bytes option allows the setting of the same base for all the numbers, so sorting or numerical comparison will be easier. For example, bytes=b presents all values in bytes, bytes=k in kilobytes, and so on.

> For the full list of arguments for each Cat API endpoint, please refer to the official Elasticsearch documentation available at: https://www.elastic.co/guide/en/elasticsearch/reference/2.2/cat.html.

The examples

When we wrote this book, the Cat API had twenty-two endpoints. We don't want to describe them all –it would be a repeat of information contained in the documentation and it doesn't make sense. However, we didn't want to leave this section without an example regarding the usage of the Cat API. Because of this, we decided to show how easily you can get information using the Cat API compared to the standard JSON API exposed by Elasticsearch.

Getting information about the master node

The first example shows how easy it is to get information about which node in our cluster is the master node. By calling the /_cat/master REST endpoint we can get information about the nodes and which one of them is currently being elected as a master. For example, let's run the following command:

```
curl -XGET 'localhost:9200/_cat/master?v'
```

The response returned by Elasticsearch for my local two-node cluster looks as follows:

```
id                    host      ip        node
Cfj3tzqpSNi5SZx4g8osAg 127.0.0.1 127.0.0.1 Skin
```

As you can see in response, we've got the information about which node is currently elected as the master: we can see its identifier, IP address, and name.

Getting information about the nodes

The /_cat/nodes REST endpoint provides information about all the nodes in the cluster. Let's see what Elasticsearch will return after running the following command:

```
curl -XGET 'localhost:9200/_cat/nodes?v&h=name,node.role,load,uptime'
```

In the preceding example, we have used the possibility of choosing what information we want to get from the approximately seventy options of this endpoint. We have chosen to get only the node name, its role— whether the node is a data or client node -, node load, and its uptime.

And the response returned by Elasticsearch looks as follows:

```
name node.role load uptime
Skin d         2.00   1.3h
```

As you can see, the /_cat/nodes REST endpoint provides all the requested information about the nodes in the cluster.

Retrieving recovery information for an index

Another nice example of using the Cat API is getting information about the recovery of a single index or all the indices. In our case, we will retrieve recovery information for a single library index by running the following command:

```
curl -XGET 'localhost:9200/_cat/recovery/library?v&h=index,shard,time,type,stage,files_percent'
```

The response for the preceding command looks as follows:

```
index    shard time type  stage files_percent
library 0      75   store done  100.0%
library 1      83   store done  100.0%
library 2      88   store done  100.0%
library 3      79   store done  100.0%
library 4      5    store done  100.0%
```

Warming up

Sometimes, there may be a need to prepare Elasticsearch to handle your queries. Maybe it's because you heavily rely on the field data cache and you want it to be loaded before your production queries arrive, or maybe you want to warm up your operating system's I/O cache so that the data indices files are read from the cache. Whatever the reason, Elasticsearch allows us to use so called warming queries for our types and indices.

Defining a new warming query

A warming query is nothing more than the usual query stored in a special type called `_warmer` in Elasticsearch. Let's assume that we have the following query that we want to use for warming up:

```
curl -XGET localhost:9200/library/_search?pretty -d '{
  "query" : {
    "match_all" : {}
  },
  "aggs" : {
    "warming_aggs" : {
      "terms" : {
        "field" : "tags"
      }
    }
  }
}'
```

To store the preceding query as a warming query for our `library` index, we will run the following command:

```
curl -XPUT 'localhost:9200/library/_warmer/tags_warming_query' -d '{
  "query" : {
    "match_all" : {}
  },
  "aggs" : {
    "warming_aggs" : {
      "terms" : {
        "field" : "tags"
      }
    }
  }
}'
```

The preceding command will register our query as a warming query with the `tags_warming_query` name. You can have multiple warming queries for your index, but each of these queries needs to have a unique name.

We can not only define warming queries for the entire index, but also for the specific type in it. For example, to store our previously shown query as the warming query only for the book type in the library index, run the preceding command not to the /library/_warmer URI but to /library/book/_warmer. So, the entire command will be as follows:

```
curl -XPUT 'localhost:9200/library/book/_warmer/tags_warming_query' -d '{
  "query" : {
    "match_all" : {}
  },
  "aggs" : {
    "warming_aggs" : {
      "terms" : {
        "field" : "tags"
      }
    }
  }
}'
```

After adding a warming query, before Elasticsearch allows a new segment to be searched on, it will be warmed up by running the defined warming queries on that segment. This allows Elasticsearch and the operating system to cache data and, thus, speed up searching.

Just as we read in the *Full text searching* section of *Chapter 1, Getting Started with Elasticsearch Cluster*, Lucene divides the index into parts called segments, which once written can't be changed. Every new commit operation creates a new segment (which is eventually merged if the number of segments is too high), which Lucene uses for searching.

 Please note that the Warmer API will be removed in the future versions of Elasticsearch.

Retrieving the defined warming queries

In order to get a specific warming query for our index, we just need to know its name. For example, if we want to get the warming query named as tags_warming_query for our library index, we will run the following command:

```
curl -XGET 'localhost:9200/library/_warmer/tags_warming_query?pretty'
```

The result returned by Elasticsearch will be as follows:

```
{
    "library" : {
        "warmers" : {
            "tags_warming_query" : {
                "types" : [ "book" ],
                "source" : {
                    "query" : {
                        "match_all" : { }
                    },
                    "aggs" : {
                        "warming_aggs" : {
                            "terms" : {
                                "field" : "tags"
                            }
                        }
                    }
                }
            }
        }
    }
}
```

We can also get all the warming queries for the index and type using the following command:

```
curl -XGET 'localhost:9200/library/_warmer?pretty'
```

And finally, we can also get all the warming queries that start with a given prefix. For example, if we want to get all the warming queries for the library index that start with the tags prefix, we will run the following command:

```
curl -XGET 'localhost:9200/library/_warmer/tags*?pretty'
```

Deleting a warming query

Deleting a warming query is very similar to getting one; we just need to use the DELETE HTTP method. To delete a specific warming query from our index, we just need to know its name. For example, if we want to delete the warming query named tags_warming_query for our library index, we will run the following command:

```
curl -XDELETE 'localhost:9200/library/_warmer/tags_warming_query'
```

We can also delete all the warming queries for the index using the following command:

```
curl -XDELETE 'localhost:9200/library/_warmer/_all'
```

And finally, we can also remove all the warming queries that start with a given prefix. For example, if we want to remove all the warming queries for the library index that start with the tags prefix, we will run the following command:

```
curl -XDELETE 'localhost:9200/library/_warmer/tags*'
```

Disabling the warming up functionality

To disable the warming queries totally but to save them in the _warmer index, you should set the index.warmer.enabled configuration property to false (setting this property to true will result in enabling the warming up functionality). This setting can be either put in the elasticsearch.yml file or just set using the REST API on a live cluster.

For example, if we want to disable the warming up functionality for the library index, we will run the following command:

```
curl -XPUT 'localhost:9200/library/_settings' -d '{
  "index.warmer.enabled" : false
}'
```

Choosing queries for warming

Finally, we should ask ourselves one question: which queries should be considered as candidates for warming. Typically, you'll want to choose ones that are expensive to execute and ones that require caches to be populated. So you'll probably want to choose queries that include aggregations and sorting based on the fields in your index. This will force the operating system to load the part of the indices that hold the data related to such queries and improve the performance of consecutive queries that are run. In addition to this, parent-child queries and nested queries are also potential candidates for warming. You may also choose other queries by looking at the logs, and finding where your performance is not as great as you want it to be. Such queries may also be perfect candidates for warming up.

For example, let's say that we have the following logging configuration set in the elasticsearch.yml file:

```
index.search.slowlog.threshold.query.warn: 10s
index.search.slowlog.threshold.query.info: 5s
index.search.slowlog.threshold.query.debug: 2s
index.search.slowlog.threshold.query.trace: 1s
```

And we have the following logging level set in the `logging.yml` configuration file:

```
logger:
    index.search.slowlog: TRACE, index_search_slow_log_file
```

Notice that the `index.search.slowlog.threshold.query.trace` property is set to `1s` and the `index.search.slowlog` logging level is set to `TRACE`. This means that whenever a query is executed for longer than one second (on a shard, not in total), it will be logged into the slow log file (the name of which is specified by the `index_search_slow_log_file` configuration section of the `logging.yml` configuration file). For example, the following can be found in a slow log file:

```
[2015-11-25 19:53:00,248][TRACE][index.search.slowlog.query]
took[340000.2ms], took_millis[3400], types[], stats[], search_
type[QUERY_THEN_FETCH], total_shards[5], source[{"query":{"match_
all":{}},"aggs":{"warming_aggs":{"terms":{"field":"tags"}}}}], extra_
source[],
```

As you can see, in the preceding log line, we have the query time, search type, and the query source, which shows us the executed query.

Of course, the values can be different in your configuration but the slow log can be a valuable source of the queries that have been running too long and may need to have some warm up defined; maybe these are parent-child queries and need some identifiers to be fetched to perform better, or maybe you are using a filter that is expensive when you execute it for the first time.

There is one thing you should remember: don't overload your Elasticsearch cluster with too many warming queries because you may end up spending too much time in warming up instead of processing your production queries.

Index aliasing and using it to simplify your everyday work

When working with multiple indices in Elasticsearch, you can sometimes lose track of them. Imagine a situation where you store logs in your indices or time-based data in general. Usually, the amount of data in such cases is quite large and, therefore, it is a good solution to have the data divided somehow. A logical division of such data is obtained by creating a single index for a single day of logs (if you are interested in an open source solution used to manage logs, look at the Logstash from the Elasticsearch suite at `https://www.elastic.co/products/logstash`).

However, after some time, if we keep all the indices, we will start having a problem in taking care of all that. An application needs to take care of all the information, such as which index to send data to, which to query, and so on. With the help of aliases, we can change this to work with a single name just as we would use a single index, but we will work with multiple indices.

An alias

What is an index alias? It's an additional name for one or more indices that allows us to use these indices by referring to them with those additional names. A single alias can have multiple indices as well as the other way round; a single index can be a part of multiple aliases.

However, please remember that you can't use an alias that has multiple indices for indexing or for real-time GET operations. Elasticsearch will throw an exception if you do this. We can still use an alias that links to only a single index for indexing, though. This is because Elasticsearch doesn't know in which index the data should be indexed or from which index the document should be fetched.

Creating an alias

To create an index alias, we need to run the HTTP POST method to the _aliases REST end-point with a defined action. For example, the following request will create a new alias called week12 that will include the indices named day10, day11, and day12 (we need to create those indices first):

```
curl -XPOST 'localhost:9200/_aliases' -d '{
  "actions" : [
    { "add" : { "index" : "day10", "alias" : "week12" } },
    { "add" : { "index" : "day11", "alias" : "week12" } },
    { "add" : { "index" : "day12", "alias" : "week12" } }

  ]
}'
```

If the week12 alias isn't present in our Elasticsearch cluster, the preceding command will create it. If it is present, the command will just add the specified indices to it.

We would run a search across the three indices as follows:

```
curl -XGET 'localhost:9200/day10,day11,day12/_search?q=test'
```

If everything goes well, we can instead run it as follows:

```
curl -XGET 'localhost:9200/week12/_search?q=test'
```

Isn't this better?

Sometimes we have a set of indices where every index serves independent information but some queries should go across all of them; for example, we have dedicated indices for countries (country_en, country_us, country_de, and so on). In this case, we would create the alias by grouping them all:

```
curl -XPOST 'localhost:9200/_aliases' -d '{
  "actions" : [
    { "add" : { "index" : "country_*", "alias" : "countries" } }
  ]
}'
```

The last command created only one alias. Elasticsearch allows you to rewrite this to something less verbose:

```
curl -XPUT 'localhost:9200/country_*/_alias/countries'
```

Modifying aliases

Of course, you can also remove indices from an alias. We can do this similarly to how we add indices to an alias, but instead of the add command, we use the remove one. For example, to remove the index named day9 from the week12 index, we will run the following command:

```
curl -XPOST 'localhost:9200/_aliases' -d '{
 "actions" : [
    { "remove" : { "index" : "day9", "alias" : "week12" } }
  ]
}'
```

Combining commands

The add and remove commands can be sent as a single request. For example, if you would like to combine all the previously sent commands into a single request, you will have to send the following command:

```
curl -XPOST 'localhost:9200/_aliases' -d '{
  "actions" : [
```

```
    { "add" : { "index" : "day10", "alias" : "week12" } },
    { "add" : { "index" : "day11", "alias" : "week12" } },
    { "add" : { "index" : "day12", "alias" : "week12" } },
    { "remove" : { "index" : "day9", "alias" : "week12" } }
  ]
}'
```

Retrieving aliases

In addition to adding or removing indices to or from aliases, we and our applications that use Elasticsearch may need to retrieve all the aliases available in the cluster or all the aliases that an index is connected to. To retrieve these aliases, we send a request using the HTTP GET command. For example, the following command gets all the aliases for the day10 index and the second one will get all the available aliases:

```
curl -XGET 'localhost:9200/day10/_aliases'
curl -XGET 'localhost:9200/_aliases'
```

The response from the second command is as follows:

```
{
  "day12" : {
    "aliases" : {
      "week12" : { }
    }
  },
  "library" : {
    "aliases" : { }
  },
  "day11" : {
    "aliases" : {
      "week12" : { }
    }
  },
  "day9" : {
    "aliases" : { }
  },
  "day10" : {
    "aliases" : {
      "week12" : { }
    }
  }
}
```

You can also use the `_alias` endpoint to get all aliases from the given index:

```
curl -XGET 'localhost:9200/day10/_alias/*'
```

To get a particular alias definition, you can use the following:

```
curl -XGET 'localhost:9200/day10/_alias/day12'
```

Removing aliases

You can also remove an alias using the `_alias` endpoint. For example, sending the following command will remove the client alias from the data index:

```
curl -XDELETE localhost:9200/data/_alias/client
```

Filtering aliases

Aliases can be used in a way similar to how views are used in SQL databases. You can use a full Query DSL (discussed in detail in *Chapter 3, Searching Your Data*) and have your filter applied to all count, search, delete by query, and so on.

Let's look at an example. Imagine that we want to have aliases that return data for a certain client so we can use it in our application. Let's say that the client identifier we are interested in is stored in the `clientId` field and we are interested in the `12345` client. So, let's create the alias named `client` with our data index, which will apply a query for `clientId` automatically:

```
curl -XPOST 'localhost:9200/_aliases' -d '{
  "actions" : [
    {
      "add" : {
        "index" : "data",
        "alias" : "client",
        "filter" : { "term" : { "clientId" : 12345 } }
      }
    }
  ]
}'
```

So when using the defined alias, you will always get your request filtered by a term query that ensures that all the documents have the `12345` value in the `clientId` field.

Aliases and routing

In the *Introduction to routing* section of *Chapter 2, Indexing Your Data*, we talked about routing. Similar to aliases that use filtering, we can add routing values to the aliases. Imagine that we are using routing on the basis of user identifier and we want to use the same routing values with our aliases. So, for the alias named `client`, we will use the routing values of `12345`, `12346`, and `12347` for querying, and only `12345` for indexing. To do this, we will create an alias using the following command:

```
curl -XPOST 'localhost:9200/_aliases' -d '{
  "actions" : [
    {
      "add" : {
        "index" : "data",
        "alias" : "client",
        "search_routing" : "12345,12346,12347",
        "index_routing" : "12345"
      }
    }
  ]
}'
```

This way, when we index our data using the `client` alias, the values specified by the `index_routing` property will be used. At the time of querying, the values specified by the `search_routing` property will be used.

There is one more thing. Please look at the following query sent to the previously defined alias:

```
curl -XGET 'localhost:9200/client/_search?q=test&routing=99999,12345'
```

The value used as a routing value will be `12345`. This is because Elasticsearch will take the common values of the `search_routing` attribute and the query routing parameter, which in our case is `12345`.

Zero downtime reindexing and aliases

One of the greatest advantages of using aliases is the ability to re-index the data without any downtime from the system using Elasticsearch. To achieve this, you would need to interact with your indices only through aliases—both for indexing and querying. In such a case, you can just create a new index, index the data here, and switch aliases when needed. During indexing, aliases would still point to the old index, so the application could work as usual.

Summary

In this chapter, we discussed Elasticsearch administration. We started by learning how to perform backups of our indices and how to monitor our cluster health and state using its API. We controlled cluster shard rebalancing and learned how to adjust shard allocation according to our needs. We've used the CAT API to get information about Elasticsearch in human-readable form and we've warmed up our queries to make them faster. Finally, we've used aliases to allow a better management of our indices and to have more flexibility.

In the next and final chapter of the book, we will focus on a hypothetical online library store to see how to make Elasticsearch work in practice. We will start with a brief introduction and hardware considerations. We will tune a single instance of Elasticsearch and properly configure our cluster by discussing each of its parts and providing a proper architecture. We will vertically expand the cluster and prepare it for both high querying and high indexing load. Finally, we will learn how to monitor such a prepared cluster.

11
Scaling by Example

In the previous chapter, we discussed Elasticsearch administration. We started with discussion about backups and how we can do them by using available API. We monitored the health and state of our clusters and nodes and we learned how to control shard rebalancing. We controlled the shard and replicas allocation and used human friendly Cat API to get information about the cluster and nodes. We saw how to use warmers to speed up potentially heavy queries and we used index aliasing to manage our indices more easily. By the end of this chapter, you will have learned the following topics:

- Hardware preparations for running Elasticsearch
- Tuning a single Elasticsearch node
- Preparing highly available and fault tolerant clusters
- Expanding Elasticsearch vertically
- Preparing Elasticsearch for high query and indexing throughput
- Monitoring Elasticsearch

Hardware

One of the first decisions that we need to make when starting every serious software project is a set choices related to hardware. And believe us, this is not only a very important choice, but also one of the most difficult ones. Often the decisions are made at early project stages, when only the basic architecture is known and we don't have precise information regarding the queries, data load, and so on. Project architect has to balance precaution and projected cost of the whole solution. Too many times it is an intersection of experience and clairvoyance, which can lead to either great or terrible results.

Physical servers or a cloud

Let's start with a decision: a cloud, virtual, or physical machines. Nowadays, these are all valid options, but it was not always the case. Sometime ago the only option was to buy new servers for each environment part or share resources with the other applications on the same machine. The second option makes perfect sense as it is more cost-effective but introduces risk. Problems with one application, especially when they are hardware related, will result in problems for another application. You can imagine one of your applications using most of the I/O subsystem of the physical machine and all the other applications struggling with lots of I/O waits and performance problems because of that. Virtualization promises application separation and a more convenient way of managing resources, but you are still limited by the underlying hardware. Every unexpected traffic could be a problem and affect service availability. Imagine that your ecommerce site suddenly gains massive number of customers. Instead of being glad that the spike appeared and you have more potential customers, you search for a place where you can buy additional hardware that will be supplied as soon as possible.

Cloud computing on the other hand means a more flexible cost model. We can easily add new machines whenever we need. We can add them temporarily when we expect a greater load (for example, before Christmas for an ecommerce site) and pay only for the actually used processing power. It is just a few clicks in the admin panel. Even more, we can also setup automatic scaling, that is new virtual machines can appear automatically when we need them. Cloud-based software can also shut them down when we do not need them anymore. The cloud has many advantages, such as lower initial cost, ability to easily grow your business, and insensitivity to temporal fluctuations of resource requirements, but it also has several flaws. The costs of cloud servers rise faster than that of physical machines. Also, mass storage, although practically unlimited, has worse characteristics (number of operations per seconds) than physical servers. This is sometimes a great problem for us, especially with disk based storage such as Elasticsearch.

In practice, as usual, the choice can be hard but going through a few points can help you with your decision:

- Business requirements may directly point for your own servers; for example, some procedures related to financial or medical data automatically exclude cloud solutions hosted by third-party vendors

- For proof of concept and low/medium load services, the cloud can be a good choice because of simplicity, scalability, and low cost

- Solutions with strong requirements connected with I/O subsystems will probably work better on bare metal machines where you have greater influence what storage type is available to you

- When the traffic can greatly change within a short time, the cloud is a perfect place for you

For the purpose of further discussion, let's assume that we want to buy our own servers. We are in the computer store now and let's buy something!

CPU

In most cases, this is the least important part. You can choose any modern CPU model but you should know that more number of cores means a higher number of concurrent queries and indexing threads. That will lead to being able to index data faster, especially with complicated analysis and lots of merges.

RAM memory

More gigabytes of RAM is always better than less gigabytes of RAM. Memory is necessary, especially for aggregation and sorting. It is less of a problem now, with Elasticsearch 2.0 and doc values, but still complicated queries with lots of aggregation require memory to process the data. Memory is also used for indexing buffers and can lead to indexing speed improvements, because more data can be buffered in memory and thus disks will be used less frequently. If you try to use more memory than available, the operating system will use the hard disks as temporary space (it starts swapping) and you should avoid this at all cost. Note that you should never try to force Elasticsearch to use as much as possible memory. The first reason is Java garbage collector – less memory is more GC friendly. The second reason is that the unused memory is actually used by the operating system for buffers and disk cache. In fact, when your index can fit in this space, all data is read from these caches and not from the disks directly. This can drastically improve the performance. By default, Elasticsearch and the I/O subsystem share the same I/O cache, which gives another reason to leave even more memory for the operating system itself.

In practice, 8GB is the lowest requirement for memory. It does not mean that Elasticsearch will never work with less memory, but for most situations and data intensive applications, it is the reasonable minimum. On the other hand, more than 64GB is rarely needed. In lieu, think about scaling the system horizontally instead of assigning such amounts of memory to a single Elasticsearch node.

Mass storage

We said that we are in a good situation when the whole index fits into memory. In practice this can be difficult to achieve, so good and fast disks are very important. It is even more important if one of the requirements is high indexing throughput. In such a case, you may consider fast SSD disks. Unfortunately, these disks are expensive if your data volume is big. You can improve the situation by avoiding using RAID (see `https://en.wikipedia.org/wiki/RAID`), except RAID 0. In most cases, when you handle fault tolerance by having multiple servers, the additional level of security on the RAID level is unnecessary. The last thing is to avoid using external storage, such as **network attached storage (NAS)** or NFS volumes. The network latency in such cases always kills all the advantages of these solutions.

The network

When you use Elasticsearch cluster, each node opens several connections to other nodes for various uses. When you index, the data is forwarded to different shards and replicas. When you query for data, the node used for querying can run multiple partial queries to the other nodes and compose reply from the data fetched from the other nodes. This is why you should make sure that your network is not the bottleneck. In practice, use one network for all the servers in the cluster and avoid solutions in which the nodes in the cluster are spread between data centers.

How many servers

The answer is always the same, as it depends. It depends on many factors: the number of request per seconds, the data volume, the level of the query's complexity, the aggregations and sorting usage, the number of new documents per unit of time, how fast new data should be available for searching (the refresh time), the average document size, and the analyzers used. In practice, the handiest answer is - test it and approximate.

The one thing that is often underestimated is data security. When you think about fault tolerance and availability, you should start from three servers. Why? We talked about the split brain situation in the *Master election configuration* section of *Chapter 9, Elasticsearch Cluster in Detail*. Starting from three servers we are able to handle a single Elasticsearch node failure without taking down the whole cluster.

Cost cutting

You did some tests, considered carefully planned functionalities, estimated volumes and load, and went to the project owner with an architecture draft. "Its too expensive", he said and asked you to think about servers once again. What can we do?

Let's think about server roles and try to introduce some differences between them. If one of the requirements is indexing massive amounts of data connected with time (maybe logs), the possible way is having two groups of servers: hot nodes, when new data arrives, and cold nodes, when old data is moved. Thanks to this approach, hot nodes may have faster but smaller disks (that is, solid state drives) in opposite to the cold nodes, when fast disks are not so important but space is. You can also divide your architecture in to several groups as master servers (less powerful, with relativly small disks), data nodes (bigger disks), and query aggregator nodes (more RAM). We will talk about this in the following sections.

Preparing a single Elasticsearch node

When we talk about *vertical scaling,* we often mean adding more resources to the server Elasticsearch is running on. We can add memory or we can switch to a machine with a better CPU or faster disk storage. Of course, with better machines we can expect an increase in performance; depending on our deployment and its bottlenecks, it can be a small or large improvement. However, there are limitations when it comes to vertical scaling. For example, one of the limitations is the maximum amount of physical memory available for your servers or the total memory required by the JVM to operate. When having large data and complicated queries, you can very soon run into memory issues and adding new memory may not help at all. In this section, we will try to give you general advice on where to look and what to tune when it comes to a single Elasticsearch node.

The thing to remember when tuning your system is performance tests, ones that can be repeated under the same circumstances. Once you make a change, you need to be able to see how it affects the overall performance. In addition to that, Elasticsearch scales great. Using that knowledge, we can run performance tests on a single machine (or a few of them) and extrapolate the results. Such observations may be a good starting point for further tuning.

Also keep in mind that this section doesn't contain a deep dive into all performance related topics, but is dedicated to showing you the most common things.

The general preparations

Apart from all the things we will discuss in this section, there are three major, operating system related things you need to remember: the number of allowed file descriptors, the virtual memory, and avoiding swapping.

Note that the following section contains information for Linux operating systems, but you can also achieve similar options on Microsoft Windows.

Avoiding swapping

Let's start with the third one. Elasticsearch and Java Virtual Machine based applications, in general, don't like to be swapped. This means that these applications work best if the operating system doesn't put the memory that they use in the swap space. This is very simple, because, to access the swapped memory, the operating system will have to read it from the disk, which is slow and which would affect the performance in a very bad way.

If we have enough memory, and we should have if we want our Elasticsearch instance to perform well, we can configure Elasticsearch to avoid swapping. To do that, we just need to modify the `elasticsearch.yml` file and include the following property:

```
bootstrap.mlockall: true
```

This is one of the options. The second one is to set the property `vm.swappiness` in the `/etc/sysctl.conf` file to `0` (for complete swap disabling) or `1` for swapping only in emergency (for Kernel versions 3.5 and above).

The third option is to disable swapping by editing `/etc/fstab` and removing the lines that contain the `swap` word. The following is an example `/etc/fstab` content:

```
LABEL=cloudimg-rootfs  /   ext4  defaults,discard  0 0
/dev/xvdb swap swap defaults 0 0
```

To disable swapping we would just remove the second line from the above contents. We could also run the following command to disable swapping:

```
sudo swapoff -a
```

However, remember that this effect won't persist between logging off and back in to the system, so this is only a temporary solution.

Also, remember that if you don't have enough memory to run Elasticsearch, the operating system will just kill the process when swapping is disabled.

File descriptors

Make sure you have enough limits related to file descriptors for the user running Elasticsearch (when installing from official packages, that user will be called `elasticsearch`). If you don't, you may end up with problems when Elasticsearch tries to flush the data and create new segments or merge segments together, which can result in index corruption.

To adjust the number of allowed file descriptors, you will need to adjust the `/etc/security/limits.conf` file (at least on most common Linux systems) and adjust or add an entry related to a given user (for both soft and hard limits). For example:

```
elasticsearch soft nofile 65536
elasticsearch hard nofile 65536
```

It is advised to set the number of allowed file descriptors to at least `65536`, but even more can be needed, depending on your index size.

On some Linux systems, you may also need to load an appropriate limits module for the preceding setting to take effect. To load that module, you need to adjust the `/etc/pam.d/login` file and add or uncomment the following line:

```
session required pam_limits.so
```

There is also a possibility to display the number of file descriptors available for Elasticsearch by adding the `-Des.max-open-files=true` parameter to Elasticsearch startup parameters. For example, like this:

```
bin/elasticsearch -Des.max-open-files=true
```

When doing that, Elasticsearch will include information about the file descriptors in the logs:

```
[2015-12-20 00:22:19,869][INFO ][bootstrap                ] max_open_
files [10240]
```

Virtual memory

Elasticsearch 2.2 uses hybrid directory implementation, which is a combination of `mmapfs` and `niofs` directories. Because of that, especially when your indices are large, you may need a lot of virtual memory on your system. By default, the operating system limits the amount of memory mapped files and that can cause errors when running Elasticsearch. Because of that, we recommend increasing the default values. To do that, you just need to edit the `/etc/sysctl.conf` file and set the `vm.max_map_count` property; for example, to a value equal to `262144`.

You can also change the value temporarily by running the following command:

```
sysctl -w vm.max_map_count=262144
```

The memory

Before thinking about Elasticsearch configuration related things, we should remember about giving enough memory to Elasticsearch. In general, we shouldn't give more than 50-60 percent of the total available memory to the JVM process running Elasticsearch. We do that because we want to leave memory for the operating system and for the operating system I/O cache. However, we need to remember that the 50-60 percent figure is not always true. You can imagine having nodes with 256GB of RAM and having indices of 30GB in total on such a node. In such circumstances, even assigning more than 60 percent of physical RAM to Elasticsearch would leave plenty of RAM for the operating system. It is also a good idea to set the Xmx and Xms properties to the same values to avoid JVM heap size resizing.

Another thing to remember are the so called compressed oops (`http://docs.oracle.com/javase/7/docs/technotes/guides/vm/performance-enhancements-7.html#compressedOop`), the ordinary object pointers. Java virtual machine can be told to use them by adding the `-XX:+UseCompressedOops` switch. This allows Java virtual machine to use less memory to address the objects on the heap. However, this is only true for heap sizes less than or equal to 31GB. Going for a larger heap means no compressed oops and higher memory usage for addressing the objects on the heap.

Field data cache and breaking the circuit

As we know, by default the field data cache in Elasticsearch is unbounded. This can be very dangerous, especially when you are using aggregations and sorting on many fields that are analysed, because they don't use doc values by default. If those fields are high cardinality ones, then you can run into even more trouble. By trouble we mean running out of memory.

We have two different factors we can tune to be sure that we don't run into out of memory errors. First of all, we can limit the size of the field data cache and we should do that. The second thing is the circuit breaker, which we can easily configure to just throw exceptions instead of loading too much data. Combining these two things together will ensure that we don't run into memory issues.

However, we should also remember that Elasticsearch will evict data from the field data cache if its size is not enough to handle aggregation requests or sorting. This will affect the query performance because loading the field data information is not very efficient and is resource intensive. However, in our opinion, it is better to have our queries slower than having our cluster blown up because of out of memory errors.

The field data cache and caches in general were discussed in the *Elasticsearch caches* section of *Chapter 9, Elasticsearch Cluster in Detail*.

Use doc values

Whenever you plan to use sorting, aggregations, or scripting heavily, you should use doc values whenever you can. This will not only save you the memory needed for the field data cache, because of fewer objects produced, it will also make the Java virtual machine work better with lower garbage collector time. Doc values were discussed in the *Mappings Configuration* section of *Chapter 2, Indexing Your Data*.

RAM buffer for indexing

In the *Elasticsearch caches* section of *Chapter 9, Elasticsearch Cluster in Detail*, we also discussed. There are a few things we would like to mention. First of all, the more RAM for the indexing buffer, the more documents Elasticsearch will be able to hold in memory. So the more memory we have for indexing, the less often the flush to disk will happen and fewer segments will be created. Because of that, your indexing will be faster. But of course, we don't want Elasticsearch to occupy 100 percent of the available memory. Keep in mind that the RAM buffers are set per shard, so the amount of memory that will be used depends on the number of shards and replicas that are assigned on the given node and on the number of documents you index. You should set the upper limits so your node doesn't blow up when it has multiple shards assigned.

Index refresh rate

Elasticsearch uses Lucene and we know it by now. The thing with Lucene is that the view of the index is not refreshed when new data is indexed or segments are created. To see the newly indexed data, we need to refresh the index. By default, Elasticsearch does that once every second and the period of refresh is controlled by using the `index.refresh_interval` property, specified per index. The lower the refresh rate, the sooner the documents will be visible for search operations. However, that also means that Elasticsearch will need to put more resources in to refreshing the index view, meaning that the indexing and searching operations will be slower. The higher the refresh rate, the more time you will have to wait before being able to see the data in the search results, but your indexing and querying will be faster.

Thread pools

We haven't talked about thread pools until now, but we would like to mention them now. Each Elasticsearch node holds several thread pools that control the execution queues for operations such as indexing or querying. Elasticsearch uses several pools to allow control over how the threads are handled and much the memory consumption is allowed for user requests.

> Java virtual machine allows applications to use multiple threads - concurrently running multiple application tasks. For more information about Java threads, refer to `http://docs.oracle.com/javase/7/docs/api/java/lang/Thread.html`.

There are many thread pools (we can specify the type we are configuring by specifying the `type` property). However, for performance, the most important are:

- `generic`: This is the thread pool for generic operations, such as node discovery. By default, the `generic` thread pool is of type `cached`.

- `index`: This is the thread pool used for indexing and deleting operations. Its type defaults to `fixed`, its `size` to the number of available processors, and the size of the queue to `200`.

- `search`: This is the thread pool used for search and count requests. Its type defaults to `fixed` and its `size` to the number of available processors multiplied by 3 and divided by 2, with the size of the queue defaulting to `1000`.

- `suggest`: This is the thread pool used for suggest requests. Its type defaults to `fixed`, its `size` to the number of available processors, and the size of the queue to `1000`.

- `get`: This is the thread pool used for real time `get` requests. Its type defaults to `fixed`, its `size` to the number of available processors, and the size of the queue to `1000`.

- `bulk`: As you can guess, this is the thread pool used for bulk operations. Its type defaults to `fixed`, its `size` to the number of available processors, and the size of the queue to `50`.

- `percolate`: This is the thread pool for percolation requests. Its type defaults to `fixed`, its `size` to the number of available processors, and the size of the queue to `1000`.

Before Elasticsearch 2.1, we could control the type of the thread pool. Starting with Elasticsearch 2.1 we can no longer do that. For more information please refer to the official documentation - `https://www.elastic.co/guide/en/elasticsearch/ reference/2.1/breaking_21_removed_features.html`.

For example, if we want to configure the thread pool for indexing operations to have a size of `100` and a queue of `500`, we will set the following in the `elasticsearch. yml` configuration file:

```
threadpool.index.size: 100
```

```
threadpool.index.queue_size: 500
```

Also remember that the thread pool configuration can be updated using the cluster update API. For example, like this:

```
curl -XPUT 'localhost:9200/_cluster/settings' -d '{
 "transient" : {
  "threadpool.index.size" : 100,
  "threadpool.index.queue_size" : 500
 }
}'
```

In general, you don't need to work with the thread pools and their configuration. However, when configuring your cluster, you may want to put more emphasis on indexing or querying and, in such cases, giving more threads or larger queues to the prioritized operation may result in more resources being used for such operations.

Horizontal expansion

Elasticsearch is a highly scalable search and analytics platform. We can scale it both horizontally and vertically. We discussed how to tune a single node in the *Preparing a single Elasticsearch node* section earlier in this chapter and we would like to focus on horizontal scaling now; how to handle multiple nodes in the same cluster, what roles should they have, and how to tune the configuration to have a highly reliable, available, and fault tolerant cluster.

You can imagine vertical scaling like building a sky scrapper – we have limited space available and we need to go as high as we can. Of course, that is expensive and requires a lot of engineering done right. On the other hand, we have horizontal scaling, which is like having many houses in a residential area. Instead of investing into hardware and having powerful machines, we choose to have multiple machines and our data split between them. Horizontal scaling gives us virtually unlimited scaling possibilities. Even with the most powerful hardware, the time comes when a single machine is not enough to handle the data, the queries, or both of them. In such cases, spreading the data among multiple servers is what saves us and allows us to have terabytes of data in multiple indices spread across the whole cluster, just like the one in the following image:

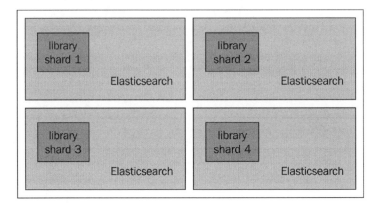

We have our 4 nodes cluster with the library index created and built of four shards.

If we want to increase the querying capabilities of our cluster, we can just add additional nodes, for example, four of them. After adding new nodes to the cluster, we can either create new indices that will be built of more shards to spread the load more evenly or add replicas to the already existing shards. Both options are viable. This is because we don't have the possibility of splitting shards or adding more primary shards to an existing index. We should go for having more primary shards when our hardware is not enough to handle the amount of data it holds. In such cases, we usually run into out of memory situations, long shard query execution time, swapping, or high I/O waits. The second option, that is having replicas, is the way to go when our hardware is happily handling the data we have but the traffic is so high that the nodes just can't keep up.

The first option is simple, but let's looks at the second case - having more replicas. So with four additional nodes, our cluster would look as follows:

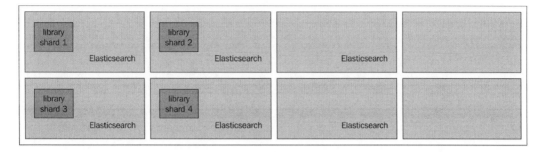

Now, let's run the following command to add a single replica:

```
curl -XPUT 'localhost:9200/library/_settings' -d '{
  "index" : {
   "number_of_replicas" : 1
  }
}'
```

Our cluster view would look more or less as follows:

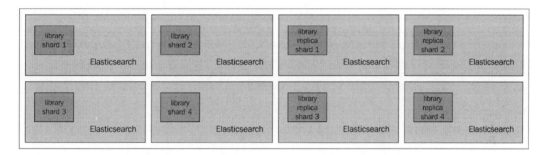

As you can see, each of the initial shards building the library index has a single replica stored on another node. The nice thing about shards and their replicas is that Elasticsearch is smart enough to balance the shards in a single index and put them on separate nodes. For example, you won't ever end up in a situation where you have a shard and its replicas on the same node. Also, Elasticsearch is able to round robin the queries between the shards and their replicas, which means that all the nodes will be hit by the queries and we don't have to care about that. Because of that, we are able to handle almost double the query load compared to our initial deployment.

Automatically creating the replicas

Let's stay a bit longer around replicas. Elasticsearch allows us to automatically expand replicas when the cluster is big enough. This means that the replicas can be created automatically when new nodes are added to the cluster. You can wonder where such functionality can be useful. Imagine a situation where you have a small index that you would like to be present on every node so that your plugins don't have to run distributed queries just to get the data from it. In addition to that, your cluster is dynamically changing, that is you add and remove nodes from it. The simplest way to achieve such functionality is to allow Elasticsearch to automatically expand the replicas. To do that, we need to set `index.auto_expand_replicas` to `0-all`, which means that the index can have 0 replicas or be present on all the nodes. So if our small index is called `shops` and we would like Elasticsearch to automatically expand its replicas to all the nodes in the cluster, we would use the following command to create the index:

```
curl -XPOST 'localhost:9200/shops/' -d '{
 "settings" : {
  "index" : {
   "auto_expand_replicas" : "0-all"
  }
 }
}'
```

We can also update the settings of that index if it is already created by running the following command:

```
curl -XPUT 'localhost:9200/shops/_settings' -d '{
 "index" : {
  "auto_expand_replicas" : "0-all"
 }
}'
```

Redundancy and high availability

The Elasticsearch replication mechanism not only gives us ability to handle higher query throughput, but also gives us redundancy and high availability. Imagine an Elasticsearch cluster hosting a single index called `library` that is built of 2 shards and 0 replicas. Such a cluster would look as follows:

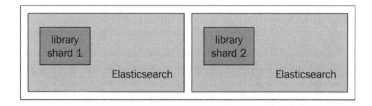

Now what happens when one of the nodes fail? The simplest answer is that we lose about 50 percent of the data and, if the failure is fatal, we lose that data forever. Even when having backups, we would need to spin up another node and restore the backup and that takes time. During that time, your application, or parts of it that are based on Elasticsearch, can't work correctly. If your business relies on Elasticsearch, downtime means money loss. Of course, we can use replicas to create more reliable clusters that can handle the hardware and software failures. And one thing to remember is that everything will fail eventually – if the software won't, hardware will. For example, some time ago Google said that in each of their clusters, during the first year at least 1000 machines will fail (you can read more on that topic at http://www.cnet.com/news/google-spotlights-data-center-inner-workings/). Because of that, we need to be ready to handle such cases.

Let's look at the same cluster but with one replica:

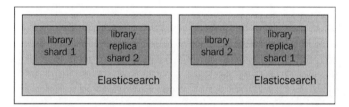

Now losing a single Elasticsearch node means that we still have the whole data available and we can work on restoring the full cluster structure without downtime. Of course, this is only a very small cluster built of two Elasticsearch nodes clusters. The larger the cluster, the more replicas, the more failure you will be able to handle without worrying about the data loss. Of course you will have lower performance, depending on the percentage of nodes that fail, but the data will still be there and the cluster will be operational.

That's why, when designing your architecture and deciding on the number of nodes and indices and their architecture, you should take into consideration how many nodes, failure you want to live with. Of course, you can't forget about the performance part of the equation, but redundancy and high availability should be one of the factors of the scaling equation.

Cost and performance flexibility

The default distributed nature of Elasticsearch and its ability to scale horizontally allows us to be flexible when it comes to performance and costs that we have when running our environment. First of all, high end servers with high performance disks, numerous CPU cores, and a lot of RAM are still expensive. In addition to that, cloud computing is getting more and more popular and if you need a lot of flexibility and don't want to have your own hardware, you can choose solutions such as Amazon (http://aws.amazon.com/), Rackspace (http://www.rackspace.com/), DigitalOcean (https://www.digitalocean.com/), and so on. They do not only allow us to run our software on rented machines, but also allow us to scale on demand. We just need to add more machines which is a few clicks away or can even be automated with some degree of work.

Using a hosted solution with one click machine renting allows having a truly horizontally scalable solution. Of course, that's not cheap – you pay for the flexibility. But we can easily sacrifice performance if costs are the most crucial factor in our business plan. Of course, we can also go the other way. If we can afford large bare metal machines, Elasticsearch clusters can be pushed to hundreds of terabytes of data stored in the indices and still get decent performance (of course with a proper hardware and property distributed).

Continuous upgrades

High availability, cost and performance flexibility, and virtually endless growth are not the only things worth talking about when discussing the scalability side of Elasticsearch. At some point in time, you will want to have your Elasticsearch cluster upgraded to a new version. It can be because of bug fixes, performance improvements, new features, or anything that you can think of. The thing is that when you have a single instance of each shard, without replicas, an upgrade means unavailability of Elasticsearch (or at least its parts) and that may mean downtime of the applications that use Elasticsearch. This is another reason why horizontal scaling is so important; you can perform upgrades, at least to the point where software such as Elasticsearch supports. For example, you can take Elasticsearch 2.0 and upgrade to Elasticsearch 2.1 with only rolling restarts (getting one node out of the cluster, upgrading it, bringing it back, and continuing with the next node until all the nodes are done), thus having all the data still available for searching and indexing happening at the same time.

Multiple Elasticsearch instances on a single physical machine

Having a large physical machine with lot of memory and CPU cores has advantages and some challenges. First of all, if you decide to run a single Elasticsearch node on that machine, you will sooner or later run into garbage collection issues, you will have lots of shards on a single node which will require a high number of I/O operations for the internal Elasticsearch communication (retrieving cluster statistics), and so so. What's more, you usually shouldn't go above 31GB of heap memory for a single JVM process because you can't use compressed ordinary object pointers (`https://docs.oracle.com/javase/7/docs/technotes/guides/vm/performance-enhancements-7.html`).

In such cases, you can either run multiple Elasticsearch instances on the same bare metal machine, run multiple virtual machines and a single Elasticsearch inside each one, or run Elasticsearch in a container, such as Docker (`http://www.docker.com/`). This is out of the scope of the book, but, because we are talking about scaling, we thought it may be a good thing to mention what can be done in such cases.

> There is also the possibility of running multiple Elasticsearch servers on a single physical machine without running multiple virtual machines. Which road to take - virtual machines or multiple instances - is really your choice. However, we like to keep things separate and because of that we usually go for dividing any large server into multiple virtual machines. When dividing one large server into multiple smaller virtual machines, remember that the I/O subsystem will be shared across those smaller virtual machines. Because of that, it may be good to wisely divide the disks between the virtual machines.

Preventing a shard and its replicas from being on the same node

There is one additional thing worth mentioning. When you have multiple physical servers divided into virtual machines, it is crucial to ensure that the shard and its replica don't end up on the same physical machine. By default, Elasticsearch is smart enough to not put the shard and its replica on the same Elasticsearch instance, but it doesn't know anything about bare metal machines, so we need to tell it. We can tell Elasticsearch to separate the shards and replicas by using cluster allocation awareness. In our previous case, we had three physical servers. Let's call them: `server1`, `server2`, and `server3`.

Now for each Elasticsearch on a physical server, we define the `node.server_name` property and we set it to the identifier of the server (the name of the property can be anything we want). So for example, for all Elasticsearch nodes on the first physical server, we would set the following property in the `elasticsearch.yml` configuration file:

```
node.server_name: server1
```

In addition to that, each Elasticsearch node (no matter on which physical server) needs to have the following property added to the `elasticsearch.yml` configuration file:

```
cluster.routing.allocation.awareness.attributes: server_name
```

It tells Elasticsearch not to put the primary shard and its replicas on the nodes with the same value in the `node.server_name` property. This is enough for us and Elasticsearch will take care of the rest.

Designated node roles for larger clusters

There is one more thing that we want to discuss and emphasise. When it comes to large clusters, it is important to assign roles to all the nodes in the cluster. This allows for a truly fully fault tolerant and highly available Elasticsearch cluster. The roles we can assign to each Elasticsearch node are as follows:

- Master eligible node
- Data node
- Query aggregator node

By default, each Elasticsearch node is both master eligible (it can serve as a master node), can hold data, and work as a query aggregator node. You may wonder why that is needed. Let us give you a simple example: if the master node is under a lot of stress, it may not be able to handle the cluster state related command fast enough and the cluster could become unstable. This is only a single, simple example and you can think of numerous others.

Because of that, most Elasticsearch clusters that are larger than a few nodes, usually look like the one presented in the following picture:

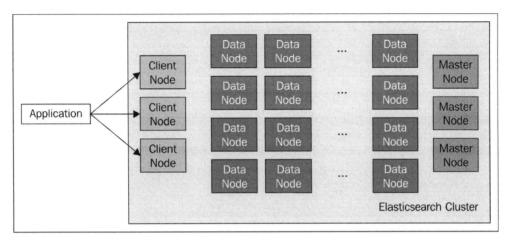

As you can see, our hypothetical cluster contains three client nodes (because we know that there will be a lot of queries), a large number of data nodes because the amount of data will be large, and at least three master eligible nodes that shouldn't be doing anything else. Why three master nodes when Elasticsearch will only use a single one at any given time? Again, because of redundancy and to be able to prevent split brain situations by setting `discovery.zen.minimum_master_nodes` to 2, which would allow us to easily handle the failure of a single master eligible node in the cluster.

Let us now give you snippets of the configuration for each type of node in our cluster. We already talked about that in the *Understanding node discovery* section in *Chapter 9, Elasticsearch Cluster in Detail*, but we would like to mention that once again.

Query aggregator nodes

The query aggregator nodes configuration is quite simple. To configure those, we just need to tell Elasticsearch that we don't want those nodes to be master eligible or to hold data. This corresponds to the following configuration snippets in the `elasticsearch.yml` file:

```
node.master: false
node.data: false
```

Data nodes

Data nodes are also very simple to configure. We just need to tell that they should not be master eligible. However, we are not big fans of default configurations (because they tend to change) and thus our Elasticsearch data nodes configuration looks as follows:

```
node.master: false
node.data: true
```

Master eligible nodes

We've left the master eligible nodes to the end of the general scaling section. Of course, such Elasticsearch nodes shouldn't be allowed to hold data, but, in addition to that, it is a good practice to disable HTTP protocol on such nodes. This is done to avoid accidentally querying those nodes. Master eligible nodes can use less resources than data and query aggregator nodes and because of that we should ensure that they are only used for master related purpose. So our configuration for master eligible nodes looks more or less as follows:

```
node.master: true
node.data: false
http.enabled: false
```

Preparing the cluster for high indexing and querying throughput

Until this chapter, we mostly talked about different functionalities of Elasticsearch, both in terms of handling queries, indexing data, and tuning. However, running a cluster in production is not only about using this great search engine, but also about preparing the cluster to handle both the indexing and querying load. Let's now summarize the knowledge we have and see what are the things we need to care about when it comes to preparing the cluster for high indexing and querying throughput.

Indexing related advice

In this section, we will look at the indexing related advice around tuning Elasticsearch. Each production environment data is different, index rate is different, and user's behavior is different. Take that into consideration and run performance tests on your environment. This will give you the best idea about what to expect and what works the best in the case of your system.

Index refresh rate

One of the general things you should pay attention to is the index refresh rate. We know that refresh rate specifies how fast the documents will be visible for search operations. The equation is quite simple - the faster the refresh rate, the slower the queries will be and the lower the indexing throughput. If we can allow ourselves to have a slower refresh rate, such as `10s` or `30s`, go for it. It will put less pressure on Elasticsearch, Lucene, and hardware in general. Remember that by default the refresh rate is set to `1s`, which basically means that the index searcher object is reopened every second.

To give you a bit of insight into what performance gains we are talking about, we did some performance tests including Elasticsearch and different refresh rates. With the refresh rate of `1s` we were able to index about 1000 documents per second using a single Elasticsearch node. Increasing the refresh rate to `5s` gave us increase in indexing throughput of more than 25 percent and we were able to index about 1250 documents per second. Setting the refresh rate to `25s` gave us about 70 percent of more throughput as compared to `1s` refresh rate, which was about 1700 documents per second on the same infrastructure. It is also worth remembering that increasing the time indefinitely doesn't make much sense, because after a certain point (depending on your data load and the amount of data you have) the increase of performance is negligible.

Some performance comparisons related to indexing throughput and index refresh rate can be found in the blog post at `http://blog.sematext.com/2013/07/08/elasticsearch-refresh-interval-vs-indexing-performance/`.

Thread pools tuning

By default, Elasticsearch comes with very good defaults when it comes to all thread pools configuration. You should remember that tuning the default thread pools configuration should be done only when you really see that your nodes are filling up the queues and they have still processing power left that could be designated to the processing of the waiting operations or when you want to increase the priority of one or more operations.

For example, if you did your performance tests and you saw your Elasticsearch instances not being saturated 100 percent, but on the other hand you experienced a rejected execution error, then that is a point when you should start adjusting the thread pools. You can either increase the amount of threads that are allowed to be executed at the same time or increase the queue. Of course, you should also remember that increasing the number of concurrently running threads to very high numbers will lead to many CPU context switches (`http://en.wikipedia.org/wiki/Context_switch`) which will result in a performance drop.

Automatic store throttling

Before Elasticsearch 2.0, we had to care about how our segment process was configured and how much disk I/O merging could use in general, but that changed. Right now Elasticsearch looks at how I/O subsystem behaves and adjusts the throttling and merging process if the merges are falling behind the indexing. So, we no longer need to automatically adjust throttling for disk based operations. You can read more about the related changes on GitHub at `https://github.com/elastic/elasticsearch/pull/9243`.

Handling time-based data

When you have time-based data, such as logs for example, the architecture of your indices plays a very important role. Let's assume that we have logs indexed into Elasticsearch. These usually come in large numbers, are constantly indexed, and are time related (an event that is logged happened at a certain point in time). The assumption is that you have a certain retention to your data and a time that you would like the data to be present and searchable in Elasticsearch. After that time, you just delete the data and forget about it.

With such assumptions in mind, you could just create a single index with lot of shards and try to index large amounts of logs there. However, that's not the perfect solution. First of all, because of merges – the larger the index gets, the more expensive the merges are. Elasticsearch needs to merge larger and larger segments and more I/O and CPU is required to handle them. This means slowdowns. In addition to that, deletes will be expensive because you will have to delete the data either by using TTL or by using delete by query plugin – both expensive to use in terms of performance and will cause even more merging. And this is not everything – during querying you will have to run through the whole index to get even the smallest slice of the data. So, are there better index architectures for time-based data?

Yes, one of the most common and best solutions is to use time based indices. Depending on the data volume, you can have daily, weekly, monthly, or even hourly indices. The downside is the number of shards you will have when the number of indices grow, but apart from that there are only pros: you can control each index, change the number of shards if that is needed, and have faster merging because the indices will be smaller compared to only one big index. What's more, deleting data won't be painful at all – the idea is to delete the whole indices; for example, a day worth of data in case of daily indices. Queries will also benefit – you can just run the query on a single time based index to narrow down the search results. Finally, Elasticsearch, by default, will create the indices for us. For example, when using daily indices, we can have names such as `logs_2016-01-01`, `logs_2016-01-02`, and so on.

The only thing we need to care about is providing the index name on the basis of the date and creating templates to configure each newly created index and Elasticsearch will do the rest.

Multiple data paths

With the release of Elasticsearch 2.0, we were given the ability to specify multiple `path.data` properties in our `elasticsearch.yml` pointing to different directories on different physical devices. Elasticsearch can now leverage that by putting different shards on different devices and using the multiple paths in the most efficient way. Because of that, we can parallelize writing to disks if we have more than a single disk. This is especially useful for high indexing use cases where you index a lot of data.

Data distribution

As we know, each index in the Elasticsearch world can be divided into multiple shards and each shard can have multiple replicas. In cases when you have multiple Elasticsearch nodes (and you will probably have in production), you should think about the number of shards and replicas and how that will affect your nodes. Data distribution may be crucial to even the load on the cluster and not have some nodes doing more work than the other ones.

Let's take the following example. Imagine we have a cluster that is built of 4 nodes and it has a single index called `book` built of 3 shards and one replica. Such a deployment will look as follows:

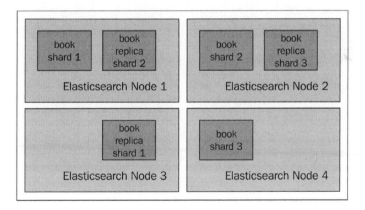

As you can see, the first two nodes have two physical shards allocated to them, while the last two nodes have only one shard allocated each. The actual data allocation is not even. When sending the queries and indexing data, we will have the first two nodes do more work than the other two - this is what we want to avoid. One option is to have the book index have two shards and one replica, so it looks as follows:

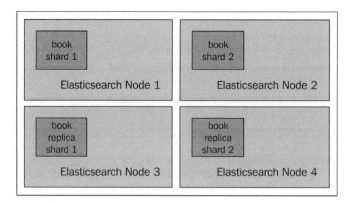

This architecture will work and it is perfectly fine. We don't have to have primary shards on all our nodes, we can have replicas, depending on what bottle neck we expect. For querying we may want to have more replicas, for indexing more primaries.

We can also have our primary shards split evenly, like in the following image:

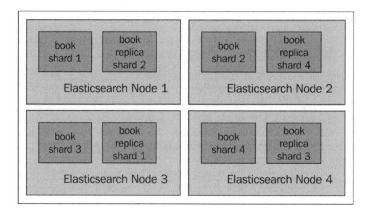

The thing to remember though is that in both cases we will end up with even distribution of shards and replicas and Elasticsearch will do similar amount of work on all the nodes. Of course, with more indices (like having daily indices) it may be trickier to get the data evenly distributed and it may not be possible to have evenly distributed shards, but we should try to get to such point.

One more thing to remember when it comes to data distribution and shards and replicas is that when designing your index architecture, you should remember what you want to achieve. If you are going for a very high indexing use case, you may want to spread the index into multiple shards to lower the pressure that is put on the CPU and the I/O subsystem of the server. This is also true for running expensive queries, because with more shards you can lower the load on a single server. However, with the queries there is one more thing - if your nodes can't keep up with the load caused by queries, you can add more Elasticsearch nodes and increase the number of replicas so that the physical copies of the primary shards are placed on those nodes. That will make indexing a bit slower but will give you the capacity to handle more queries at the same time.

Bulk indexing

This is very obvious advice, but you would be surprised how many Elasticsearch users forget about indexing data in bulks instead of sending the documents one by one. So the advice here is to do bulks instead of one by one indexing whenever possible. The thing to remember though is not to overload Elasticsearch with too many bulk requests and to keep them under a reasonable size (do not push millions of documents in a single request). Remember about the bulk thread pool and its size and try to adjust your indexers not to go beyond it or you will first start to queue these requests and, if Elasticsearch will not be able to process them, you will quickly start seeing rejected execution exceptions and your data won't be indexed.

Just as an example, we would like to show results of tests we did some time ago for the two types of indexing: one by one and bulks. In the following image, we have the indexing throughput when running indexation one document by one:

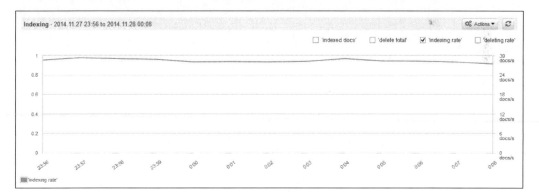

In this next image, we do the same, but instead of indexing documents one by one, we index them in batches of 10 documents (which is still a relatively low number of documents in a bulk):

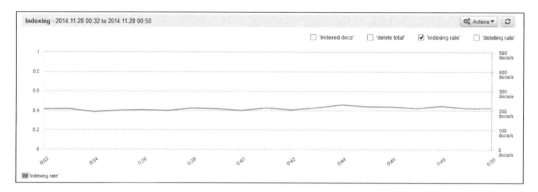

As you can see, when indexing documents one by one, we were able to index about 30 documents per second and it was stable. The situation changed with bulk indexing and batches of 10 documents; we were able to index slightly more than 200 documents per second. So the difference can be clearly seen.

Of course this is a very basic comparison of indexing speed. To show the real difference, we should use dozens of threads and push Elasticsearch to its limits. However, the preceding comparison should give you a basic view of the indexing throughput gains when using bulk indexing.

RAM buffer for indexing

Remember, the more available RAM for the indexing buffer (the `indices.memory.index_buffer_size` property), the more documents Elasticsearch can hold in memory. However, we don't want to have Elasticsearch occupy 100 percent of the available memory. The indexing buffer can help us with delaying the flush to disk, which will mean less I/O pressure and less merges. You can read more about indexing buffer configuration in *Chapter 9, Elasticsearch Cluster in Detail*.

Advice for high query rate scenarios

One of the great features of Elasticsearch is its ability to search and analyze the data that was indexed. However, sometimes it is necessary to adjust Elasticsearch and our queries to not only get the results of the query, but also get them fast (or in a reasonable amount of time). In this section, we will look at the possibilities of preparing Elasticsearch for high query throughput use cases, but not just that. We will also look at general performance tips when it comes to querying.

Shard request cache

The purpose of the shard request cache is to cache aggregations, suggester results, and numbers of hits (it will not cache the returned documents and thus only works with `size=0`). When your queries use aggregations or suggestions, it may be a good idea to enable this cache (it is disabled by default) so that Elasticsearch can re-use the data stored there. The best thing about the cache is that it promises the same near real-time search as a search that is not cached. You can read more about caches and the shard request cache in particular in *Chapter 9, Elasticsearch Cluster in Detail*.

Think about the queries

This is the most general advice we can actually give – you should always think about optimal query structure, filter usage, and so on. For example, let's look at the following query:

```
{
  "query" : {
   "bool" : {
    "must" : [
     {
      "query_string" : {
       "query" : "mastering AND department:it AND category:book",
       "default_field" : "name"
      }
     },
     {
      "term" : {
       "tag" : "popular"
      }
     },
     {
      "term" : {
       "tag" : "2014"
      }
     }
    ]
   }
  }
}
```

It returns the book matching a few conditions. However, there are a few things we can improve in the preceding query. For example, we can move the static things such as the tag, department, and category field related conditions to the filter section of the Boolean query, so that the next time we use some parts of the query we save CPU cycles and re-use the information stored in cache. That static filtering information is also not relevant when it comes to scoring. Because of that we can move those static elements to the filter section and omit scoring calculation for them. For example, this is how the optimized query will look like:

```
{
  "query" : {
   "bool" : {
    "must" : [
      {
       "query_string" : {
        "query" : "mastering",
        "default_field" : "name"
       }
      }
    ],
    "filter" : [
      {
       "term" : {
        "tag" : "popular"
       }
      },
      {
       "term" : {
        "tag" : "2014"
       }
      },
      {
       "term" : {
        "department" : "it"
       }
      },
      {
       "term" : {
        "category" : "book"
       }
      }
    ]
   }
  }
}
```

As you can see, there are a few things that we did. We still used the `bool` query, but we introduced the use of the `filter` section. We used filtering for the static, non-analyzed fields. This allows us to easily re-use the filters in the next queries that we execute. Because of such query restructuring, we were able to simplify the main query. This is exactly what you should be doing when optimizing your queries or designing them - have optimization and performance in mind and try to keep them as optimal as they can be. This will result in faster execution of the queries, lower resource consumption, and better health of the whole Elasticsearch cluster.

Parallelize your queries

One thing that is usually forgotten is the need of parallelizing queries. Imagine that you have a dozen nodes in your cluster but your index is built of a single shard. If the index is large, your queries will perform worse than you expect. Of course you can increase the number of replicas, but that won't help. A single query will still go to a single shard in that index, because replicas are not more than the copies of the primary shard and they contain the same data (or at least they should). This is also true not only for indices having one shard but also if you have more than one shard, but they are very large, you can still have performance related problems. It is said that the query is only as fast as the slowest partial query response.

Of course, the parallelization also depends on the use case. If you run a lot of queries to Elasticsearch, you may not need to parallelize the queries, especially when the shards are small enough and you don't see problems at shard level. In general, look at your Elasticsearch nodes and see if they have unused CPU cores and, if that's the case, you may have room for improvement and parallelization.

Field data cache and breaking the circuit

We have two different factors we can tune to be sure that we don't run into out of memory errors. First of all, we can limit the size of the field data cache. The second thing is the circuit breaker, which we can easily configure to just throw an exception instead of loading too much data. Combining these two things will ensure that we don't run into memory issues. Even if you are using `doc` values a lot, you may still run into out of memory issues. For example, for analysed fields, which can't use `doc` values and will use, field data cache – configure the field data cache and circuit breakers correctly. You can read more about how to configure them in *Chapter 9, Elasticsearch Cluster in Detail*.

Keep size and shard size under control

When dealing with some of the queries that use aggregations, we have the possibility of using two properties: `size` and `shard_size`. The `size` parameter defines how many buckets should be returned by the final aggregation results; the node that aggregates the final results will get the top buckets from each shard that returns the result and will only return the top `size` of them to the client. The `shard_size` parameter tells Elasticsearch about the same but at the shard level. Increasing the value of the `shard_size` parameter will lead to more accurate aggregations (like in the case of significant terms aggregation) at the cost of network traffic and memory usage. Lowering that parameter will cause aggregation results to be less precise, but we will benefit from lower memory consumption and lower network traffic. If we see that the memory usage is too large, we can lower the `size` and `shard_size` properties for problematic queries and see if the quality of the results is still acceptable.

Monitoring

Elasticsearch monitoring APIs expose a lot of information, both about the search engine itself as well as about the environment, such as the operating system. We saw that in *Chapter 10, Administrating Your Cluster*. Because of this and the ease of retrieving this information, numerous applications were built – ones that allow us to do monitoring and beyond. Some of these applications are simple and just read the data in real time without any persistent storage, while others allow us to read historical data about our cluster behavior. In this chapter, we will only slightly touch the top of the pile of information about such applications, but we strongly advise you to get familiar with some of them as they can make your everyday work with Elasticsearch easier.

We chose three examples of monitoring solutions which take a different approach of integration with Elasticsearch. The first two tools are available as Elasticsearch plugins and the third takes a different approach to integration.

Elasticsearch HQ

This tool is available as an Elasticsearch plugin but can also be downloaded separately as a JavaScript application run in a browser.

Elasticsearch HQ uses JavaScript and AJAX techniques where data is fetched periodically from the cluster, prepared for visualization on the browser side, and shown to the user.

The tool allows us to track statistics on a particular node. The browser can present vital information about the cluster and particular nodes. The following screenshot shows the graphical user interface from Elasticsearch HQ:

We have the basic information about the cluster, the number of nodes, and Elasticsearch health. We can also see which node we are looking at and some statistics about the node, which include the memory usage (both heap and non-heap), the number of threads, Java virtual machine garbage collector work, and so on. The plugin also presents simplified information about schema and shards and allows execution of simple queries.

In order to install Elasticsearch HQ, one should just run the following command:

```
bin/plugin install royrusso/elasticsearch-HQ
```

After that, the GUI will be available at `http://localhost:9200/_plugin/hq/`.

One thing to remember is that Elasticsearch HQ doesn't persist the fetched data anywhere, so the data is only fetched when your browser is running and has Elasticsearch HQ opened. If something has happened in the past, you won't be able to diagnose it.

Marvel

Marvel is the tool created by the Elasticsearch team. In the current version, it is built as a plugin for a visualization platform called Kibana (`https://www.elastic.co/products/kibana`).

 Kibana is out of the scope of this book. You can find more about Kibana on official product page available at `https://www.elastic.co/`.

Marvel also visualizes basic information about clusters and nodes by drawing nice graphs that are dynamically updated over time. The main difference from Elasticsearch HQ is that the performance data is stored on the server side (in the same or external Elasticsearch cluster), so historical data is available. The example screenshot is presented next:

The installation procedure for Marvel contains three steps:

```
bin/plugin install license
bin/plugin install marvel-agent
```

And finally, the third step is to install the Marvel plugin in Kibana by running the following command:

```
bin/kibana plugin --install elasticsearch/marvel/latest
```

SPM for Elasticsearch

This tool presents a different approach than the previously mentioned tools. SPM is a **Software as a Service (SaaS)** solution created for monitoring Elasticsearch installations of any size and allows monitoring several clusters and different technologies. Though its roots are SaaS-based, it is also available on premises, which means that you can run SPM on your own machines without the need for sending your metrics to cloud.

Information is sent by simple client software installed on the Elasticsearch machine to the SPM servers. The main advantage is the possibility of storing information for a wider range of time and seeing what was happening in the past. You can create your own dashboards and correlate metrics with logs between multiple applications (SPM allows you to monitor a wide variety of applications).

The following screenshot shows the dashboard of SPM for Elasticsearch:

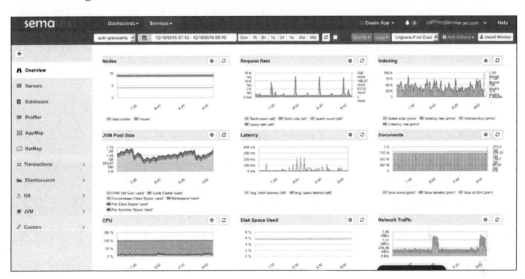

The overview dashboard shown in the preceding screenshot provides information about the cluster nodes, the request rate and latency, the number of documents in the indices, CPU usage, load, memory details, Java virtual machine memory, the disk space usage, and finally network traffic. You can get detailed information about each of these elements by going into the tab dedicated to it.

You can find additional information about SPM installation and available options at `http://sematext.com/spm/index.html`.

Summary

In this chapter, we focused on scaling and tuning Elasticsearch. We started with the hardware preparations and decisions we need to make. Next, we tuned a single Elasticsearch node as much as we could and after that we configured the whole cluster to work as well as it could. We discussed vertical expansion possibilities and we learned how to monitor our cluster once it hits the production environment.

So now we have reached the end of the book. We hope that it was a nice reading experience and that you found the book interesting. Since the previous edition of the book, Elasticsearch has changed a lot. Not only when it comes to versions, but also when it comes to functionalities. Some of the features are no longer there, some of them were moved to plugins, and of course new features were added. We really hope that you have learned something from this book and now you will find it easier to use Elasticsearch every day – no matter if you are a beginner in this world or a semi–experienced Elasticsearch user. As the authors of this book, but also as Elasticsearch users ourselves, we tried to bring you, our readers, the best reading experience we could. Of course Elasticsearch is more than we described in the book, especially when it comes to monitoring and administration capabilities and API. However, the number of pages is limited and if we were to describe everything in great details we would have ended up with a book one thousand pages long. We need to remember that Elasticsearch is not only user friendly but also provides a large amount of configuration options, querying possibilities, and so on. Due to that, we had to choose which functionalities to describe in greater details, which had to be only mentioned, and which had to be totally skipped. As with the two previous editions of the book you are holding, we hope that we made the right choice and that you are happy about what you've read.

We would also like to say that it is worth remembering that Elasticsearch is constantly evolving. When writing this book, we went through a few stable versions finally making it to the release of Elasticsearch 2.2. Even back then we knew that new features and improvements were coming, like some of the changes mentioned in the book that will be part of the next release, or at least they are planned to be. Be sure to check the official documentation of Elasticsearch periodically for the release notes for new versions of Elasticsearch, if you want to be up to date with the new features being added. We will also be writing about new features that we think are worth mentioning on `www.elasticsearchserverbook.com`. So if you are interested, visit the site from time to time.

Once again thank you for the time you've spent with the book.

Index

Symbols

_all field 84, 85
_source field 85

A

advices, for high query rate scenarios
  about 498
  circuit, breaking 501
  field data cache 501
  queries 499-501
  queries, parallelizing 501
  shard request cache 499
  shard size, controlling 502
  size, controlling 502
aggregation engine
  working 277
aggregations
  about 273
  children aggregation 322
  date histogram 312
  general query structure 274-276
  geo distance aggregations 313, 314
  geohash grid aggregation 315
  global aggregation 315, 316
  nested aggregation 323
  nesting aggregations 326
  reverse nested aggregation 324, 325
  sampler aggregation 321
  significant terms aggregation 316-318
  types 278
aggregation, types
  buckets 278, 294
  metrics 278
  pipeline 278

Amazon
  URL 488
Amazon S3
  URL 423
Analyze API
  URL 75
analyzers
  default analyzers 76
  defining 73-75
  out-of-the-box analyzers 72
  using 71
Apache Lucene
  about 195, 197
  architecture 2-4
  document 2
  field 2
  glossary 2-4
  scoring 227
  term 2
  token 2
  tokenizer 4
  URL 2
Apache Lucene scoring
  about 227
  default scoring formula 228, 229
  document matching, factors 228
  relevant documents 229, 230
Apache Solr
  URL 265
Apache Solr synonyms
  equivalent synonyms 266
  expand property 266
  explicit synonyms 265, 266
  using 265
Apache Tika
  URL 244

arbitrary geo shapes
about 363, 364
envelope 364
example usage 366
multipolygon 365
point 364
polygon 365
storing, in index 367-369
attributes, index structure mapping
boost 65
coerce 68
copy_to 65
doc_values 64
format 69
format, reference link 69
ignore_malformed 68-70
include_in_all 65
index 64
index_name 64
null_value 65
numeric_resolution 70
precision_step 68, 69
store 64
Azure
URL 423

B

basic queries
about 116
common terms query 119, 120
exists query 119
fuzzy query 130-132
identifiers query 129
match all query 118
match query 121
missing query 119
more like this query 134-136
multi match query 124, 125
prefix query 129
query string query 125-127
range query 133
regular expression query 134
simple query string query 128
term query 116, 117
terms query 117

type query 118
wildcard query 132, 133
batch indexing
used, for speeding up indexing process 80
bool query
about 137
boost parameter 138
disable_coord parameter 138
filter parameter 138
minimum_should_match parameter 138
must_not section 137
must section 137
should section 137
used, for explicit filtering 165-169
boosting query 140
boost_mode parameter
avg value 257
max value 257
min value 257
multiply value 256
replace value 256
sum value 256
bucket aggregations
ordering 326-329
buckets 276
buckets aggregations
about 294
date range aggregation 305-308
filter aggregation 294, 295
filters aggregation 296, 297
histogram aggregation 310, 311
ip_range aggregation 308, 309
missing aggregation 309, 310
range aggregation 301, 302
terms aggregation 298, 299
bulk indexing
data, preparing 81

C

caches
about 412
avoiding, scenarios 417
fielddata cache 412
fielddata, using with doc values 413
indexing buffers 416

node query cache 416
shard request cache 414
Cat API
about 456
common arguments 458, 459
defining 456-458
examples 459, 460
using 458
children aggregation 322, 323
client node 393
cluster
about 9
configuring 12
directory layout 15
installing 12
settings API 418
system-specific installation and
configuration 18
cluster health API
about 428
additional parameters 429
information details, controlling 429
cluster rebalancing
controlling 454
defining 454
implementing 455
settings 455
cluster wide allocation
about 446, 447
allocation awareness 447, 448
allocation awareness, forcing 449
filtering 449
CMS system
URL 22
common terms query 119-121
completion suggester
about 376, 377
custom weights 380
data, indexing 377, 378
indexed data, querying 378, 379
compound queries
about 137
bool query 137, 138
boosting query 140
constant_score query 141
dis_max query 139
indices query 141, 142

configuration options, phrase suggester
max_errors 376
separator 376
configuration options, term suggester
analyzer 373
field 373
size 373
sort 373
suggest_mode 373
text 373
constant_score query 141
content, searching in different languages
about 243
data, querying 247
document language, detecting 244
languages, handling 243
mappings 245-247
multiple languages, handling 243
queries, combining 249, 250
sample document 244, 245
context suggester
about 381
geo location context, using 384-387
types 381
using 381-383
context switches
reference link 493
core types, index structure mapping
about 63
binary 69
boolean 68
common attributes 64, 65
date 69, 70
number 67, 68
string 65-67
count to it field 30
create, retrieve, update, delete (CRUD)
URL 21

D

data
_all field 84, 85
_source field 85
default sorting 186
indexing 82-84
internal fields 86

manipulating, with REST API 21
preparing, for bulk indexing 81
querying, in child documents 216-218
querying, in parent documents 219, 220
sorting 186
storing, in Elasticsearch 22
data node 392
data querying, cases
identified language, using 247, 248
unknown language, using 248
data sets
background sets 319
foreground sets 319
data sorting
about 186
behavior for missing fields, specifying 191
default sorting 186
dynamic criteria 191, 192
fields, selecting 187-189
mode 189, 190
scoring, calculating 192
data, that is not flat
arrays 205
data 204, 205
dynamic behavior 208
indexing 204
mappings 206
object indexing, disabling 209
objects 205
date histogram aggregations
about 312
time zones 312, 313
DEB package
used, for installing Elasticsearch 19
default indexing 90
derivative aggregation
about 340
URL 340
designated nodes roles, for larger clusters
about 490, 491
data nodes 492
master eligible nodes 492
query aggregator nodes 491
DigitalOcean
URL 488

directory layout, cluster
bin 15
config 15
data 15
lib 15
logs 15
modules 15
plugins 15
work 15
disk-based shard allocation
about 443
configuring 444
disabling 444
dis_max query 139
Docker
reference link 489
document
about 7, 8
automatic identifier creation, creating 25
creating 22, 24
deleting 31
non-existing documents,
        dealing with 28, 29
partial documents, adding 29
retrieving 25, 26
updating 26-28
document type 8
double type
URL 68
dynamic templates
about 405-407
matching pattern 408
target field definition, writing 408

E

Elasticsearch
about 1, 6
caches 412
configuration files, localization 20
configuring 16, 17
document 7, 8
document type 8
example data 98, 99
hardware preparations 473

index 7
indexing 10, 11, 50
installing 12
installing, with DEB package 19
installing, with RPM package 18
key concepts 7
Kibana, URL 504
mapping 8
monitoring 502
paging 101, 102
parameters, passing to script fields 110, 111
plugins 408
querying 97-101
reference documentation, URL 376
result size, controlling 101, 102
return fields, selecting 105, 106
running 13, 14
score, limiting 104
script fields, using 108, 110
scripting capabilities 230
searching 10, 11
shutting down 15
source filtering 106, 107
spatial capabilities 355
URL 12, 78
version value, returning 103, 104
Elasticsearch cluster
preparing, for high indexing 492
preparing, for high querying 492
Elasticsearch HQ tool
using 503
Elasticsearch indexing
about 50
indices, creating 52
replicas 50, 51
shards 50, 51
Elasticsearch infrastructure
cluster 9
gateway 10
key concepts 9
node 9
replica 9
shard 9
Elasticsearch, monitoring
about 502
Elasticsearch HQ tool, using 502, 503

Marvel tool, using 504
SPM tool, using 505
Elasticsearch time machine
about 421
old snapshots, deleting 427
parameters 426
snapshot repository, creating 422, 423
snapshot, restoring 425, 426
snapshots, creating 424
exists query 119
Explain API
URL 272
explain information
about 267
field analysis 267-269
query, explaining 269-272

F

factors, for score property calculation
coord 228
document boost 228
field boost 228
inverse document frequency 228
length norm 228
query norm 228
term frequency 228
FastVectorHighlighter
URL 172
Fedora Linux
URL 18
fielddata cache
about 412
circuit breakers 413
size, controlling 412
filtering
about 449
exclude parameter 450
include parameter 450
require parameter 450
filters
language stemming filters 5
lowercase filter 5
synonyms filter 5

full text searching
  about 2
  Apache Lucene, architecture 2-4
  Apache Lucene, glossary 2-4
  indexing 5, 6
  input data analysis 4, 5
  querying 5, 6
  query relevance 6
  scoring 6
function score query
  about 255
  decay functions 261
  field_value_factor function 258
  random_score function 260
  script_score function 259
  structure 256, 257
  weight factor function 258
function_score query
  URL 262
fuzzy query 130

G

gateway
  about 10
  recovery options 401
**general preparations, single Elasticsearch
    node**
  about 478
  file descriptors 479
  swapping, avoiding 478
  virtual memory 479, 480
Geo 292
geo distance aggregations 313, 314
geo_field properties 357
geohash grid aggregation
  about 315
  URL 315
GitHub
  automatic store throttling, URL 494
  URL 411
global aggregation 315, 316
Groovy
  URL 230

H

**hardware preparations, for running
    Elasticsearch**
  about 473
  cloud 474, 475
  cost cutting 477
  CPU 475
  mass storage 476
  network 476
  physical servers 474, 475
  RAM memory 475
  servers counting 476
HDFS
  URL 423
highlighted fragments
  controlling 175
highlighter type
  selecting 172, 173
highlighting
  about 169, 170
  Apache Lucene, using 172
  custom query 179, 180
  field configuration 172
  global settings 175, 176
  highlighter type, selecting 172, 173
  HTML tags,, configuring 173, 175
  local settings 175, 176
  matching need 176-178
  Postings highlighter 180-183
  using 170, 171
horizontal expansion
  about 483-485
  continues upgrades 488
  cost and performance flexibility 488
  designated nodes roles for larger
    clusters 490
  high availability 486, 487
  multiple Elasticsearch instances,
    on single physical machine 489
  redundancy 486, 487
  reference 487
  replicas, automatic creation 486
HTTP module
  properties, URL 399

HTTP transport settings, adjusting
 HTTP, disabling 398
 HTTP host 399
 HTTP port 398
 node 398
HyperLogLog++ algorithm
 URL 283

I

identifiers query 129
index
 about 7
 segments 4
 speeding up, batch indexing used 80
 structure, modifying, with update API 221
index alias
 about 465
 and routing 470
 and zero downtime reindexing 470
 commands, combining 467
 creating 466
 defining 466
 filtering 469
 modifying 467
 removing 469
 retrieving 468, 469
indexation 4
indexing related advices
 about 492
 automatic store throttling 494
 bulk indexing 497, 498
 data distribution 495-497
 index refresh rate 493
 multiple data paths 495
 RAM buffer, used for indexing 498
 thread pools, tuning 493
 time-based data, handling 494
index structure mapping
 about 61, 62
 core types 63
 fields 63
 IP address type 70
 multi fields 70
 token count type 71
 types 62, 63
 types definition 62, 63

index structure, modifying
 existing index fields, modifying 223, 224
 mappings 222
 new field, adding 222
index structure, parent-child relationship
 about 214
 child mappings 214
 children documents 215
 parent document 215
 parent mappings 214
index-time boosting
 defining, in mappings 263
 using 262
indices, Elasticsearch indexing
 automatic creation, altering 53, 54
 creating 52
 deleting 55
 newly created index, settings 55
indices query 141, 142
indices settings API 418, 419
indices stats API
 about 430
 defining 432
 docs 431
 get 431, 432
 indexing 431, 432
 search 431, 432
 store 431
internal fields
 _field_names 86
 _id 86
 _type 86
 _uid 86
inverted index
 about 3
 URL 7

J

Java
 installing 12
 URL 2
JavaScript Object Notation (JSON)
 URL 8, 13
Java threads
 URL 482

Java Virtual Machine (JVM) 17
JMeter
  URL 417
Joda Time library
  URL 307

K

Kibana
  about 504
  URL 504

L

language analyzer
  URL 72
language detection
  URL 244
Levenshtein algorithm
  URL 122
Linux
  Elasticsearch, configuring as
    system service 20
  Elasticsearch, installing 18
Logstash
  URL 465
Lucene Javadocs
  URL 229
Lucene query syntax 47, 48

M

mappings
  about 8, 206
  analyzers, using 71
  configuration 56
  field of existing index, modifying 223, 224
  final mappings 207
  index structure mapping 61
  new field, adding to existing index 222, 223
  sending, to Elasticsearch 207
  similarity models 76
  type determining mechanism 56
Marvel tool
  using 504

master node 392, 393
match all query 118
matching pattern, dynamic templates
  match 408
  unmatch 408
match query
  about 121
  Boolean match query 121, 122
  match phrase prefix query 124
  phrase match query 123
Maven
  URL 411
merge policy
  about 87
  properties 87, 88
merge scheduler 88
metrics aggregations
  about 278
  avg 278, 279
  extended statistics 281, 282
  field cardinality aggregation 283
  field value statistics 281, 282
  geo bounds aggregation 292
  max 278, 279
  min 278, 279
  missing values 279
  percentile ranks aggregation 286
  percentiles aggregation 284, 285
  scripted metrics aggregation 292, 293
  scripts, using 280
  sum 278, 279
  top hits aggregation 287-291
  value count aggregation 283
Microsoft Windows platform
  file handles, URL 17
missing query 119
more like this query 134, 136
moving avg aggregation
  about 341
  future buckets, predicting 342
  models 343
  models, URL 343
  URL 341
multi match query 124, 125

multiple Elasticsearch instances, on single physical machine
about 489
replicas, preventing on same node 489
shard, preventing on same node 489, 490
multiple indices
URL 37
multiterm 193
multivalued field 7
Mustache
URL 230

N

native code, using
factory implementation 238, 239
native script implementation 239, 240
plugin definition 240, 241
plugin, installing 242
script, running 242
nested aggregation 323, 324
nested objects
nested queries 213
score_mode property, setting 213
URL 209
using 209-213
nesting aggregations 326-329
network attached storage (NAS) 476
node
about 9
cluster name, setting 394
discovery
about 392
HTTP transport settings, adjusting 398
roles 392
types 392
Zen discovery 395
node roles
client node 393
configuring 394
data node 392, 393
master node 392, 393
nodes info API
about 433
extensive information, returning 434
requisites 433

NoSQL
URL 21
number, index structure mapping
byte 67
double 68
double, URL 68
float 68
integer 67
long 67
short 67

O

object indexing
disabling 209
official repository
URL 409
OpenJDK
URL 12
optimistic locking
URL 32
options, term suggester
lowercase_terms 373
max_edits 373
min_word_len 374
prefix_len 374
shard_size 374
out-of-the-box analyzers
keyword 72
language 72
pattern 72
simple 72
snowball 72
standard 72
stop 72
whitespace 72

P

parameters, Boolean match query
analyzer 121
cero_terms_query 122
fuzziness 122
lenient 122
max_expansions 122
operator 121

prefix_length 122
zero_terms_query 122
parameters, fuzzy query
boost 131
fuzziness 131
max_expansions 132
prefix_length 132
value 131
parameters, more like this query
analyzer 135
boost 135
boost_terms 135
fields 135
include 135
in_term_freq 135
like 135
max_query_terms 135
max_word_len 135
min_doc_freq 135
minimum_should_match 135
min_word_len 135
stop_words 135
unlike 135
parameters, query string query
allow_leading_wildcard 126
analyzer 126
analyze_wildcard 127
auto_generate_phrase_queries 127
boost 127
default_field 126
default_operator 126
enable_position_increments 126
fuzziness 127
fuzzy_max_expansions 126
fuzzy_prefix_length 126
lenient 127
locale 127
lowercase_expand_terms 126
max_determined_states 127
minimum_should_match 127
phrase_slop 127
query 126
time_zone 127

parameters, range query
gt 133
gte 133
lt 133
lte 133
parent aggregations 330
parent-child relationship
data indexing 214
index structure 214
performance considerations 221
querying 216
using 213
pattern analyzer
URL 72
percolator
about 345
combining, with other
  functionalities 353, 354
exploring 350, 351
index 346
indexed documents percolation 355
matching queries count, obtaining 354
preparing 347-349
returned results size, controlling 352
using, for and score calculation 352, 353
phrase match query
analyzer 123
slop 123
phrase suggester
about 374, 375
configuration 376
pipeline aggregations
about 330
data, gaps 330
other aggregations, referencing 330
parent aggregation family 330
sibling aggregation family 330
types 330, 331
URL 330
pipeline aggregations, types
average bucket aggregations 331, 332
bucket script aggregation 336, 337
bucket selector aggregation 334, 335
cumulative sum aggregation 333, 334

derivative aggregation 340
max_bucket 331, 332
min_bucket 331, 332
moving avg aggregation 341
serial differencing aggregation 338-340
sum_bucket 331, 332

plugins
about 408
basics 409
installing 409, 411
removing 411

PostingsHighlighter
about 180-182
URL 172

prefix query 129

Q

queries
selecting, for warming 464, 465

query boosts
about 250
adding, to queries 250-253
applying, to document 250
score, modifying 254
used, for influencing scores 250

querying process
about 111
data, in child documents 216-218
data, in parent documents 219, 220
query logic 111, 112
search execution preference,
    specifying 113, 114
search shards API, specifying 114-116
search type, specifying 112

query parser
URL 48

query rewrite
about 193
Apache Lucene, using 195-197
prefix query, example 193, 194
properties 197-199

query string query
about 125, 126
running, against multiple fields 128

R

Rackspace
URL 488

RAID
URL 476

range aggregation
about 301, 302
keyed buckets 303

range query 133

recovery process
about 400
delayed allocation 403, 404
gateway recovery options 401
index recovery prioritization 404
indices recovery API 401, 403

regular expression query
about 134
URL 134

replicas, Elasticsearch indexing
about 50, 51
write consistency, controlling 52

REST API
about 21, 22
data, storing in Elasticsearch 22
documents, deleting 31
documents, retrieving 25, 26
documents, updating 26, 27
URL 22
used, for data manipulation 21
versioning 32

results
explicit filtering, bool query used 165-169
filtering 164
query context 165

reverse nested aggregation 324, 325

rewrite property, values
constant_score 197
constant_score_boolean 197
scoring_boolean 197
top_terms 198
top_terms_blended freqs 198
top_terms_boost_N 198

right query
results, limiting to given tags 152
selecting 151

use cases 152
values in range, searching 152
routing
about 89-93
default indexing 90
default searching 90, 91
fields 94, 95
parameters 93, 94
RPM package
used, for installing Elasticsearch 18

S

sample
bounding box filtering 360-362
distance-based sorting 358, 360
distance, limiting 362
sampler aggregation 321, 322
score
about 227
influencing, with query boosts 250
modifying 254
score_mode parameter
about 257
avg value 257
first value 257
max value 257
min value 257
multiple value 257
sum value 257
score, modifying
about 254
boosting query 255
constant_score query 254
function score query 255
script fields
parameters, passing to 110
selecting 108, 110
scripting capabilities
about 230
languages, Groovy 237
native code, using 238
other than embedded languages,
    using 237
parameters, using 236

querying, scripts used 235
script execution, available objects 230-232
script, types 232
script properties
file 235
id 235
inline 235
lang 235
params 235
script 235
scripts, scripted metrics aggregation
combine_script 292
init_script 292
map_script 292
reduce_script 292
script types
about 232
indexed scripts 234, 235
in file scripts 232, 233
inline scripts 232, 233
Scroll API
about 388
problem definition 388
problem definition, solution 388, 389
searching 90, 91
segment merging
about 86, 87
merge policy 87
merge policy, basic properties 87
merge scheduler 88
need for 87
throttling 89
shard allocation
cancelling 452
forcing 452
IP address, using for 443
multiple commands per HTTP request 453
operations, allowing on primary shards 453
shard and replica allocation
allocation throttling 445, 446
cluster wide allocation 446, 447
configuration 441
controlling 440
controlling, explicitly 440
index, creating 441, 442

node attributes, requiring 443
node parameters, specifying 441
nodes, excluding 442
number of shards and replicas
   per node 445
rolling restarts, handling 453, 454
shards and replicas, moving
   manually 451
shard request cache
about 414
configuring 414, 415
enabling 414, 415
per request shard request cache,
   disabling 415
usage monitoring 415
shards
about 7-9, 50, 51
moving 451
write consistency, controlling 52
sibling aggregations 330
significant terms aggregation
about 317, 318
multiple value, analyzing 319, 320
significant terms, selecting 319
similarity models
about 76
BM25 similarity, configuring 79
default similarity, configuring 78
DFR similarity, configuring 79
IB similarity, configuring 80
information-based model 78
Okapi BM25 model 78
per-field similarity, setting 77
randomness model, divergence 78
simple query string query
about 128
URL 128
single Elasticsearch node
circuit, breaking 480
doc values, using 481
field data cache 480
general preparations 478
index refresh rate 481
RAM buffer, used for indexing 481
thread pools 482, 483
tuning 477

snapshots
additional parameters 425
creating 424
snowball analyzer
URL 72
Software as a Service (SaaS) 505
source filtering 106
span queries
performance considerations 151
span 143
span containing query 150
span first query 144
span multi query 151
span near query 145, 147
span not query 148, 149
span or query 147
span term query 143
span within query 149
using 142
spatial capabilities
about 355
example data 356
geo_field properties 357
mappings preparation 356
SPM tool
URL 505
standard analyzer
URL 72
state and health, cluster
cluster health API 428
cluster state API 435
cluster stats API 436
indices recovery API 437, 438
indices segments API 439
indices shard stores API 439
indices stats API 430
monitoring 427
nodes info API 433, 434
nodes stats API 434, 435
pending tasks API 436
status code definition
URL 84
stemming
URL 73
stop analyzer
URL 72

stop words
  URL 119
suggesters
  freq property 372
  response 371, 372
  score property 372
  suggestions, including 370
  text property 372
  types 369
  URL 369, 374
  using 369
synonym rules
  Apache Solr synonyms, using 265
  defining 265
  WordNet synonyms, using 267
synonyms
  about 263
  filtering 263
  index-time synonyms expansion 267
  in mappings 264
  query-time synonym expansion 267
  rules, defining 265
  storing, in filesystem 265
synonyms filter
  using 263
**system-specific installation and
        configuration**
  about 18
  Elasticsearch, configuring as system
        service on Linux 20
  Elasticsearch, installing on Linux 18
  Elasticsearch, using as system service
        on Windows 20

T

T-Digest algorithm
  URL 284
templates
  about 405
  example 405, 406
term query 116
terms aggregation
  about 298, 299
  approximate counts 299
  minimum document count 300

terms query 117
term suggester
  about 372
  configuration options 373
  options 373, 374
thread pools
  about 482
  bulk 482
  generic 482
  get 482
  index 482
  percolate 482
  search 482
  suggest 482
throttling 89
time zones
  URL 313
tree-like structures
  analysis 203, 204
  data structure 202
  indexing 201
type determining mechanism
  about 56
  disabling 57, 58
  tuning, for dates 59-61
  tuning, for numeric types 58, 59
type property, values
  fvh 173
  plain 172
  postins 173
type query 118
types, suggesters
  completion 369, 376
  context 369, 381
  phrase 369, 374
  term 369, 372

U

Unicast
  URL 392
update API
  used, for modifying index structure 221
update settings API
  about 417
  cluster settings API 418
  indices settings API 418, 419

URI query string parameters
about 41
analyzer property 42
analyze_wildcard property 47
default operator 42
default search field 42
explain parameter 42, 43
fields returned 45
lowercasing terms expansion 46
per shard results, limiting 46
prefix queries analysis 47
query 42
results, sorting 45
results window 46
search timeout 45
search type 46
unavailable indices, ignoring 46
wildcard queries analysis 47
URI request query
analyzing 40, 41
Lucene query syntax 47, 48
parameters 41
sample data 34
URI search 35-37
used, for searching 34
URI search
about 35, 37
Elasticsearch query response 38, 39
URL 47

V

Validate API
using 183-186
values, has_child query parameter
avg 217
max 217
min 217
none 217
sum 217
values, in range
lower scoring partial queries,
    ignoring 154-156
Lucene query syntax, using in queries 157
matched documents, boosting 153

prefixes, used for providing autocomplete
    functionality 159
searching 152
similar terms, finding 160
spans 160-162
user queries without errors,
    handling 157-159
values, score_mode property
avg 213
max 213
min 213
none 213
sum 213
versioning
about 32
from external system 33
usage example 32, 33
vertical scaling 477

W

warming query
about 460
defined warming queries,
    retrieving 462, 463
defining 461, 462
deleting 463
warming up functionality, disabling 464
wildcard query 132
Windows
Elasticsearch, configuring as
    system service 20
WordNet
URL 267

Z

Zen discovery
about 395
cluster state updates control 397
fault detection ping settings 397
master election configuration 395, 396
master unavailability, dealing with 398
unicast, configuring 396

Thank you for buying
Elasticsearch Server
Third Edition

About Packt Publishing

Packt, pronounced 'packed', published its first book, *Mastering phpMyAdmin for Effective MySQL Management*, in April 2004, and subsequently continued to specialize in publishing highly focused books on specific technologies and solutions.

Our books and publications share the experiences of your fellow IT professionals in adapting and customizing today's systems, applications, and frameworks. Our solution-based books give you the knowledge and power to customize the software and technologies you're using to get the job done. Packt books are more specific and less general than the IT books you have seen in the past. Our unique business model allows us to bring you more focused information, giving you more of what you need to know, and less of what you don't.

Packt is a modern yet unique publishing company that focuses on producing quality, cutting-edge books for communities of developers, administrators, and newbies alike. For more information, please visit our website at www.packtpub.com.

About Packt Open Source

In 2010, Packt launched two new brands, Packt Open Source and Packt Enterprise, in order to continue its focus on specialization. This book is part of the Packt Open Source brand, home to books published on software built around open source licenses, and offering information to anybody from advanced developers to budding web designers. The Open Source brand also runs Packt's Open Source Royalty Scheme, by which Packt gives a royalty to each open source project about whose software a book is sold.

Writing for Packt

We welcome all inquiries from people who are interested in authoring. Book proposals should be sent to author@packtpub.com. If your book idea is still at an early stage and you would like to discuss it first before writing a formal book proposal, then please contact us; one of our commissioning editors will get in touch with you.

We're not just looking for published authors; if you have strong technical skills but no writing experience, our experienced editors can help you develop a writing career, or simply get some additional reward for your expertise.

Mastering Elasticsearch

Second Edition

ISBN: 978-1-78355-379-2   Paperback: 434 pages

Further your knowledge of the Elasticsearch server by learning more about its internals, querying, and data handling

1. Understand Apache Lucene and Elasticsearch's design and architecture.

2. Design your index, configure it, and distribute it, not only with assumptions, but with the underlying knowledge of how it works.

3. Improve your user search experience with Elasticsearch functionality and learn how to develop your own Elasticsearch plugins.

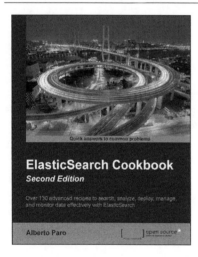

ElasticSearch Cookbook

Second Edition

ISBN: 978-1-78355-483-6   Paperback: 472 pages

Over 130 advanced recipes to search, analyze, deploy, manage, and monitor data effectively with ElasticSearch

1. Deploy and manage simple ElasticSearch nodes as well as complex cluster topologies.

2. Write native plugins to extend the functionalities of ElasticSearch to boost your business.

3. Packed with clear, step-by-step recipes to walk you through the capabilities of ElasticSearch.

Please check **www.PacktPub.com** for information on our titles

Learning Big Data with Amazon Elastic MapReduce

ISBN: 978-1-78217-343-4   Paperback: 242 pages

Easily learn, build, and execute real-world Big Data solutions using Hadoop and AWS EMR

Learning Big Data with Amazon Elastic MapReduce

Easily learn, build, and execute real-world Big Data solutions using Hadoop and AWS EMR

Amarkant Singh   Vijay Rayapati

1. Learn how to solve big data problems using Apache Hadoop.

2. Use Amazon Elastic MapReduce to create and maintain cluster infrastructure for big data analytics.

3. A step-by-step guide exploring the vast set of services provided by Amazon on the cloud.

Building Web and Mobile ArcGIS Server Applications with JavaScript

ISBN: 978-1-84969-796-5   Paperback: 274 pages

Master the ArcGIS API for JavaScript, and build exciting, custom web and mobile GIS applications with the ArcGIS Server

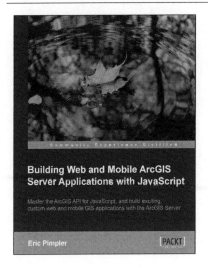

Building Web and Mobile ArcGIS Server Applications with JavaScript

Master the ArcGIS API for JavaScript, and build exciting, custom web and mobile GIS applications with the ArcGIS Server

Eric Pimpler

1. Develop ArcGIS Server applications with JavaScript, both for traditional web browsers as well as the mobile platform.

2. Acquire in-demand GIS skills sought by many employers.

3. Step-by-step instructions, examples, and hands-on practice designed to help you learn the key features and design considerations for building custom ArcGIS Server applications.

Please check **www.PacktPub.com** for information on our titles

16590697R00307

Printed in Great Britain
by Amazon